*Landlords and Tenants in
Mid-Victorian Ireland*

Landlords and Tenants in Mid-Victorian Ireland

W. E. VAUGHAN

CLARENDON PRESS · OXFORD

OXFORD
UNIVERSITY PRESS

Great Clarendon Street, Oxford OX2 6DP

Oxford University Press is a department of the University of Oxford
It furthers the University's objective of excellence in research, scholarship,
and education by publishing worldwide in

Oxford New York

Athens Auckland Bangkok Bogotá Buenos Aires Calcutta
Cape Town Chennai Dar es Salaam Delhi Florence Hong Kong Istanbul
Karachi Kuala Lumpur Madrid Melbourne Mexico City Mumbai
Nairobi Paris São Paulo Singapore Taipei Tokyo Toronto Warsaw

with associated companies in Berlin Ibadan

Oxford is a registered trade mark of Oxford University Press
in the UK and in certain other countries

Published in the United States
by Oxford University Press Inc., New York

© W.E. Vaughan 1994

The moral rights of the author have been asserted
Database right Oxford University Press (maker)

Reprinted 1999

All rights reserved. No part of this publication may be reproduced,
stored in a retrieval system, or transmitted, in any form or by any means,
without the prior permission in writing of Oxford University Press,
or as expressly permitted by law, or under terms agreed with the appropriate
reprographics rights organisation. Enquiries concerning reproduction
outside the scope of the above should be sent to the Rights Department,
Oxford University Press, at the address above

You must not circulate this book in any other binding or cover
and you must impose this same condition on any acquirer

ISBN 0-19-820356-X

Printed in Great Britain
on acid-free paper by
Biddles Short Run Books
King's Lynn

FOREWORD

THIS study is limited to certain aspects of relations between landlords and tenants in mid-nineteenth-century Ireland: evictions, rents, tenant right, estate management, agrarian outrages, and conflicts between landlords and tenants are the main topics. The landlords and tenants whose relations form the connection between these subjects were the owners of landed estates on the one hand and the tenants of agricultural holdings on the other. Relations between tenants and sub-tenants, between the owners of great estates and middlemen, between farmers and labourers, and between town tenants and their landlords are occasionally referred to, but they are not part of the main theme. The subjects examined were largely determined by the interpretation of relations between landlords and tenants that was enshrined in J. E. Pomfret's *The Struggle for Land in Ireland, 1800–1923*, published in 1930.[1]

A few quotations from Pomfret illustrate his ideas. 'The landlords as a class were alien and absentee, and had little interest either in the welfare of the peasants or in the improvement of their property'; 'the tenants never allowed an unwarranted eviction to pass without retribution, and any move toward a general clearance seriously disturbed the peace of the community'; the landlord 'was able to capitalize the desire of the peasant to obtain land at any price and as a result a rent was extorted that was out of proportion to the yield'.[2] These three quotations are from Pomfret's first chapter, which covered the period 1800 to 1850; but at the end of his second chapter, entitled 'The Magic of Laissez Faire, 1850–1870', he compared Ulster with the rest of Ireland in terms that showed he regarded high rents and frequent evictions as endemic and persistent:

In the only region where customary rights were permitted anything resembling free play, there was agricultural prosperity. Contrast the two situations: on the one hand there was the subtle withdrawal of customary privileges, the ceaseless demand for higher rents, the perennial notice to quit and the cruel eviction; while on the other the tenants enjoyed within reasonable bounds security of tenure, fair rents, the recognition of their interest in the holding and the right to sell or to bequeath that interest.[3]

There were some lighter shades in Pomfret. After the famine, for example, he admitted that 'arrears of rent became less frequent and the wholesale evictions of former years were no longer heard of. But the relief was only temporary for the return of bad seasons following the year 1857 revealed

[1] (Princeton, NJ, 1930). [2] Ibid. 27, 25, 19. [3] Ibid. 57–8.

suffering and made it apparent that as yet there was no real margin of subsistence for the Irish peasant' (p. 41). He was more enthusiastic, however, about the period from 1867 to 1877: 'throughout the period there were less than five hundred evictions during any single year. Crops were good, prices high, rents were paid without difficulty, there were no wholesale evictions and in consequence little crime.'[4]

It is difficult now, looking back to the 1960s and early 1970s, to recapture the power of this interpretation, which gave the predatory landlord a central place in nineteenth-century Irish history. It was what most people believed; it was a belief shared by many who shared few other beliefs; it had a powerful teleological attraction in that it explained the land war and the abolition of landlordism. As an orthodoxy it had the attributes that keep orthodoxies going: it explained what had happened; it was unchallenged; it could cope with exceptions to the rules it proclaimed; it was a convenient generalization for scholars; it concealed with plausible decency an epistemological black hole. In Pomfret it had an expositor who added to its strength: he wrote well; he was easy to understand; his reliance on the British parliamentary papers was a guarantee of his objectivity. There was more to Pomfret, however, than his style and his sources. He was an outsider, unconnected with any Irish faction; he was a distinguished scholar who became the twenty-first president of the College of William and Mary; he was supported in his conclusions within a few years by Elizabeth R. Hooker's *Readjustments of Agricultural Tenure in Ireland*.[5]

The following study did not begin with landlords and tenants; it began with an attempt to compare Ulster with the rest of the country. The new departure, the land war, the victory of Parnellism, the rise of unionism were seen as events whose influence was still powerfully felt even in the second half of the twentieth century. Their impact on Ulster and Ulster's impact on them seemed a worthwhile subject to study. The existence of the tenant-right custom in Ulster seemed to separate that province from the others; even before 1870 the Ulster tenants appeared to enjoy in practice what was virtually fixity of tenure, fair rents, and free sale. When the land war began, many Ulster tenants were sympathetic to the land league, but the land league did not sweep them into the arms of Parnell. If the tenant-right custom played a part in the fateful denouement of the 1880s, it seemed an obvious starting-point for a study of Ulster and Ireland.

Preliminary work on the Ulster custom, using easily accessible sources, such as the British parliamentary papers, showed that Ulster tenants had indeed enjoyed something remarkable. They bought and sold farms for sums of money that would have paid for the fee simple; the privilege was not confined to leaseholders, but was enjoyed by yearly tenants as well; nor

[4] Ibid. 102.   [5] (Chapel Hill, NC, 1938).

was it confined to Protestant tenants in the north and east of the province, but enjoyed by Catholic tenants in Donegal, Cavan, and Monaghan as well. That was interesting, but there were problems. For one thing tenant right was not as cut and dried as Pomfret thought; that, however, was not as puzzling as the fact that many of the attributes that the custom conferred on Ulster seemed to be enjoyed by tenants all over the country. In the sources used by Pomfret, particularly in the parliamentary papers but also in the pamphlets, there were many statements that rents were moderate, that the value of improvements was not absorbed by rent increases, and that evictions were rare all over the country.

Among the most puzzling of the sources was a report produced for the government by the poor law inspectors in 1870 on the existing relations between landlords and tenants.[6] It had been said, and often repeated, that one of Gladstone's mistakes in 1870 was that he had not set up a royal commission on the land question and that he lacked the sort of heavy, accurate missiles that a commission would have given him. But here in volume xiv of the House of Commons sessional papers for 1870 was something like a royal commission; but it did not provide the materials for the damning indictment of landlordism that Gladstone needed. Indeed, on reading the poor law inspectors' reports one might well wonder what there was to legislate for. If Gladstone was resolved to do or die on behalf of the Irish tenants, his dauntless courage was vitiated not so much by his ignorance of the terrain that lay before him or by the reluctance of the men he led, but by the curious absence of the Russian guns. Equally puzzling was the fact that in the same volume of the House of Commons sessional papers was a report, also by the poor law inspectors, on the conditions of the agricultural labourers in Ireland.[7] This was much more substantial stuff: here were deeply felt grievances; here were grievances felt by large numbers; here were grievances palpable and present, and not remote or anticipated; here were outspoken statements by the poor law inspectors. Yet Gladstone hardly mentioned the labourers in his great speech introducing the land bill, and Pomfret did not include the report in his bibliography.

There seemed to be something wrong with Pomfret. That was not in itself deeply worrying. After all Pomfret was not Holy Writ; and even if he were, there were good precedents for producing a new translation, whether it was called the Authorized Version, the Revised Version, or even the Revised Standard Version. (More worrying perhaps was K. H. Connell, who had delivered himself of some very strong opinions on the highness of rents.[8] Connell was not in the 1960s Holy Writ; he was something more; he was

[6] *Reports from Poor Law Inspectors in Ireland as to the Existing Relations between Landlord and Tenant in Respect of Improvements on Farms, etc.* [C 31], HC 1870, xiv. 37.
[7] *Reports from Poor Law Inspectors on the Wages of Agricultural Labourers in Ireland* [C 35], HC 1870, xiv. 1. [8] Below, p. 46.

fast becoming the subject of Holy Writ.) Even more worrying was the fact that Pomfret represented the verdict of history; he was the scholarly exposition of what everyone knew. In this troublesome predicament certain comforting aphorisms suggested themselves. Two swallows, for example, do not make a summer; of course there were exceptions—the existence of good landlords had always been recognized—but they were exceptions, and bad landlords were the rule. That there was no smoke without a fire seemed a comforting thought. Why should so many nineteenth-century witnesses condemn the landlords? There must have been something in it. The sources, even the parliamentary papers, which Pomfret had lauded and which seemed so impressive a body of contemporary testimony, might be biased towards the landlords; perhaps Pomfret was right not to take much notice of what was said by landlords' sycophants.

The obvious course, however, was to go beyond the consolation of philosophy to the collections of estate papers that had accumulated in public repositories since the days of Pomfret. Olive Robinson's work on County Londonderry was a welcome exemplar, but the task was daunting.[9] The rentals and accounts for the most part had to be made to talk; apart from marginal comments, they did not speak for themselves; an acquaintance with double-entry book-keeping was necessary. A slide-rule made it relatively easy to calculate the size of rent increases of individual holdings and to compare them with the tenement valuation; but even a slide-rule could not solve the conundrum of the results it helped to elicit. An examination of the rentals of over fifty estates, covering the period between the famine and the land war, made it clear that rents had not increased frequently; that rent increases had been about 20 per cent; that evictions had not been common. At that point it seemed easy to say that Pomfret had got it wrong; certainly it was obvious that if he had used rentals he would have come to radically different conclusions. A doubt, however, remained.

In using rentals and the tenement valuation to measure rents it was impossible not to become interested in agricultural incomes. It now seems incredible that the search began with rents and not with agricultural incomes; but there were good excuses for this. First, nobody had produced calculations of the value of agricultural output; secondly, Pomfret and most of the sources he used did not start from agricultural prices, yields, and incomes—instead they relied very heavily on what people said about rents. Rents were discussed in a sort of economic limbo. Before the question of rents could be resolved, however, there had to be a measure of the tenants' capacity to

[9] Olive Robinson, 'The London Companies as Progressive Landlords in Nineteenth-Century Ireland', *Econ. Hist. Rev.* 2nd ser. 15: 1 (Aug. 1962), 103–18; see also ead., 'The London Companies and Tenant Right in Nineteenth-Century Ireland', *Agric. Hist. Rev.* 18 (1970), 54–63.

pay them. The possibility existed that a rent increase of 20 per cent, small thought it seemed, may in fact have been high. The only guide available was Thomas Barrington's index of agricultural prices, which was based on nineteenth-century agricultural prices.[10] Barrington was reassuring because he showed that prices had gone up; but the problem was what weight to assign to the different commodities in his index. How to do that was suggested to the author by Mícheál O Suilleabháin's discussion paper on calculating Irish agricultural output, which was read at the annual conference of the Economic and Social History Society of Ireland in October 1970. What was particularly attractive about calculating agricultural output was that the agricultural statistics, which had begun in 1847, and the prices series in the Cowper commission could be used to produce calculations for every year of the period between the famine and the land war.

These calculations, however, were anything but satisfying. If they had shown that landlords and tenants had kept pace with each other that would have been a serious modification of Pomfret's picture but it would have been credible. Instead they showed, especially if the starting-point was the early 1850s, that tenants had done much better than landlords, which seemed incredible. Pomfret might have been mistaken, but at least his views as a whole were sensible. Rents that lagged considerably behind agricultural incomes seemed to be the triumph of arithmetic over history. At that point B. L. Solow's *The Land Question and the Irish Economy, 1870–1903*[11] appeared and illuminated much that had been dark, inexplicable, and confused. Where Pomfret had been enveloped in tradition, Mrs Solow was breezily iconoclastic; where Pomfret wandered about, she kept to the point and stuck to her arguments. A historian might have thought that her sources were rather sparse; that her arguments were exiguously covered with facts; but the point that was obvious to anyone in the know was that her sources and facts covered the parts that decency and necessity required to be covered. In a short, well-written, and readable book she estimated the movement of rents, calculated the value of agricultural output, cast a cold eye on evictions, said some provocative things about Irish agriculture, made sense of tenant right, and challenged three generations of muddle, exaggeration, and tendentiousness.

Mrs Solow's book was published in 1971; it was followed in 1975 by James S. Donnelly's *The Land and the People of Nineteenth-Century Cork*,[12] which covered the rural economy, including the vicissitudes of landlords and tenants in Cork, from the end of the French wars to the early 1890s. For Donnelly evictions were rare after 1854 and rent increases were such that 'tenant farmers, not landlords, received the lion's share of the benefits

[10] Thomas Barrington, 'A Review of Irish Agricultural Prices', *Jn. Stat. Soc. Ire.* pt. 101 [1925–7], 249–80.
[11] (Cambridge, Mass., 1971). [12] (London, 1975).

accruing from price and production increases between 1851 and 1876'. Professor Donnelly, however, turned the nineteenth century on its head by going further and arguing that the land war was caused by prosperity: 'In a very real sense, the land war was a product not merely of agricultural crisis, but also of a revolution of rising expectations.'[13]

In a few short years, therefore, much had changed in the aspect of landlord and tenant relations. By the mid-1970s the work of Solow, Donnelly, and the present author had coincided to challenge ideas that had been long and passionately held. The fact that all three had arrived at these conclusions independently, practically unknown to each other, using different methods and sources, and covering different aspects of the subject seemed reassuring. (The fact that two of those concerned were Americans seemed a just and ironic balancing of Hooker and Pomfret.)

The new ideas on landlords and tenants have sometimes been treated as a new orthodoxy. To do so is wrong, for they have few of the attributes of orthodoxy. They are based on empirical methods and not on a priori assumptions; they are tinged with scepticism and purged of faith; they have not been received as dogmatic by all of the faithful; they open rather than conceal the subject; they offer no comfort to those who like certainty. What follows is an attempt to see certain aspects of the land system without a teleological bias; the land war is not forgotten, but it is not treated as the culmination of thirty years of estate management. If this work has a preoccupation, as opposed to a theme, it is with power: the power to evict; the power to make tenants pay their rents; the power to keep everyone quiet—and possibly happy; the power to keep opponents from organizing; the power to use or thwart the state in all of its forms, especially in its local power; the power of inertia and routine.

[13] Ibid. 200, 189, 250.

ACKNOWLEDGEMENTS

I WISH to thank the following for allowing me to use collections of manuscripts in their care: the Board of Trinity College, Dublin; the Director of the National Archives, Dublin; the Council of Trustees of the National Library of Ireland; the Deputy Keeper of the Records, the Public Record Office of Northern Ireland. I wish to thank the following depositors of private collections in the Public Record Office of Northern Ireland for permission to use their collections: Messrs E. D. Atkinson & Son (solicitors, Portadown); representatives of the late R. H. Blackwood Esq; representatives of the late W. J. Boyd (solicitor, Ballycastle); the marchioness of Dufferin and Ava; the earl of Erne; Roger Hall Esq; F. E. Hart Esq; representatives of the late Sir John Heygate; representatives of the late Major-General R. K. Hezlett; Messrs Martin, King, French & Ingram (solicitors, Limavady); Messrs Orr & Rountree (solicitors, Omagh); Hermione, countess of Ranfurly; Major J. E. Shirley; Dr Jean Whyte; Messrs Wilson & Simms (solicitors, Strabane).

I also wish to thank the following: the staffs of the National Archives, of the National Library, of the Public Record Office of Northern Ireland, and of the Library of Trinity College, Dublin; the Arts and Social Sciences Benefaction Fund, Trinity College, Dublin for a grant towards making the index; Helen Litton for making the index; Dr Andrew Harrison for information about the Dufferin estates; Dr W. H. Crawford for information about newly acquired collections in the Public Record Office of Northern Ireland; R. A. J. Hawkins for his careful reading of the text; Mrs Peggy Morgan for typing an earlier version of the text; Davison & Associates for supplying a photograph of the Kildare Street Club; Dr Edward McParland for designing the dust-jacket and for many other kindnesses.

20 July 1993

W. E. V.
Ballinamallard
Co. Fermanagh

CONTENTS

List of Tables	xvi
Abbreviations	xvii
1. Landlords and Tenants	1
2. Evictions	20
i. Numbers, Fluctuations, and Incidence	20
ii. Evictions and Estate Management	29
iii. Obstacles to Evictions	34
iv. 'So Untruly and Unjustly Represented'	39
3. The Movement and Level of Rents	44
i. A Contemporary Puzzle	44
ii. The Significance of Rent Increases	49
iii. Fixing Rent Increases	55
iv. The Obstacles to Rent Increases	63
4. The Tenant-Right Custom	67
i. What was Tenant Right?	67
ii. The Extent of Tenant Right	76
iii. Tenant Right and Prosperity	80
iv. Tenant Right and Estate Management	87
v. The Land Act of 1870	93
5. Estate Management	103
i. Ideas and Means	103
ii. Arrears and the Payment of Rents	113
iii. Estate Expenditure	117
iv. Why did Landlords not Spend More on Improvements?	124
v. Landlords' Indebtedness	130
6. Agrarian Outrages	138
i. 'A Bould Intrepid Gentry'	138
ii. What were Agrarian Outrages?	141
iii. Threatening Letters	150
iv. What Caused Agrarian Outrages?	156
v. The Importance of Agrarian Outrages	161

7. Resistance to Landlordism	177
i. Principles of Aggregation	177
ii. The Concealment of Criminals	184
iii. Ribbonism	189
iv. Why was there no Mass Movement against Landlordism before 1879?	202
v. What Caused the Land War?	208
8. Conclusion	217

Appendices — 229

1. Eviction Statistics, 1849–1887 — 229
2. Civil Bill Ejectments and Ordinary Civil Bills, 1866–1886 — 232
3. Counties Ranked According to Evictions, 1851–1880 — 233
4. Counties Ranked According to Evictions during Four Periods, 1849–1882 — 235
5. Fieris, Haberes, and Warrants Issued to Special Bailiffs for the Ejectment of Cottiers and Town Tenants, 1863–1886 — 237
6. The Movement of Rents on Eleven Estates — 238
7. Arrears on Twelve Estates — 241
8. Rent Receipts on Twelve Estates — 244
9. Agricultural Output, Rents, Potatoes, and the Cost of Labour, 1850–1886 — 247
10. The Tenement Valuation — 251
11. The Trinity College, Dublin leasing powers act (14 & 15 Vict., c. cxxviii (1 Aug. 1851) — 256
12. Rents Based on the TCD Leasing Powers Act — 261
13. Alternative Methods of Increasing Rents, 1850–1886 — 263
14. Counties Ranked According to Valuation of Land per Acre, Percentage of Land under Tillage, and Valuation of Holdings — 267
15. Counties Ranked According to Quality of their Rural Housing in 1851 and 1881 — 269
16. Counties Ranked According to the Quality of their Land and Houses — 271
17. Compensation under Sections 3, 4, and 7 of the Land Act, 1870 — 273
18. Expenditure on Nine Estates, 1850–1880 — 277
19. Agrarian Outrages and Other Outrages Returned by the Constabulary, 1844–1893 — 279

20. Counties Ranked According to Serious Crime, 1851–1880   281
21. Counties Ranked According to Agrarian Outrages, 1851–1880   283
22. Counties Ranked According to Agrarian Outrages Committed during Four Crises, 1848–1882   285
23. Spearman Ranking Coefficients of County Ranks   287

Select Bibliography   289

Index   323

LIST OF TABLES

1. Recipients of agricultural incomes, 1865   8
2. Deaths caused by gunshot wounds   145
3. Firings at the person, 1869–1878   146
4. Agrarian outrages, 1871   147
5. Agrarian outrages, 1848–1880   149
6. Recipients of threatening letters, 1863   154
7. Threatening letters, 1863   155
8. Causes of agrarian outrages, 1848–1880   158

ABBREVIATIONS

ABBREVIATIONS listed below consist of (a) the relevant items from the list in *Irish Historical Studies*, supplement 1 (Jan. 1969) and (b) abbreviations, on the same model, for sources and works not included in the *Irish Historical Studies* list.

Agric. Hist. Rev.   *Agricultural History Review* (Oxford, 1953–)

AHR   *American Historical Review* (New York, 1895–)

Bateman, *Great Landowners* (1883)   John Bateman, *The Great Landowners of Great Britain and Ireland* (4th edn. London, 1883); repr. with introduction by David Spring (Leicester, 1971)

Bence-Jones, *Ir. Country Houses*   Mark Bence-Jones, *Burke's Guide to Country Houses,* i. *Ireland* (London, 1978)

Bessborough Comm. Report, Minutes of Evidence, pts. i & ii, etc.   *Report of Her Majesty's Commission of Inquiry into the Working of the Landlord and Tenant (Ireland) Act, 1870, and the Acts Amending the Same* [C 2779], HC 1881, xviii. 1 (earl of Bessborough, chairman)
    Minutes of Evidence, pt. i [C 2779-I], HC 1881, xviii. 73
    Minutes of Evidence and Appendices, pt. ii [C 2779-II], HC 1881, xix. 1
    Index to Minutes of Evidence and Appendices [C 2779-III], HC 1881, xix. 825

Campbell, *Ir. Land*   George Campbell, *The Irish Land* (London and Dublin, 1869)

Census Ire.	*Census of Ireland* (published as volumes of the British House of Commons Sessional Papers, 1822–1913)
Comerford, *Fenians*	R. V. Comerford, *The Fenians in Context: Irish Politics and Society* (Dublin, 1985)
Cork Hist. Soc. Jn.	*Journal of the Cork Historical and Archaeological Society* (Cork, 1892–)
Cowper Comm. Report, Minutes of Evidence, etc.	*Report of the Royal Commission on the Land Law (Ireland) Act, 1881, and the Purchase of Land (Ireland) Act, 1885* [C 4969], HC 1887, xxvi. 1 (Earl Cowper, chairman) *Minutes of Evidence and Appendices* [C 4969-I], HC 1887, xxvi. 25 *Index to Evidence and Appendices* [C 4969-II], HC 1887, xxvi. 1109 *Separate Report by Thomas Knipe* [C 5015], HC 1887, xxvi. 1241
Davitt, *Fall of Feudalism*	Michael Davitt, *The Fall of Feudalism in Ireland: Or the Story of the Land League Revolution* (London and New York, 1904)
De Moleyns, *Landowner's Guide* (1872)	Thomas de Moleyns, *The Landowner's and Agent's Practical Guide* (6th edn. Dublin, 1872)
Denton, *Farm Homesteads of England*	J. Bailey Denton, *The Farm Homesteads of England* (London, 1864)
Devon Comm. Report, Minutes of Evidence, etc.	*Report from Her Majesty's Commissioners of Inquiry into the State of the Law and Practice in Respect to the Occupation of*

                                Land in Ireland [605], HC 1845, xix. 1 (earl of Devon, chairman)

                                    Minutes of Evidence, pt. i [606], HC 1845, xix. 57

                                    Minutes of Evidence, pt. ii [616], HC 1845, xx. 1

                                    Minutes of Evidence, pt. iii [657], HC 1845, xxi. 1

                                    Appendix to Minutes of Evidence, pt. iv [672], HC 1845, xxii. 1

                                    Index to Minutes of Evidence, pt. v [673], HC 1845, xxii. 225

Donnell, *Practical Guide*	Robert Donnell, *Practical Guide to the Law of Tenant Compensation and Farm Purchase under the Irish Land Act* (London, 1871)
Donnelly, *Land and People of Cork*	J. S. Donnelly, jun. *The Land and the People of Nineteenth-Century Cork* (London, 1975)
Econ. Hist. Rev.	*Economic History Review* (London, 1927–)
Endowed Schools Comm., 1857–8, Report, Evidence, Appendix	*Report of Her Majesty's Commissioners Appointed to Inquire into the Endowments, Funds, and Actual Condition of All Schools Endowed for the Purpose of Education in Ireland* ... [2336-I], HC 1857–8, xxii, pt. i, p. 1 (marquis of Kildare, chairman)
	evidence, vol. i [2336-II], ibid., pt. ii, p. 1
	evidence, vol. ii with index [2336-III], ibid., pt. iii, p. 1
	papers [appendix] accompanying report, vol. iii [2336-IV], ibid., pt. iv, p. 1
Godkin, *Land War in Ire.*	James Godkin, *The Land War in Ireland* (London, 1869)

Griffith, *Instructions*	Sir Richard Griffith, *Instructions to Valuators and Surveyors Appointed under 15th and 16th Vict., cap. 63, for the Uniform Valuation of Lands and Tenements in Ireland* (Dublin, 1853)
Hansard 3	*Hansard's Parliamentary Debates*, 3rd ser. 1830–91 (vols. i–cxcix, London, 1831–91)
Hist. Jn.	*The Historical Journal* (Cambridge, 1958–)
Hoppen, *Elections, Politics, and Society*	K. Theodore Hoppen, *Elections, Politics, and Society in Ireland, 1832–1885* (Oxford, 1984)
ICR	Chief Secretary's Office, Irish Crime Records
IHS	*Irish Historical Studies: The Joint Journal of the Irish Historical Society and the Ulster Society for Irish Historical Studies* (Dublin, 1938–)
ILT	*The Irish Law Times and Solicitor's Journal: A Weekly Newspaper, and Gazette of Legal Proceedings* (Dublin, 1868–)
Ir. Econ. & Soc. Hist.	*Irish Economic and Social History: The Journal of the Economic and Social History Society of Ireland* ([Dublin and Belfast], 1974–)
Jn. Stat. Soc. Ire.	*Journal of the Statistical and Social Inquiry Society of Ireland* (Dublin, 1861–)
Judicial Statistics, Ire.	*Judicial Statistics, Ireland* (published annually as volumes of the British House of Commons Sessional Papers, from 1864)
Lords' Sel. Comm. on Land Tenure, 1867	*Report from the Select Committee of the House of Lords on the*

	Tenure (Ireland) Bill [HL]; together with the Proceedings of the Committee, Minutes of Evidence, Appendix, and Index, HC 1867 (518), xiv. 423 (marquis of Clanricarde (who sat as Lord Somerhill), chairman)
Lords' Sel. Comm. on the Land Act, 1872	*Report from the Select Committee of the House of Lords on the Landlord and Tenant (Ireland) Act, 1870; together with the Proceedings of the Committee, Minutes of Evidence, Appendix, and Index,* HC 1872 (403), xi. 1 (Lord Chelmsford, chairman)

Lords' Sel. Comm. on the 1881 Land Act, First Report, etc.	*First Report from the Select Committee of [the] House of Lords on the Land Law (Ireland) Act; together with Proceedings of the Committee, Minutes of Evidence, Appendix, and Index,* HC 1882 (249), xi. 1 (Earl Cairns, chairman)
	   Second Report, ibid. (379), 547
	   Third Report, HC 1883 (204), xiii. 443
	   Fourth Report, and index, ibid. (279), 653

MacLagan, *Land Tenure in Ire.*	Peter MacLagan, *Land Tenure and Land Culture in Ireland* (London and Edinburgh, 1869)
O'Brien, *Parnell & his Party*	Conor Cruise O'Brien, *Parnell and his Party, 1880–90* (Oxford; 1957; corrected impression, 1964)
OP	Chief Secretary's Office, Official Papers
Pomfret, *Struggle for Land in Ire.*	John E. Pomfret, *The Struggle for Land in Ireland, 1800–1923* (Princeton, NJ, 1930)

Poor Law Inspectors' Reports, 1870	Reports from Poor Law Inspectors in Ireland as to the Existing Relations between Landlord and Tenant in Respect of Improvements on Farms, etc. [C 31], HC 1870, xiv. 37
Return of Evictions, 1849–80	Return, 'by Provinces and Counties (Compiled from Returns made to the Inspector-General, Royal Irish Constabulary) of cases of evictions which have come to the knowledge of the constabulary in each of the years 1849 to 1880, inclusive', HC 1881 (185), lxxvii. 725
RP	Chief Secretary's Office, Registered Papers
Samuelson, *Land and Tenantry of Ire.*	Bernhard Samuelson, *Studies of the Land and Tenantry of Ireland* (London, 1870)
Sel. Comm. on County Monaghan, 1852	Report from the Select Committee on Outrages (Ireland); together with the Proceedings of the Committee, Minutes of Evidence, Appendix and Index, HC 1852 (438), xiv. 1 (Joseph Napier, chairman)
Sel. Comm. on Land Tenure, 1865	Report from the Select Committee on the Tenure and Improvement of Land (Ireland) Act; together with the Proceedings of the Committee, Minutes of Evidence, Appendix, and Index, HC 1865 (402), xi. 341 (John Francis Maguire, chairman)
Sel. Comm. on Westmeath, 1871	Report from the Select Committee on Westmeath, etc. (Unlawful Combinations); together with the Proceedings of the Committee, Minutes of Evidence, and

	Appendix [and index], HC 1871 (147), xiii. 547 (marquis of Hartington, chairman)
Stephens, *Book of the Farm*	Henry Stephens, *The Book of the Farm* (2nd edn. 2 vols., Edinburgh and London, 1851)
Thompson, *Ire. in 1839 and 1869*	H. S. Thompson, *Ireland in 1839 and 1869* (London and Dublin, 1870).
Thom's Directory	*Thom's Almanac and Official Directory of the United Kingdom and Ireland* (Dublin, 1845–)
Thornley, *Isaac Butt*	David Thornley, *Isaac Butt and Home Rule* (London, 1964)
Trench, *Realities of Ir. Life*	William Steuart Trench, *Realities of Irish Life* (London, 1868)
Vaughan, *Derryveagh Evictions*	W. E. Vaughan, *Sin, Sheep and Scotsmen: John George Adair and the Derryveagh Evictions, 1861* (Belfast, 1983)
VO Dublin	Valuation Office, Ely Place, Dublin
Walker, *Election Results, 1801–1922*	Brian M. Walker (ed.), *Parliamentary Election Results in Ireland, 1801–1922* (Dublin, 1978)
Whyte, *Indep. Ir. Party*	J. H. Whyte, *The Independent Irish Party, 1850–9* (Oxford, 1958)

I
Landlords and Tenants

ONE of the most familiar pictures of the land war was an illustration in the *Illustrated London News* of January 1881, showing the burning of the duke of Leinster's lease at a land league meeting.[1] Solemn-looking men, heavily bearded, burning a piece of paper, assumed a specious ferocity because they were burning the lease on a '98 pike. As an image of revolution it was not striking; certainly it was not as striking as Delacroix's *Liberty Leading the People*. The picture, however, did suggest one thing about the land system: compared with other forms of wealth, landed property and the relationship between landlords and tenants were remarkably public. Estates were concentrated in easily identified territorial blocks, often comprising dozens of townlands. The greater estates were often distributed through two or three counties. The duke of Leinster had 73,000 acres in Kildare and Meath; the marquis of Downshire had 115,000 acres in Antrim, Down, Kildare, King's County, and Wicklow; the earl of Erne had 40,000 acres in Donegal, Fermanagh, Mayo, and Sligo.[2]

The most visible aspect of the estates was their mansion houses, ranging from great palaces like Castletown, Powerscourt, and Castle Coole to substantial houses, perhaps little bigger than rectories, like Woodbrook in Roscommon, but forming centres of employment and social power.[3] The houses of the gentry were not for the most part sited conspicuously on hills or precipitous cliffs (Lord Palmerston at Classiebawn was one of the few landlords whose front door could be seen from the public road); but the paraphernalia of demesnes were strikingly visible: the demesne walls stretching for miles at Carton; gate lodges, better than many farmers' houses, at Powerscourt; model villages such as Adare and Caledon, and Coolattin where 'the houses are all bright and fresh as a new pin, having been only recently erected or restored by the great lord of the land, Earl Fitzwilliam';[4] the plantations at Baltiboys in Wicklow, 'the handsome seat

---
[1] *Illustrated London News*, 8 Jan. 1881; see T. W. Moody and F. X. Martin, *The Course of Irish History*, rev. and enlarged edn. (Cork, 1987), 290; see also the dust-jacket of C. H. E. Philpin (ed.), *Nationalism and Popular Protest in Ireland* (Cambridge, 1987).
[2] Bateman, *Great Landowners* (1883).
[3] David Thomson, *Woodbrook* (Harmondsworth, 1975).
[4] John Forbes, *Memorandums made in Ireland in the Autumn of 1852* (London, 1853), i. 41.

of Colonel Smith', who is better known as the husband of the diarist, Mrs Smith.[5]

The bigger houses of the gentry were considerable centres of employment and consumption, often resembling small villages; in County Fermanagh, for example, Belle Isle, Colebrooke, and Castle Archdale were almost as substantial additions to the countryside as the villages of Lisbellaw, Brookeborough, and Ballinamallard. Lord Clonbrock in County Galway spent several thousand pounds a year on his house, stables, garden, farm, and woods; in the 1850s he spent about £3,500 annually, which rose to £5,300 by 1880. The main items of expenditure were servants' wages and food, and repairs. Some money found its way to workers outside the house—carpenters, plumbers, and plasterers; in the 1859 account, for example, 5s. 5d. was paid for 'killing 130 bats'.[6] Such establishments were like small factories: twenty men and women were employed constantly on the demesne farm at Woodstock, County Wicklow, the men earning about 1s. 2d. a day and the women 8d. in the 1860s.[7] How many of the 28,000 first-class houses returned in the 1871 census were like Woodstock and Powerscourt? Mark Bence-Jones has 2,000 houses in his masterly survey of country houses;[8] in a return of mansion houses published in 1906 there were only about 1,600.[9]

The actual working of the land system was remarkably visible. Rents were collected twice a year, often in hotels; evictions and debt collections were not only public, but occasionally sensational. The details of landlordism became more public than in the eighteenth century: the government and tenement valuations itemized every estate in the country; parliament published statistics of evictions, agrarian crimes, and legal transactions relating to estates. Parliamentary inquiries and royal commissions investigated many aspects of estate management. The process of administrative revelation gathered pace in the 1870s, with inquiries into absenteeism and the size of estates; from the mid-1870s the size of most estates could be found in *Thom's Directory*, giving match-making dowagers' gossip a precision unknown in the eighteenth century.

Estates were owned by individuals, although the interests of heirs might be protected by family settlements; but there was no attempt to hide ownership behind trusts or corporations. Not only were peers' titles

---

[5] James Fraser, *A Guide to the County of Wicklow. With a large Map of the County, and Twenty-One Wood-Engravings* (Dublin, 1851), 114; see also David Thomson and Moyra McGusty (eds.), *The Irish Journals of Elizabeth Smith, 1840–1850* (Oxford, 1980), 58.
[6] Clonbrock accounts, 1850–67 (NLI, MS 19510).
[7] See e.g. Tottenham wages-book, 1863 (ibid. MS 5721).
[8] Bence-Jones, *Ir. Country Houses*, p. vii.
[9] *Return of Untenanted Lands in Rural Districts, Distinguishing Demesnes on which there is a Mansion House...* HC 1906 (250), c. 177.

territorially eponymous, taking the names of mountains, rivers, lakes, and counties (only the duke of Leinster, two royal princes, and a royal bastard diffused their nobility through whole provinces), but in return families gave their names to towns and streets: Hillsborough and Parsonstown; Farnham Street in Cavan and Belmore Street in Enniskillen. Although Ireland had fewer hotels than England taking their names from the local gentry, there were some: the Ram Arms in Gorey, the Kenmare Arms in Kenmare, the Ranfurly Arms in Dungannon, and the Headfort Arms in Kells.[10]

Residence on estates was considered an important part of a landlord's duty; even critics of landlordism, like A. M. Sullivan, extolled the virtues of a resident gentry.[11] In practice, of course, residence was not of great importance to tenants, for some of the best-managed estates were owned by absentees, or virtual absentees: the duke of Devonshire's estates in Cork and Waterford; the Murray Stewart estate in Donegal; the London companies' estates in County Londonderry. The importance of a resident gentry, however, was probably exaggerated. According to Sir Thomas Larcom, the under-secretary, County Leitrim was always a turbulent county (it ranked twenty-eighth in the 1860s when counties were ranked according to the prevalence of crime[12]), but 'by far the most troublesome and turbulent thing in it was the noble earl of that name'.[13] Residence probably meant most to those who busied themselves with the polemics of the land question and who saw it as a bulwark of landlordism, for proximity 'brings cleanliness and order, because it brings observation and encouragement'.[14] If residence mattered economically it was more important to shopkeepers and agricultural labourers than to tenants. One thing that did matter was a supply of local magistrates, who were recruited from the gentry. A miller in County Westmeath in 1873, who wanted to evict a sub-tenant, had to bring his case six times to the petty sessions before he got an ejectment warrant.[15] There was a strong feeling among country people that personal contact was effective in getting things done. An old woman, a tenant of Lord Gosford at Arva, went all the way from Arva, County Cavan, to Markethill in County Armagh in 1858, to ask the agent to transfer her tenancy to her son, which was a piece of business that could have been arranged by writing a letter.[16]

According to a return made in 1872, 46 per cent of estates had resident landlords; 25 per cent had landlords resident elsewhere in Ireland; 23 per

---

[10] [P. D. Hardy,] *Hardy's Tourist Guide through Ireland: In Four Tours*... (Dublin, 1858), at 356.   [11] A. M. Sullivan, *New Ireland* (London, 1877), i. 271.
[12] See below, App. 20.   [13] Larcom papers (NLI, MS 7634, p. 1).
[14] Benjamin Disraeli, *Sybil, or the Two Nations* (Harmondsworth, 1980), 226.
[15] National Archives, OP 1872/3/5.
[16] Gosford rental (County Cavan), 1858 (PRONI, D1606/7C/43, p. 8).

cent were owned by absentees or public institutions.[17] Many contemporaries seem to have ignored the fact that residence was impractical for many landlords. For one thing, they could not live simultaneously on all their estates. Lord Downshire had houses at Hillsborough, Dundrum, and Blessington, but none on his estates in Antrim, Kildare, and the King's County. Lord Belmore admitted that he had never lived on his Tyrone estate, preferring, as one would expect, to live at Castle Coole.[18] If Lord Dunraven devoted himself to his County Limerick estate, it was at the expense of being an absentee from his much more valuable estate in Wales. The social and political leadership that went with landlordism drew landlords away from their estates. The marquis of Dufferin was almost continuously in office for thirty years, as chancellor of the duchy of Lancaster, governor-general of Canada, ambassador in St Petersburg and Constantinople, viceroy of India, and finally ambassador in Paris and Rome. The earl of Mayo was chief secretary of Ireland on three occasions and viceroy of India, 1869–72. Lord Belmore was governor of New South Wales, 1867–72; Marie Edmé Patrice Maurice de MacMahon, a Waterford landlord, was better known as the victor of Magenta and Solferino. It is remarkable, therefore, how many men of great wealth chose the gentrified equivalent of living over the shop. Of the 8,412 landlords returned in the 1861 census, for example, 8,159 were born in Ireland, which implied that their mothers spent a short time there at least once in their lives.[19] Also noticeable was the tendency of the gentry to marry their neighbours, as good a test as any of their attachment to their localities.

There was more to landlordism than the mere payment of rents. Land conferred social and political power. At general elections until 1880, for example, landlords played an important part in returning members to parliament; a substantial proportion of those returned were landlords, or landlords' relations.[20] In local government landlords dominated county administration until 1898, and the poor law boards until the 1880s.[21] They played a large part in the administration of justice through the petty sessions until the very end of the union. They were also one of the sources of spectacle in rural society. In the absence of religious processions and long-established civic traditions, the hunt, the assizes, a son's coming of age, a daughter's marriage ('the brilliant edition of a universal fact'), or a

---

[17] *Return, for the Year 1870, of the Number of Landed Proprietors in Each County, Classed According to Residence, Showing the Extent of Land Held by Each Class* . . . p. 8, HC 1872 (167), xlvii. 782.
[18] *Lords' Sel. Comm. on the 1881 Land Act, Second Report*, 43.
[19] *Census Ire.*, 1861, pt. v, pp. 502, 530–3 [3204-IV], HC 1863, lxi.
[20] Whyte, *Indep. Ir. Party*, 90; Thornley, *Isaac Butt*, 207; O'Brien, *Parnell & his Party*, 15–18; Hoppen, *Elections, Politics, and Society*, 152–70.
[21] William L. Feingold, *The Revolt of the Tenantry: The Transformation of Local Government in Ireland, 1872–1886* (Boston, 1984).

funeral was a spectacle. When the earl of Bandon was buried in 1877, the hearse was drawn by six black horses, and followed by the earl's coach ('containing a page in charge of the coronet on a crimson velvet cushion'), mounted constabulary, estate workmen, gardeners, and the tenantry 'on horse-back'.[22]

Land, or rather its possession through several generations, conferred gentility. Old landlords could confirm the gentility of those who aspired to it. A merchant already prominent in New Ross's municipal politics, S. F. McCormick, wanted to be added to the commission of the peace for Wexford; but the lieutenant of Wexford, Lord Carew, would not put his name forward. 'I have the pleasure of knowing Mr McCormick and am aware that he is a highly respectable merchant and gentleman,' wrote Carew, 'but I understand that he is engaged in a retail trade and consequently I cannot appoint him.' On hearing this McCormick in his fury revealed even more complicated layers of snobbery: one of Carew's latest appointments was a New Ross shopkeeper 'at whose shop a purchaser could buy a halfpennyworth of thread', while McCormick was the sole proprietor of a grain-importing firm that had just brought in a cargo of Indian corn worth £8,000.[23]

The illustration in the *Illustrated London News* pointed to another characteristic of the land question; for the burning of a legal document symbolized the nature of the struggle between landlords and tenants, which was a strange mixture of the commonplace and the *outré*. An impression of irrepressible conflict was created by incidents such as the Derryveagh evictions, by tyrannical landlords such as the third earl of Leitrim, and by the assassination of landlords, agents, and bailiffs. By the 1870s it was well established, at least in the writings and speeches of those who represented the tenants, that tenants were rackrented; that they had been evicted in hundreds of thousands; that they lived in fear of eviction; that they were poor, wretched, and prone to violence. The land question had been given, in typical Victorian fashion, an ancient pedigree, stretching back for centuries. J. P. Prendergast's *Cromwellian Settlement*, published in 1865, was the history not just of confiscation, but also of the eviction of a whole people. Not only was the land system seen as oppressive, it was seen as peculiar to Ireland. Fr. Lavelle's *Irish Landlord since the Revolution*, for example, put Irish land tenure in its European context. Beside these highly coloured notions went a prosaic demand for legal reform such as compensation for improvements, regulation of rents, the legalization of tenant right, and ending of 'capricious' evictions. The legal framework was important, but it is difficult to reconcile the relative triviality of tenurial

---

[22] *Extracts from Public Journals in Memory of Francis Bernard, Third Earl of Bandon* (Dublin, 1877), 24–5.   [23] National Archives, RP 1876/16878.

adjustments with the profound issues raised by Lavelle. Nor was it easy to see the connection between politicians' rhetoric and the mundane details of land bills. Even Gladstone was carried away by rhetoric, not only in his great speech introducing the land bill in 1870, but also in private, telling Lord Dufferin that if the bill succeeded in Ireland it would be 'a blessing for the remaining years of life and for the hour of death to us all'.[24] Yet the land act, important though it was, was not a ringing declaration of rights, but an ordinary, complicated piece of legislation, more like a truck act or a factory act than the Gettysburg address.

Rural society was apparently divided into three groups, defined by their relationship to the ownership and occupation of land: the landlords, who owned the land; the tenants, who occupied it; and the labourers, who worked on the larger farms. The landlords were the most visible but smallest of the three groups, numbering about 6,500 at most in the official returns of landowners made in the 1870s—if it is assumed that the smallest estate entitling its owner to be considered a landlord was 500 acres. In fact, most of the country was covered by much larger estates: about 48 per cent by estates of 5,000 acres and upwards, which were owned by only 700 landlords.[25] Other measures of the numbers of landlords give different figures: 8,412 landlords were returned in the 1861 census;[26] there were almost 4,000 justices of the peace in 1880, a good measure of the number of established, potentially active gentry in the country.[27]

The tenants were a much larger group, amounting to about 500,000 in the 1860s. Their numbers were variously estimated: in 1861 there were 610,000 holdings, 554,000 occupiers, and according to the census 440,697 farmers, including 27,388 women.[28] (According to a return of leaseholders and yearly tenants in 1870 there were 680,000 tenements.[29]) On the whole the most realistic estimate of the tenants' numbers lies somewhere between the farmers in the census and the occupiers, that is, about half a million. The tenants were the entrepreneurs of rural society, making decisions about the use of land, what to grow, and what to buy and sell. As a group they were perhaps more varied than the landlords, ranging from wretchedly small tenants in the west, living in single-room cottages, to large graziers such as Edward Delany of Woodtown in County Meath.[30]

---

[24] Gladstone to Dufferin, 16 Feb. 1870 (PRONI, D1071H/B/G).
[25] *Thom's Directory, 1881*, 721.
[26] *Census Ire., 1861*, pt. v, p. 502 [3204-IV], HC 1863, lxi.
[27] *Thom's Directory, 1881*, 1255-70.
[28] *Agricultural Statistics, Ire., 1861*, pp. x–xii [3156], HC 1863, lxix. 556-8; *Census Ire., 1861*, pt. v, p. 466 [3204-IV], HC 1863, lxi.
[29] *Returns Showing the Number of Agricultural Holdings in Ireland, and the Tenure by which they are Held by the Occupiers*, pp. 16-17 [C 32], HC 1870, lvi. 752-3.
[30] Vaughan, 'Farmer, Grazier and Gentleman: Edward Delany of Woodtown, 1851-99', *Ir. Econ, & Soc. Hist.* 9 (1982), 53-74.

Most tenants had the same tenure, a yearly tenancy, which did not vary from place to place. About 20 per cent had leases, but the remainder held by the year.[31] Looked at superficially the yearly tenancy was a poor thing: tenants could be evicted with only six months' notice to quit; rents could be increased annually; and evicted tenants had no right to compensation for improvements. A yearly tenancy was not, however, a tenancy at will. A yearly tenant could not just be thrown out by force (occasionally the fate of caretakers), but only by due legal process. Nor could the rent be increased at the mere will of the landlord. The law presumed that a yearly tenancy persisted unchanged from year to year: it did not expire at the end of each year, but continued from year to year, unless surrendered by the tenant. If the landlord wanted to change it, he could do so only by going into court; once, therefore, a yearly tenancy was established, it could be changed only by mutual consent, or by litigation. The landlord had in effect given his land away and could recover it only through the courts.[32]

The third group in the countryside was the agricultural labourers, whose plight was virtually ignored by advocates of land reform; compared, for example, with the accumulation of blue books on tenants, those devoted exclusively to the labourers were few before 1880.[33] Yet in 1861 they were more numerous than farmers: there were 890,520 farm servants, labourers, herds, and ploughmen compared with 440,697 farmers.[34] The term labourer was almost something to be ashamed of; many returned themselves in the census as 'landholders', even if they held only a small patch of land; the grown-up sons of farmers, who were in effect labourers, often described themselves as 'farmers'. The labourers were by far the poorest group in rural society. Their numbers fell sharply after the late 1840s, on account of the famine, the reduced demand for labour, and the attractions of emigration; they had the worst houses; their wages increased, but usually not as rapidly as agricultural prices; their wages were the lowest in the United Kingdom, the highest in Ireland being lower than the lowest in Britain. They had only a small share of the land; many were 'indoor'

---

[31] *Returns Showing the Number of Agricultural Holdings in Ireland* ... HC 1870, lvi. 737. Of the 661,931 tenements enumerated, 135,392 had leases (pp. 16–17).

[32] Below, pp. 21–3.

[33] For an exception see *Reports from Poor Law Inspectors on the Wages of Agricultural Labourers in Ireland* [C 35], HC 1870, xiv. 1; for a comprehensive survey of labourers see David Fitzpatrick, 'The Disappearance of the Irish Agricultural Labourer, 1841–1912', *Ir. Econ. & Soc. Hist.* 7 (1980), 66–92; John W. Boyle, 'A Marginal Figure: The Irish Rural Laborer', in Samuel Clark and James S. Donnelly, jun. (eds.), *Irish Peasants: Violence and Political Unrest, 1780–1914* (Manchester, 1983), 311–38.

[34] *Census Ire., 1861*, pt. v, pp. 466, 475 [3204-IV], HC 1863, lxi; not all were agricultural labourers, however; if the farmers (440,697) are multiplied by 1.8, which is the multiple used by Fitzpatrick for 1861 (see Fitzpatrick, 'The Disappearance of the Irish Agricultural Labourer', 88), there were 793,255.

TABLE 1. Recipients of agricultural incomes, 1865

Recipients	£ million	%
Landlords	14.7	33
Tenants	23.1	52
Landless labourers	6.8	15
TOTAL	44.6	100

Note: This table is based on the assumption that landlords received rent and 15% of profits; that tenants received 85% of profits and 45% of wages; that landless labourers received 55% of wages. The division of wages between tenants and landless labourers is based on the assumption that in 1861 the agricultural labour force was 1,234,000, consisting of 554,000 occupiers (45%) and 680,000 landless labourers (55%). The figure of 1,234,000 follows David Fitzpatrick ('The Disappearance of the Irish Agricultural Labourer', 88), who has put historians in his debt by sorting out farmers, false farmers, landed labourers, and landless labourers.

servants who lived in their masters' houses; the remainder seem to have been distributed between the 281,000 'landless' households that existed in the countryside in 1861 and the 113,000 small occupiers who were not returned as farmers in the census.[35]

The apparent threefold division of rural society coincided with the three factors of production in agriculture (land, labour, and capital) and their rewards (rent, wages, and profits). In 1865, for example, agricultural output was £44.6 million, which was divided: £11.6 million rent, £20.6 million profits, and £12.4 million wages.[36] The actual distribution, however, was not as simple as the theoretical threefold division implies. First, the tenants provided much of the labour themselves; secondly, many landlords were farmers in their own right, probably farming about 15 per cent of the land;[37] thirdly, rents were distributed among groups other than landlords: the government, local authorities, mortgagees, and members of landlords' families. Finally, there was more sub-letting than was recorded in rentals and valuation books. Table 1, which makes allowances for the fact that many landlords were farmers, that many tenants were labourers, and that many labourers had land, shows how agricultural income was distributed among the three main groups in the countryside.

Even assuming that the landlords' share was divided among a group much larger than the landlords themselves, their share was impressive. They appropriated a large agricultural surplus equivalent to, for example,

---

[35] *Census Ire., 1861*, pt. v, pp. 455, 466 [3204-IV], HC 1863, lxi; *Agricultural Statistics, Ire., 1861*, p. xii [3156], HC 1863, lxix. 558.   [36] See below, App. 9.
[37] This estimate is based on a sample of demesnes in *Return of Untenanted Lands in Rural Districts, Distinguishing Demesnes on which there is a Mansion House* ... HC 1906 (250), c. 177.

the sum annually spent on the upkeep of the Royal Navy.[38] The extraction of such a sum and its distribution had certain consequences. It meant that landlords and tenants were the pivots on which a large number of transactions turned: income flowed into the tenants' hands, and out again to labourers, shopkeepers, and landlords; from landlords it went to mortgagees, poor law boards, the Irish church, grand juries, and to the government. The land system seemed to be a pyramid, with money flowing upwards to the landlords; it was, in fact, more like a circle, with landlords and tenants at the centre. (There was the additional irony that some tenants were indirectly their landlords' creditors: through insurance companies, the banks, and the Representative Church Body.[39]) Any interruption of the flow of money to the centre created a crisis that was not entirely under the control of either landlords or tenants.

The extraction of such large sums acted as an incentive to production, forcing tenants to use their land vigorously; it also created a fund from which investment in agriculture could come. It was, however, a relatively inflexible system: rents could go up; having gone up, they could fall only if landlords gave abatements. If prices went up, tenants did well in the short run; when they fell, they lost immediately. On the whole a system like this probably favoured tenants, especially in good times; a sharecropping system would probably have taken more, but would at least have made landlords more sensitive to falling prices. The economic reality, however, was simple, but not widely recognized: tenants could pay low rents indefinitely; but they could not, for any length of time, pay rents that were too high.

While every aspect of the land question attracted public attention— poor rates, encumbered landlords, the tenement valuation, institutional landowners (such as Trinity College, Dublin), limited owners, and land registration—most attention was given to the pivot of the system, the relationship between landlords and tenants. Should this be endlessly negotiable, based on contract, and assuming a *tabula rasa* in social relations? Or should it be restricted by reasonable rules, recognizing the force of prescription, and admitting the importance of status? Both sides claimed to serve the public good; both claimed that more food could be produced; the advocates of tenurial reform argued that security of tenure would make the countryside more peaceful. The advocates of freedom of contract

---

[38] The richest 5% of the rural population received about 45% of agricultural output. This figure is based on the assumption that the richest 40,000 families in 1865 appropriated the whole agricultural rental and 43% of profits; for other European countries see Peter H. Lindert and Jeffrey G. Williamson, 'Reinterpreting Britain's Social Tables, 1688–1913', *Explorations in Economic History*, 20: 1 (Jan. 1983), 96.

[39] For the RCB see L. P. Curtis, jun., 'Incumbered Wealth: Landed Indebtedness in Post-Famine Ireland', *AHR* 85: 2 (Apr. 1980), 332–67.

had perhaps a wider concept of the public good: if large-scale sheep-farming could reduce the price of woollen socks even by a small fraction of a farthing, sweeping changes in rural society might be justified, even required. Both sides, however, had one thing in common: land was private property, whether sold as fee simple, as tenant right, or as unexhausted improvements. There was no demand for land to be communally controlled, except possibly to prevent subdivision. Even the sternest advocate of the rights of tenants did not suggest that tenants who had been rescued from rapacious landlords should be similarly protected from other creditors. Irish tenants were not to be given inalienable land like American Indians, or communally controlled land like Russian serfs. Nor was there any suggestion that the community as a whole had any specific rights, except possibly to agricultural efficiency. The land for the people, when that cry came to predominate, meant the transfer of the fee simple to the present occupiers.

The tendency to concentrate strongly on the relationship between landlords and tenants was most dramatically exemplified by the neglect of farm labourers. They were worse off than the tenants; they could be thrown out of their cottages with a few weeks' notice; many were casually employed (six months' notice would have been an unimaginable luxury for them); they were numerous; but little was done for them, and only lip-service was paid to them during the land war.[40] The reasons for their neglect were various. First, they were a transient group. They were much younger than the farmers, suggesting that labouring was a prelude either to emigration or to inheriting a farm. They seem to have moved on from place to place. Conditions of work on estate farms such as Powerscourt or Woodstock were good; in the Woodstock accounts, for example, it was noted that Thomas Keady was 'not well' for most of the second half of 1860, but he still got his wages of 6s. a week.[41] Yet labourers did not stay for more than a few years: the old family retainer did not exist among the Tottenham labourers. Secondly, the labourers did not have the vote until 1885. Thirdly, they were either too like small farmers to be consciously separated from them;[42] or they lived on large farms, where disputes with their masters were no doubt bitter, frequent, and personal, but not amenable to collective expression.

The division between landlords and tenants was not the only one in rural society. Although labourers were not organized, they did have common

---

[40] Samuel Clark, *Social Origins of the Irish Land War* (Princeton, NJ, 1979), 113–19, 210, 298; for a different view see Paul Bew, *Land and the National Question in Ireland, 1858–82* (Dublin, 1978), 174–5; for labourers' organizations in the 1870s see Pamela L. R. Horn, 'The National Agricultural Labourers' Union in Ireland, 1873–9', *IHS* 17: 67 (Mar. 1971), 340–52. [41] Tottenham wages book, 1860 (NLI, MS 5720).
[42] See Fitzpatrick, 'The Disappearance of the Irish Agricultural Labourer', 82–3.

grievances: reaping-machines, for example, were attacked;[43] disputes between tenants and sub-tenants were frequent.[44] Nor were the tenants united, or even potentially united. There were differences between big and small farmers; disputes between neighbours caused many outrages; there were also local differences: between upland and lowland farmers and between Protestants and Catholics in the north. One great, potential division in the countryside, however, had been removed in 1846 when the corn laws were repealed.

Were Irish landlords peculiarly isolated in rural society? Or to use the phrase beloved of contemporaries, were they alien and absentee? Like many glib phrases this one improved with repetition; like many political clichés it had a grain of truth that was too commonplace to be of much value. Any small group can be described as alien, especially if it is well off, specialized, or privileged. Graziers like Delany of Woodtown, with his gig, his railway shares, and his pretensions, must have seemed strange to small farmers. Priests, with their black clothes, inverted collars, and celibacy hardly blended into the landscape (unneutered celibacy in a pastoral society might qualify as one of the more successful social eyecatchers). Public-spirited publicans, sporting their PLGs and TCs (poor law guardians and town commissioners), must have seemed pretentious to many of their neighbours. By certain criteria the landlords were certainly alien, or rather, could plausibly be shown to be so. For one thing they were largely Protestant; in the 1861 census 48 per cent were Church of Ireland and 43 per cent were Roman Catholics, but this apparent equality did not reflect the fact that most of the big landlords were Protestant. Catholic landlords were not immune from quarrelling with their tenants: William Scully is perhaps the most notorious example; but in 1860 John Whyte was memorialized by 'the Catholics of Banbridge, assembled at a public meeting', because he intended to ask the parish priest to give up his farm. 'If, under similar circumstances, a Protestant landlord acted towards us, as it is said you intend to do,' he was told, 'we would look upon his conduct as harsh and ungenerous.'[45] Presbyterians were very poorly represented among landlords, accounting for only 7 per cent, which suggests that the Irish gentry agreed with Charles II that Presbyterianism was no religion for a gentleman.[46]

The landlords were not as 'culturally' Irish as they had allegedly been in the eighteenth century. Of those who went to university, for example, only a minority went to Trinity; indeed, going to Trinity was almost

---

[43] Clark, *Social Origins*, 210; John W. Boyle, 'A Marginal Figure', 316–17.
[44] Below, pp. 143, 146, 147, 149, 155.
[45] Petition of Banbridge Catholics to John Whyte, 25 Nov. 1860 (PRONI, D2918/3/9/12); see also Hoppen, *Elections, Politics, and Society*, 122–5.
[46] *Census Ire., 1861*, pt. v, pp. 502, 508 [3204-IV], HC 1863, lxi.

accidental among the socially prominent. Lord O'Neill, who had 66,000 acres in County Antrim, was a Trinity graduate, but he had not been the heir apparent of the Chichester estate when he was a youth.[47] Whether a university education made any difference is not certain. Provost Mahaffy, an interested party, thought it did.[48] The reality, however, was that many landlords did not go to university. On the other hand, many were members of Dublin clubs, especially the Kildare Street, suggesting some cultural mediation between London and the localities: 41 per cent were members of Dublin and London clubs; a mere 16 per cent were members only of Dublin clubs.[49]

As very rich people landlords must have seemed different from their tenants. Yet all sections of the upper classes had so much in common by the 1870s that it is doubtful if country people could distinguish, merely on sight, landlords from RMs, bank managers, and solicitors. Country people were indeed supposed to be connoisseurs of blood; Sir Francis Head found them discriminating, especially a man in Galway who had found the 'lord liftinant' a plain man with no 'affictation';[50] Lord John Manners, who would have known what he was talking about, admired 'the veneration generally felt for rank and station by the Irish peasantry'.[51] (These remarks reflect one of the minor advantages of the gentry: they were the touchstone that exposed the baseness of pretension.) What is clear is that the landlords were not a highly refined élite, compounded of ivory and rose petals. Their amusements were the same as their tenants'; in 1869 the fortunes of Lord Lurgan's greyhound, Master Magrath, attracted as much attention as the impending land bill. Landlords and tenants did not, for the most part, speak different languages. There was considerable evidence of close personal contact between landlords and country people. Miss Hinds, a County Cavan landlord, gave a lift to an old man on her way home from Ballyconnell on the day she was murdered;[52] when Arthur Shaen Bingham and his mother were attacked in County Mayo in October 1881, they were with a farmer's daughter, to whom they had given a lift.[53] Lord Mayo helped with hay-making, bought heifers at the Ballinasloe fair, took up wood-turning, and liked potato cakes 'hot off the girdle'.[54]

---

[47] See also W. W. Hunter, *A Life of the Earl of Mayo, Fourth Viceroy of India* (London, 1875), i. 34.
[48] W. B. Stanford and R. B. McDowell, *Mahaffy: A Biography of an Anglo-Irishman* (London, 1971), 124-5; see also Hoppen, *Elections, Politics, and Society*, 116.
[49] These figures are based on a sample of landowners in Bateman, *Great Landowners* (1883); see also Hoppen, *Elections, Politics, and Society*, 119, 127.
[50] Sir Francis B. Head, bt., *A Fortnight in Ireland* (London, 1852), 211.
[51] John Manners, 7th duke of Rutland, *Notes of an Irish Tour in 1846*, new edn. (London, 1881), 107. [52] National Archives, convict reference files, 1856/D/26.
[53] Ibid. ICR, return of outrages, 1881.
[54] W. W. Hunter, *A Life of the Earl of Mayo*, i. 18, 22, 75.

Measured by electoral success landlords kept a grip on many tenants until 1874. One of their achievements was to capture the new rural electorate established in 1850, in spite of the set-back in the 1852 general election. The landlords were strongly Tory. A sample from Bateman's *Great Landowners*, using clubs as a test of politics, showed that only about one-eighth of them were members of the Reform and Brooks's, while nearly one-third were in the Carlton.[55] Most Irish Catholics who were politically active were Liberals. Making an alliance with these was the challenge that faced the landlords as a political élite; this in its way was more important than the details of estate management; that landlords in the end failed was not by any means predictable, even in 1880. Parnell's belief that Irish landlords would espouse home rule when the land question was settled was not unrealistic. That would have been only one of the minor political apostasies of nineteenth-century Britain, certainly not more remarkable than Peel's repeal of the corn laws, Disraeli's extension of the franchise, or Gladstone's disestablishment of the Irish church. Viewed as a political élite, however, apostasy was not among the landlords' talents. The nineteenth-century landlords had little of their ancestors' theological nimbleness, for example; more should have become Catholics, if they had cared about governing the country.

The landlords' visible importance enhanced the land question's importance. Land and its ownership seemed to touch all aspects of rural life. Land was a source of income, a source of political power, and the great source of food, fuel, space, and sport. Neither chapel nor meeting-house, presbytery nor manse, could be built without some landlord's co-operation. Taxes on land supported county government, workhouses, dispensaries, and (in the form of a rent-charge) the Irish church. Rents supported important institutions: Trinity College, Dublin owned almost 200,000 acres, which made it one of the greatest landowners in the British isles. Estates in County Londonderry supported the gormandizing of London merchants. Rents supported endowed schools, such as those at Enniskillen, Armagh, and Dungannon, which like the seven cities of Greece that gave birth to Homer simultaneously claimed to be the Eton of Ireland. Taxes on land, including income tax, poor rates, grand jury cess, tithe rent-charge, and institutional rents amounted to over £2 million in the late 1860s.

Although the land question was constantly before the public, it did not make much of a head of steam between 1848 and 1879; only at the general election of 1880 did it proceed vigorously, its furnaces stoked by the agricultural depression and its valves nicely adjusted by the engineers of the new departure. The importance of the land question can be exaggerated. It had to jostle with other issues, even when it seemed to reign supreme.

[55] Bateman, *Great Landowners* (1883); see also Hoppen, *Elections, Politics, and Society*, 127.

In June 1880, for example, a delegation of tenants waited on James Wann, Lord Gosford's agent; they had not come to demand a rent reduction, as one might have expected, but to ask for his support for an intermediate school, so that their children would 'receive a better classical education than that afforded by a national school'.[56] The land question had to contend with a growing interest in foreign affairs: the Crimean war, the Indian mutiny, the American civil war, the Italian question, especially the predicament of Pius IX, who suffered the attentions of an Italian crow-bar brigade at the Porta Pia on 20 September 1870. Interest in foreign affairs was not confined to an élite of priests and middle-class newspaper readers. In 1870, for example, a crowd gathered in the County Fermanagh village of Kesh, whose population was 296, not to protest against the shortcomings of the land act, but to pass a resolution supporting the king of Prussia.

The landlords were not as strong in the countryside as they appeared. They differed from English landlords in two respects. First, they did not control the constabulary in their counties; secondly, they did not, with exceptions, appoint even the clergy of the Irish church, for most ecclesiastical patronage was in the gift of the Crown or the bishops. The duke of Leinster was unusual in having the advowson of Maynooth (he was also a visitor of the Royal College of St Patrick, a combination of functions that must have made him one of the ecclesiastical curiosities of Christendom). In any case, most tenants were not members of the Irish church: in 1861 only 10 per cent were, while 77 per cent were Roman Catholics, and 12 per cent were Presbyterians.[57] Most landlords had to live with priests and ministers who were not beholden to them, or even likely to be friendly. Priests organized much of the opposition to landlords, especially in the years 1849–52; they shared electoral influence with the landlords; the most voluminous indictment of landlordism was written by the parish priest of Partry, Fr. Lavelle.

The constabulary were superficially more respectful and obliging, but they were not the servants of the landlords. They were controlled by the government, paid for by the Treasury, recruited from all over the country, free from local ties, and officered by men who considered themselves to be at least the equals of the gentry. As magistrates the landlords were restricted in two ways: at the petty sessions by stipendiary magistrates, who were paid, made a career of their position, and reported regularly to the Castle; at the quarter sessions by the assistant barristers, who were professional lawyers and who usually presided. In the enforcement of the law, landlords were at a further disadvantage because of the practical distinction between the criminal and civil law. The constabulary enforced the

---

[56] Wann's letter-book, 4 June 1880 (PRONI, D1606/5/5, p. 340).
[57] *Census Ire.*, 1861, pt. v, p. 502 [3204-IV], HC 1863, lxi.

former, but the latter, which affected the administration of estates, was enforced by the sub-sheriff and his bailiffs (who were described by one lord chancellor as 'the bravest of living things').[58] The constabulary would protect the sheriff, but they did not directly enforce the civil law.

In 1857 the *Annual Register* drew its readers' attention to 'a social revolution in Ireland' when it reported that 'a remarkable contrast to the former state of religious animosity in Ireland' was presented at a dinner where the Tipperary tenantry of Captain Robert Jocelyn Otway, RN, welcomed that 'gallant officer' on his return from the Black Sea. The company included all creeds and classes, parsons and priests fraternizing with each other 'in a spirit of charity and goodwill': the rector of Templederry, Revd W. T. Jordan, who 'filled the chair', proposed 'the catholic clergy' and the health of Fr. Kenyon; in reply Fr. Kenyon—'so well known for his active and energetic participation in the agitations of the troublous year 1848'—proposed 'the protestant clergy'.[59] The *Annual Register* was right to note a change in Ireland, and shrewdly made its point by describing a convivial gathering in what its readers would have known as the most turbulent county in Ireland. By 1857 any of the measurable characteristics of landlord-tenant relations showed a great improvement since the early 1850s: evictions had dwindled to a very small fraction of their numbers in the early 1850s; crime, including agrarian outrages, had fallen below its pre-famine level; on individual estates not only had arrears accumulated during the famine begun to fall, but rents were rising.[60]

As if to match the amelioration of relations between landlords and tenants, the fortunes of the independent Irish party declined: internal squabbles, failure to secure even a modest measure of reform, and the difficulties of organizing such a party in the political circumstances of the 1850s led to the return of only thirteen 'independents' at the general election of 1857, compared with forty-eight in 1852.[61] While the party's internal tensions probably adequately accounted for its failure, the agricultural prosperity of the mid-1850s must also have hastened its decline. The occurrence of dramatic events outside Ireland such as the Crimean war and the Indian mutiny distracted public attention from the land question: fewer pamphlets, for example, on the problems of Irish land were published in the mid- and late 1850s than in the early 1850s.[62]

Where the *Annual Register* erred perhaps, was in its timing of the social

---

[58] Sir John Ross, bt., *Pilgrim Scrip: More Random Reminiscences* (London, 1927), 140.
[59] *Annual Register*, 1857, pt. ii, p. 28; for more on Fr. Kenyon, see James O'Shea, *Priest, Politics and Society in Post-Famine Ireland: A Study of County Tipperary, 1850–1891* (Dublin and Atlantic Highlands, NJ, 1983), 54–5, 57, 154.
[60] See below, Apps. 6 and 7.   [61] Whyte, *Indep. Ir. Party*, 90, 165.
[62] R. D. C. Black, *A Catalogue of Pamphlets on Economic Subjects, Published between 1760 and 1900 ... in Irish Libraries* (Belfast, 1969), 367–424.

revolution: the land question did not fade away after 1857 and the recovery had in fact occurred much earlier than 1857. Almost two years before, the *Irish Farmers' Gazette* had closed the year 1855 with a paean of praise for Irish agriculture: 'each succeeding year seems more eventful than the last, and gives practical proofs of the rapid strides improved agriculture is making in Ireland': Irish short-horns were 'not behind' those of Britain in breeding; Irish sheep were 'progressing'; 'in pigs, we have nothing to desire'; in the cultivation of roots and green crops 'we shine preeminently'.[63] Even before 1855 the *Irish Farmers' Gazette* had discerned signs of improvement. In 1851, when evictions, while not as high as in 1850, exceeded 8,000, the *Farmers' Gazette* noticed reassuring signs of vitality in land and people: in May a 'common-sized' hen laid an egg 'of the prodigious girth of 7¾ inches'; in June a salmon in the River Shannon got away after exhausting three fishermen in a twenty-three hours' struggle; in August an 'enormous fleece of wool' weighing 18 lbs was taken from a ram near Hillsborough; in October at the Belturbet Agricultural Society's Show, not only did the splendid bull 'Tenant Right' excite universal admiration, but the object of 'greatest curiosity' at the show was 'an immense-sized' child, who was only 4 years old, but weighed 7 stoné.[64]

Calculations of agricultural output make the same point: that prosperity returned to Ireland even before the mid-1850s. Between 1852 and 1853 there was a dramatic increase, over 40 per cent, followed by the remarkably good years of 1854 and 1855, when the Crimean war caused an increase in agricultural prices, especially grain prices.[65] Although the high levels of the years 1854–5 were not maintained, generally good years followed, establishing a pattern of high agricultural incomes that was in strong contrast to the late 1840s and early 1850s. While calculations of agricultural output firmly suggest that 1853—the year before the Crimean war—was the turning-point, there are enough problems associated with the calculation of agricultural output, however, to induce caution.[66] The recovery in agriculture may indeed have occurred even earlier than 1853. Sir John Benn-Walsh, who visited his Irish estates every year between 1848 and 1853, recorded in his journal in 1851 that he left Ireland that year 'with far more hope & in better spirits than on any of the three former occasions since the potato failure'.[67] His description of the condition of his estates in the following year, 1852, shows that improvement was well under way: 'It seems universally admitted that the country has greatly improved; prices are really good for stock, butter, pigs, & sheep, and while

---

[63] *Irish Farmers' Gazette*, 29 Dec. 1855, p. 711.
[64] Ibid. 31 May, 7 June, 26 July, 4 Oct., pp. 261, 271, 361, 476.
[65] See below, App. 9.   [66] Below, pp. 247–8.
[67] James S. Donnelly, jun., 'The Journals of Sir John Benn-Walsh Relating to the Management of his Irish Estates, 1823–64', *Cork Hist. Soc. Jn.* 70: 230 (1974), 117.

in the old days of outdoor relief there were 30,000 souls on the lists out of a population of 70,000 there are now not more than 1,500.'[68] (William Allingham had also noted that the peasantry believed that Ireland would flourish in 1852.[69])

The rentals of individual estates show that rents were being paid punctually before 1853: on the Blacker and Inchiquin estates rent receipts equalled annual rents as early as 1848; on the Clonbrock estate in Galway and the Erne estate in Donegal receipts equalled annual rents in 1849; on the Murray Stewart estate in Donegal, where farms were miserably small, remote, and on poor land, rents were paid punctually in 1850 for the first time since the beginning of the famine; in 1852 rents on the Ashtown estate in Galway were not only paid punctually, but exceeded the annual rental by nearly 50 per cent, almost wiping out the arrears accumulated in the previous years. It is true, however, that similar signs of recovery did not appear on other estates until the mid-1850s: rent receipts approached annual rents on the Knox estate in Roscommon and on the Pratt estate in Cavan only in 1853 and 1854.[70]

Recovery, therefore, took place over a six-year period, 1848–54, but it is remarkable how quickly many tenants recovered from the effects of the famine.[71] Recovery, however, in the more substantial sense that tenants not only paid current rents but began to pay off the arrears accumulated during the famine certainly did not occur on some estates until the war years 1854–5; on the Garvagh estate in Londonderry and on the Midleton estate in Cork, for example, this was true. A sacerdotal squabble in a minor Asiatic city not only united Turk and Christian in an inept war, but also eradicated the lingering effects of the famine on many Irish estates; less directly, one of the least glorious casualties of the war was the movement to reform the land system. Recovery from the effects of the famine in the 1850s was more than the mere exhausting of the terrible impetus of the years 1847–9, for the rise in prices and incomes in 1853 was unexpected and dramatic, thus dispelling the gloom that had hung over the whole of agricultural production in the late 1840s. The basis of Irish agricultural prosperity between the early 1850s and the late 1870s was the increased value of livestock and livestock products, especially store cattle and butter. The importance of cereals, however, must not be forgotten: much of the prosperity of the years 1854–5 was based on high cereal prices. This, of course, was a temporary phenomenon,

---

[68] Ibid. 119.
[69] William Allingham, 'Irish Ballad Singers and Irish Street Ballads', *Household Words*, 4: 94 (Jan. 1852), 365.
[70] See below, App. 8; Murray Stewart rentals (County Donegal), 1847–50 (NLI, MSS 5467–9); Pratt rentals (County Cavan), 1850–64 (ibid. MS 3122).
[71] Donnelly, *Land and People of Cork*, 145.

and the value of wheat production, for example, began to fall after 1856; but the fact remains that the 'conversion' from tillage to pasture was spread over a number of years and the transition was eased by the windfall years in the mid-1850s.

The effects of agricultural prosperity were most noticeable on rents. Not only were famine arrears cleared off, but on some estates even pre-famine arrears were cleared—on the Erne estate in Donegal, for example. Most unexpected, however, was the fact that rents actually began to rise, which could not have been foreseen in 1851 or 1852, except in rare circumstances. Between 1851 and 1860 rents on the Pratt estate in County Cavan increased by 29 per cent and rents on the Murray Stewart estate in County Donegal increased by 21 per cent.[72] It would be misleading to say that the changed aspect of estate management—rentals not only cleared of arrears, but actually buoyant—was the basis of a resurgence of landlord influence in the 1850s, best exemplified by the dissolution of the tenant league in 1858, but also by the fact that the Tories won a majority of seats in Ireland in the 1859 general election, which was the only time they did so between 1832 and 1921.[73] For one thing, not all Irish landlords were Tories; also, the Tory victory in 1859 owed as much to the disarray of those who had opposed the landlords in 1852 as it did to the strength of landlordism in 1859. But landlordism was stronger in 1859 than it had been in 1849; many hopelessly insolvent landlords had been replaced by newcomers who bought estates offered for sale by the encumbered estates court; the laws governing landlord and tenant relations were still unchanged in spite of the electoral successes of the independent Irish party; evictions and agrarian crime had fallen dramatically, and the countryside was more peaceful than it had been for twenty years.

A closer look, however, at landlord-tenant relations at the end of the 1850s suggests that the progress of the last seven or eight years had limitations. First, it would have been in the landlords' interest if the independent Irish party had secured some measure of reform. If, for example, tenants had been empowered to claim compensation for improvements made without their landlords' permission, landlords would have been forced to take a serious interest in agricultural improvement. At the very least, such a measure would have removed the issue from discussion, with the possible result that more important problems would have been tackled.[74] Secondly, while landlords had done relatively well with rents, by 1859 rent increases had begun to fall behind increases in the value of agricultural output, and the major change in the distribution of agricultural incomes that was the

---

[72] Pratt rentals (County Cavan), 1850–64 (NLI, MS 3122); Murrary Stewart rentals (County Donegal), 1850–9 (ibid. MSS 5470, 5473–7).
[73] Walker, *Election Results, 1801–1922*, 193.   [74] Below, pp. 127–8.

most important development between the famine and the land war began decisively and almost unnoticed in the mid-1850s.[75]

Progress between the early 1850s and the mid-1870s was not uninterrupted. The early 1860s were marked by agricultural depression: the beginning of 1860 'was marked by a great dearth of fodder and loss of cattle in many districts of the west and south of Ireland';[76] the potato crop was poor in 1860; in 1861 its yield was the lowest recorded since 1847; in 1862 it was better, but not good. Oats were below average in 1861 and 1862; wheat was below average in 1860, 1861, and 1862; the value of butter fell in 1862 and 1863; the value of cattle fell in 1861 and 1862.[77] Arrears increased; evictions increased in the years 1861–4; agrarian outrages increased in 1862–4.[78] From 1864, however, prosperity returned, and remained until 1877, except in 1867, when the value of agricultural output fell;[79] but the fall in 1867 did not have any great effect on evictions or agrarian outrages, although arrears increased on some estates. A poor potato crop in 1871 and a bad one in 1872 seem to have been cushioned by the general prosperity.[80]

[75] See below, App. 9.
[76] *Annual Report of the Commissioners for Administering the Laws for Relief of Poor in Ireland* ... p. 7 [2966], HC 1862, xxiv. 549.
[77] For a comprehensive survey see James S. Donnelly, jun., 'The Irish Agricultural Depression of 1859–64', *Ir. Econ. & Soc. Hist.* 3 (1976), 33–54 and id., *Land and People of Cork*, 146–8; see also William Neilson Hancock, *Report on the Supposed Progressive Decline of Irish Prosperity* (Dublin, 1863). [78] See below, Apps. 7, 1, and 19.
[79] See below, App. 9; see also Donnelly, *Land and People of Cork*, 148–50.
[80] See below, App. 9.

2
Evictions

i. Numbers, Fluctuations, and Incidence

In September 1853 the sub-sheriff of County Galway, escorted by eleven constables, ejected forty-two families in the townland of Kilcoosh, which had just been bought in the encumbered estates court by J. N. Gerrard of Gibstown, County Meath. There was no trouble when the sheriff demanded possession and the tenants were allowed to remain on their farms as caretakers until they had harvested their crops. They were warned, however, that the sub-sheriff would have to return and 'put them all out if they remained there'. The tenants promised that they would 'be totally cleared off and cause him no further trouble' by 1 November. They did not keep their promise and on 11 November the sub-sheriff had to go out again, escorted by thirty-six constables. At Kilcoosh they were confronted by 'upwards of 400 men and women assembled, who evinced a determination of resistance'. When the landlord's steward tried to level some of the houses 'the mob got so outrageous that Mr O'Hara [the sub-sheriff] thought it advisable not to persevere further as he was decidedly of opinion if he did, the loss of life would be the result.' A fortnight later he set out again, this time escorted by forty constables and fifty-five soldiers of the 33rd regiment from Athlone. The tenants were cowed by this display of force and thirty-one houses were unroofed, and only ten families were left as caretakers. The valuation records show that all of the caretakers were later removed.[1]

In the years after the famine there was nothing exceptional about the Kilcoosh evictions. They were not even exceptional in the east riding of Galway in the early 1850s: in 1850 J. C. R. Burke evicted fifty-two families and levelled forty houses, and Elizabeth West evicted forty-one families and levelled their houses.[2] In the west riding even larger evictions took place: in 1851 on the Martin estate over 400 families were evicted and 267 houses levelled.[3] If there was anything remarkable about the Kilcoosh evictions it was the relative prosperity of the tenants, for the police reported

---

[1] National Archives, RP 1853/10655; VO Dublin: cancelled books for County Galway/Mountbellew/Clonkeen; below, p. 183; see also James S. Donnelly, jun., 'Landlords and Tenants', in Vaughan (ed.), *A New History of Ireland*, v. *Ireland under the Union, I. 1801–70* (Oxford, 1989), 342.
[2] National Archives, RP 1850/16482, C187.   [3] Ibid. OP 1851/28.

that they were 'in most comfortable circumstances, [and] always paid their rent, poor rates, and taxes'.[4]

It would be hard to exaggerate the emotional significance of evictions in nineteenth-century Ireland. The family thrown out of its home in bad weather, with no refuge but the workhouse, was well depicted in prose and verse, in paintings, and in illustrations in periodicals such as the *Illustrated London News*.[5] The emotion generated explained the obsession with security of tenure in the writings and speeches of those who advocated reform of the law of landlord and tenant. Sir John Gray, the editor of the *Freeman's Journal*, devoted ten of the forty-four pages of his pamphlet on the land question, published in 1869, to evictions.[6] Emotion may also have caused the exaggeration that seemed to accompany estimates of the number of evictions. The constabulary recorded the eviction of 68,767 families in the thirty-two years 1849–80—or 344,711 persons.[7] Although these figures have shortcomings, it is unlikely that they seriously underestimate the number of actual evictions;[8] but Fr. Thomas Meagher, giving evidence to the Cowper commission in 1886, claimed that 900,000 families had been evicted during the previous fifty years.[9] Assuming that the number of persons in each family was the same as in the constabulary's returns, Fr. Meagher believed that four and a half million people had been evicted since 1836. Michael Mulhall, the author of a dictionary of statistics that went through several editions, estimated that 363,000 families were evicted between 1849 and 1882. He was quite clear that he meant families and not individuals, for he stated that the 'number of persons actually evicted was over 2 millions'.[10] (Mulhall's 'families' seem in fact to have been the constabulary's 'persons'; such a slip is significant in a compiler of statistics as careful and as experienced as Mulhall.)

Before the land act of 1870 ejectment procedures were simple and swift. They varied slightly, according to the tenure and size of holdings, but all were analogous to those used for the ejectment of yearly tenants, who could be ejected if their rent fell into one year's arrears or after the expiry of six months' notice to quit. The forcible removal of the tenant by the sub-sheriff, assisted if necessary by the constabulary, could take place only with the sanction of a court, and after 1851 for yearly tenants this usually

---

[4] Ibid. RP 1853/10655.
[5] *Illustrated London News*, 20 Mar. 1880; see also Lady Butler's painting *The Eviction* (Irish Folklore Commission), which was reproduced on the jacket of Cecil Woodham-Smith's, *The Great Hunger: Ireland 1845–9* (London, 1962).
[6] Sir John Gray, *The Irish Land Question: Speech of Sir John Gray, Delivered in the Free Trade Hall, Manchester, on 18 October 1869* (Dublin and London, 1869), 14–23.
[7] *Return of Evictions, 1849–80*, see below, App. 1.   [8] Below, pp. 229–30.
[9] *Cowper Comm., Minutes of Evidence*, 444.
[10] Michael G. Mulhall, *Dictionary of Statistics* (London, 1884), 175.

meant the 'civil bill' court.[11] Depending on the grounds for ejectment, the landlord had a choice of procedures: if he wished to eject for non-payment, the tenant was served with a process stating the amount of rent and costs due; if he wanted to get rid of a tenant who was not in arrears, he had to give six months' notice to quit, followed by a process for overholding. Both processes summoned the tenant to appear in court to show why he had not paid his rent, or given up the holding. The difference between them, however, was important: the ejectment for non-payment could be stopped by the tenant paying his arrears and costs; the ejectment for overholding could be stopped only if the landlord gave up the case or the tenant got out. When the case came to trial, its outcome depended largely on technicalities; there was no jury in civil bill cases; the court had no power to withhold an ejectment decree—if the proper forms had been observed.

If the court decided in the landlord's favour, he was given an ejectment decree, which was an order to the sheriff to give the landlord possession of the holding. It was at this point that the scene described above took place, when the sub-sheriff set out, often but not always escorted by the constabulary, to enforce the decree. The decree had to be executed within a certain period—it could not be held indefinitely as a threat to the tenant. It had to be executed on a weekday between 9 a.m. and 3 p.m.; it could not, after 1848, be executed on Christmas Day or Good Friday. The landlord or his agent had to inform the relieving officer at least forty-eight hours before the eviction took place; failure to do so could lead to a fine of £20. The amount of force that could be used was strictly regulated. It was, for example, a misdemeanour to unroof a house while it was still occupied.[12] The sub-sheriff and his escort did nothing more than give possession to the landlord's bailiffs: they did not, for example, unroof the house of the evicted tenant. If that was done, it was done by the landlord's bailiffs and it was done to what had just become the landlord's property.

Even when tenants were ejected they were not always thrown out on the road. Some were readmitted as caretakers, like those at Kilcoosh; some were readmitted as full tenants. A tenant evicted for non-payment had six months in which to redeem his holding by paying arrears and costs, even though he was actually put out of possession. Between 1849 and 1880

---

[11] 14 & 15 Vict., c. 57 (1 Aug. 1851); De Moleyns, *Landowner's Guide* (1872), 161–92; on ejectment procedures see J. W. Carleton, *The Jurisdiction and Procedure of the County Courts in Ireland* (Dublin, 1878); William Dwyer Ferguson and Andrew Vance, *The Tenure and Improvement of Land in Ireland* ... (Dublin, 1851); Joseph Smith Furlong, *The Law of Landlord and Tenant, as Administered in Ireland*, 2nd edn. by R. Digues La Touche (2 vols.; Dublin, 1869); Francis Nolan and Robert Romney Kane, *The Statutes Relating to the Law of Landlord and Tenant in Ireland since 1860* (Dublin, 1871); Bram Stoker, *The Duties of Clerks of Petty Sessions in Ireland* (Dublin, 1879).

[12] 11 & 12 Vict., c. 47 (14 Aug. 1848).

over 20 per cent of evicted tenants were readmitted as caretakers or tenants.[13] (The difference between a caretaker and a tenant was an important one: the former could be removed without notice and 'on the failure of gentler means, force may be used'; a tenant had to be given notice to quit and could not be removed without the judicial process already described.[14])

Fluctuations in the number of evictions between the famine and the land war followed a pattern. They were high in the late 1840s and early 1850s; by 1853 they had fallen to their lowest level since 1846 and they remained low until 1861 when they began to increase, almost doubling between 1861 and 1864, when they reached a peak. Then they fell again and remained low until the late 1870s; from 1878 they increased rapidly until they reached a peak of over 5,000 in 1882; again they fell, but not to the low level of the 1870s.[15] The period between the famine and the land war, in spite of the high numbers in the early 1860s, was a period of stability between two great crises, with 1853 and 1878 marking the turning-points: the former marked the end of the famine and the latter the beginning of the land war.

The peak of 1,600 in 1864 was unimpressive compared with 14,000 in 1850 and 5,000 in 1882. The crisis of the 1860s did not persist for long, lasting four years, compared with eight years between 1846 and 1853 and ten years between 1878 and 1887. The total evictions in the three periods make the same point: 70,000 families were evicted between 1846 and 1853, 30,000 between 1878 and 1887, but only 5,000 between 1861 and 1864.[16] It is worth noting that evictions during the land war and its aftermath, in spite of the land league, the land act of 1881, the arrears act of 1882, and the fact that the agricultural crisis of the late 1870s, though bad, was not as bad as the famine, were almost half the number that occurred during the famine.

If the fluctuations of evictions are compared with those of arrears and the value of agricultural output, their cause is apparent. Evictions were frequent when arrears were high and output low: in the early 1850s, early 1860s, and late 1870s. They fell when arrears fell and output increased: in the mid-1850s and mid-1860s.[17] Other evidence confirmed the connection between evictions and arrears. An examination of evictions on individual estates showed that most tenants who were threatened with eviction were in arrears.[18] It also showed that most tenants who were threatened were not actually removed. The judicial statistics show that most ejectments were for non-payment and not for overholding; in 1864, for example,

---

[13] *Return of Evictions, 1849–80*, 3; see below, App. 1.
[14] De Moleyns, *Landowner's Guide* (1872), 62.   [15] See below, App. 1.
[16] Ibid.   [17] See below, Apps. 7 and 9.
[18] W. E. Vaughan, 'A Study of Landlord and Tenant Relations in Ireland between the Famine and the Land War, 1850–78' (Ph.D. thesis, University of Dublin, 1974), 157–9.

civil bill ejectments entered for non-payment outnumbered those for overholding. In County Mayo, one of the worst-affected counties, there were 516 ejectments for non-payment and only 83 for overholding.[19]

Much contemporary attention was attracted by the problem of the solvent, improving tenant who was capriciously evicted. Most of the bills introduced in parliament in the 1850s and 1860s, as well as the land act of 1870 itself, were founded on the belief that the most pressing problem of landlord–tenant relations was the landlords' power to evict yearly tenants on six months' notice to quit. The other form of ejectment, for non-payment, was not given as much attention as the notice to quit, which could be served so easily, printed on the back of rent receipts, and falling on the tenants like snowflakes, or 'thick as autumnal leaves that strow the brooks in Vallombrosa'.[20] There is no doubt, however, that eviction was generally a form of insolvency. The problem, in so far as eviction was the most important aspect of the land question, was the feckless, unfortunate, or improvident tenant who was evicted because he could not pay his rent. Yet to isolate the landlords' power of eviction, it was necessary, unconsciously or deliberately, to ignore the fact that eviction was not usually different from any of the other debt-collection measures provided by the law.

The famine and its aftermath were probably the worst period for evictions in the nineteenth century; certainly, the eight years 1846–53, with an estimated 70,000 evictions, were worse than any period for which statistics exist. Beginning in 1846, which was probably not untypical of pre-famine years, evictions increased annually until 1850, when they reached a peak of 14,336.[21] How many solvent tenants like those at Kilcoosh were evicted? The rentals show that many tenants were in arrears, although it is surprising that arrears were not higher;[22] the returns of evictions in the Kilrush union show that most were evicted for non-payment;[23] the number of ordinary civil bill decrees greatly exceeded those for ejectment in 1846–50, suggesting that indebtedness of all kinds increased greatly during the

---

[19] *Judicial Statistics, Ire.*, *1864*, p. 136 [3563], HC 1865, lii. 842; see also below, Apps. 1 and 2. For the connection between poverty and evictions, see below, App. 23.

[20] A. M. Sullivan, *New Ireland* (London, 1877), i. 353; see also *Paradise Lost*, i. 302. In 1876 5,531 notices to quit were issued; in the same year there were 553 evictions (*Return 'of the Number of Stamps for Notices to Quit Issued by Each Stamp Distributor in Ireland from the Time of the Adoption of the Distinctive Die* [16 Oct. 1875] *to 1880*...' p. 1, HC 1881 (53), lxxvii. 755; see also below, App. 1). Assuming that there were ten notices to quit for every eviction, 530,000 were served in the ten years 1850–9, 97,000 in the years 1860–9, 69,000 in the years 1870–9, and 290,000 in the years 1880–7. The total served between 1850 and 1886 comes almost to a million, which is an impressive figure. Before concluding that Sullivan and others were right, however, it should be remembered that almost 3 million ordinary civil bill processes were served in the ten years 1870–9, which makes the 69,000 notices to quit served in the same period appear insignificant (see below, App. 2).

[21] See below, App. 1.   [22] See below, App. 7.

[23] *Reports and Returns Relating to Evictions in the Kilrush Union*, pp. 8–19 [1084], HC 1849, xlix. 322–31.

famine.²⁴ Yet returns of ejectments for the three years 1846-8 showed that those for overholding were slightly more numerous than those for non-payment. In other words, more than half of those ejected were solvent. Before concluding that this was so, it must be remembered that before 1851 landlords often had to use notices to quit to proceed against insolvent tenants, because yearly tenants, holding without written agreements, could not be proceeded against for non-payment.²⁵ It is probable, therefore, that many ejectments for overholding were for non-payment of rent, and that a majority of those evicted were insolvent.

The effects of a large number of evictions on a locality were drastic. When the report on the Kilrush evictions was presented to parliament, its voluminous recital of thousands of evictions in one poor law union moved Sir Robert Peel to doubt 'that the records of any country, civil or barbarous, present materials for such a picture as is set forth in the statement of Captain Kennedy'.²⁶ The absolute numbers evicted in Kilrush were horrifying enough—2,700 families between 1847 and 1850, or 18 per cent of the union's population in three years; but the concentration of the evictions in certain areas and the apparent laying waste of parts of the countryside made them worse.²⁷ Even the 70,000 evictions that took place in the whole country between 1846 and 1853 would not have threatened or even seriously modified the structure of rural society if they had been evenly spread throughout the whole country. They were not, however, evenly spread. Some counties had more than others: Tipperary, the worst county in 1849-53, had nineteen times as many evictions as Fermanagh, which had the fewest evictions.²⁸

A large proportion of the evictions in the late 1840s and early 1850s were clearances, either on one estate or in one locality. How many clearances were there in the late 1840s and early 1850s? Quarterly returns of evictions made by the constabulary have survived for eleven of the sixteen quarters of 1850-3. In those eleven quarters there were 141 clearances where more than forty families were removed simultaneously from the

---

²⁴ A Return 'Giving, in Tabular Form, the Number of Original Civil Bill Ejectment Processes Entered, and the Number of Copies Served in Each of the Years 1844, 1845, 1846, 1847, 1848, 1849, and 1850...' HC 1851 (322), l. 335. A Return 'Giving, in Tabular Form, the Number of Original Civil Bill Ejectment Processes Entered, and the Number of Copies Served in Each of the Years 1844, 1845, 1846, 1847, 1848, 1849, and 1850...' HC 1851 (322), l. 335; Returns 'from the Courts of Queen's Bench, Common Pleas, and Exchequer in Ireland, of the Number of Ejectments Brought in Those Courts Respectively, for the Last Three Years, Beginning with Hilary Term 1846, and Ending with Hilary Term 1849; ... and, from the Assistant Barristers' Court of Each County of Ireland, of the Number of Civil Bill Ejectments...' HC 1849 (315), xlix. 235.

²⁵ J. C. Brady, 'Legal Developments, 1801-79', in Vaughan (ed.), *A New History of Ireland*, v. *Ireland under the Union, 1*. 457.   ²⁶ Hansard 3, cv. 1287.

²⁷ *Report from the Select Committee on Kilrush Union; together with Proceedings of the Committee, Minutes of Evidence, Appendix, and Index*, pp. 2, 249, HC 1850 (613), xi. 550, 797.   ²⁸ Below, p. 235.

same estate. In the third quarter of 1852, for example, 289 families (1,441 persons) were evicted and 197 houses levelled on Sir Samuel O'Malley's estate in County Mayo.[29] By inference it is plausible to assume that in the whole four years 1850–3 there were 200 such clearances, each one on average involving the removal of eighty families. If evictions for the years 1846–9 contained the same number of clearances, there were at least 220 in those years. Putting the two figures together suggests that there were over 400 clearances between 1846 and 1853. In other words, clearances accounted for almost half of the 70,000 evictions during the famine and its aftermath.

After 1853 the concentration of evictions in certain counties and on individual estates became less pronounced. The difference between the 'best' and the 'worst' counties in the decade 1861–70 was much less than in 1849–53. Kilcoosh may have been one of the last post-famine clearances; certainly from 1854 the annual returns of evictions could not have contained many clearances, for few counties returned numbers large enough to contain a clearance. County Clare, where evictions had been numerous in the early 1850s—there were 1,576 in 1850—never returned more than a hundred between 1853 and 1880; indeed evictions in Clare rarely exceeded forty a year, except in a few bad years in the early 1860s.[30]

Not only were clearances rare after 1853, they were also well publicized. The Derryveagh evictions in County Donegal, when J. G. Adair evicted forty-seven families in April 1861, were no worse than those at Kilcoosh, or indeed than hundreds of famine clearances, but they were widely discussed.[31] The small clearance at Partry, when the bishop of Tuam, Lord Plunket, evicted several families, also received elaborate attention in press and parliament. Fr. Lavelle's personality and his vigorous advocacy of the tenants' cause may have explained some of the attention they received; the Derryveagh evictions helped to keep alive the interest in Partry—until the events following the attack on Fort Sumter by the Confederates distracted attention from both.[32] There was also a scandalous piquancy attaching to both Partry and Derryveagh that lightened, without mitigating, them. One of Lord Plunket's tenants was apparently evicted 'for conduct of the grossest indecency, conduct which I dare not venture to describe'.[33] The Christian Brothers in Partry disliked the ladies of Plunket's family passing in front

---

[29] National Archives, RP 1850/16482, C187; OP 1851/28; RP 1852/C268; 1853/11351; see also James S. Donnelly, jun., 'Landlords and Tenants', in Vaughan (ed.), *A New History of Ireland*, v. *Ireland under the Union*, I. 342.

[30] *Return of Evictions, 1849–80*, passim.   [31] Vaughan, *Derryveagh Evictions*, 11–14.

[32] The Derryveagh evictions were carried out on 8–10 April 1861; Fort Sumter was attacked on 12 April.

[33] See *Daily Express*, 23 Nov. 1859 in National Archives, RP 1861/7272.

of their school, and to discourage them 'recourse was had to a device which ... though not decent, was certainly ingenious'.[34]

Other evictions were controversial not so much because of their harshness, but because they challenged notions about the proper management of estates. The evictions on the Pollok estate in County Galway, for example, were debated in parliament. What was at issue was not that Allan Pollok, who had acquired a large estate in County Galway through the encumbered estates court, was trying to clear his estates of hundreds of families, but that he was trying to get them to give up their farms and to work as labourers.[35] (The valuation books and the census returns show roughly what happened on his estate: holdings disappeared, but the people remained.[36]) In 1857 in the King's County a large number of evictions were reported by the constabulary: 242 compared with nine in the previous year and thirty-eight in the next—a clear sign that a clearance had taken place.[37] The cause was apparently the breaking of leases on the Digby estate by the agent, William Steuart Trench. The tenants were not actually removed, but their leases were replaced by yearly tenancies.[38] Again, these evictions attracted attention; partly because they showed how tenants could fall foul of the law and partly because of the agent's flamboyance.

The publicity given to clearances after 1853 and the relative obscurity of those that happened before—very few famine clearances were mentioned in parliament, for example[39]—is not easily explained. The typical eviction after 1853 was not a clearance; nor was it the capricious removal of solvent, improving tenants, but the final blow to an insolvent tenant. Evictions, therefore, were likely to be more common in depressed years—in the early 1860s, for example; they were also likely to be more frequent in certain counties—they were ten times more frequent in Leitrim in the 1860s than in Londonderry.[40] Whether small holdings were more likely to be evicted than large ones is less clear; the rentals show that even the larger holdings were often in arrears in bad years. To some extent, the attention given to the Derryveagh evictions was a distraction from the real problem, which was the eviction of insolvent tenants in depressed years. The eviction of insolvent tenants, however, did not take place without bitterness. In November 1863 two tenants in the townland of Crumlin near Roscrea

---

[34] 'Lex', *Doings in Partry: A Chapter of Irish History in a Letter to the Rt. Hon. the Earl of Derby, KG* (London, 1860).
[35] *Hansard* 3, cxli. 1707–18; cxlii. 697–712; National Archives, RP 1856/15416.
[36] VO Dublin: cancelled books for County Galway/Glenamaddy/Creggs & Ballynakill; *Census Ire., 1881*, iv. *Province of Connacht*, pp. 19–23 [C 3268], HC 1882, lxxix.
[37] National Archives, RP 1874/685, p. 25.
[38] Godkin, *Land War in Ire.*, 391; Trench, *Realities of Ir. Life*, 311–31.
[39] For a rare example, see *Hansard* 3, xcvii. 856–8.
[40] See below, Apps. 1 and 3. Leitrim had 37 evictions per 1,000 holdings in 1861–70; Londonderry had only 4.

were evicted for non-payment. Although they had only 20 acres each they owed arrears of £50 and £60. According to the constabulary they blamed 'agricultural disappointments' for their failure, which was not surprising given the badness of the previous seasons; but they also blamed their landlord, who had raised their rent to 'more than its value about six years ago'; also they did not like the agent, who was 'considered very harsh'. (They had been much happier under their former landlord, Lord Portarlington.)[41] This case shows that resentment was stirred up by the kind of eviction that could have taken place under any of the proposed tenant-right legislation of the 1850s and 1860s, and even under the land act of 1881.

Even collusive evictions, where tenants' convenience was the landlord's aim, could cause trouble by creating a vacuum into which contending forces rushed. Two brothers, James and Florence Donoghue, inherited the leasehold of a farm in the townland of Rusheenbeg near Killarney, under Daniel Coltsman of Flesk Castle. Florence 'became dissipated and improvident and failed in the payment of his proportion of the rent'; James, finding that he was liable for his brother's arrears, asked the landlord 'to protect him from ruin' by evicting both of them. A chapel and a school, sub-let by the Donoghues to Fr. Shanahan and his clerk Darby Sullivan, had also to be ejected in July 1859 when all parties gave up possession. The priest and the clerk were readmitted as caretakers and James Donoghue was given the land for six months subject to redemption. At the end of the six months, however, a row began: the landlord wanted to let the ground for the chapel and the school directly to the priest at 2s. a year, with a lease, in which eschatological possibilities were nicely balanced—'for ever (if wanted so long) for the purposes of a chapel'. The clerk opposed this arrangement and had to be forcibly removed, refusing even 'a garden and a better house' as the price of his acquiescence. The rest of the land was let to the former tenant, James Donoghue, at the old rent, and he gave his brother £120 as 'tenant right' to emigrate.[42] What had started as a landlord's attempt to sort out a family dispute ended as a row; what was superficially a landlord–tenant dispute seems in fact to have been a dispute between the parish priest and Darby Sullivan.

What were the effects of evictions? At one level this question is almost unanswerable. During the famine and its aftermath 70,000 families were thrown out of their homes by legal process; between 1854 and 1878 there were 700 or 800 evictions returned annually; between the mid-1860s and mid-1870s there were on average fewer than 500 annually, implying that only one tenant out of every thousand was removed per year. The famine clearances were like a great natural disaster: hopeless problems of coping

[41] National Archives, RP 1863/9788. [42] Ibid. RP 1860/13318.

with distress were created; since whole communities were uprooted, there were few neighbours left to give the evicted shelter. The social landscape of those who remained was transformed: many, who were well placed in rural society before the famine, were now at the bottom of the landholding hierarchy. They had survived, indeed; but many not very different from themselves had not. Like those who survived an earthquake or an epidemic, many must have had tormenting memories, a sense of guilt, and a fear of a recurrence. A striving to make sense of their predicament in terms of human responsibility was not an unpredictable phenomenon.

ii. Evictions and Estate Management

The judicial statistics and estate papers show that threats of eviction exceeded evictions. Notices to quit and ejectment processes exceeded the number of ejectment decrees, which in turn exceeded the number of executions made by the sub-sheriff and the number of evictions returned by the constabulary. In 1869, for example, 3,232 civil bill ejectment processes were served, 1,890 decrees were granted, 683 were executed; in the same year only 372 evictions were returned by the constabulary.[43] The diminishing rate of implementation at each successive stage of the legal procedure suggests that threats of eviction were much more frequent, and possibly more important, than actual evictions.

Why did landlords threaten tenants with eviction? Two ejectment books of Earl Fitzwilliam's estate in the counties of Wicklow and Wexford have survived, showing not only the number of notices to quit served annually during the period 1845–86 but also in many cases the reasons for their service.[44] The number served varied from year to year; 1850 was one of the busiest—about 200 were served. Most were served on tenants who were in arrears, which is surprising, since after 1851 it would have been easier to use ejectments for non-payment. Arrears, however, were not the only reason: tenants were served with notices for sub-letting, non-residence, bad farming, and admitting squatters or lodgers. Some tenants were threatened for less predictable reasons: one 'for beating his wife and drunken rows'; another for snaring hares; another because he was 'not thought to be steady'. The supervision of farming seems to have been strict, if conventional: in 1867 several tenants were served with notices for selling hay off their farms; another 'for not managing the place as a farmer should'. The two most important things to emerge from these books were: first, very few of those served with notices were actually removed; secondly, the same names appeared over and over again—whatever the

---

[43] *Judicial Statistics, Ire., 1869*, pp. 209–12 [C 227], HC 1870, lxiii. 961–4; see below, Apps. 1 and 2.

[44] Fitzwilliam ejectment books, 1845–60, 1861–86 (NLI, MSS 4972, 4992).

value of threats of eviction, they were not a cure for certain kinds of agrarian recidivism.

Lord Fitzwilliam was a paternal landlord who interfered in his tenants' affairs; other landlords may have interfered less, but they also used threats of eviction for a variety of purposes. Probably the most important use, as on the Fitzwilliam estate, was to keep estates free of arrears, either by getting rid of defaulting tenants or by putting pressure on those who were slow in paying.[45] As the gale day approached, preparations for initiating ejectment procedures would be made. In May 1874 William Wann's letter to the solicitor of the commissioners of endowed schools, whose estate near Coalisland he had managed for years, was not untypical: some of the tenants had not paid their rents in the previous year and legal proceedings were necessary, especially against '*one* of them I know to be a notorious usurer and has little mercy and is reputed to be wealthy'.[46] On the Hodson estate in County Cavan in 1864 the agents started legal proceedings because they thought it was 'unjust on the part of the tenants not paying up', when the season had been a good one for flax and cereals.[47]

Threats of eviction were also used to prevent sub-letting and to encourage consolidation.[48] The latter depended on the notice to quit, either to intimidate intruders, as Wann tried to do in the Gartlaney case described below,[49] or to wipe the tenurial slate clean so that holdings could be rearranged, as John George Adair used it in 1860 when at the 'unanimous wish of the tenants' he served notices to quit on all his Derryveagh tenants in order 'to survey and rearrange, in the most equitable and convenient way, the various holdings'.[50] Some landlords went further. Lord Leitrim ordered his agent to tell a tenant that 'if his house is not in perfect repair within three months from this date that I will make him pay double rent and evict him out of the land'.[51] Lord George Hill built shops for his tenants on his County Donegal estate, but to keep them in business he suppressed rivals: a tenant whose lodger set up as a baker was served with a notice to quit; a tenant who had got a spirits licence at Buncrana petty sessions was evicted when he opened a public house.[52] Tenants who trespassed on bogs,[53] who kept goats contrary to their landlords' wishes,[54] or who were poachers were threatened with eviction.

---

[45] For a discussion of arrears see below, pp. 113–17.
[46] Wann's letter-book, 1 May 1874 (PRONI, D1606/5/5, p. 143).
[47] Hodson rentals and agents' report, 1863 (NLI, MS 16419, p. 113); see also ibid. 167.
[48] For the prevention of subdivision on County Cork estates, see Donnelly, *Land and People of Cork*, 159–63. [49] Below, pp. 39–43.
[50] Vaughan, *Derryveagh Evictions*, 21.
[51] Leitrim rent-ledgers (County Leitrim), 1864–9 (NLI, MS 5802, p. 40).
[52] *Report from the Select Committee on Destitution (Gweedore and Cloughaneely); together with the Proceedings of the Committee, Minutes of Evidence, Appendix, and Index*, p. 283, HC 1857–8 (412), xiii. 387.
[53] Wann's letter-book, 30 Aug. 1859 (PRONI, D1606/5/4, p. 75).
[54] Annesley letter-book, 7 July 1847 (PRONI, D1854/6/6, p. 40).

When landlords intervened in family disputes, or in disputes between tenants, the notice to quit was their sanction. The smooth working of the tenant-right custom partly depended on the agent's power to enforce his decisions by serving notices to quit.[55] If, on occasion, the tenant's right to dispose of his farm to his heirs was limited by the landlord's power, almost as often his wishes were enforceable only by the same means. On the Hodson estate in County Cavan, for example, the agents were 'obliged to evict John Wallace in order to rid him from the ill-treatment he received from his son-in-law . . . ; we got possession after the January session and have reinstated Wallace'.[56] The power of eviction was not, therefore, always used to thwart tenants, for it was a means of settling rows quickly and cheaply.

The notice to quit, which was only one means of initiating ejectment proceedings, was an administrative maid-of-all-work, offering a quick, effective means of settling disputes. It put the landlord in a privileged position in rural society: he could threaten poachers, trespassers, drunkards, bad farmers, wife-beaters, and undutiful children, either without recourse to the courts, or for offences that would not have been punishable by the courts. The power to evict also put landlords' debts in a relatively privileged position: the law provided them with four distinct means of recovering rents, two of which were forms of ejectment: distraint for one year's arrears, an ordinary civil bill as for any other debt, a civil bill ejectment when arrears reached one year's rent, and the notice to quit. (The last took longer than the process for non-payment to enforce, but was absolutely certain in its operation, unless there were legal hitches, and did not involve a six months' wait to see if the evicted tenant could redeem his holding.) Ejectment, moreover, was more useful than either distraint or an ordinary civil bill, for land, unlike the goods seizable by distraint or civil bill decree, could not be spirited away.[57] Distraint, which in theory was a formidable power, was in practice much less useful than ejectment: the constabulary were forbidden by their standing orders to assist at distraints;[58] and distraint was so complicated that it was risky for landlords to use it. No distress could be made until the day after the rent was due; only one year's rent could be distrained; 'the distress should be reasonable, and not excessive';[59] tenants could retaliate with actions of replevin to try the legality of the distresses and with actions for excessive distress.[60]

---

[55] Below, pp. 87–93.
[56] Hodson rentals and agents' report, 1861 (NLI, MS 16419, p. 3).
[57] Gosford letter-book, 21 Feb. 1877 (PRONI, D1606/5A/4, p. 133).
[58] *Standing Rules and Regulations for the Government and Guidance of the Royal Irish Constabulary*, 3rd edn. (Dublin, 1872), 310; *The Constabulary Manual; or Guide to the Discharge of Police Duties* (Dublin, 1866), 5, 9.
[59] De Moleyns, *Landowner's Guide* (1872), 135.
[60] Ibid. 277; see also Ferguson and Vance, *The Tenure and Improvement of Land in Ireland*, 217.

That these powers were useful cannot be denied; that they were used moderately by many landlords and abused by others cannot be denied either. Lord Leitrim served all his tenants annually with notices to quit and kept them in a permanent state of insecurity.[61] On the other hand, the power of the landlord was flexible, arbitrary, and irresponsible—just what was needed on occasion to settle disputes or to intimidate trouble-makers who might have annoyed and defied their neighbours for years. The rentals and other estate papers suggest that landlords did not press their tenants for rents, especially in bad years; in the early 1850s and early 1860s arrears were allowed to mount; some pressing was done, no doubt, when times improved. The rentals also show that the misfortunes of tenants were noted as an excuse for not forcing them to pay punctually. It also appears that on many estates tenants were not generally proceeded against until they were more than one year in arrears: a return of civil bill ejectments for the years 1866–73 shows that the majority of decrees for non-payment were for more than one year's rent. In County Westmeath, for example, two-thirds owed more than one year's rent.[62]

If the power to evict had been seriously modified before 1870 it is doubtful if evictions would have been rarer, for it is probable that insolvency would have thinned the ranks of the tenantry even if they had enjoyed the three Fs (fixity of tenure, fair rents, and free sale), or even if they had owned their holdings. The thinning might have been slower; there might have been fewer disputes and they might have been less publicized; but many insolvencies could not have been prevented. What is surprising is that there were not more evictions after the early 1850s; if landlords had been anxious to get rid of vulnerable or lazy tenants, they could have evicted many more for non-payment of rent. It is also arguable that there might have been more removals if landlords had not enjoyed such reassuringly wide powers. Such powers, however, had to be used sparingly. Eviction was too extreme in its effects to be used often; compared with the results implied by the service of a notice to quit, the offences punished were often trivial. Even eviction for arrears was too drastic an exercise of personal power to be entirely desirable. In practice, the landlord may have only speeded up the inevitable; he may have been only one—and by no means the most pressing—of several creditors; but the final ruin of insolvent tenants would have been less invidious if the machinery that effected that ruin had been better concealed, had worked more slowly, and had been less obviously under the control of one driver. The fact that landlords enjoyed special powers was not ultimately a source of strength; if their debts and property were given the protection of special procedures, they

---

[61] National Archives, RP 1869/5078.
[62] *Return 'in Tabular Form, of the Number of Original Civil Bill Ejectment processes Entered, Heard, and Decided on* [1866–70], . . .' p. 90, HC 1875 (260), lxii. 92.

could be deprived of them without danger to property as a whole. The landlords were weak as property owners because they could be separated from other creditors in rural society.

Could the system have worked without such sweeping powers? At first sight the answer would seem to be that it could not. An agent faced with a numerous tenantry led by a small knot of trouble-makers would have felt powerless without the power of eviction. It might be argued, too, that landownership was more than the mere collection of rents, and landlords expected deference—electoral power, frequent and visible marks of respect, and personal popularity—as well as income. The possession of a great power to do harm, exercised with restraint, or not exercised at all, was a considerable enhancement of landlords' prestige. Estates probably could have been managed by other means: nominally high rents, for example, discounted for prompt payment and good behaviour, would have been a practicable substitute for the power of eviction; rents could have been secured by deposits or sureties like other debts; in any case, landlords could have used ordinary debt-collecting procedures, which no doubt could have been greatly improved if landlords had put their political power behind reform. Above all, landlords could have achieved much the same results by a large expenditure on their estates, like English and Scots landlords. Deference, like obedience, was a complex phenomenon, depending on ostentatious display, sympathetic anticipation of change, the cultivation or snubbing of the right people, judicious absences as well as residence, and political power outside the localities, as well as fear and gratitude. As for securing and maintaining political power, the threat of eviction was not decisive. At most it could be used to control stragglers, but not against concerted opposition from tenants who had made up their minds, as in the general elections of 1852 and 1868.[63] As long as tenants were led by landlords in politics, the notice to quit was only one of several electioneering weapons. Once those conditions changed, it could at most only retard change, or inflict damage, but not decisively, on opponents.

The notice to quit, however, was not a mere legal technicality in the management of estates that could have been either done without or seriously modified. It could have been done without as a means of social control; but the power to evict was inseparable from the whole system of landed property based on great, tenanted estates. The law presumed that a yearly tenancy existed from year to year until either the landlord or the tenant wanted to change its terms.[64] If the landlord wanted to increase the rent, he could only do it with the consent of the tenant—or if the tenant

---

[63] J. H. Whyte, 'Landlord Influence at Elections in Ireland, 1760-1885', *English Historical Review*, 80: 317 (Oct. 1965), 740-60; for an account that puts greater weight on landlords' threats, see Hoppen, *Elections, Politics and Society*, 147-51.

[64] De Moleyns, *Landowner's Guide* (1872), 63.

did not agree, by ejecting him. If the landlord's power to evict had been abolished, or even seriously modified, his power to adjust rents would have been reduced. The problem with proposals to change the existing law in favour of the tenants was that piecemeal or 'moderate' compromises were almost impossible, for change at one point in the system could not be confined to that point, but would have effects throughout the whole. The management of an estate was not the exercise of absolute legal rights; rather it was the negotiation of a series of obstacles that had to be overcome at a certain price. Any curtailment of the landlord's power to evict increased those obstacles and influenced the degree to which he could increase rents or enforce their collection. A reform that prevented capricious evictions, or prevented threats of eviction, would have affected rents: fixity of tenure was inseparable from fair rents and free sale. Nor could the effects of reform have been restricted: the tenants freed from the interference of their landlords might have been surprised when they found that they could not evict the sub-tenants.

iii. Obstacles to Evictions

On 14 August 1868 William Scully, a Tipperary landlord, was shot and seriously wounded while trying to serve ejectment processes on tenants in the townland of Ballycohey in the south riding of the county. His bailiff Darby Gorman and a constable, Samuel Morrow, died of gunshot wounds.[65] Efforts to detect the perpetrators were unsuccessful;[66] in the end the Ballycohey tenants were not evicted, for Charles Moore of Moorefort, County Tipperary, bought the townland from Scully to prevent further trouble.[67] For A. M. Sullivan the 'battle' of Ballycohey was not only a successful resistance to eviction, contrasting with the helplessness of the Derryveagh tenants evicted only seven years before, but it also 'passed the Irish land act of 1870' and 'evictions of the old character and extent will henceforth hardly be attempted'.[68] The argument that violence was the only obstacle to evictions in the absence of legal security of tenure was not an implausible one before 1870. There were, however, more prosaic obstacles to evictions than murderous attacks.

The law itself, in spite of the apparent ease with which landlords could evict, gave the tenants some protection. In the absence of a lease or written agreement the law presumed the existence of a yearly tenancy; but a yearly tenancy, 'outliving often, like other frail existences, its more robust brethren',[69] could not be terminated at the mere word of the landlord. If a

---

[65] A. M. Sullivan, *New Ireland* (London, 1877), ii. 350–71; Homer E. Socolofsky, *Landlord William Scully* (Lawrence, Kan., 1979), 39–64.
[66] National Archives, RP 1869/5522.
[67] Sullivan, *New Ireland*, i. 373; Socolofsky, *Landlord William Scully*, 61.
[68] Sullivan, *New Ireland*, 364, 369.   [69] De Moleyns, *Landowner's Guide* (1872), 63.

landlord tried to throw out a tenant without legal authority, magistrates and constabulary were obliged to protect the tenant. In May 1863 a large force of constabulary was requisitioned by William Marshall Day, a justice of the peace in County Galway, to protect a tenant against Richard St George of Headford Castle, who was about to evict him without notice. The constabulary and thirty men in the employment of the tenant anticipated the arrival of the landlord's men and 'no steps were taken to force the cattle off the land'.[70]

The use of force, even when exercised legally, had to be exercised with care; an act of 1848, for example, made it a misdemeanour to unroof, pull down, or demolish a tenant's house 'whilst such person or any of his family shall be actually within the same'.[71] If a landlord or one of his servants struck a tenant in the course of an eviction, or while serving a notice to quit or ejectment process, they were liable to be prosecuted. In May 1865, while serving an ejectment process, William Scully struck Bridget Teahan, the wife of one of his tenants, Patrick Teahan, in the townland of Gortnagap. According to Scully, Bridget Teahan caught him

> by the cape coat which he then wore, and dragged him with great violence... to the ground, and in so doing memorialist [Scully] lost his footing, and fell sideways upon one knee, Bridget Teahan shouting loudly for help and retaining her hold.... The houses of the two other Teahans are within twenty-five yards... of said Patrick Teahan's house; that memorialist fearing his life was in danger and especially whilst in such a position and believing from experience of the character of the Teahans that he would be fatally injured in case the Teahans arrived up before he could disengage himself and retire, memorialist did upon the impulse of the moment raise a short stick which he had in his hand and made a blow at said Bridget Teahan's hands or arms to make her release her hold of your memorialist and in doing so said Bridget Teahan who at that moment put herself into a stooping position to drag memorialist from the door received the blow intended for her hands or arms on the forepart of her head with the end of said stick which cut her.

Scully was sued by the Teahans and had to pay Bridget damages of £80. He was also prosecuted for assault and convicted at Kilkenny summer assizes in 1865. (Bridget Teahan denied that she attacked him first, claimed that she had suffered a miscarriage as a result of the struggle, and medical evidence showed that she had been struck with 'a sharp instrument' and not with a stick.) Scully was sentenced to twelve months' imprisonment. He appealed unsuccessfully to the lord-lieutenant, Lord Wodehouse, for a reduction of his sentence: he had, he claimed, 'for some years past been of nervous and delicate constitution of health' and the prison diet was 'wholly unsuited to his constitution and former habits of life'.[72]

---

[70] National Archives, RP 1863/4082.   [71] 11 & 12 Vict., c. 47 (14 Aug. 1848).
[72] National Archives, convict reference files, 1865/S/25.

Even if a landlord was not prosecuted for assault, he might suffer equally embarrassing sanctions. James Blake, a County Galway landlord, was removed from the commission of the peace in 1848, because his sons had levelled some houses without legal authority.[73] If a landlord or agent failed to inform the relieving officer of their intention to evict, they were liable to be fined £20.[74] Complaints of such irregularities were investigated by the constabulary and the poor law authorities. The earl of Orkney's agent in County Kerry apologized to the Tralee board of guardians in 1861 for what seems to have been a genuine misunderstanding: 'I trust the board will be so good as to overlook it as they rest assured I would be the last wilfully to omit such wise provision of the law, or want of respect to your board.'[75]

Large-scale evictions required large forces of constabulary: 200 at Derryveagh in April 1861, and fifty-one when Lord Leitrim evicted a priest from a chapel in west Galway.[76] Relations between evicting landlords and constabulary and officials such as sub-sheriffs and RMs were often strained. It is impossible to read the files of the Derryveagh evictions without sensing the official hostility towards Adair: gossip about him was recounted with gusto, his motives were impugned, and he was accused of lying.[77] Likewise, some of the most searching criticism of Lord Leitrim came from policemen and poor law officers.[78] Whether officials were as nauseated by eviction as was alleged is not clear: during the Derryveagh evictions it was reported that the constabulary wept, and A. M. Sullivan claimed that sub-sheriffs, who had usually to carry out the evictions, found them 'far more painful to their feelings' than their duties at public hangings.[79]

Even if the landlords were not deterred by the legal risks of evictions and the lukewarmness of officials who had to do some of the dirty work, many must have been deterred by the publicity that the simultaneous removal of twenty or thirty families attracted. The Kilrush evictions were discussed in parliament and the names of the tenants and landlords were published in a parliamentary paper that ran to almost sixty pages;[80] the evictions on the Pollok estate were discussed in parliament;[81] the Partry evictions were discussed in parliament, three pamphlets were written about

---

[73] *Papers Relating to Proceedings for the Relief of the Distress, and State of the Unions and Workhouses in Ireland, Fifth Series, 1848*, p. 467 [919], HC 1847-8, lv. 495; see also National Archives, OP 1848/11.   [74] 11 & 12 Vict., c. 47 (14 Aug. 1848).
[75] National Archives, RP 1861/6554.
[76] Vaughan, *Derryveagh Evictions*, 11; National Archives, RP 1863/7182.
[77] Vaughan, *Derryveagh Evictions*, 43.
[78] Below, pp. 103-4; see also National Archives, RP 1869/5078.
[79] Sullivan, *New Ireland*, i. 252.
[80] *Reports and Returns Relating to Evictions in the Kilrush Union*, pp. 1-57 [1089], HC 1849, xlix. 315-71; Hansard 3, cv. 1286-95.
[81] Hansard 3, cxli. 1707-18; cxlii. 697-712; National Archives, RP 1856/15416.

them, and a French bishop preached a sermon on them;[82] the Kilkee evictions by the Marquis Conyngham were described in detail in a pamphlet of fifty-seven pages.[83] The power of parliament to order the publication of official returns exposed the administration of individual estates to public view, with an authority that was not easily impugned: in the 1860s the Law Life Society's management of its large estate in the west riding of Galway was exposed with embarrassing details, as were the evictions carried out by William Steuart Trench in the barony of Farney in the 1850s.[84] These are only some of the major examples of publicity; many others are to be found in the newspapers, in the pages of evidence presented to select committees and royal commissions, and in contemporary works, where even the eviction of a single tenant might attract considerable attention.[85] In none of the cases mentioned above did publicity, or the threat of it, stop the evictions. The printed word, or the attention of the newspapers came too late. Even the spoken word, powerfully and promptly administered, did not always work. Fr. Lavelle's sermons did not prevent the Partry evictions, although he assured his congregation that the tenants would not be removed until he was 'stretched'. After the Partry evictions took place without the necessary formality of Lavelle's 'stretching', his stream of vituperation flowed strongly: Lord Plunket was a drunkard, the son of a charity boy, and a disgrace to the episcopate and the human race.[86]

Even relatively routine ejectments could lead to embarrassing incidents. In 1875 the agent of the Berridge estate in the west riding of Galway, near Oughterard, brought an ejectment against tenants whose leases had expired—not to remove them but to rearrange their holdings.[87] The tenants were on the point of signing caretakers' agreements when the curate of the parish appeared and told them that it was 'the advice of Archbishop MacHale, Mr Isaac Butt, and himself that the tenants should not sign caretakers' agreements and that he would not allow them to do so'. The

---

[82] Hansard 3, clxiv. 413–36; Fr. Patrick Lavelle, *The War in Partry; or, Proselytism and Eviction on the Part of Bishop Plunket of Tuam* (Dublin, 1861); id., *Partry and Glenveagh: A Letter to the Rt. Hon. E. W. Cardwell, MP, Chief Secretary for Ireland* (Dublin, 1861); 'Lex', *Doings in Partry*; see also Desmond Bowen, *Souperism: Myth or Reality: A Study in Souperism* (Cork, 1970), 166–9.

[83] Sylvester Malone, *Tenant Wrong in a Nutshell; or, a History of Kilkee in Relation to Landlordism during the Last Seven Years* (Dublin, 1867); see also Vaughan, *Derryveagh Evictions*, 11–14.

[84] Return 'of all Civil Bill Ejectments Entered at the Suit of the Law Life Society before the Chairman of Quarter Sessions...' HC 1864 (275), l. 663; Return 'of Ejectment Processes in the Barony of Farney Entered at Quarter Sessions...' [1846–56], HC 1866 (178). lviii. 95.

[85] Godkin, *Land War in Ire.*, 338–41; Samuelson, *Land and Tenantry of Ire.*, 4–5.

[86] National Archives, RP 1861/7272.

[87] Ibid. 1875/17226; see also Dufferin to Brinsley Sheridan, 6 Feb. 1881 (PRONI, D1071/B/E3/12/4).

sub-sheriff and the agent were then obliged to remove the tenants, although their furniture was left in the houses. When the sub-sheriff left, some of the tenants broke into their houses and had to be removed again. At this second eviction, one of the tenants, who seemed 'to be in apparently good health, ... took suddenly ill and expired shortly after'. A coroner's jury held an inquest the following day and brought in a verdict of manslaughter against Berridge's bailiff, Bartly Murphy. The coroner ignored the verdict as improper, for the dead man was aged 85, he had received no ill-treatment from Murphy, and some of the jurymen were related to him. The agent was able to retrieve the situation by playing on the feelings of the dead man's son. He appealed to him to sign the caretaker's agreement in order to be able to have his father's wake in his own house. The son yielded and 'with tears in his eyes looked at the priest as though imploring him to give his consent'; the agent turned on the priest and asked him 'was it possible that he intended to be the means of keeping the people out of their houses for the night, and finally he gave his consent'. The agreements were signed and the tenants were readmitted. The valuation books show, moreover, that the agent was not trying to deceive them, for they were still there years later.[88]

The effects of such publicity and embarrassment in deterring evictions in the first place should not be underestimated, especially on a class that was not only socially prominent but also professed ideals of benevolent paternalism. Adair persisted with the Derryveagh evictions, in spite of public opprobium, but he did not carry out the evictions that he had planned at the same time in Ballylehane in the Queen's County.[89] Even if individual landlords were unmoved by the threat of publicity, landlords as a whole seem to have been hostile to any of their fellows who stirred up trouble. A meeting of magistrates in north Donegal publicly condemned Adair; the grand jury of County Kilkenny indicted Scully for the assault of Mrs Teahan; and at least one Donegal landlord regarded the third earl of Leitrim as the cause of the land act of 1870.[90]

There were other obstacles to evictions as well as publicity and embarrassment. Evictions were often financially unrewarding. An insolvent tenant, evicted for non-payment, would probably leave unpaid arrears that would be lost. On the Pratt estate in County Cavan in 1863, for example, a tenant whose rent was only £16. 14s. 6d. was evicted and arrears of £50. 3s. 6d. were lost.[91] Law costs could be high. Scully's quarrel with the Teahans was exceptional, but he claimed that he had lost £500 in costs

---

[88] VO Dublin: cancelled books for County Galway/Oughterard/Wormhole.
[89] Vaughan, *Derryveagh Evictions*, 61.
[90] William Hart to G. V. Hart, jun., 9 Apr. 1878 (PRONI, D3077/F/6/120).
[91] See townland of Corrinseca in Pratt rental (County Cavan), 1850–64 (NLI, MS 3122, p. 254).

and damages.⁹² It was better for both parties if tenants could be made to pay, and complicated arrangements were often made to pay back the arrears over many years. When a holding became vacant, it was not always easy to find another suitable tenant, in spite of the demand for farms. In the 1850s talk of consolidation was common, small tenants were seen as a liability, and the future seemed to lie with large farms. Landlords who could take large farms into their own hands could do well; the townland of Kilcoosh, for example, mentioned at the beginning of this chapter, remained untenanted for over thirty years.⁹³ The number of landlords, however, who could profitably manage large farms was small. Farming may have been fashionable but its successful practice remained elusive.⁹⁴

The fashion for large farms did not survive unchallenged, for by the 1860s the *Farmers' Gazette* was describing capitalist farming, stall-feeding, and large farms as an *ignis fatuus*: small farms were now growing more cereals and green crops than large farms.⁹⁵ The belief that there were thousands of English and Scots farmers ready to take vast tracts of Irish land was exaggerated: in 1851 there were 579 English and Scots farmers in Ireland; by 1861 they had increased, but only to 886.⁹⁶ The small farmers who survived the famine were remarkably resilient; instead of becoming the victims of further clearances, they paid their rents punctually, paid off their famine rears, and paid rents that were as high, if not higher, than those paid by large farmers.⁹⁷ In the end the main obstacle to evictions on a large scale was an insuperable one—the existing tenants were the only ones available.

iv. 'So Untruly and Unjustly Represented'

Even against an experienced agent, defiant tenants could achieve notable successes, as was shown by the struggle between an agent and a family in County Tyrone between 1867 and 1871. The royal school in Dungannon was supported by an estate of 3,891 acres near Coalisland, managed by William Wann for the commissioners of endowed schools.⁹⁸ Wann, who was also Lord Gosford's agent in Armagh and Cavan, kept a copy of his correspondence during his long career, and it forms one of the most detailed and revealing accounts of estate management between the famine and the land war.⁹⁹ He lived at Markethill near Lord Gosford, and as far

---

⁹² National Archives, convict reference files, 1865/S/25. ⁹³ Above, p. 20.
⁹⁴ For a young man who did not know what to do with a lactometer see *Irish Farmers' Gazette*, 22 Sept. 1855, p. 505. ⁹⁵ Ibid. 17 Jan. 1863, p. 25.
⁹⁶ *Census Ire., 1851*, pt. vi, p. 653 [2134], HC 1856, xxi. 797; *Census Ire., 1861*, p. 533 [3204-IV], HC 1863, lxi.
⁹⁷ Vaughan, 'A Study of Landlord and Tenant Relations in Ireland', p. viii.
⁹⁸ *Endowed schools Comm., 1857–8, Appendix*, 22–4.
⁹⁹ Wann's letter-books, 1846–81 (PRONI, D1606/5/3–5); Gosford letter-books, 1848–78 (ibid. D1606/5A/1–4).

as the Dungannon estate was concerned he was an absentee agent working through a resident bailiff. Whether because he was an absentee, or because he seems to have referred so many decisions to the commissioners through their secretary William Cottar Kyle, and their solicitor John Collum, he found the school tenants difficult to manage: he was criticized by the royal commission in 1857 for serving the tenants annually with notices to quit; he found it difficult in 1859 to increase the rents even by a small amount. In 1873 after his worst struggle with them, he mournfully noted: 'I receive from the *same number* of tenants in Cavan as in the school lands over £4,000 *a year* for Lord Gosford and for the last twenty years, the trouble I have had with the *entire estate* would fall far short of what I experienced in Gartlaney's case.'[100]

The Gartlaneys were a family that had clashed with Wann on several occasions, especially when he tried to increase the rents in 1859.[101] Their leader seems to have been Michael Gartlaney, who was big, violent, and truculent. On one occasion he and the bailiff, Pirie, came to blows; but as Wann pointed out, 'any force Pirie could use against a man of Gartlaney's size would be very futile indeed.'[102] The cause of the most serious dispute between Wann and the Gartlaneys, which lasted from 1867 to 1871, was Wann's attempt to evict Michael's brother, Owen, from a small holding, formerly held by another brother, Laurence. Laurence had died in November 1867, leaving his widow Eliza in possession of two farms, one in the townland of Aughamullen where she lived, and the other, about 4 acres, in Kingsisland. Wann decided that Eliza could keep the former, but must give up the Kingsisland holding to an adjoining tenant, since it was his policy to consolidate holdings.[103] Eliza did not object to this arrangement, although she was not allowed to sell the Kingsisland holding, for her husband had got it free of tenant right.[104] Before the arrangement was completed, however, her brother-in-law Owen seized Kingsisland 'clandestinely, contrary to this order, and refuses to give it up.'[105] Michael supported his brother, telling Wann 'in the most violent and insulting manner that "Kingsisland would never be given up"'.[106] Wann had to begin ejectment proceedings against the nominal tenant of the Kingsisland holding, Eliza Gartlaney, by serving a notice to quit in April 1868.[107]

The case came before the assistant barrister in January 1869. The proceedings should have been a straightforward end to a transaction already too long protracted; but things went unexpectedly wrong.

---

[100] Wann's letter-book, 12 Feb. 1873 (ibid. D1606/5/5, p. 95).
[101] Below, pp. 64–5; Wann's letter-book, 14 Nov. 1860 (ibid. D1606/5/4, pp. 97–8).
[102] Ibid., p. 303 (17 Jan. 1868).   [103] Ibid., p. 300 (11 Dec. 1867).
[104] For tenant right and estate management, see below, pp. 87–93.
[105] Wann's letter-book, 19 Feb. 1868 (PRONI, D1606/5/4, pp. 305–6).
[106] Ibid., p. 301 (14 Jan. 1868).   [107] Ibid., p. 328 (16 Dec. 1868).

The Gartlaneys had *three solicitors* employed to defend the ejectment for the plot of ground at Kingsisland. The barrister saw the case clearly and was with us every step till at last a point was raised that *the stamp* on my power of attorney was defective. The opposing solicitor said there should be two stamps on it.[108]

The case was adjourned until the next quarter sessions and the Gartlaneys celebrated their victory by giving Wann 'considerable' abuse outside the courthouse in Dungannon.

When the case came on in April 1869, fortune again favoured the Gartlaneys: the chairman who had presided in January had been transferred to Cavan and his successor was unfamiliar with the case. On this second occasion, the Gartlaneys were represented by four solicitors and 'a new defence was set up that the commissioners of education had *no power to depute anyone* to sign notices to quit and that therefore on that ground also the notice to quit was bad'.[109] A new notice to quit had to be served, to run from April to November 1870. Possession would not be obtained until January 1871 at the earliest, over three years after the beginning of the dispute.

During this long interval Michael Gartlaney seems to have made, on several occasions, a suggestion to Wann that illuminated the whole transaction: Michael wanted 'his sister-in-law Eliza eject[ed] from Aughamullan for the advantage of his *friends*'.[110] The Gartlaneys had convinced themselves of the justice of their claims to their sister-in-law's farms. First, Catherine Gartlaney, the mother of Michael, Owen, and the dead Laurence, 'stated that her son Laurence... had done her injustice and by way of recompense gave her this lot [Kingsisland]'.[111] Secondly, they argued that Kingsisland had passed from their father to Catherine and that the dead Laurence was never its tenant.[112] (Their claim to Eliza's farm in Aughamullan was presumably an extension of their claim to Kingsisland.)

Finally in January 1871 Wann obtained an ejectment decree for the Kingsisland holding—more than three years after the death of Laurence Gartlaney, and two years after the first appearance in court.[113] The Gartlaneys, however, did not give up even at this point; they appealed against the ejectment decree to the assizes,[114] but the judge upheld it in spite of 'considerable hard swearing by six witnesses' called by the appellants.[115] Before the passing of the land act of 1870 this would have been the end of the case. The sub-sheriff of County Tyrone would have evicted Owen

---

[108] Ibid., p. 330 (14 Jan. 1869).
[109] Ibid., p. 336 (14 Apr. 1869). An agent's powers were a nice point, once legal proceedings started; see Furlong, *The Law of Landlord and Tenant*, 2nd edn. by Digues La Touche, i. 617–18.
[110] Wann's letter-book, 29 Apr. 1870 (PRONI, D1606/5/4, p. 372); see also ibid. 5, p. 2.
[111] Ibid. 4, p. 346 (7 Aug. 1869). [112] Ibid. 5, p. 23 (1 Jan. 1871).
[113] Ibid., p. 26 (27 Jan. 1871). [114] Ibid.
[115] ibid., p. 30 (13 Mar. 1871).

Gartlaney from Kingsisland, protected if necessary by the constabulary. By delaying the eviction, however, the Gartlaneys were able to claim compensation for improvements under section 4 of the act and by 'firm swearing' they were able to convince the court that the Kingsisland improvements were worth £70.[116] This was an enormous sum for a farm of 4 acres, whose rent was only £2. 18s. 6d.—far more than the value of its fee simple.

Wann had won a pyrrhic victory. When he approached the tenant of the adjoining holding to whom he had meant to give the Kingsisland holding four years before, he was offered only £20. 'I am almost certain he told me', wrote Wann, 'more than once within the last few years that he could have got it from Gartlaney at or about £30.'[117] Assuming that Wann accepted the £20, the estate had lost the balance of £50 paid as compensation as well as legal costs. The Gartlaneys were beaten indeed but they had done very well, holding the farm rent-free, and going off with £70 for their 'improvements'. As Wann admitted, they had fought with energy worthy of a better cause. They had, it is true, been lucky, for the passing of the land act could not have been foreseen in 1867; but they had helped themselves—'by no small amount of false swearing', according to Wann.[118]

In 1873, two years after the end of the affair, he complained to the commissioners' secretary:

I may now tell you that the perpetual worry and annoyance which I so long endured in Gartlaney's case had a very bad effect on my health, so much so, that I was obliged to put myself into the doctor's hands. My best and most honest intentions to truly discharge my duties to all parties, so untruly and unjustly represented to the commissioners and your frequent calls for reports on the subject, which I could quite understand on your part, had me often on the point of resigning long since.[119]

In some ways the case was exceptional, for few tenants were as tough as the Gartlaneys; few could have mustered four solicitors in their defence; few would have embarked on such an ambitious act of defiance. Wann was peculiarly vulnerable: he was a scrupulous man; he did not have a good solicitor; he was the servant of a public corporation whose board included the primate, the archbishop of Dublin, and the lord chancellor, which made the risks of publicity more embarrassing. Yet in other ways the Gartlaney case was as typical of the realities of estate management as the case described at the beginning of the chapter, where forty-two families were evicted and a whole townland depopulated.[120] Both were routine in the sense that neither attracted much attention; both could have illustrated arguments for and against the existing land laws. The Gartlaneys' legal

---

[116] Ibid., p. 54 (3 July 1871).
[118] Ibid., p. 55 (4 July 1871).
[120] Above, p. 20.
[117] Ibid., p. 77 (12 Feb. 1872).
[119] Ibid., pp. 94–5 (12 Feb. 1873).

prowess was exceptional, but many ejectments were dismissed by the courts, suggesting that in spite of the apparent simplicity of the law, many agents became muddled over technicalities. In 1869, for example, 2,757 ejectment cases were entered in the chairmen's courts; only 1,890 decrees were granted; the remaining third were either held over, dismissed, or otherwise disposed of.[121] The Gartlaney case illustrated two aspects of landlord–tenant relations often concealed by contemporary partisanship. First, ejectment was not a straightforward, mechanical procedure that an agent could apply without compunction. Secondly, the Gartlaney case had only the form, but not the substance, of a landlord–tenant dispute. It was in reality a family dispute into which the agent was drawn. If Wann had been as unscrupulous as his opponents, he would have let Michael Gartlaney have his way, for it did not matter to him who had Aughamullen so long as Kingsisland went to a neighbouring tenant.

[121] *Judicial Statistics, Ire.*, 1869, p. 212 [C 227], HC 1870, lxiii. 964. See also *Returns 'from the Clerks of the Peace of the Several Counties and Counties of Cities in Ireland, of the Number of Civil Bill Ejectments Entered for Hearing in the Courts of the Assistant Barristers, or Chairmen, for Five Years Previous to 1 Jan. 1851 . . . [and] for Five Years Previous to 1 Jan. 1861 . . . Distinguishing the Number of Same Decreed, Dismissed, and Nilled in Each Respective Year'*, HC 1861 (552), li. 677.

3
The Movement and Level of Rents

i. A Contemporary Puzzle

Rents were the most important aspect of landlord–tenant relations. Few tenants were evicted, or even threatened with eviction, but all paid rent. Rents could be increased frequently, even annually, if tenants did not have leases. Rent, even a low rent, was a large proportion of a tenant's income, and a fall in prices, or a farming disaster, such as the death of a cow, would make punctual payment difficult. There is much information on rents in the evidence collected by official inquiries such as the Devon and Bessborough commissions and in the mass of contemporary pamphlets and books. While much of this is useful, as historical evidence it is inevitably coloured by the circumstances that produced it. The appointment of a royal commission, for example, presided over by a great nobleman such as the duke of Richmond and Gordon, sustained the assumption that there was a weighty problem to investigate, an assumption that was not challenged by many of the witnesses who gave evidence.

The writers of pamphlets and books on the land question were less burdened by the panoply of state, and often, like George Campbell, brought a refreshingly new point of view to Irish problems.[1] Pamphlets and books, however, tended to be written at times when controversy was most acute: Campbell's *The Irish Land* was published in 1869, William O'Connor Morris's *Letters on the Land Question of Ireland* was published in 1870, and Finlay Dun's *Landlords and Tenants in Ireland* in 1881. While none of these was as tendentious as William Steuart Trench's *Realities of Irish Life* (1868), Fr. Lavelle's *The Irish Landlord since the Revolution* (1870), or William Bence Jones's *The Life's Work in Ireland of a Landlord who Tried to Do his Duty* (1880), they all suffered from the weakness of any inquiry that proceeded by asking direct questions: not only was there a risk of receiving misleading answers, but the questions themselves imposed a rigid simplicity on complicated matters.

A contradictory picture of rents comes from these sources. There were estates where rent increases occurred infrequently, usually preceded by a valuation of the whole estate. On the Salters' estate in County Londonderry, for example, rents were unchanged from 1853 to 1878.[2] After an increase,

---

[1] For Campbell's influence on Gladstone see E. D. Steele, 'Ireland and the Empire in the 1860s. Imperial Precedents for Gladstone's First Land Act', *Hist. Jn.* 11: 1 (1968), 64–83.
[2] *Bessborough Comm., Minutes of Evidence*, pt. i, p. 324.

tenants were often confident that their rents would not be increased again for a long time; Lord Arran's agent, for example, after an increase in 1860 promised that rents would not be increased again for twenty-one years.³ On other estates it was alleged, however, that there were no fixed periods for revaluations and that rents were increased 'just as the landlord or his agent take the whim into their heads': a tenant of Lord Gosford's claimed that his rent had been increased three times in eight years,⁴ and on another estate it was claimed that the rent had been increased five times between 1865 and 1880.⁵ There was also debate about the size of rent increases. On some estates, increases were small; between 9 and 12 per cent on the Blakiston-Houston estate in 1876.⁶ On others they were enormous: the earl of Castlestuart was accused of increasing some of his rents by 500 per cent.⁷ On estates in Gweedore, County Donegal, investigated by a select committee in 1857, increases as high as 100 per cent were reported.⁸ It was typical of the controversy that attended such investigations that Lord George Hill, one of the Donegal landlords accused of increasing his rents by large amounts, told the select committee that 'a single tenant has never complained to me of his rent'.⁹

There was debate, too, about the level of rents when compared with the tenement valuation, which had been made in the 1850s and 1860s under the supervision of Sir Richard Griffith as a basis for local taxation.¹⁰ Examples of rents that were as much as 100 per cent above the valuation were produced;¹¹ but the opposite was also noted: Lord Downshire 'charges 33 per cent less for his land than it is worth'; and the Salters' rents were said to be 16 per cent below the valuation.¹² The question that was perhaps most variously answered concerned the effect of rents on tenants' improvements. Tenants, it was claimed, feigned poverty to avoid rent increases,¹³ or bribed bailiffs not to report their improvements to the agent.¹⁴ As one tenant told Murrough O'Brien: 'if they saw you getting anyway comfortable, or clane, or snug, they'd raise the rent on you saying you were too well off.'¹⁵ Even landlords admitted that occasionally rents were increased because of tenants' improvements.¹⁶ On the other hand, it was strongly asserted by some of the poor law inspectors, whose reports on the

---

³ Ibid. 487.   ⁴ Ibid. 212.   ⁵ Ibid. 168.   ⁶ Ibid. 256.   ⁷ Ibid. 206.
⁸ *Report from the Select Committee on Destitution (Gweedore and Cloughaneely); together with the Proceedings of the Committee, Minutes of Evidence, Appendix, and Index*, pp. 19, 57, 60-1, 66, 89, 129, 136, HC 1857-8 (412), xiii.   ⁹ Ibid. 291.
¹⁰ Vaughan, 'Richard Griffith and the tenement valuation' in G. L. Herries Davies and R. Charles Mollan (eds.), *Richard Griffith, 1784-1878* (Dublin, 1980), 103-33; below, App. 10.   ¹¹ *Bessborough Comm., Minutes of Evidence*, pt. i, pp. 233, 328-9, 401.
¹² Godkin, *Land War in Ire.*, 315; *Bessborough Comm., Minutes of Evidence*, pt. i, p. 324.
¹³ *Lords' Sel. Comm. on the Land Act, 1872*, 272.
¹⁴ MacLagan, *Land Tenure in Ire.*, 37-8.
¹⁵ Murrough O'Brien's commonplace book, p. 117 (MS in private possession).
¹⁶ *Poor Law Inspectors' Reports, 1870*, 38.

land question in 1870 are one of the least contentious sources, that 'it is CERTAINLY NOT the usual practice on any well regulated estate ... to increase the annual rent *in consequence* of these, except upon the expiration of leases.'[17]

One point about which there was little debate, however, was the fact that rents in Ireland were lower than in England. Two Englishmen, who published studies of the land question in 1869 and 1870, believed that rents were low: according to Bernhard Samuelson Irish rents could have been increased by 30 per cent if revalued by a 'disinterested' authority;[18] H. S. Thompson believed that the ratio of rent in Ireland and England was 5 : 8.[19] Samuelson also pointed out that rents varied 'incredibly' from one farm to another, even on the same estate, often by as much as 15s. or £1 an acre—a variation that could not be explained on 'economical grounds'.[20]

The great mass of evidence accumulated and published in the second half of the nineteenth century suggests that rent increases were frequent and infrequent, high and low, arbitrary and predictable; that rents were above and below the tenement valuation; that they did and did not absorb the value of tenants' improvements. How is the typical and the general to be selected from such a mass of apparently contradictory evidence? If it is assumed that rents were high, much of the evidence can be used to illustrate convincingly that they were. J. E. Pomfret believed that after the famine there was a 'ceaseless demand for higher rents'.[21] K. H. Connell, in two articles published in 1957 and 1962, argued that 'after the famine, as before, the central force in the Irish economy was the drive for rent, and so insistently was it applied that profit as a spur to the tenant farmer was ... rubbed away, almost to unreality'; until the land acts of 1870 and 1881 'the social and economic life of the countryside was geared to an elastic rent'.[22] These conclusions seem to be based on two closely related assumptions about the weight to be attached to contemporary statements: that complaints about high rents had a wider application than the actual rents complained of; that examples of moderate rents were *sui generis* and not representative. An alternative approach, and superficially at least, an obvious one, would be to give the same weight to all examples.[23] B. L. Solow in *The Land Question and the Irish Economy*, published in 1971, came to conclusions radically different from those of Pomfret and Connell by

[17] Ibid. 96; see also 37, 69, 140. [18] Samuelson, *Land and Tenantry of Ire.*, 28.
[19] Thompson, *Ire. in 1839 and 1869*, 46.
[20] Samuelson, *Land and Tenantry of Ire.*, 27.
[21] Pomfret, *Struggle for Land in Ire.*, 58.
[22] K. H. Connell, 'Peasant Marriage in Ireland after the Great Famine', *Past & Present*, no. 12 (Nov. 1957), 79; id., 'The Potato in Ireland', ibid. 23 (Nov. 1962), 69.
[23] See Cormac Ó Gráda, 'Agricultural Head Rents, Pre-Famine and Post-Famine', *Economic and Social Review*, 5:3 (Apr. 1974), 390, where an average increase of 33.7% between 1850 and 1870 was calculated by using the Bessborough commission.

using parliamentary papers and official statistics to show that rents increased by just under 30 per cent between the early 1850s and 1880.[24]

This solution, however, while an obvious one, is not without difficulties, for it is difficult to determine the weight to be attached to contemporary statements about rents within the context of the evidence itself. The problem can be solved by going outside the body of contemporary comment to the archival evidence of the period such as estate accounts, rentals, and correspondence, much of which has become available only since the 1930s when Pomfret's book was published. In any case, estimates of rents based only on parliamentary papers and contemporary pamphlets cannot be regarded as anything more than hypothetical and provisional until estate papers have been examined. The estate papers are not without weaknesses as historical sources: they are likely to give more weight to the difficulties of landlords than to the feelings of tenants; the larger estates and Ulster estates are better represented than small estates and estates outside Ulster; the collections that have survived in public repositories are not, even when taken together, a random sample in the statistical sense.[25] They have, however, certain undeniable strengths: their availability was not determined by the crises of the land question itself; they were not prepared with the intention of being made public or used to sustain a particular case; they were not likely to have been falsified, except through fraud, which at least might be said to be neutral in the debate between landlord and tenant; they describe a whole range of actual transactions, and not just those that make a point.

Professor J. S. Donnelly and Olive Robinson used rentals in their studies of estates in Cork and Londonderry. Both show that rent increases were small. Donnelly found that there was 'the stability of rents on many Cork estates', although he found that there were 'extremely large' rent increases on the Benn-Walsh and Cave estates. More typical, however, 'were landowners whose rent increases ranged from 20 to 30 per cent', which was 'well within the limits of the price and production increments of the time'.[26] The work of Donnelly, Robinson, and Solow suggests, therefore, that

---

[24] See B. L. Solow, *The Land Question and the Irish Economy, 1870–1903* (Cambridge, Mass., 1971), 67–70, where 'a close reading' of the parliamentary papers gave a rent increase of 12% between 1865 and 1880 and an implied increase of just under 30% between 1852 and 1880.

[25] Below, pp. 290–3; for an impressive range of rentals and accounts of County Cork estates see Donnelly, *Land and People of Cork*, 387–92; for the London companies' archives see Olive Robinson, 'The London Companies as Progressive Landlords in Nineteenth-Century Ireland', *Econ. Hist. Rev.* 2nd ser. 15: 1 (Aug. 1962), 103–18; ead., 'The London Companies and Tenant Right in Nineteenth-Century Ireland', *Agric. Hist. Rev.* 18 (1970), 54–63.

[26] Donnelly, *Land and People of Cork*, 191, 192, 193, 194. See also Robert Brian MacCarthy, *The Trinity College Estates, 1800–1923: Corporate Management in an Age of Reform* (Dundalk, 1992), 188.

Pomfret was exaggerating; the work of Donnelly and Robinson even suggests that Solow's estimate of 30 per cent is too high.

A study of over fifty collections of rentals suggests that rents increased by about 20 per cent between the early 1850s and the late 1870s.[27] There were some collections of estate papers that revealed substantial rent increases between the early 1850s and the late 1870s. The rentals of part of the Archdale estate in County Fermanagh,[28] while not as vigorously managed as the Leitrim estates in the counties of Donegal and Leitrim,[29] increased from about £7,000 in the early 1850s to over £10,000 in the late 1870s, or by 40 per cent. (During the same period the Erne rents in the same county increased by only 20 per cent—from just under £12,000 to just over £14,000.[30]) The eleven estates whose rents are summarized below were chosen to represent the larger group of over fifty estates whose rentals have survived.[31] The highest increases on the eleven estates were on the Hall estate in County Down, where rents increased by just over 30 per cent by the early 1870s, and on the Crofton estate in County Roscommon, where they increased by 29 per cent between the early 1850s and the late 1870s. The middling increases were on the Garvagh estate in Londonderry, where they increased by about 25 per cent, and on the Ashtown estate in County Galway, where they just reached 24 per cent by 1873. The lowest increases were on the Blacker and Midleton estates, where they were almost negligible; on the Hamilton estate where they were only 3 per cent; and on the Erne estate in County Donegal, where they were only 15 per cent. Taking the eleven estates as a whole the average increase was just under 20 per cent. The pace of the rent increases varied slightly from decade to decade; they were brisker in the 1850s than in the 1860s, and unexpectedly slow in the 1870s.

Average rent increases of only 20 per cent suggest that allegations of rackrenting must be treated with caution. The evidence of the rentals, however, does more than merely alter the weight that should be attached to contemporary statements: it largely explains the complexity of that evidence. Behind the averages there was a great variety of experience. Not only did rent increases vary from estate to estate, but even on the same estate some individual rents might be increased by trifling amounts, while others were increased by larger amounts. Most rents were increased only once between the famine and the land war; many were not increased at all; but some were increased more than once. When rents were compared with

---

[27] For the collections used, see below, App. 6 and pp. 290–3. See also W. E. Vaughan, 'A study of Landlord and Tenant Relations in Ireland between the Famine and the Land War' (Ph.D. thesis, University of Dublin, 1974), 49.
[28] Archdale rentals and accounts (Counties Fermanagh and Tyrone), (PRONI, D704/9–82).
[29] Leitrim rentals (NLI, MSS 179–80, 3803–12 5790–2, 5794–802).
[30] Erne rentals and accounts (County Fermanagh), (PRONI, D1939/4/2–9).
[31] See below, App. 6.

the tenement valuation the same variety was found; even on estates where average rents were just above or below the valuation, there were nearly always some high and some low rents. On Lord Belmore's estate at Beragh, County Tyrone, rents were revalued in 1854. Although the new rents were on average about the same as the tenement valuation (about 1 per cent below, in fact), some townlands were as much as 14 per cent above, and one was 23 per cent below it.[32] On the Dunraven estate in County Limerick, owned by one of the country's model landlords, Charles Brassington's valuation showed that rents were 'manifestly low and unequal', although some tenants were paying a 'full rent'.[33] Even on well-run estates, tenants could point to inequalities that could be passed off as acts of tyranny because their rationale was obscure. Any inquiry into rents, if it simply asked tenants about their rents, inevitably revealed hundreds of anomalies. By the same means inquiries addressed to landlords tended to elicit information about rents as a whole, with anomalies hidden behind averages. Although anomalies' importance should not be underestimated, the averages at least give a general picture of the pattern that affected the great mass of the tenants.[34]

ii. The Significance of Rent Increases

What is to be made of a rent increase of 20 per cent? This was not the sort of increase that usually provoked complaints; but a landlord in County Westmeath was shot in April 1868 for trying to increase a rent by 13 per cent, from £1. 2s. 11d. to £1. 6s.[35] Rents came from the margin between the tenant's cost of production and the value of his produce. These are easy enough to understand and not impossible to calculate; the real problem is how to divide the margin between rent and profit. In theory rents could advance to the point where the tenant had nothing but a labourer's wages and a very small return on his capital. Much contemporary comment implied that this was the point that rents had reached; much of that comment also implied that there were rules that should have restrained rents before they reached that point. There were in fact no rules that could be applied. It was clear that the tenant had to get something more than

---

[32] Belmore rentals (County Tyrone), (PRONI, D1716/24); see also Lindsay Proudfoot, 'The Management of a Great Estate: Patronage, Income and Expenditure on the Duke of Devonshire's Irish Property, c. 1816–1891', *Ir. Econ. & Soc. Hist.* 13 (1986), 40.

[33] Dunraven papers (PRONI, D3196/F/17/11).

[34] The rentals support Solow's opinion that 'What the Irish tenant faced was not impersonal market forces but a bewildering array of prices and practices, varying from landlord to landlord.... The charging of fair rents instead of competitive equilibrium rents may avoid social unrest on the grand scale, but it does not necessarily promote amity and content' (Solow, *The Land Question and the Irish Economy*, 44).

[35] *Sel. Comm. on Westmeath*, 1871, 69.

the current rate of interest paid on deposit accounts by the commercial banks; it was also clear that he had to get something to compensate for the risks he was taking—at the very least there had to be something for contingencies. But beyond that it is difficult to go; whether the tenant should get 5 per cent, or 10 per cent, or even 15 per cent was a matter that could not be resolved by rules or theories.

Tests of rent can be devised. First, rents can be compared with agricultural output, giving a rough estimate of the changing fortunes of landlords and tenants. The value of agricultural output increased by about 70 per cent between the early 1850s and the mid-1870s, which suggests that a rent increase of 20 per cent favoured the tenants.[36] Secondly, rents on individual estates can be compared with each other. If rents increased by 50 per cent on the Leitrim estate in County Donegal, where the holdings were small and the land 'rocky, intersected with bog and mountain', the much smaller increases on the Erne estate in the same county were obviously moderate.[37] On the Crosbie estate in County Kerry the agent, George Frederick Trench, described the method he used for revaluing farms. His calculations were based on Griffith's valuation: 25 per cent was added to bring Griffith's valuation up to the letting value at the time when it was made; 73 per cent was added for the increase in prices that had taken place since the making of the valuation; 5s. an acre were deducted to allow for increases in the cost of production.[38] If this method had been applied to the Clonbrock estate in County Galway, for example, the rental in the late 1870s would have been 50 per cent higher than it was.[39] There was nothing intrinsically fair, or unfair, about Trench's calculations, or Lord Leitrim's exactions, but they offer a measure for other estates.

Thirdly, rents can be measured by using the rules laid down in the Trinity College, Dublin, leasing powers act.[40] The college had an estate of about 200,000 acres, much of which was let to large lessees like Lord Leitrim in County Donegal or Sir James Stronge in County Armagh. The leasing powers act regulated the lessees' rents by taking the government or tenement valuation as their starting-point, by assigning weights to five agricultural commodities, and by making rents fluctuate with the prices of the five commodities.[41] The act is a good measure of rents. It was constructed by parties who were well matched; the government and Sir Richard

---

[36] See below, App. 9.   [37] National Archives, RP 1869/5078; see below App. 6.

[38] George F. Trench, *Are the Landlords Worth Preserving? or, Forty Years' Management of an Irish Estate* (Dublin, 1881), 30–1.

[39] See below, App. 6; in the 1870s the rental was about £10,700; assuming that tenanted land amounted to 28,500 acres, valued at £10,700, the rent would have been £16,000 if Trench's method had been applied.   [40] 14 & 15 Vict., c. cxxviii (1 Aug. 1851).

[41] See below, Apps. 11 and 12; see also W. J. Lowe, 'Landlord and Tenant on the Estate of Trinity College, Dublin, 1851–1903', *Hermathena*, 120 (1976), 5–24, and MacCarthy, *The Trinity College Estates*, 27–32.

Griffith were involved; the 'tenant' side was represented by substantial landlords and the 'landlord' side was represented by the college's board, who were not incapable of making nice calculations. The act has the edge on agricultural output because it has a starting-point for rents as well as a measure of price increases; it is, however, not as sensitive a measure of fluctuations as output, because its five weighted commodities are cruder than the range of commodities used in calculating output. It is better than Trench's method because it was not a private landlord's arbitrary concoction, put together without an umpire. The TCD act suggested that rents should have increased by about 50 per cent between 1851 and 1876.

Fourthly, the tenement valuation can be used to compare rents in the 1850s and 1870s. Griffith's prices for agricultural commodities were among the lowest recorded between the famine and the land war;[42] in other words, in any year after 1852 rents that were close to the valuation would almost certainly have been 'fair' by Griffith's standards.[43] By the 1870s price increases had made the tenement valuation anachronistic, and a new one was planned. In 1877 a bill was prepared, but nothing was done to implement it.[44] According to John Ball Greene, Griffith's successor at the Valuation Office, 33 per cent should have been added to the valuation to get the letting value in the 1870s.[45] The prices used in the 1877 bill, however, suggest that the new valuation would have been much more than 33 per cent above the old one. The price of oats was 58 per cent above the 1852 price; butter was 86 per cent; cereals as a whole were 46 per cent above the 1852 prices, and livestock products 81 per cent. Assuming that production costs rose by the same amounts the new valuation could have been in some cases 80 per cent above the tenement valuation.[46]

By the mid-1870s rents that were only 20 per cent above their 1850 level were much lower than any of these tests would have suggested. The tests, however, rest on certain assumptions, which arbitrarily resolve the problem of dividing the agricultural surplus between rents and profits. If the value of agricultural produce increased by 70 per cent between the 1850s and the 1870s, should rents have increased by 70 per cent? The assumption that they should have is based on nothing more profound than the simple fact that if they had, landlords and tenants would have got proportionate shares of the increased prosperity. It could be argued that rents should have increased more rapidly than the value of agricultural produce because the supply of land was limited while the amount of

[42] Griffith, *Instructions*, 2; 15 & 16 Vict., c. 63 (30 June 1852); *Cowper Comm., Minutes of Evidence*, 960–7. [43] See below, App. 10.
[44] *A Bill to Amend the Law Relating to the Valuation of Rateable Property in Ireland*, HC 1877 (bill 102), vii. 425. [45] *Bessborough Comm., Minutes of Evidence*, pt. i, p. 31.
[46] See the calculations below in App. 10.

capital was increasing.[47] If increased value, on the other hand, was created by applying more labour (or the same amount of more highly paid labour) and more capital in the form of better buildings or artificial manures, rent increases that kept pace with output would have reduced the tenants' return on their capital. The idea that rents should have increased in line with the tests is also based on the assumption that rents equal to the tenement valuation in the early 1850s gave the tenants an adequate return on their capital.[48] The tenement valuation of land, excluding buildings, was £9.1 million; actual rents in the early 1850s were just over £10 million; the tests assume, for the sake of being generous to the tenants, that if agricultural output had continued at the levels of 1850, 1851, and 1852, £9.1 million is a better starting-point than £10 million.

Landlords and tenants shared in the prosperity created by the demand for agricultural products in Britain; but tenants did rather better because actual rents lagged behind potential rents. When landlords increased their rents they were taking a share of the prosperity that was created outside Irish agriculture. Far from taking advantage of their tenants' improvements, they did not take anything like a proportionate share of the income created by price increases. Although this imbalance was at its most extreme in the 1870s, its origins lay in the 1850s, especially in the three years 1853–5, when landlords failed to increase their rents by amounts that would have given them a proportionate share of the new prosperity. The belief that landlords rackrented their tenants became one of the most deeply ingrained beliefs of Irish people. To challenge this belief was not easy: it was not only accepted by historians such as Pomfret but sustained by a collective memory that cared little for nice distinctions or complicated calculations. If the rackrenting landlord had not been such a substantial figure in Irish history, rackrenting landlords might have been turned into rather slothful landlords without the tests mentioned above.

The criticism of Mrs Solow's work by V. G. Kiernan is an example of the scepticism that can be provoked by questioning traditional ideas. She is 'a "revisionist" from conservative America'; 'a good deal of her evidence is culled from answers to commissions of inquiry by land agents and others with an interest in saying what landowners wanted said'; the tenants' case went by default because 'one may wonder what became of tenants who said all they wanted to say'.[49] This is not a fair description of Solow's clear, elegantly written book. Even a cursory reading of the evidence heard

---

[47] Avner Offer, 'Ricardo's Paradox and the Movement of Rents in England, c. 1870–1910', *Econ. Hist, Rev.* 2nd ser. 33: 2 (May 1980), 236–52.
[48] See below, App. 10.
[49] V. G. Kiernan, 'The Emergence of a Nation', in C. H. E. Philpin (ed.), *Nationalism and Popular Protest in Ireland* (Cambridge, 1987), 30.

by the royal commissions or select committees shows that the tenants and their representatives were not among the most taciturn people of their day. Solow's missiles were nicely fashioned, well aimed, and accurate; as for 'culling' parliamentary papers, that is what Pomfret did. Solow's achievement was to see the contradictions in contemporary statements and to have the confidence to speak her mind. Her missiles may have been too light to pierce the armour of received ideas; no historian who was learning history in Ireland in the 1970s would have dared to challenge the idea that rents were high by using her method of calculating rent increases; her book's appearance, nevertheless, was an encouraging experience for those who were trying to make sense of the land question.

If historians have problems, they are less than those of contemporaries, whose empirical tools were crude and difficult to apply. Even to establish the size of rent increases was not easy; rentals were more obviously reliable than much of the evidence collected by contemporaries, but they were not widely available. Few attempts to calculate the value of agricultural output were made: Léonce de Lavergne was a rare example in the 1850s;[50] Hancock's estimates in 1863 were useful but not complete;[51] the discussions preceding 1870 rarely referred to such calculations (a short passage in Gray's pamphlet in 1869 was typical, and not very helpful);[52] Grimshaw's calculations for the Cowper commission were crude, and not as good as Hancock's.[53] It is an astonishing fact that there is so little about agricultural output or incomes in contemporary writing; there is a great deal about rents, but only fragmentary references to prices and yields, certainly before 1879. Contemporaries' ignorance of the Trinity College, Dublin leasing powers act, which was rescued from oblivion by W. J. Lowe in 1976, was typical, for the act was hardly ever referred to as a standard for measuring rent, except in the privacy of the college's board room.[54] How rents could be discussed without constant references to prices and production is a mystery, which must stand as one of the triumphs of faith over reason.

The problems faced by historians, nevertheless, are considerable. Arguments based on statistical material are technical, dull, and esoteric; their reception varies from the uncritical to the invincibly sceptical; they can be

---

[50] Léonce de Lavergne, *The Rural Economy of England, Scotland, and Ireland* (Edinburgh and London, 1855), 351.

[51] William Neilson Hancock, *Report on the Supposed Progressive Decline of Irish Prosperity* (Dublin, 1863), 37–8.

[52] Sir John Gray, *The Irish Land Question: Speech of Sir John Gray, Delivered in the Free Trade Hall, Manchester, on 18 October 1869* (Dublin and London, 1869), 34; see also Samuelson, *Land and Tenantry of Ire.*, 18, where there is a description of a farm near Oldcastle whose tenant had a balance of £75 after paying rent of £33 and all other expenses.

[53] *Cowper Comm., Minutes of Evidence*, 952–6.

[54] Lowe, 'Landlord and Tenant on the Estate of Trinity College, Dublin', 5–24.

easily misunderstood.⁵⁵ The tests that can be applied to rents have weaknesses as well as strengths. Calculations of agricultural output are not easy to make;⁵⁶ the agricultural statistics on which they are based, although they are a monument to the Irish government's efforts to provide accurate information, changed slightly from time to time and present certain difficulties.⁵⁷ The price series that is available is not perfect either, if only because it was based on Dublin prices for the most part.⁵⁸ Even crude modern estimates of agricultural output, however, are better than those available to contemporaries. The agricultural statistics, whatever their shortcomings, were not compiled for the use of those interested in the land question; the price series, reproduced in the Cowper commission and compiled by the *Irish Farmers' Gazette*, was based on actual market prices, which were collected and published years before their relevance to the crisis of 1879 was foreseeable.⁵⁹

Even the tenement valuation, which was so often appealed to by contemporaries, was one of the most mysterious fiscal institutions of its day. In some respects Sir Richard Griffith was clear in his ideas; his analysis of 'local circumstances' was good; but on many points he was contradictory and confused.⁶⁰ Criticism of the tenement valuation, however, was fiercest after 1879 when the land league tried to make it a standard for rents;⁶¹ its use for that purpose, however, was not wrong, certainly not before 1879— if it was remembered that it was made in the 1850s and early 1860s and based on prices that were low by the early 1870s. The TCD leasing powers act, which is the simplest and most easily applied of all the tests, did not work smoothly on the college's estates.⁶² The friction between the college's board and its lessees, however, was caused more by the timing of the increases than by the method of their calculation. The main cause of the trouble in the 1880s, for example, was the fact that the lessees were paying

---

⁵⁵ See K. Theodore Hoppen, *Ireland since 1800: Conflict and Conformity* (London and New York, 1989), 100, where calculations based on output calculations by Michael Turner suggest that farmers' profits increased only slightly between 1852–4 and 1872–4 (in real terms they actually fell slightly). Apart from the difficulties connected with Turner's calculations, which have been discussed elsewhere (see W. E. Vaughan, 'Potatoes and Agricultural Output', *Ir. Econ. & Soc. Hist.* 17 (1990), 79–92), it is worth noting that Hoppen's calculations, if they had been published in the 1970s, would have surprised historians reared on Pomfret's *Struggle for Land in Ire.* The idea that tenants were only just behind landlords in the race for income would have been novel. (The idea that agricultural labourers were slightly ahead of farmers in the race would, one suspects, have been even more novel.)

⁵⁶ See below, App. 9.

⁵⁷ William Neilson Hancock, *Report on the Supposed Progressive Decline of Irish Prosperity* (Dublin, 1864), 37–8. ⁵⁸ *Cowper Comm., Minutes of Evidence*, 960–1.

⁵⁹ *Irish Farmers' Gazette*, 1 Nov. 1879, p. 375.

⁶⁰ Griffith, *Instructions*, 36–44; W. E. Vaughan, 'Richard Griffith and the Tenement Valuation', 103–33.

⁶¹ For a vigorous critique arising out of the land war see James F. V. Fitzgerald, *A Practical Guide to the Valuation of Rent in Ireland* (Dublin, 1881).

⁶² Lowe, 'Landlord and Tenant on the Estate of Trinity College, Dublin', 10–19.

during a time of depression rents fixed in the 1860s. If the rents had been adjusted upwards and downwards annually, instead of every ten years, there would have been less criticism in the 1880s. The real weakness of the TCD leasing powers act as a measure of rents was its exclusion of the most dynamic commodities: of store cattle and sheep, for example; nor did it make any allowance for the increase in livestock and the decline in tillage. Both of these shortcomings meant that it underestimated the prosperity of the decades between the famine and the land war. This is hardly a weakness, however, for sustaining the argument that rents were lower than they might have been. The most reassuring thing about the tenement valuation and the TCD leasing powers act was their independence of the debate on the land question. They were related to it, but not created by it; they could be used tendentiously, but their origin was not tendentious.

The tests may have weaknesses, but they all point in the same direction: rents could have been higher. The margin of difference between actual rents and potential rents based on the tests is great; even allowing for the fact that actual rent increases might have been higher than the 20 per cent suggested by the rentals and that measures of potential rent might exaggerate the increase in prosperity, the idea that rents increased faster than agricultural prosperity seems unlikely. It is arguable that a measure of land reform that would have adjusted rents might have benefited landlords; at any rate, they could hardly have fared worse. If landlords had been forced to use the TCD leasing powers act their rents would have been much higher by 1876; between 1851 and 1860, for example, the college's rents from its main estate had increased by 40 per cent;[63] this was not directly comparable with what ordinary landlords could have done, but by 1876 Hancock estimated that the college's rents should have been increased by 46 per cent under the leasing powers act.[64] There is evidence in the 1850s that Griffith was thinking of a method of adjusting the tenement valuation by collecting agricultural prices, whose publication and enforcement would have transformed estate management.[65] Even without this, there was much that landlords could have done to adjust rents more flexibly.

iii. Fixing Rent Increases

The timing of rent increases was apparently arbitrary. It was rare for all rents to be increased at the same time. It did happen, however; there were simultaneous increases on most of the holdings on the Pratt estate in

---

[63] TCD rentals, 1852–80 (TCD, MUN/V/78/6–9).

[64] Report on revision of rents under the Trinity College leasing and perpetuity act, 1851, by William Neilson Hancock (TCD, MUN/P/22/204, p. 29; this was in fact a very tentative estimate based on only one or two commodities: see below, App. 12.

[65] *A Bill to Provide for the Taking and Regulating Returns of the Average Prices of Agricultural Produce in Ireland*, HC 1854 (bill 101), i. 21.

County Cavan in 1855, on the Murray Stewart estate in County Donegal in 1859, and on the Dungannon Royal School estate in 1859–60.[66] These were only a minority, however, and the majority of rent increases took place sporadically and individually rather than simultaneously and collectively. Some landlords and agents were clear enough about why they increased rents. In 1864 Wann decided to increase the rents on Lord Gosford's County Cavan estate because 'their markets now are as good as ours and they have a railway not far distant'. He had not, he wrote, increased them earlier, for 'these last few years was not the time to make an increase and only for the flax crop difficulty would have been [found] in collecting rents'.[67] Lord Belmore was less clear why he had not increased rents on his estate at Beragh: his agent believed that 'in some respect it was underlet' but Belmore 'did not think it was wise to attempt to raise the rents', although he thought an increase would have been 'not unreasonable if the good times up to 1877 had continued'.[68] Landlords occasionally followed each other; in 1866 Sir Thomas Bateson decided to have part of his estate in County Londonderry revalued: 'as the Salters' Company have lately increased their rental, Sir Thomas Bateson is of opinion that the present is a suitable occasion to have the work done.'[69]

The principles on which increases were calculated were obscure. A very small number of farms were let by proposal. On Lord Powerscourt's estate in County Wicklow, there were thirteen applications for a farm in Ballyman and the tenders ranged from £2 to £2. 13s. an Irish acre.[70] The proposals were often complicated, covering not only the new rent, but arrears, improvements, tenure, and the payment of taxes as well. In 1861 Charles Devlin on the Johnston estate in County Armagh offered to pay not only the rent but the sum of £8. 5s. 4d. 'in discharge of the arrears of rent due on said farm' and to give his sister Anne Devlin the sum of £36 'with the agent's permission'.[71] Some proposals were neither detailed nor complicated; an applicant for a farm on the Powerscourt estate simply proposed to pay 'whatever rent the guardians approve of.'[72]

The grounds on which landlords accepted or rejected proposals varied; but one thing was clear: there was a prejudice against taking the highest bidder. (The same prejudice, of course, deplored the auctioning of farms as 'altogether reprehensive, as there is a great risk of getting insufficient tenants, mere adventurers, probably'.[73]) On the Powerscourt estate Lord Powerscourt's guardians 'had regard to the character and solvency of the

[66] Pratt rentals, 1850–64 (NLI, MS 3122); Murray Stewart rentals, 1858–9 (ibid. MS 5476).
[67] Gosford letter-book, 26 Oct. 1864 (PRONI, D1606/5A/2, p. 376).
[68] *Lords' Sel. Comm. on the 1881 Land Act, Second Report*, 48.
[69] Spotswood's letter-book, 29 Oct. 1866 (PRONI, D1062/1/8A, p. 69).
[70] Powerscourt requests-book, 1852–6 (NLI, MS 16378, no. 788).
[71] Johnston tenancy agreements (County Armagh), 1861 (National Archives, M3514).
[72] Powerscourt requests-book, 1850–2 (NLI, MS 16377, no. 537).
[73] D. G. F. MacDonald, *Estate Management . . .* 10th edn. (London, 1868), 363.

parties making application rather than to the amount of the several offers for same'. There were, for example, several offers for Kilmacanogue farm: two from 'most respectable old tenants' who offered less than the previous rent, two who offered the same rent, and two who offered more but were not 'well known'. In the end the farm went to John Sutton of Blackditch 'who proposed the largest rent of any except the two last mentioned'.[74] There was a prejudice in favour of local men or existing tenants of good character. A tenant on the Powerscourt estate was given a farm not only because he was the brother-in-law of the late tenant, but also because of 'the land applied for being the nearest to his holding'.[75] On the Fitzwilliam estate a prospective tenant was viewed with suspicion because 'he writes from Rathnew which is not a very tempting place to get a tenant from'.[76] One kind of outsider, however, was welcome on that estate, especially in the early 1850s, for the agent believed that 'Lord Fitzwilliam would approve of letting a farm to an Englishman of capital and skill and could now let one of light land well adapted for sheep and that grows good turnips.'[77]

The letting of farms by proposal implied the operation of market forces, which was simple in principle. Most rents were not, however, fixed by proposal but by attempts to simulate market forces, ranging from formally made valuations to rough rule-of-thumb comparisons with other estates and vague references to the 'custom of the country'.[78] The general valuation of an estate was occasionally followed by the increase of rents; the increases on the Dungannon Royal School estate and on the Gosford estate in County Cavan, already referred to, were preceded by valuations.[79] This was not, however, the invariable practice: most rents were not increased on the Powerscourt estate after its valuation by the firm of Brassington & Gale in 1853.[80] Occasionally a valuation led to reductions of rent, or at least to a redistribution of the burden. Lord Fitzwilliam's agent, Robert Chaloner, claimed that the valuation carried out by Samuel Nicholson in 1851 'was decided on with a view of lowering such farms as were too high and those persons that have been lowered say nothing while those [who] have been raised speak loudly'.[81]

Valuators were members of firms that specialized in surveying and valuing.

---

[74] Powerscourt requests-book, 1852–6 (NLI, MS 16378, no. 1249).
[75] Powerscourt requests-book, 1850–2 (ibid. MS 16377, no. 583); for the clannishness of landlords and tenants, see *Hansard 3*, clxiv. 423.
[76] Robert Chaloner's letter-book, 29 May 1852 (NLI, MS 3987, p. 404).
[77] Ibid. 335–6 (27 Nov. 1850).
[78] *Report from the Select Committee on General Valuation etc. (Ireland); together with the Proceedings of the Committee, Minutes of Evidence, and Appendix*, p. 178, HC 1868–9 (362), ix. 190; see also George Birmingham, *The Bad Times* (London, 1914), 40.
[79] Above, p. 56; below, pp. 64–5.
[80] Brassington & Gale's valuation of the Powerscourt estate, 1853 (NLI, MS 2740); Powerscourt rent-ledgers, 1845–54 (ibid. MSS 3164, 3172).
[81] Robert Chaloner's letter-book, 28 Apr. 1852 (ibid. MS 3987, p. 395).

Some were based in Dublin, with clients all over the country. The firm of Brassington & Gale, who were land surveyors, valuators, and 'agents for the purchase of landed estates' at 52 Upper Sackville Street, valued estates (including the Crown's lands) as widely separated from each other as the Powerscourt estate in Wicklow, the Dunraven estate in County Limerick, and the Gosford estate in County Cavan.[82] Other valuators were local men such as Richmond, who valued the Gosford estates in County Armagh and worked as well in the counties of Down and Fermanagh.[83] Valuators built up their clientele by recommendations from one agent to another, or from that great school of valuation the Valuation Office in Dublin, presided over by Sir Richard Griffith. Samuel Nicholson, who valued the Fitzwilliam estate, was recommended by Griffith, 'which', said the agent, 'is all that I know about him'.[84] The cost of a general valuation was considerable; Nicholson's was 3 per cent of the Fitzwilliam rental,[85] and the valuation of the Bateson estate cost 1s. 9d. an acre.[86]

Some landlords and agents valued their farms themselves without the interposition of an apparently impartial outsider. Valuations on the Leitrim estate in County Donegal were made directly under the third earl's supervision, and the agent's field notes were sent directly to him.[87] Sir John Benn-Walsh seems to have taken the leading part in valuing farms on his estates in Cork and Kerry in the early 1850s.[88] One of the main reasons, however, for employing a professional valuator was to give the new rents the authority of being fixed by an impartial and disinterested outsider. 'I kept aloof from the valuation,' protested Wann when a row broke out on the Dungannon Royal School estate. 'Richmond being a professional man I in no way interfered with him. My feeling is that the agent of an estate should not be its valuator.'[89] Richmond's independence was, on one occasion at least, an embarrassment to Wann. Wann employed him in 1851 to revalue cut-away bog; but he had 'gone over all and made very large abatements'. Wann was put out because he had no instructions from Lord Gosford and did not know 'what to say to him'. The news of the abatements

[82] Above, p. 49; below, p. 64.
[83] Wann's letter-book, 19 Dec. 1860 (PRONI, D1606/5/4, p. 109).
[84] Robert Chaloner's letter-book, 18 Feb. 1850 (NLI, MS 3987, p. 297).
[85] Ibid. 333 (9 Nov. 1850).
[86] Spotswood's letter-book, 12 Dec. 1866 (PRONI, D1062/1/8A, p. 71).
[87] Leitrim estate reports (County Donegal), 18 Oct. 1864 (NLI, MS 13339(6)).
[88] James S. Donnelly, jun. 'The Journals of Sir John Benn-Walsh Relating to the Management of his Irish Estates, 1823–64', *Cork Hist. Soc. Jn.* 80: 231 (1975), 34: 'I went out straight to Grange and had a long conference with Callaghan of Classis. He holds 57 acres of the prime part of Grange at only 17s. per acre. Last year when I raised all the other tenants, I could not see him, as he was lying in a dangerous state from a fall from his horse. He is a good tenant but a hard swearing, lying Irishman. I told him that I should expect £80 per annum or 28s. per acre, or if he did not choose to give it, I should advertise the farm. He made a piteous complaint. I gave him till Saturday.' (See ibid. 37 for Callaghan's acceptance.)
[89] Wann's letter-book, 23 Oct. 1861 (PRONI, D1606/5/4, p. 138).

leaked out and 'every man seemed to know exactly' what they were.[90] Wann persisted, however, in allowing Richmond to work independently; in 1859–60 when he wanted to increase the rents on the Dungannon school estate Richmond was employed. Wann was not, on that occasion, aware of any tenant's valuation until he 'got the reference book from Mr R[ichmond] *for all*';[91] Richmond in turn supported Wann by declaring in writing that the valuation of 'the entire estate' was his own 'without being prejudiced by any person'.[92] ('It is not', said Wann, 'the poorest that grumble most.')

The way in which valuations were made was not clear. The valuator had to fix a point somewhere between the cost of production and the value of the farm's produce, leaving the tenant his profits and the landlord his rent. This was an obscure business if only because there were no rules that could be applied. The prices ascribed to agricultural products, the costs of production, and the return on capital were all potentially matters of debate, for the calculation of each affected the shares enjoyed by landlord and tenant. It was possible to settle these matters, as was done on Scottish estates, but on Irish estates they were not even defined.[93] In 1872 Sir Charles Compton Domvile employed Thomas Fitzgerald to value his estate in County Dublin. The existing rents were only 20 per cent above the tenement valuation and Fitzgerald suggested an increase of 50 per cent, which brought them to almost twice the level of the tenement valuation. Sir Charles asked Fitzgerald for the 'basis' of his valuation; Fitzgerald replied that the 'basis' on which he valued was the knowledge that he had acquired 'after five and twenty years of practice and experience in every county in Ireland'; he had 'never tabulated it' and could not help Sir Charles.[94]

The methods used were probably the same as those used by Griffith's valuators and described by the English authority on valuation, J. S. Bayldon. Valuators were supposed to calculate the value of the gross produce and costs of production on sample farms on the best and worst lands on an estate; the remaining farms were valued by comparison with the sample lots. On the best land, one-third of the gross produce was allowed for rent; on medium land, one-quarter; and on poor land, one-fifth.[95] Griffith's valuators seem to have worked in the same way. In the *Instructions* there were specimen calculations of the gross and net produce of the best tillage land and superior grassland.[96] The valuation, therefore, was essentially a

---

[90] Gosford letter-book, 22 May 1851 (ibid. D1606/5A/1, p. 150).
[91] Wann's letter-book, 19 Dec. 1860 (ibid. D1606/5/4, p. 108).
[92] Ibid. 115 (25 Feb. 1860).
[93] *Chambers's Encyclopedia* (London, 1868), iv. 311–12.
[94] Thomas Fitzgerald to Sir Charles Compton Domvile, 9 May 1872 (NLI, Domvile papers, MS 11305).
[95] J. S. Bayldon, *Art of Valuing Rents and Tillages*... 6th edn. (London, 1844).
[96] Griffith, *Instructions*, 29, 32–3.

ranking system and as such was easy enough to put into practice. How individual valuators made the basic calculations that fixed the high, middle, and low points of the scale is not clear, except that Griffith's valuation seems to have played a part in many of them.[97]

Griffith was probably exaggerating when he claimed in 1869 that the tenement valuation had 'nearly put an end to all other valuation', that it was used as a standard everywhere, and that 'at present there are scarcely any valuators employed in Ireland'.[98] Ten years before, in the late 1850s, he had claimed that landlords had adopted his valuation as the basis of rents on their estates, 'increasing the amount of the valuation of each tenement by a proportionate addition or percentage so as to meet their own views of the actual rent value'.[99] There is some evidence to support these claims. A textbook on valuation, for example, published in 1853 'with copious instructions as to the qualifications and duties of valuators', was so closely based on Griffith's own *Instructions* that it looked like a plagiarism.[100] There was also a remarkable resemblance between the tenement valuation and the private valuations carried out in the 1850s. Nicholson's valuation of the Fitzwilliam estate in 1851, Brassington & Gales's valuation of the Powerscourt estate in 1853, and Rutledge's valuation of the Belmore estate in County Tyrone in 1854 were all close to the tenement valuation.[101] Not only were the actual values close but the order in which the farms were ranked according to acreable value were very close.[102] Also the correspondence of the Valuation Office shows that Griffith and his staff were willing to give advice to individual landlords about rents on their estates.[103] That landlords relied on the tenement valuation is also clear from the evidence of some of the estate papers. In 1872 Alexander Spotswood used it to check a new valuation of part of the Bateson estate in County Londonderry.[104] On the dozens of holdings valued on the Gosford estate, presumably by Richmond, the tenement valuation was carefully noted.[105] It seems to have played a part in the calculation of rent increases

[97] See e.g. survey of the Westropp estate in Counties Clare and Limerick by Robert L. Brown, 1871–7 (NLI, MS 5397).
[98] *Report from the Select Committee on General Valuation etc. (Ireland)* ... p. 47, HC 1868–9 (362), ix. 59; see *Census Ire.*, 1861, pt. v, p. 472 [3204–IV], HC 1863, lxi.
[99] Griffith to Lord Wrottesley, 8 Apr. 1858 (National Archives, OL 2/16, p. 85); see also Valuation Office letter-registers, 1852 (ibid. OL 2/28, nos. 5248, 5311, 5553).
[100] John Lanktree, *The Elements of Land Valuation, With Copious Instructions as to the Qualifications and Duties of Valuators* (Dublin, 1853).
[101] Samuel Nicholson's valuation of the Fitzwilliam estates, 1851 (NLI, MS 4977); Brassington & Gale's valuation of the Powerscourt estate, 1853 (ibid. MS 2740); Rutledge's valuation of the Belmore estate, 1854 (PRONI, D 1716/box 24).
[102] Vaughan, 'Richard Griffith and the Tenement Valuation', 115.
[103] For examples see Valuation Office letter-register, 1852 (National Archives, OL 2/28, nos. 5248, 5553).
[104] Spotswood's letter-book, 23 Mar. 1873 (PRONI, D1062/1/8A, p. 112).
[105] Gosford valuations & surveys (ibid. D1606/12/7, nos. 302, 305, 321, 324).

on the Butler estate at Castle Crine in County Clare in the 1870s[106] and on the estates managed by Robert L. Brown in the counties of Clare and Limerick.[107]

The pattern of rent increases that prevailed on most estates had disadvantages for both landlords and tenants. First, arbitrary and sporadic rent increases tended to annoy the tenants. Given that rent took a large proportion of agricultural output, even moderate increases had a considerable effect on the tenants' incomes. The tenant in County Donegal who was 'a very irritable man' and who 'fell into a passion, and ... suddenly died' when his rent was increased, was exceptional, but his reaction may have been only an exaggerated form of what many tenants felt.[108] Secondly, sporadic rent increases did not produce increases in total incomes commensurate with their size. The calculations below[109] show that while rents went up by 20 per cent, the total rents paid during the thirty years 1850–79 were only about 10 per cent higher than they would have been if not increased at all. Thirdly, sporadic increases, especially those not based on a thorough valuation, tended to produce uneven levels of rents throughout an estate. At any one time, some tenants would be paying rents that were not only above the average of the estate, but well above many of the lowest rents. The grumbling that this caused was exacerbated by the absence of any rationale in the existing level of rents. Because rents were not generally fixed by regular market transactions, the portion of agricultural output that should have been taken by rent was virtually an uncharted landscape whose main features were discerned only through a fog of tradition, rumour, and envy. Even when careful valuations were made, their rationale was not explained and they were presented to the tenants as a sort of talisman. Edward Curling, Lord Dunraven's agent, who took the price of butter as the standard for raising and lowering rents, was exceptional in his understanding of the need to make clear the basis of rents.[110]

If landlords had applied to their estates other systems of increasing rents, they would not only have avoided many potential disputes with their tenants, but they would also have increased their incomes. If they had, for example, adopted the system of fluctuating rents recommended by Henry Stephens, they would have fared much better.[111] Sporadic increases of 20

---

[106] Butler rent-roll (County Clare), 1878 (NLI, MS 5422).
[107] Above n. 97.
[108] *Report from the Select Committee on Destitution (Gweedore and Cloughaneely)* ... p. 61, HC 1857–8 (412), xiii. 165. [109] pp. 265–6.
[110] *Sel. Comm. on Land Tenure, 1865*, 211.
[111] Stephens, *Book of the Farm*, ii. 498–503; see also John M. Wilson (ed.), *The Rural Cyclopedia, or a General Dictionary of Agriculture* ... (Edinburgh, 1851), iv. 37–42; C. S. Orwin and E. H. Whetham, *History of British Agriculture, 1846–1914* (London, 1964), 167.

per cent increased total incomes by only 10 per cent during the period 1850–79, but the TCD system would have increased them by 32 per cent; rents based on agricultural output would have increased incomes by 21 per cent; rents based on profits would have increased them by 30 per cent. Expressed as actual income over thirty years the differences were more dramatic: sporadic increases yielded an extra £30 million; the TCD system would have yielded an extra £100 million; rents based on profits would have yielded an extra £90 million; rents based on agricultural output would have yielded an extra £60 million.[112] The advantages of such a system far transcended the increased rentals that it would have given. Landlords and tenants would have received 'their just shares of profit and loss from the general improvement of agriculture, without influencing the gain or loss due to the tenant for his peculiarly good or bad management'.[113]

Fluctuating rents, based on clearly understood principles, would have given estate management a flexibility that it lacked, but needed. Increases in prosperity would have been accompanied by rent increases that came quickly and not four or five years later when the prosperity had been so long established that tenants regarded it as normal. More importantly, immediate relief would have been given in bad years, especially in the early 1860s and late 1870s. (It is perhaps worth noting that flexible rents would have given the tenants substantial reductions between 1876 and 1879; rents based on agricultural output, for example, would have fallen by almost 30 per cent.) Thirdly, such a system would have made clear the mechanism on which rents depended, and the effects of market changes would have been mediated explicitly and predictably.

What were the obstacles in the way of such a system? According to Stephens 'the difficulty of determining the statistical fact of the *annual average acreable produce of grain and of stock-feeding crops in each county*, is the only considerable obstacle to the adoption of this theory of grain rent in practice'.[114] This was not, however, an obstacle in Ireland, for the agricultural statistics gave these statistics not only for counties but also for baronies and poor law unions. All that was lacking was a reliable and generally acceptable series of agricultural prices for each locality, and it was not difficult to get those. A weightier objection to its application in Ireland was that Irish tenants were too numerous, too ignorant, and too illiterate to accept without constant grumbling such a complicated idea.[115]

---

[112] See below, App. 13.   [113] Stephens, *Book of the Farm*, ii. 501.   [114] Ibid.

[115] See e.g. William Robert Anketell, *Landlord and Tenant: Ireland. Letters by a Land Agent*... (Belfast, 1869), 7–8, where a County Down landlord's failure to work a system of triennial increases is described. 'It is just possible', wrote Anketell of corn and valuation rents, 'that a Scotch brain might survive the mental tension required, but no Irish brain could' (p. 21); see Donnelly, *Land and People of Cork*, 194, for Sir John Benn-Walsh basing rent increases 'upon the number of stock the tenants already possessed as well as upon his agent's conviction that stocking ratios could be greatly improved under the spur of higher rents'.

There was no reason, however, why tenants, even the most backward, should not have grasped its principles: fluctuating prices were part of the experience of any farmer who bought and sold livestock. The fishermen of Hare Island who mystified the magistrates at Shreelane petty sessions with references to the 'boat's share' knew all that was needed to understand the value of land as a factor of production and the practice of a fluctuating rent.[116] That there would have been grumbling was inevitable; after all the TCD leasing powers act caused a deal of grumbling in the 1880s among tenants who were not numerous, ignorant, or illiterate; but such a system would have narrowed its scope and forced it to concentrate on prices, costs, and the return on capital—the prosaic business of agriculture rather than the emotive issue of land tenure. The system could have been simplified in practice: a part of the rent could have fluctuated with the price of butter or beef, making unnecessary complicated calculations of agricultural output.

iv. The Obstacles to Rent Increases

'It is not incorrect to suppose', William Wann told the commissioners for endowed schools, whose estate he managed in County Tyrone, 'that tenants don't like an increase of rent no matter how fair it might be.'[117] The returns of agrarian crime suggest, however, that rent increases were not a major cause of outrages before 1879 and that opposition to them often took less dramatic forms.[118] When the tenants on the Shirley estate in County Monaghan wanted a reduction of rent, a crowd of them confronted the new agent, William Steuart Trench, and fell on their knees before him.[119] On the Gosford estate in County Armagh a petition for a rent reduction used language that was fulsome even by the generous standards of the nineteenth century: the tenant referred to himself as 'a poor worn slave', implored his lordship's 'humane protection', claimed he would 'always esteem it his greatest happiness to pay rent to the most noble earl', and concluded by wishing 'many happy days and more titles to the name of Gosford'.[120]

Tenants could make nuisances of themselves by petitioning, and writing to the newspapers. Although there was no doubt that in a protracted struggle a landlord could get his rents increased by evicting recalcitrant tenants, widespread and concerted resistance could be a nuisance. If tenants got wind of an impending increase, they could let their rents fall into arrears and defy the landlord to evict them. He would then not only be

---

[116] Edith Somerville and Martin Ross, *Further Experiences of an Irish RM* (New York, 1927), 85–102.
[117] Wann's letter-book, 19 Dec. 1859 (PRONI, D1606/5/4, p. 81).
[118] Below, p. 158.   [119] Trench, *Realities of Ir. Life*, 60.
[120] Gosford valuations and surveys (PRONI, D1606/12/7/305).

in the invidious position of having to evict them but would also risk losing the arrears. A rent increase of 25 per cent would not compensate in the short term for the loss of several years' rents—or for the embarrassment that might be felt by a landlord who relied on a steady income to meet the demands of encumbrancers.[121] He might, too, be left with vacant farms surrounded by hostile neighbours.

When Wann wanted to increase the rents on Lord Gosford's estate in County Cavan in 1864 he decided that it would be imprudent to mention the new valuation until he had collected the current rents in January 1865. When the valuation was completed in 1865, he did not reveal the new rents until after the 1865 rents had been collected in January 1866, because he wanted to have them 'fully collected first' and to 'have a good talk with the tenants and prepare them for subsequently ... agreeing to the new rent'.[122] Even when most of the tenants agreed to pay the new rents in 1866, he was still worried, for newspapers in Cavan were carrying reports that the crops had not been saved and that it was 'openly hinted' that landlords would be asked for rent reductions.[123] What was going on in Wann's mind was revealed in 1868 when the sale of the Cavan estate, to pay off Lord Gosford's debts,[124] was discussed. He hoped to get twenty-five years' purchase because he had succeeded in collecting the increased rent 'these last two years and up to last November there is not *six pence* of arrears'; also, when the rents had been increased in 1866 'there was no semblance of a combination'.[125]

Wann was not only thinking of the effects on the value of the Cavan estate that a botched attempt to increase the rents would have, he was probably also remembering the trouble he had had on the Dungannon Royal School estate in 1859 when he had raised the rents there. Although the royal commission on endowed schools noted that 'the tenants appear to be industrious, and the spirit of insubordination ... seems to have disappeared', Wann was worried about the proposed increases.[126] 'In order to make the intended rise in the school lands not too bitter for them ... it might not be a bad arrangement to have it understood with the valuator that in future the board would pay the *entire of the poor rates*.'[127] His diplomacy did not work, for there was resistance; in December 1860 one-sixth of the tenants did not pay, and twenty-eight memorialized the board, asking for a reduction of the new valuation. None of the tenants had agreed to pay the new rents, and if ejectment proceedings were started for

[121] Below, p. 118.
[122] Gosford letter-book, 7 Oct. 1865 (PRONI, D1606/5A/3, pp. 4–5); ibid. 3, p. 27; ibid. 2, p. 384.
[123] Ibid. 3, p. 84 (1 Oct. 1866). [124] Below, p. 136.
[125] Gosford letter-book, 19 Oct. 1868 (PRONI, D1606/5A/3, p. 198).
[126] *Endowed Schools Comm., 1857–8, Appendix*, p. 22.
[127] Wann's letter-book, 19 Dec. 1859 (PRONI, D1606/5/4, p. 81).

arrears, only the old rents could be recovered.[128] The dispute dragged on for years, a new valuation of part of the estate was made, some rents were reduced, and the tenants whose rents had not been revalued demanded another valuation. Part of the trouble, of course, was that the rent increases coincided with the bad years of the 1860s; but there was also 'pretty clear[ly] a *combination amongst them to resist payment*'.[129] (One of the leaders was Michael Gartlaney, who was to prove himself a most redoubtable troublemaker a few years later.[130]) In this particular dispute Wann had a weapon that was exceptional. During the dispute a 'middleman' offered to take the school lands at a much higher rent than was paid by the tenants. Wann did not hesitate to spread the good news: in September 1863 he told the commissioners that the news 'had been previously conveyed to them but *I repeated it* . . . so that the offer of £1,000 a year over the present rental is by *no means a secret to them*'.[131] It is worth noting that the dispute had been about an increase of 22 per cent and that the new rents were only 18 per cent above the valuation. The rent offered by the 'middleman' would have been 80 per cent above the valuation.[132]

The danger of a combination among the tenants and possibly a rent strike was obviously an obstacle to general increases over a whole estate. Sporadic increases, therefore, had at least the advantage of not generating widespread opposition. The experience of Wann on the Gosford and Dungannon Royal School estates shows that increasing rents required diplomacy, good timing, and determination. In theory the landlord had powerful weapons in his arsenal, but the tenants were not defenceless, and the position of the two parties was more evenly balanced than their purely legal relationship would suggest. How far the threat of opposition inhibited landlords and agents is not clear; Wann was cautious by nature, for in 1857 he told a correspondent that it was better for a landlord 'to set his lands at a moderate rent and be paid than to subject them to [a] sharper figure and render the payments uncertain'.[133] Yet in 1859 he tried to increase the rents on an estate that had a turbulent history without even taking the precaution of serving notices to quit.[134] Beyond suggesting that fears of concerted opposition probably accounted for the rarity of simultaneous rent increases, it is difficult to argue that such fears alone accounted for the relative smallness of rent increases as a whole. There are enough examples of large rent increases to suggest that landlords could have gone much further than they did.

Although agents complained that rents were hard to collect, there is

---

[128] Ibid. 104 (11 Dec. 1860). [129] Ibid. 207 (8 Dec. 1863).
[130] Above, pp. 39–43.
[131] Wann's letter-book, 14 Sept. 1863 (PRONI, D1606/5/4, p. 197).
[132] Ibid. 101 (22 Nov. 1860). [133] Ibid. 17 (13 Apr. 1855).
[134] Ibid. 105 (11 Dec. 1860).

little evidence to show that tenants normally resisted their payment. The tables below[135] show that on a group of estates whose rentals have survived, rents were paid punctually except in bad years, such as the early 1850s and early 1860s, and even then receipts did not fall dramatically below the annual rent due. The judicial statistics of debt recovered through the courts confirm this impression. The amount of rent for which civil bill decrees were granted in 1869, for example, was only £26,000 out of a rental of over £10 million; civil bill decrees for ordinary debts amounted to £169,000, which was nearly seven times as much as the rent recovered.[136] Concerted opposition by tenants was probably no more important as a cause of moderate rents than the unimaginative way in which rents were adjusted. The failure of landlords to exploit their estates to the full may have influenced the efficiency with which land was used. One of the arguments in favour of a tenancy system was that it acted as a spur to economic efficiency. 'Under a system of competitive rents, a farmer is unlikely to acquire more land than at any time it is worth his while to have ... land is allocated in the economically most efficient manner.'[137] Mrs Smith of Baltiboys made the same point more emphatically—as was her habit. 'As a general rule,' she wrote in her journal, 'and for the sake of the tenant himself he should be very strictly dealt with both as to his rent being paid to the day and that being fully high for the value of the land. All human beings requiring a stimulus to exertion and the farmer almost more than any other man of business needing to employ more both of mind and body to enable him to do justice to his holding.'[138] Certainly the argument that higher rents would have encouraged more intensive farming was as sound as its opposite, that security of tenure and compensation for improvements would have increased output. There is a final point. If actual rents were less than potential rents, what became of the uncollected balance? This unobtrusive aspect of rents, ignored by many contemporaries who were obsessed with rackrenting, was profoundly and pervasively important in landlord–tenant relations.

[135] See below, Apps. 7 and 8.
[136] *Judicial Statistics, Ire.*, 1869, pp. 212–13 [C 227], HC 1870, lxiii. 964–5.
[137] Raymond D. Crotty, *Irish Agricultural Production: Its Volume and Structure* (Cork, 1966), 93.
[138] David Thomson and Moyra McGusty (eds.), *The Irish Journals of Elizabeth Smith, 1840–1850* (Oxford, 1980), 58.

4
The Tenant-Right Custom

i. What Was Tenant Right?

Tenant right was, according to the lawyers Ferguson and Vance, 'a phantom that melts away under every attempt to define it and that, chameleon-like, appeared to assume a different aspect every time it presents itself'.[1] Contemporary definitions ranged from the simple right of an outgoing tenant to sell his improvements to what became known as the three Fs—fair rent, fixity of tenure, and free sale. Mountifort Longfield, a judge of the landed estates court, told a select committee in 1865 that tenant right was 'the custom of a tenant holding from year to year at a moderate rent and with security of tenure depending upon the honour of the landlord': when such a tenant 'wants' to quit, he may sell his tenant right 'for sometimes as much as £800'.[2] The tenant-right custom, according to W. D. Henderson, was the three Fs.[3] Even landlords and agents went beyond the right to sell improvements. Fitzherbert Filgate, Lord Downshire's agent, thought that tenant right included 'fair' rents;[4] Robert Russell, a County Donegal agent, thought that it included fixity of tenure.[5]

There were enough contradictions in definitions of tenant right in the 1850s to justify the cautious, but capacious, definition put forward by Ferguson and Vance: the right of a tenant to continue in possession as long as he paid his rent or until the landlord required possession; the right of an outgoing tenant to sell 'all the interest in the farm recognized by custom to belong to him'.[6] But what did this mean? The first right conferred nothing remarkable on a tenant; the second did not explain what the custom allowed him to sell. Was it his improvements, or something more? William Neilson Hancock, brother of Lord Lurgan's agent John Hancock and professor of political economy in Dublin University (1845–51), argued that

---

[1] William Dwyer Ferguson and Andrew Vance, *The Tenure and Improvement of Land in Ireland, Considered with Reference to the Relation of Landlord and Tenant and Tenant Right* (Dublin, 1851), 300–16; see also B. L. Solow, *The Land Question and the Irish Economy, 1870–1903* (Cambridge, Mass., 1971), 24–32.
[2] *Sel. Comm. on Land Tenure*, 1865, 190.
[3] W. D. Henderson, *Lecture on the History and Origin of Ulster Tenant Right, Delivered before the National Reform Union, Manchester, 20 March 1877* (Manchester, 1877), 8.
[4] *Lords' Sel. Comm. on Land Tenure*, 1867, 190.   [5] Ibid. 88.
[6] Ferguson and Vance, *The Tenure and Improvement of Land in Ireland*, 302; see 300–1 for several different definitions of tenant right.

the real basis of tenant right was the sale of permanent improvements;[7] William Sharman Crawford, the advocate of tenant-right legislation, allowed outgoing tenants to receive payments from their successors only if they had 'expended labour or capital in some form so as to increase the value of the premises'.[8]

The weight of contemporary opinion, however, supported the assertion that tenant right was more than the sale of improvements. Longfield was quite clear that tenant right and compensation for improvements 'are totally different things';[9] the inquiries made by the poor law inspectors in 1869-79 showed that tenant right was more than improvements.[10] It was also clear that the sums paid for tenant right were much greater than the value of improvements and that farms offered for sale were often dilapidated.[11] That the custom gave tenants the right to sell something more than their improvements does not seem to be seriously in doubt; but did it also give them security of tenure and fair rents? Lord Dufferin thought it was only an impediment and not an obstacle to evictions;[12] there was only a likelihood and not a certainty, according to David Ross, that the tenant would not be evicted.[13] The same point was made by H. S. Thompson, who visited Ireland on the eve of the land act of 1870: far from giving the tenants security of tenure, *'it acts precisely the other way, and makes it easier for the landlord to remove an objectionable tenant'*.[14]

The argument that the custom gave tenants fair rents was even more complicated. First, rents were said to be lower in Ulster than in the other provinces[15]—at least 20 per cent under the full competition rent;[16] rent was spread more evenly over holdings;[17] and, according to William O'Connor Morris, there were hardly any complaints of rackrenting in Ulster.[18] Secondly, there were statements about how the custom regulated rents: they

---

[7] William Neilson Hancock, *The Tenant Right of Ulster, Considered Economically...* (Dublin, 1845), 33-4.

[8] B. A. Kennedy, 'Select Documents XXIII: Sharman Crawford on Ulster Tenant Right', *IHS* 13: 53 (Mar. 1963), 247.

[9] *Sel. Comm. on Land Tenure*, 1865, 14; see also *Lords' Sel. Comm. on Land Tenure*, 1867, 98, 215. [10] *Poor Law Inspectors' Reports*, 1870, 4.

[11] *Sel. Comm. on Land Tenure*, 1865, 61-2; *Lords' Sel. Comm. on Land Tenure*, 1867, 5, 14; *Poor Law Inspectors' Reports*, 1870, 102, 139; Solow, *The Land Question and the Irish Economy*, 26. [12] *Sel. Comm. on Land Tenure*, 1865, 78.

[13] David Ross, 'The Tenant Right of Ulster, What it is, and How Far it should be Legalized and Extended to the Other Provinces of Ireland', *Jn. Stat. Soc. Ire.* 3: 24 (July 1863), 391.

[14] Thompson, *Ire. in 1839 and 1869*, 94.

[15] *Bessborough Comm., Minutes of Evidence*, pt. i, p. 178; Thompson, *Ire. in 1839 and 1869*, 90-1.

[16] Frederick Temple Hamilton-Temple-Blackwood, 1st marquis of Dufferin and Ava, *Contributions to an Inquiry into the Present State of Ireland* (London, 1866), 59.

[17] Samuelson, *Land and Tenantry of Ire.*, 33.

[18] William O'Connor Morris, *Letters on the Land Question of Ireland* (London, 1870), 274.

should be fixed by valuation;[19] the valuation should allow the price of the tenant right to remain high and should not include the tenant's buildings;[20] revaluations should be infrequent.[21] The contrary, however, was asserted: there were no rules about the frequency of valuations on Ulster estates;[22] rents were as high in Ulster as anywhere else—it was even asserted that Ulster rents were about 9s. an acre higher than rents in the rest of the country.[23] Lord Dufferin claimed that there was a dynamic conflict between rents and the value of tenant right: as one went up, the other went down, 'like buckets in a well'.[24] It was admitted that rents could be increased, but not to the point where they would 'destroy' the tenant right.[25] But how could such calculations be made? Robert Donnell told a select committee that rents should be fixed so that the tenant right would sell for ten years' purchase of the rent; but that was a rare foray into explicitness.[26] George Campbell gave up in despair: the connection between rent and tenant right was 'hopelessly puzzling to an outsider', for it was arranged 'among the natives by some sort of rule of thumb which a foreigner cannot exactly understand'.[27]

An additional problem in defining tenant right was that most, but not all, of the definitions that included security of tenure and fair rents came from the later part of the period, apparently stimulated by the debates on the land act of 1870. Most of the witnesses who defined tenant right for the Devon commission a generation earlier confined themselves to the right to sell. Did the custom develop between the 1840s and 1870s? H. S. Thompson, who visited Ireland in 1839 and 1869, thought it had developed, for in 1839 it had not assumed 'its present formidable proportions'.[28] Even in the 1850s changes were noticed: a witness told a parliamentary committee that the tenant right advocated by the tenant league was not the 'old' tenant right of Ulster.[29] Lord Ranfurly's agent, Courtenay Newton, told a select committee in 1872 that the historical origin given by 'theorists' was 'all wrong', for in his youth tenant right was not 'one-seventh part of the value that it is now on several estates about me'.[30]

The problem was, however, that none of those who commented on the development of the custom described it as a progress from the right to sell to security of tenure and fair rents. Newton and Thompson were most

---

[19] Alexander G. Richey, *The Irish Land Laws* (London, 1880), 106; *Lords' Sel. Comm. on the Land Act*, 1872, 241.   [20] Ibid. 276; Donnell, *Practical Guide*, 103.
[21] *Lords' Sel. Comm. on the Land Act*, 1872, 240.
[22] *Lords' Sel. Comm. on Land Tenure*, 1867, 191.
[23] Ibid. 11, 91, 192; MacLagan, *Land Tenure in Ire.*, 7, 22; *Bessborough Comm., Minutes of Evidence*, pt. i, p. 346.   [24] *Sel. Comm. on Land Tenure*, 1865, 62.
[25] Campbell, *Ir. Land*, 48.   [26] *Lords' Sel. Comm. on Land Act*, 1872, 276.
[27] Campbell, *Ir. Land*, 48.   [28] Thompson, *Ire. in 1839 and 1869*, 98.
[29] *Sel. Comm on County Monaghan*, 1852, 68–9, 87.
[30] *Lords' Sel. Comm. on the Land Act*, 1872, 99.

impressed by the increase in its selling price. Thompson, however, also noticed that not only had it 'raised its terms', but it was also 'striving to include within its range leases which were then [1839] entirely free from any claim of the kind and other kinds of property besides land, such as mills, quarries, etc.'. He went further, but unfortunately not far enough, towards clearing up the mystery, by predicting the next stage: 'there are also not wanting indications that no long time will elapse before a strenuous attempt will be made to establish *fixity of rent*.'[31] The problem of definition was further complicated by the fact that some of the comprehensive definitions came as early as the 1840s, occasionally from sources that could not be dismissed as biased. John Hancock told the Devon commission that tenant right included 'the claim of the tenant and his heirs to continue in undisturbed possession of the farm, so long as the rent is paid'.[32]

Even a cursory examination of contemporary definitions of tenant right reveals uncertainties. Only two things are clear. First, tenants bought and sold the interest, whatever that was, of their farms. Secondly, there was a vague awareness that something was happening to tenant right, especially in the 1860s and 1870s. Estate papers help a little towards making tenant right clearer, although they are silent on its most intriguing aspects. They can, for example, resolve the difficulty about security of tenure. It is true that evictions were less common in Ulster than in the other provinces: between 1849 and 1880, out of 68,767 evictions in the whole country, only 8,791 occurred in Ulster.[33] Estate papers show, however, that tenants were occasionally evicted even when not in arrears. Tenants who made a nuisance of themselves could be 'made to sell their holdings'.[34] What was characteristic of the custom, however, was that evicted tenants were allowed to sell their tenant right. Evictions without the right to sell were rare. The Derryveagh evictions were probably the most notorious case. More typical was the Ulster agent, Alexander Spotswood, who remonstrated with his employer, Lord Garvagh, when it seemed that he would have to evict a tenant without compensation:

Since I first commenced business as an agent I have never been required to evict a tenant without compensation and as it is a most unusual proceeding... and would place your lordship in a very unpleasant position as regards public opinion in the country I would strongly advise the eviction to be deferred.[35]

[31] Thompson, *Ire. in 1839 and 1869*, 98–9.
[32] *Devon Comm., Minutes of Evidence*, pt. i, p. 483; see also William Neilson Hancock, *The Tenant Right of Ulster, Considered Economically*... (Dublin, 1845), 7–9.
[33] *Returns of Evictions, 1849–80*, 3–4.
[34] Wann's letter-book, 4 Nov. 1857 (PRONI, D1606/5/4, p. 43); for the case of a tenant in arrears being forced to sell, see Farnham requests-book, 22 Dec. 1856 (NLI, MS 3118).
[35] Spotswood's letter-book, 31 July 1861 (PRONI, D1062/1/8A, p. 45).

Estate papers are less helpful in elucidating the connection between the custom and fair rents. Rents were adjusted by valuation on many estates in Ulster; but rents were also adjusted by valuation on southern estates.[36] Rent increases were not more frequent on southern estates than on northern; nor were they higher in the south. The only differences between rents in Ulster and the rest of Ireland that can be measured were: first, rents were higher in the south when compared with the tenement valuation; secondly, they were more unevenly laid on individual holdings in the south.[37] Too much weight, however, should not be attached to these differences. There is evidence that the tenement valuation was higher in Ulster than in the rest of Ireland, which accounts for the relative lowness of rents there.[38] The apparent unevenness of rents, therefore, seems to be the only major difference between Ulster and the rest of Ireland.

Most puzzling of all is the absence of any explanation in the estate papers of how rents were adjusted in conformity with the custom. Only the right to sell emerges clearly from the estate papers—as it does from contemporary descriptions. It is tempting, therefore, to argue that tenant right was not the three Fs; at most it was one F, the right to sell. Definitions that went beyond that could be seen as mere aspirations that formed an insubstantial halo round a substantial core. The problem, however, was more complicated than this would suggest. The sums paid for tenant right were large—too large to be regarded as the tenurial equivalent of luck-pennies. In the 1870s the tenant-right prices suggested that many outgoing tenants received as much as twenty years' purchase of the rent of their holdings.[39]

In other words, tenant right was as valuable as the fee simple and tenants had as substantial an interest in their land as the landlord. It is arguable that some of the prices given to parliamentary inquiries were exaggerated by tenants who wanted to make the most of their claims; but their reliability is supported by the record of tenant-right sales on the Abercorn estates in the counties of Donegal and Tyrone between 1867 and 1887.[40] The average value of tenant right was twenty-three years' purchase, and what was even more remarkable, about one-quarter of the holdings sold for more than thirty years' purchase. If the duke of Abercorn had sold

---

[36] Above, pp. 57–61.
[37] W. E. Vaughan, 'A Study of Landlord and Tenant Relations in Ireland between the Famine and the Land War, 1850–78' (Ph.D. thesis, University of Dublin, 1974), 391, 406, 420, 433, 454, 468, 479, 488.
[38] *Report from the Select Committee on General Valuation etc. (Ireland); together with the Proceedings of the Committee, Minutes of Evidence, and Appendix*, p. 242, HC 1868–9 (362), ix. 254.
[39] Vaughan, 'A study of landlord and tenant relations in Ireland', 254, 255, 263.
[40] Tenant-right sales on the Abercorn estate, 1867–87 (PRONI, D623/B/11/4).

his estate in the 1870s, he might not have got more than twenty-three years' purchase; he might have got less; it is highly unlikely that he would have got thirty years'.[41]

Although the precise connection between rents and tenant right cannot be elucidated, it was generally agreed that the lower the rent, the higher the value of the tenant right. As Lord Dufferin said, tenant right and rents were like buckets in a well. At a dinner for his tenants in 1865 he was more expansive. He was, he said, 'content to let his land at a far lower rate than the rackrent or competition price, in order that, by leaving them a more ample margin, his tenantry may live better'; but he was forced to see his moderation

entirely neutralized by a surreptitious sale of nominal improvements, which abstracts from the pocket of his future tenant perhaps forty years' purchase of the difference between the fair rent he is content to take and the exorbitant rent he might have had from a dozen people, had he been so minded.[42]

What Dufferin was doing, or rather objecting to his tenants doing, was allowing part of the rental value of his land to be sold in the form of tenant right.

The same point was made more clearly by Charles Uniacke Townshend in his evidence to the Bessborough commission. 'The Ulster tenant-right custom means some kind of saleable interest which they would not possess if a farm was not worth more than they are paying for it.'[43] Nassau William Senior had noticed this even earlier when a landlord in County Londonderry told him about a tenant who sold his tenant right for £5 an acre:

'Such a tenant right', I said, 'implies that the rent is too low. Why do you not raise it?'

'I cannot', he answered, 'ask a larger rent than that which is usually paid in this neighbourhood for land of this quality. I should not, certainly, incur personal danger by doing so, but I should become unpopular, which might affect my position.'[44]

These three statements are remarkable, for most contemporaries tried to define the custom and rents as if they were two discrete entities, connected only by customary rules. The value of tenant right was influenced by rent, it was admitted, but it was also implied that this was only one of many things influencing it. If Dufferin, Townshend, and Senior were right the connection between rent and tenant right was not just a series of customary

---

[41] *Report from the Select Committee on* [the] *Irish Land Act, 1870; together with the Proceedings of the Committee, Minutes of Evidence, Appendix, and Index*, p. 316, HC 1878 (249), xv. 358.

[42] *Irish Farmers' Gazette*, 13 May 1865, p. 163; see also Solow, *The Land Question and the Irish Economy*, 26–9.   [43] *Bessborough Comm., Minutes of Evidence*, pt. i, p. 60.

[44] Nassau William Senior, *Journals, Conversations, and Essays Relating to Ireland* (London, 1868), ii. 171.

rules, for tenant right was actually part of the rent. The relationship between rents paid to landlords and the tenants' interest was, therefore, a dynamic one: if one moved, so did the other, and neither could be defined until the other was rendered immobile.

Much of the confusion caused by tenant right can be traced to two circumstances. First, contemporaries tried to define the custom as a series of rules, not because that was the best way to analyse it, but because they were interested in it as a model for legislation. Secondly, to have defined the custom as it actually was—a capitalization of the uncollected rental—would have discredited it as a model for legislation. It is arguable, too, that landlords put up with the custom only as long as its implications remained obscure. It worked well enough in practice, giving northern landlords security for their arrears and enabling them to get rid of obnoxious tenants; but as soon as its internal dynamic was revealed, argument and friction were produced. Only much more refined methods of adjusting rents could have established a *modus vivendi*, for only a clearly enunciated method of increasing rents would have cleared up the relationship between rents and tenant right and made it possible to establish it on estates where it did not exist or where it had been wiped out.

Were Dufferin, Townshend, and Senior right? If tenants were prepared to pay ten or twenty years' purchase for land they must have expected a return on their capital. According to Robert Donnell they expected a return of 3 per cent;[45] Mountifort Longfield, on the other hand, implied that they expected 5 per cent.[46] (The second of these agrees roughly with the rough estimate occasionally put forward that a shilling on the rent took a pound off the tenant right.) If tenants expected a return of 5 per cent, those who paid twenty years' purchase were obviously expecting a return that was as large as the rent; in other words rents could have been doubled if there had been no tenant right. The tests applied to rents below[47] suggest that rents were low by the 1870s; but could they have been increased by 100 per cent? None of the tests suggested that rents could have been doubled even in the 1870s: at most they might have been increased by 40 per cent. The tests, however, were not designed to measure the full competition rent, but merely to measure alternative ways of adjusting rents. All were based on the assumption that landlords and tenants should share proportionately in increases in the value of agricultural output. In practice it may have been possible to increase rents by much larger amounts. The middleman who offered to take the Dungannon Royal School estate was prepared to pay a rent that was 50 per cent above that paid by the tenants.[48] In a survey of estates in the counties of Limerick and Clare in

---

[45] Donnell, *Practical Guide*, 42–3.
[46] *Sel. Comm. on Land Tenure*, 1865, 2.
[47] See below, Apps. 9, 10, 12, and 13.
[48] Above, p. 65.

the 1870s it was even suggested that some of the rents could be increased by 100 per cent.[49]

Before concluding that tenant right was largely a capitalization of the margin between actual rents and the full rent, it is worth approaching tenant right from its one undoubted characteristic, which was the fact that large sums were given to outgoing tenants. If tenants were not buying a portion of the rent what were they buying? There were three possible reasons why an incoming tenant might have paid an outgoing tenant, even for land let at its full value. First, there may have been improvements such as a dwelling-house, drains, and fences. Secondly, the payment might have been a sort of blackmail for 'immunity' from outrages. Thirdly, small tenants, whose incomes were close to those of agricultural labourers and whose farms did not absorb all their labour, might have been prepared to pay something for more land, even if it yielded no extra profit.

None of these reasons operating separately, however, could have explained why tenants paid £100 or even £200 for a small farm. Although great claims were made for tenants' improvements, they do not seem to have been very valuable. Sums awarded under the land act of 1870 for improvements, for example, were not large.[50] Dwelling-houses, which were probably the most valuable assets of tenants, would not have been worth much on small farms, probably not more than £30 or £40. In any case an incoming tenant would not have wanted the house if he lived on an adjoining farm. At most, therefore, improvements on a small farm might have justified the payment of four or five years' purchase. Even on a large, well-equipped farm, it is doubtful if the buildings would have been worth more than a couple of hundred pounds; yet there are examples of tenants paying thousands for such farms.

It was hinted that incoming tenants paid outgoing tenants to go away quietly. On an estate in County Donegal, for example, the landlord bought the tenant right of a small farm for £75 and the following agreement between them was recorded:

The said Hugh Sweeney, for himself, his wife, and children, doth hereby undertake and promise and pledge his faith as an honest man, that Mr Woodhouse [the landlord] shall not get any kind of annoyance, trouble or disturbance, directly or indirectly, by acts, deeds, language, letter, notice, or otherwise, for or on account or by reason of taking said farm.[51]

Although fear of violence probably played a part in sustaining the custom, it is doubtful if such large sums would have been necessary to buy off

[49] Survey of the Westropp estate in Counties Clare and Limerick by Robert L. Brown, 1871–7 (NLI MS 5397, 68–9).
[50] See e.g. *Judicial statistics, Ire.*, 1875, pp. 77–8 [C 1563], HC 1875, lxxix. 349–50.
[51] *Report from the Select Committee on Destitution (Gweedore and Cloughaneely); together with the Proceedings of the Committee, Minutes of Evidence, and Appendix*, p. 238, HC 1857–8 (412), xiii. 342.

trouble-makers. On estates outside Ulster, where the custom did not prevail, small sums were paid to outgoing tenants, sometimes by the landlord and sometimes by the new tenant. In the Smith Barry papers it was noted that although the widow Doherty had been given £10 by the landlord when she gave up her holding, 'she was still waiting for the new tenant that he might give her a few pounds'.[52] Even if the widow got another £10 from her successor she would have ended up with a mere fraction of the tenant right. The main argument against the custom as blackmail was that most tenants who sold their farms were vulnerable or weak: widows, orphans, old men with no close relatives, or those on the verge of bankruptcy.

The argument that tenant right was sustained by intense competition for small farms is more weighty than either of the preceding. Small farmers were probably more interested in their actual incomes than in the most rational disposition of their capital and labour. If they could produce more food, have an extra pig or calf for sale, they would not carefully set that benefit against costs in the way a large farmer might. Many small farmers kept horses for which there was not enough work on their farms. Additional land, therefore, even if acquired at what was in effect the full economic rent, enabled them to spread their overheads. There is little doubt that small farms sold well; a farm on the Abercorn estate, whose rent was £15, sold for thirty-seven and a half years' purchase in 1868.[53] Their smallness, however, only added to their value; it was not the cause of it. The argument that tenant right was sustained by the land hunger of small farmers was weak, for large farms also sold well: on the same estate, a farm whose rent was £91. 4s. sold for twenty-seven and a half years' purchase in 1876.

None of these three reasons, taken separately or together, could account for the prices commonly paid for tenant right. It is possible, of course, that all three operating powerfully and simultaneously could have accounted for substantial sums. A small farm, well fenced and drained, with a good house, held by a formidable ruffian in the prime of life, might have fetched a high price, even if the rent was high; but even the most lurid accounts of the countryside do not claim, or even imply, that such circumstances were common enough to sustain a custom that was public, systematic, and routine. At the same time, it would be rash to say that tenant right was only a capitalization of the rent, for these other things played a part. What strengthens, however, the argument that tenant right was mainly a capitalization of the rent was the increase in its value between the 1840s and 1870s.[54] None of the three reasons for buying tenant right could have caused tenant right to increase so dramatically. Indeed, if tenant right had

[52] Smith Barry papers (NLI, MS 8819 (21)).
[53] Tenant-right sales on the Abercorn estate, 1867–87 (PRONI, D623/B/11/4)).
[54] Above, p. 69; see also Vaughan, 'A Study of Landlord and Tenant Relations in Ireland', 254, 263.

been sustained only by improvements, the land hunger of small farmers, and fear of retaliation, it would probably have declined between the 1840s and the 1870s, for by then there were fewer small farmers, fewer outrages, relatively more police in the countryside, and no overwhelming evidence that improvements had increased dramatically.

ii. The Extent of Tenant Right

George Campbell divided the country into three 'zones', according to the prevalence of tenant right in each. The first was Ulster, where tenant right 'has assumed a definite and recognized form, against which it is vain for landlords to contend'. The second, where 'the custom is uncertain and imperfect, but is maintained by violence' stretched from Ulster to Tipperary. The third where there were traces of tenant right, unsupported either by custom or violence and where tenants were at the mercy of their landlords, lay to the south of Tipperary and in the extreme west.[55]

If tenant right existed outside Ulster in an attenuated form, its strength inside the province also varied. According to William O'Connor Morris, it was most fully developed in the centre of the province and along its north-eastern seaboard—what he regarded as the centre of the seventeenth-century plantation. The custom was weaker on the periphery—in parts of the counties of Cavan, Donegal, and Armagh—where 'it is less thoroughly sustained by usage; the general character of the land system more nearly approaches that of the south, and evictions and clearances have been less uncommon'. O'Connor Morrris also noted that tenant right was most valuable in Antrim and Down, less valuable in Londonderry, and even less valuable in Fermanagh.[56] The poor law inspectors' reports largely support O'Connor Morris's account of tenant right in Ulster: the custom was stronger in Antrim and Down than in Cavan, Fermanagh, and Monaghan.[57] In Fermanagh, for example, there were restrictions on tenant right 'which are almost unknown and would hardly be tolerated further north'. On six of the county's largest estates its price was fixed: on the marquis of Ely's estate its price was limited to three years' purchase; on the Archdale estate it was limited to two years'.[58] What was remarkable, in the poor law inspectors' reports, was the strength they attributed to tenant right in Donegal; in west Donegal, for example, except on the Leitrim estate where it was prohibited, tenant right sold for twenty and thirty years' purchase.[59]

The poor law inspectors' reports also add some details to Campbell's

---

[55] Campbell, *Ir. Land*, 113, 6, 114, 117.
[56] William O'Connor Morris, *Letters on the Land Question of Ireland* (London, 1870), 245, 254, 265. In Antrim and Down prices ranged from seven to twenty-five years' purchase; in Londonderry from five to twenty years'; in Fermanagh from three to six.
[57] *Poor Law Inspectors' Reports, 1870*, 12–13, 101, 142.
[58] Ibid. 13. [59] Ibid.

two zones outside Ulster, although it must be admitted that they convey a more complex pattern than he does. The only area outside Ulster where, according to the poor law inspectors, tenant right prevailed over a whole district was in five unions in County Mayo: the unions of Ballina, Ballinrobe, Castlebar, Claremorris, and Swineford, where its value ranged from four to seven years' purchase.[60] Tenant right was sold openly on many individual estates in the counties of Carlow, Dublin, Kildare, and Meath, and in the Queen's County. The inspector whose report covered most of this district found 'that upon about one-third of the estates from which I have received returns, the system is either openly sanctioned, or carried out under another name'.[61]

There is evidence of sales on single estates outside this area, but they do not appear to have been numerous. The inspector whose district included County Waterford and parts of the counties of Carlow, Cork, Kilkenny, Tipperary, and Wexford believed that 'Ulster tenant right' existed on only two estates in that area: on the marquis of Ormond's in Kilkenny and on Lord Granard's in Wexford.[62] Tenant right, however, or something very like it, can be identified on other estates: on Lord Portsmouth's in Waterford, for example, where tenants were allowed to sell by auction and private treaty.[63] Sources other than the poor law inspectors' reports have information on tenant right on single estates in the 1860s. Robert Russell said that it existed on Lord Palmerston's estate at Mullaghmore, County Sligo, where it sold for £8 an acre in 1868.[64]

There is little doubt, therefore, that something like tenant right was known outside Ulster. But how different was it? The problem of describing southern tenant right is illustrated by W. J. Hamilton, the poor law inspector whose report covered County Waterford and parts of neighbouring counties: 'Ulster tenant right is not recognized in this part of the south of Ireland,' he wrote, 'but outgoing tenants frequently, if not invariably, receive payment for their goodwill, in general with the consent of the landlord, sometimes without it.'[65] How the sale of goodwill was different from 'Ulster tenant right' is not clear; but certain differences can be discerned between the south and those areas of Ulster where tenant right was very strong.

First, southern tenant right was more a matter of landlord favour or

---

[60] Ibid. 57–8. [61] Ibid. 29.
[62] Ibid. 73–4; see Donnelly, *Land and People of Cork*, 210–18 for examples of tenants selling their farms. [63] *Poor Law Inspectors' Reports*, 30.
[64] Robert Russell, *Ulster Tenant Right for Ireland: or, Notes upon Notes Taken During a Visit to Ireland in 1868* (London and Edinburgh, 1870), 45; see also Murrough O'Brien's commonplace book, 24–5 (MS in private possession), and Robert Brian MacCarthy, *The Trinity College Estates, 1800–1923: Corporate Management in an Age of Reform* (Dundalk, 1992), 198–9. For examples of southern tenant right causing crimes and at the same time establishing the fact of its existence, see National Archives, OP 1872/85, nos. 33, 34, 110.
[65] *Poor Law Inspectors' Reports*, 1870, 73.

acquiescence than of established custom: permission to sell, when given, was not given as a matter of course but as a matter of favour.[66] Secondly, tenant right outside Ulster did not have 'the certainty of a fixed price' that it had in Ulster.[67] In Ulster the poor law inspectors were able to give the current prices of tenant right, but in the south some of them found this difficult. 'The price, whether by the acre or rental, is arbitrary, varying extremely, not only on different properties, but in individual cases.'[68] Others refused to generalize, merely giving the prices of individual sales of which they had heard.[69] Thirdly, many of the sales in the south were, if not secret, at least clandestine, and landlords did not co-operate in carrying them out.[70] There was also a hint of blackmail: the payment of an outgoing tenant, according to one inspector, 'would, probably, not ordinarily amount to more than a moderate sum, barely sufficient to insure (in its literal sense) the goodwill of the outgoing tenant, a thing, in Ireland, which is always much and earnestly desired'.[71]

The contrast between Ulster and the rest of Ireland was demonstrated by the working of the land act of 1870. Both northern and southern tenants had a choice: they could claim under sections 3 and 4 for improvements and compensation for disturbance; or they could claim under sections 1 and 2 for the benefit of the Ulster custom or analogous customs; or they could claim under section 7 for payments made to their predecessors. Claims outside Ulster under sections 2 and 7 should therefore give a rough idea of the strength of tenant right. Obviously tenants would claim under sections 1 and 2 only if what they hoped to get exceeded what they were likely to get under sections 3, 4, and 7. The judicial statistics for the years 1871–8 show that most Ulster tenants claimed under the custom and that almost 60 per cent of the compensation was awarded under it. In the other three provinces, however, only two claims were made under section 2 between 1871 and 1878, and awards under section 7 for incoming payments were made only in 1871, 1875, and 1876.[72] The contemporary tendency to call tenant right the Ulster custom gave the impression that there was a sharp distinction between Ulster and the rest of Ireland; superficially the judicial statistics confirmed this, but even they suggest that there was variety within Ulster, for many Ulster tenants claimed under sections 3 and 4, like the majority in the other provinces.

---

[66] Ibid. 101; see also 23, 126, 154; see also Donnelly, *Land and People of Cork*, 217–18.
[67] Campbell, *Ir. Land*, 54.   [68] *Poor Law Inspectors' Reports, 1870*, 143.
[69] Ibid. 31.   [70] Ibid. 119; see also *Lords' Sel. Comm. on Land Tenure, 1867*, 214.
[71] *Poor Law Inspectors' Reports, 1870*, 143.
[72] *Judicial statistics, Ire., 1871*, pp. 92–4 [C 674], HC 1872. lxv; ibid. *1872*, pp. 88–91 [C 851], HC 1873, lxx; ibid. *1873*, pp. 84–7 [C 1034], HC 1874, lxxi; ibid. *1874*, pp. 79–82 [C 1295], HC 1875, lxxxi; ibid. *1875*, pp. 76–8 [C 1536], HC 1876, lxxix; ibid. *1876*, pp. 78–80 [C 1822], HC 1877, lxxxvi; ibid. *1877*, pp. 78–82 [C 2152], HC 1878, lxxix; ibid. *1878*, pp. 68–71 [C 2389], HC 1878–9, lxxvi.

Outgoing tenants in the south often received small payments from their landlords. Fourteen tenants on the Inchiquin estate in 1851 received a total of £15. 0s. 6d. and in 1852 six received £4. 17s. 6d.[73] These sums were trifling, but on other estates slightly larger payments were made.[74] Occasionally the incoming tenant was involved. On the Ashtown estate the landlord gave an outgoing tenant money to emigrate and the incoming tenant paid his arrears.[75] On some estates tenants were compensated for improvements. On the Crosbie estate in County Kerry tenants were allowed to sell not only their crops but their buildings as well; their arrears, however, were deducted. A widow who was removed in 1848 received £35. 13s. 11½d. for her house, crops, and manure; but £27. 15s. 8d. was deducted for arrears, leaving her only £7. 18s. 3½d. She was luckier than another tenant who got only 10½d. after deductions were made from her compensation of £33. 0s. 10½d.[76]

There were some examples on southern estates of landlords exercising the sort of probate jurisdiction that existed on northern estates. There was, for example, a note in the Fitzwilliam memoranda books in 1873 that the 'family of Judith Byrne have agreed about shares of her property except one son who ... won't allow the amount of £45 to stand over for three years or accept arbitration ... the son who is selected for tenant, Joseph, to pay off the one who is raising objections.'[77] The difference, however, between tenant right in the north and the *ad hoc* arrangements on southern estates was demonstrated by a similar transaction on the Powerscourt estate. An incoming tenant gave his predecessor £20, but the agent 'had nothing to do with the arrangement'.[78] In other words, creditors did not have the same protection as they enjoyed in the north.[79]

These sums were small and not comparable with the sums paid by incoming tenants in Ulster. Yet the forces that sustained tenant right in Ulster existed in the south: rents were lower than they might have been; there were small tenants anxious to get more land. That there was a disposable margin between actual and potential rents outside Ulster can hardly be doubted. The southern margin may not have been as large, but even assuming that rents in the south were higher than in the north, there should still have been a substantial margin. Sales of tenants' interests

---

[73] Inchiquin rentals (County Clare), 1851–2 (NLI, MSS 14523–4).
[74] St George rentals (Counties Leitrim, Roscommon, Tipperary, and Waterford), 1850–5 (ibid. MSS 4006–11).
[75] Ashtown rentals (County Limerick), 1850–65 (ibid. MS 5824, p. 627).
[76] Crosbie rent-ledger (County Kerry), 1844–77 (ibid. MS 5037, pp. 6, 8, 11, 17, 21, 22, 36, 78); see also Fitzwilliam memoranda book, 26 Mar. 1860 (ibid. MS 4988, p. 26).
[77] Fitzwilliam memoranda book, 25 May 1873 (ibid. MS 5995, p. 45).
[78] Powerscourt requests-book, 1852–5 (ibid. MS 16238, no. 1071); for examples of landlords refusing to recognize sales in County Cork, see Donnelly, *Land and People of Cork*, 212.
[79] Below, pp. 90–1.

under the land act of 1881, when full freedom of sale was established, suggest that tenant right was most valuable in Ulster, but not negligible elsewhere. From 1,474 sales recorded by E. C. Houston of the Irish Loyal & Patriotic Union (not, admittedly, an unbiased source), it is possible to infer that for holdings paying rents of £20 a year and less, tenant right in Ulster was about fourteen years' purchase; in Munster and Connacht it was about eleven years'; in Leinster it was eight years'.[80]

It seems reasonable to assume, therefore, that before 1881 southern tenants had a potentially valuable interest that was only partially realizable through *sub rosa* payments and small donations from landlords. The inchoate nature of southern tenant right seems to have been largely due to a lack of co-operation between landlords and tenants, for much of the flexibility and certainty of Ulster tenant right came from the power of the estate office. As the gap between rents and agricultural output widened in the mid-1860s, it is easy to understand why tenants felt insecure. It was not eviction that they feared, but rather the loss of the gains they had fortuitously made. Security of tenure was one way of preserving the status quo, not because it would prevent evictions, but because it would weaken the landlords' power to recover their position.

iii. Tenant Right and Prosperity

In 1869 Sir John Gray, one of the most distinguished advocates of tenant right, told a meeting in the Free Trade Hall, Manchester, that

> if all Ireland were brought to the same crop and food-producing condition as Ulster, where small farms abounded, and security for the tenant was the rule, the gross product of the country would be raised from £30,000,000 to £42,141,000 a year.[81]

Observers more disinterested than Sir John Gray made the same point. Peter MacLagan, MP for Linlithgowshire, believed that farming was better in Ulster and that rents were much higher there than in the rest of Ireland.[82] George Campbell, whose book on the land question influenced Gladstone,[83] thought that there was 'a wide distinction between the careful, pushing, moderately skilful Ulster farmer and the unthrifty, unskilful man of the

---

[80] *Cowper Comm., Minutes of Evidence*, 998.
[81] *The Irish Land Question: Speech of Sir John Gray, Delivered in the Free Trade Hall, Manchester, on 18 October 1869* (Dublin and London, 1869), 54; see Solow, *The Land Question and the Irish Economy*, 30–2; see the tables in Apps. 14, 15 and 16, which suggest that a strong case can be made for the relative prosperity of part of Ulster, and a plausible case for the whole province; but Leinster must not be forgotten.
[82] MacLagan, *Land Tenure in Ire.*, 7.
[83] E. D. Steele, 'Ireland and the Empire in the 1860s: Imperial Precedents for Gladstone's First Irish Land Act', *Hist. Jn.* 11: 1 (1968), 64–83.

south, the typical Irishman', for in Ulster, tenant right attracted money to the soil, while in the south the 'savings of this *"miserable"* Irish peasantry is principally employed in the large farming of Scotland through one of the leading banks, and in London City speculations through another'.[84] Even the less prosperous parts of Ulster were compared favourably with similar areas of the south. County Fermanagh, according to William O'Connor Morris, was not a wealthy county but 'contrasted with Connaught, it is another world'.[85] It was also argued that the Ulster countryside was more peaceful and that relations between landlords and tenants were better because tenant right gave outgoing tenants money to pay their debts and to go away peacefully.[86] It was even claimed that Catholics in Ulster 'have been more generally peaceable than their brethren in the rest of the island'.[87]

Tenant right was an attractive explanation of Ulster's prosperity for those who wanted to reform the law of landlord and tenant. Not only did it seem incontestable that Ulster was prosperous, but tenant right was a conservative model for reform—it seemed to work smoothly, securing the rights of tenants without limiting unduly the rights of landlords. It also fitted into a critique of classical economic theory that was becoming more powerful in the 1860s, for customary arrangements were seen as an alternative to freedom of contract.[88]

Not everyone, however, agreed that tenant right was the cause of Ulster's prosperity. Some even argued that it discouraged investment in agriculture because it consumed tenants' capital: to buy a farm they parted with ready money, or even borrowed at high rates of interest.[89] Others argued that there were other equally important causes of Ulster's prosperity. MacLagan pointed to flax and the fact that Ulstermen were of a different race. 'We can trace, even now, the origin of the different farmers in Ulster from the appearance of the holdings and townlands,' he wrote in 1869.

The orchards, and general neatness about the doors, and the tidiness and substantial comfort within, show us the descendants of the English settlers; the want of order and neatness about the offices, and the rough comfort within, disclose the Scotch origin of others; while the slovenliness about the doors, and the dirt and discomfort in the house, distinguish the descendants of the native Irish.[90]

[84] Campbell, *Ir. Land*, 157.
[85] O'Connor Morris, *Letters on the Land Question*, 240.
[86] *Lords' Sel. Comm. on Land Tenure, 1867*, 5, 11; *Bessborough Comm., Minutes of Evidence*, pt. i, p. 241.
[87] O'Connor Morris, *Letters on the Land Question*, 239; see the tables in Apps. 20, 21, and 22, which suggest that Ulster was indeed the most peaceful of the four provinces.
[88] Clive Dewey, 'Celtic Agrarian Legislation and Celtic Revival: Historicist Implications of Gladstone's Irish and Scottish Land Acts', *Past & Present*, no. 64 (Aug. 1974), 30–70.
[89] Thompson, *Ire. in 1839 and 1869*, 93; James Caird, *The Irish Land Question*, 2nd edn. (London, 1869), 12; Ferguson and Vance, *The Tenure and Improvement of Land in Ireland*, 316.
[90] MacLagan, *Land Tenure in Ire.*, 7–9.

The fact that Ulster Catholics bought and sold tenant right, and enjoyed its tenurial advantages, if not its tradition of superior hygiene, did not prevent other observers from ascribing Ulster's prosperity to 'the advancing and indomitable spirit of protestantism'.[91]

Arguments based on race and religion reveal more about the prejudices of contemporaries than about the economic effects of tenant right. The importance of flax is easier to evaluate. Flax was virtually confined to Ulster; indeed, it was largely concentrated in those Ulster counties that were regarded as most prosperous. It was a very valuable crop. The agents of Sir George Hodson's estate in County Cavan estimated in 1864 that 330 acres of flax on the estate 'not only pay the rent ... but leave a surplus of £1,500 in the pockets of the tenants'.[92] This, however, was exceptional, because 1864 was the second of four very good years for flax, when prices were good, yields high, and relatively large acreages cultivated, coinciding with a great demand for linen stimulated by the American civil war.[93]

It is possible, therefore, that visitors to Ulster in the 1860s witnessed the effects of the flax boom, as well as the effects of tenant right. Flax was an ideal crop for small farmers, requiring a lot of labour, but giving a very high acreable return. Even when yields and prices were low, an acre of flax would probably have paid the rent of a small farm. In 1861 the price and the yield were below average, but flax was still worth about £8 an acre. In a good year like 1865, it was worth about £17 an acre. In most years in the 1850s the whole crop, which occupied only a small fraction of the arable land of Ulster, would have paid at least half the rent of the province. In the 1860s it probably paid the whole rent through most of the decade. Much of the apparent prosperity of Ulster, especially during the 1860s, may be traced as convincingly to flax as to tenant right. It is not unlikely that impressions of the hard-working qualities of Ulster farmers were created by the heavy, dirty work that went with flax cultivation. Sir John Gray's belief that the value of agricultural output in Ireland would have increased by £12 million, 'if all Ireland were brought to the same crop and food-producing condition as Ulster', was a good one, if he was thinking of flax: if the other three provinces had grown as much flax as Ulster in the mid-1860s total agricultural output would indeed have been higher.

For those who advocated legislation that would protect the tenants, tenant right seemed to justify their criticisms of the existing law. These criticisms depended on each other logically and apparently empirically: first, Irish agriculture was backward, unimproved, and poor because

---

[91] Ferguson and Vance, *The Tenure and Improvement of Land in Ireland*, 318.
[92] Hodson rentals and agents' reports, 1864 (NLI, MS 16419, p. 114).
[93] *Agricultural Statistics, Ire., 1865*, p. lvii [3929], HC 1867, lxxi. 491; *Cowper Comm., Minutes of Evidence*, 962-3.

tenants did not invest in the improvement of their holdings; secondly, tenants did not invest, not because they were poor, but because they were insecure; thirdly, Ulster was prosperous, unlike the other provinces, because tenant right gave security for improvements. These criticisms were clear, logical, and apparently well founded on facts. It was clear that there was money to invest: the deposits of Irish banks more than doubled between 1859 and 1876.[94] What also seemed clear was that there was scope for improvement. Travellers in Ireland, especially Englishmen and Scots, noticed bad fences, poor housing, and careless cultivation. A survey of weeds in 1854 showed that weeding was either 'almost entirely omitted' or 'wholly neglected' on 50 per cent of farms.[95] The houses of many of the tenants were wretchedly bad: miserably cramped, badly built, and often shared with livestock. Even in 1881 over half the houses in rural districts were classified either as third class or fourth class. Admittedly, fourth-class houses had almost disappeared, but third-class houses, with only two or three rooms, were still common.[96] The evidence of photographs makes the point more forcibly, for some houses were hardly recognizable as houses at all.[97]

One of the most optimistic critics of Irish agriculture was Thomas Baldwin, whose *Handy Book of Small Farm Management* first appeared around 1870, when the debate on security of tenure was at its height. Baldwin went through the products of Irish farms and showed how their value could be increased by better management. To give only the most striking of his suggestions is enough to show his optimism. Deep tillage and early harvesting would add £5.5 million to the value of tillage; 'an improved system of feeding and managing dairy cows' would add £6 million; bringing sheep to market earlier would add £2.4 million; the drainage of 6 million acres would add £3 million. These four items alone add up to almost £17 million, which puts Baldwin well ahead of Sir John Gray; but Baldwin was not spent at that point: good imported flax seed would give better yields than home-grown seeds; the value of cattle could be increased by 20 per cent; more eggs could be exported to England,

---

[94] *Report on Certain Statistics of Banking in Ireland and Investments in Government and India Stocks, on which Dividends are Payable at the Bank of Ireland* [1859–85], p. 7 [C 4681], HC 1886, lxxi. 147.

[95] *Agricultural Statistics, Ire., 1854*, p. xxi [2017], HC 1856, liii. 21; for a discussion of improvers' views, see Jonathan Bell and Mervyn Watson, *Irish Farming: Implements and Techniques, 1750–1900* (Edinburgh, 1986), 229–38. See below, Apps. 16 and 23, where the relationship between land and houses is shown. At first sight this would suggest that certain counties were 'unimproved' and that the cause might be bad landlords. The weak correlation between good land and good housing, however, can be partly explained by the odd performance of certain counties (Kildare, Louth, Meath, and Limerick) where farms were large, land good, but where houses, presumably labourers' houses, were bad. The positions of Fermanagh, Tyrone, Wicklow, and Waterford are, however, less easy to explain.

[96] *Census Ire., 1881*, pt. ii, p. 104 [C 3365], HC 1882, lxxvi; below, pp. 126–7.

[97] Brian M. Walker, *Shadows on Glass: A Portfolio of Early Ulster Photography* (Belfast, 1976), 68–9.

which imported 1 million eggs a day. Small farmers could increase their incomes by keeping fewer horses. A horse cost £26 a year and should not, according to Baldwin, have been kept on a farm of less than 10 acres, where it could have been replaced by spade cultivation.[98] (In 1871 there were 60,000 horses on farms of less than 15 acres. Their removal would have increased the incomes of their owners by £1.6 million.[99]) Baldwin was probably the leading authority on Irish agriculture and highly respected by all parties. He had no doubt about the soundness of his ideas, for they were based on the model farm at Glasnevin where 5.5 acres produced a gross income of £77 a year and a net income, after deductions for rent, seeds, artificial fertilizers, and hired horse labour, of £45. 17s. 4d.[100]

Baldwin's suggestions were part of a critique of Irish agriculture that assumed that riches awaited any tenant who ploughed deep, improved the breed of his livestock, and practised house-feeding. 'We believe', he wrote, 'that there is no system which gives so great an income to the small farmer, so long as the extra labour which it involves comes from his own family.' The problem is not to assess the realism of Baldwin's proposals, but to assess how far insecurity of tenure before 1870 prevented tenants from improving. If it is supposed that tenants genuinely feared eviction at the end of every year, but were nevertheless determined to farm better, how did the law before 1870 affect their calculations? First, the law did not prevent deep ploughing, weeding, and proper crop rotations, since their benefits were immediate, and their implementation required no great capital outlay that was irrecoverable. Secondly, the law did not prevent tenants from improving their livestock, or keeping more pigs, poultry, and cows, for even if they were evicted they had the right to take their livestock with them. Thirdly, it did not prevent tenants from getting rid of horses that were not fully employed; indeed, if the allegation that landlords increased rents when they saw tenants thriving had any substance, getting rid of horses might have had the opposite effect.

The law before 1870 was an apparent impediment to permanent improvements such as houses, fences, and drains, for these were presumed to belong to the landlord unless there was an agreement to the contrary.[101] Yet between 1841 and 1851, 44,000 new second-class houses appeared in rural districts; whether these were newly built, or were conversions of

[98] Thomas Baldwin, *Handy Book of Small Farm Management* (Dublin, [1871]), 3, 86, 117, 121, 138–43, 159, 165–6, 171, 182.
[99] *Agricultural Statistics, Ire., 1871*, p. lxiv [C 762], HC 1873, lxiv. 438.
[100] Baldwin, *Handy Book*, 214. Baldwin believed that the income of his Glasnevin farm 'can be realised on a holding of five and a half acres of good arable land in any part of Ireland'.
[101] De Moleyns, *Landowner's Guide* (1872), 240–1; see also Joseph Smith Furlong, *The Law of Landlord and Tenant as Administered in Ireland*, 2nd edn. by Edmund R. Digues La Touche (Dublin, 1869), i. 647–9, 651–2, 654, 657–8, 663–4.

existing houses, hardly matters, for modest though many of them were, they represent a visible, tangible, long-term investment. Between 1851 and 1871 a further 33,000 appeared; but between 1871 and 1881 only 26,000 appeared, in spite of the security given by section 4 of the land act and the prosperity of the late 1860s and early 1870s.[102] Of Baldwin's major suggestions, only the drainage of 6 million acres, which was supposed to add £3 million a year to output, would have been discouraged by insecurity of tenure. Drainage was an expensive but useful improvement, which a tenant did at a certain risk before 1870, if he did not have his landlord's agreement; but a greater obstacle than the risk of expropriation was that drainage required the co-operation of several farmers.

If tenants did not do the things that Gray and Baldwin thought they should have done, the reason may have been that they did not share the ideas of those who wanted to reform the land system. Their ideas of status and convenience may, for example, have been different. Horses on small farms struck Baldwin as wasteful; but a horse, like a bull (or a son at Maynooth), was a status symbol. (If Baldwin had had to carry turf to Glasnevin from a bog several miles away he might have been less impatient with horses.) When tenants hoarded money, or left it in banks at low rates of interest, their reasons may not have been their fear of improving. As George Campbell observed: 'In the case of the Irishman, as in that of the Hindoo, it is the expense of marrying his daughters and the customary obligation of honour to do so handsomely, which weighs on the peasant.'[103]

There may also have been profound misunderstandings between the tenants and those who supported them. When the latter spoke of improvements, they meant houses, drainage, and better cultivation. It is possible that the tenants meant something different and equated improvements with the prosperity they had enjoyed since the early 1850s. James Caird noticed this in 1869. There was not, he wrote, much evidence of 'general improvement' in Irish agriculture since 1849:

> Most of the wet land is still undrained. The broken, worn, and gapped fences remain too much as before.... The people are better clothed, better housed, and better fed, not because the produce of the ground has been materially increased, but because it has become of more value, and is divided among two-thirds of the numbers who shared it then.... Yet there is a general uneasiness and discontent. With the increasing value of their property, there has arisen in the minds of the farmers a keener desire to secure it.[104]

If tenants farmed badly and kept inferior livestock, ignorance and incompetence may have been as important as insecurity of tenure; but it is

---

[102] *Census Ire., 1841*, p. 434 [504], HC 1843, li; *Census Ire., 1851*, pt. vi, p. 625 [2134], HC 1856, xxxi; *Census Ire., 1871*, pt. iii, p. 14 [C 1377], HC 1876, lxxxi; *Census Ire., 1881*, pt. ii, p. 104 [C 3365], HC 1882, lxxvi.
[103] Campbell, *Ir. Land*, 56.   [104] Caird, *The Irish Land Question*, 19, 5.

also arguable that the greatest obstacle to the kind of improvements favoured by experts was that the tenants did not need them. House-feeding may or may not have been profitable; but it was not really necessary in Ireland where mild winters made outdoor wintering possible. (Some tenants thought it was unlucky to keep cows indoors during the winter.[105]) It is also possible that some observers did not understand the foundation of the tenants' prosperity: that they had done well by rearing cattle and sheep and that grass was as good for that as green crops. As a critique of the law the tenant-right argument was sound; as a means of analysing actual landlord–tenant relations it was misconceived. As an explanation for the apparently backward state of agriculture, it was at best only a partial one.

The countryside was not inhabited by thousands of frustrated tenants, anxious to invest in drainage, farm buildings, and pedigree livestock. Even if only one-tenth of the landlords had been anxious to let tenants improve, there should have been thousands of agreements made under the land improvement act of 1860—if there had been thousands of improving tenants. This did not happen, however; in 1864, for example, only four building leases were registered.[106] Those who wanted to give the tenants security of tenure ascribed to them their own urban, middle-class values, such as the systematic use of time, a desire to experiment, a concern with appearances, and a self-consciousness of their relations with other groups in society.

A different analysis of rural society was equally plausible. It could be argued that tenants needed the stimulus of high rents and the spur of insecurity, for they were cautious, unenterprising, and careless. This argument is as difficult to evaluate as the tenant-right one. If a tenant's overheads were increased, which is what a rent increase did, would he try to maintain his profits by producing more? (The assumption that there was an unexploited capacity in Irish agriculture was common to both arguments.) It is difficult to find estates where rents were high; the estates of the third earl of Leitrim in the counties of Donegal and Leitrim are the only ones that come near to being rackrented; but unfortunately it is difficult to assess what effect this had on the productive capacity of the tenants. The only piece of evidence that suggests that there may have been something in the argument is that the smallest holdings produced much more per acre than the largest. In the 1870s holdings under 15 acres produced 137 per cent more per acre than the largest holdings.[107] It is possible that a heavy

---

[105] J. P. Sheldon, *Dairy Farming, Being the Theory, Practice, and Methods of Dairying* (London, New York, and Paris, [1879–81]), 356.

[106] *Judicial Statistics, Ire.*, 1864, p. 143 [3563], HC 1865, lii. 849; 23 & 24 Vict., c. 153 (8 Aug. 1860).

[107] This estimate is based on figures in W. E. Vaughan, 'Agricultural Output, Rents and Wages in Ireland, 1850–1880', in L. M. Cullen and F. Furet (eds.), *Ireland and France, 17th–20th Centuries: Towards a Comparative Study of Rural History* (Paris, 1980), 88.

rent would have had the same effect on large tenants as a constricted acreage had on small tenants.

iv. Tenant Right and Estate Management

Tenant right was bought and sold, used as a security for loans, and bequeathed. Its value, like the value of other property, could be realized by auction, valuation, or arbitration. It was different from other property in its foundation in custom rather than law and in its dependence on the voluntary co-operation of landlords and agents in its working. When it is remembered that ordinary landed property required courts, a system of registration, and a whole profession devoted to its orderly transfer, the working of tenant right, without any of these aids and without even a clear definition of what it was, was a remarkable example of social cohesion. In this process landlords and agents were important—and in a predicament, for they were both partisans and arbitrators. On the one hand, the agents, who usually saw to all the details, had to protect their employers' interests, which included deducting arrears from the sum realized by the sale of tenant right; on the other, they had to deal fairly with the outgoing tenant, his family, his successor, and his creditors.

Agents protected landlords' interests by dictating the means of transfer, by examining purchasers, by insisting that certain purchasers be given preference, and by deducting arrears from the purchase money. Some agents objected to auctions, for 'sweeteners' attended to put up the bidding and it was not easy to reject the highest bidder, even if he was not suitable.[108] Alexander Spotswood, who managed several estates in County Londonderry, preferred to take written proposals and to 'select from them a good tenant, always giving the farm to an adjoining tenant, provided he will give . . . a fair value'.[109] Auctions, nevertheless were common: advertisements appeared in newspapers, and a handbill survives in the Gosford rentals, referring to an outgoing tenant as the farm's 'proprietor'.[110] Some agents tried to limit the selling-price of tenant right because purchasers were tempted to borrow the purchase money at high rates of interest.[111] Since sales often took place when tenants were close to bankruptcy, any limit on the price was bound to be resented and possibly evaded. 'All such limitations are nugatory,' reported one poor law inspector, 'and invariably prove ineffectual to prevent the incoming tenant from making a secret settlement with the

---

[108] *Bessborough Comm., Minutes of Evidence*, pt. i, pp. 200, 215.
[109] Spotswood's letter-book, 17 Jan. 1871 (PRONI, D1062/1/8A, p. 99).
[110] Gosford rental (County Armagh), 1871 (ibid. D1606/7A/77).
[111] *Poor Law Inspectors' Reports*, 1870, 13, 104, 142; *Bessborough Comm., Minutes of Evidence*, pt. i, pp. 279, 284; Olive Robinson, 'The London Companies and Tenant Right in Nineteenth-Century Ireland', *Agric. Hist. Rev.* 18 (1970), 59–61; Hamilton-Temple-Blackwood, *Contributions to an Inquiry*, 60.

outgoer.'[112] (Some agents, far from trying to limit the price of tenant right, regarded such restrictions as an infringement of the 'custom'.[113])

To prevent disputes and to enable agents to make decisions without being accused of arbitrariness, rules were developed and promulgated. On the Stewart of Ards estate in County Donegal the following restrictions were enforced: if the tenant were evicted he would be allowed six and a half years' purchase less arrears; if the landlord took the land into his own hand, the tenant got ten years' purchase.[114] The ordinary, routine working of the custom is illustrated in a memoranda book of tenants' requests kept on the Farnham estate in County Cavan. When a tenant wished to sell, he applied to the agent, and was not allowed to proceed until Lord Farnham himself approved. Lord Farnham's approval was not to be taken for granted. One tenant was allowed to sell, but only 'to Philip Smith the adjoining tenant but I must know the rate of purchase. I will not allow land to be put out to the highest bidder'; another was not allowed to sell until 'the rent was paid up'; on another occasion Lord Farnham said 'I prefer one of the family as purchaser but the man must first be submitted to me.' Occasionally purchasers were turned down. In 1849 one was rejected because 'he never was able to manage the small quantity of land he had'.[115]

Landlords and agents were usually content if they got a solvent, respectable tenant; but occasionally more was required. In 1877 Wann made enquiries about a prospective purchaser of a farm near Markethill: not only did he want 'a steady, industrious well-disposed man' but he did not want one with a 'poaching propensity' because the farm was near the demesne where game was plentiful.[116] Landlords generally preferred their own tenants, not only because they knew them, but also because purchases by existing tenants led to consolidation.[117] The encouragement of consolidation was probably the most common aim of agents supervising tenant-right sales. They tried to give preference to adjoining tenants, and outgoing tenants naturally tried to evade this restriction. Defiance led to threats of eviction against the prospective purchaser. Wann wrote to a would-be purchaser in 1852: 'I beg to give you notice if you purchase William McDonnell's farm... I cannot accept you as tenant for it.... I have desired Mr Fyfe [the bailiff] if the farm goes into any other hands but Prunty's (unless McDonnell holds it himself) to hand the matter over to

[112] *Poor Law Inspectors' Reports, 1870*, 12; see also 101.
[113] *Lords' Sel. Comm. on Land Tenure, 1867*, 9–10.
[114] *Poor Law Inspectors' Reports, 1870*, 105–6; see also *Bessborough Comm., Minutes of Evidence*, pt. i, p. 256.
[115] Farnham requests-book, 12 Mar. 1849, 18 Aug. 1856, 12 Apr. 1858, 4 June 1855 (NLI, MS 3118).
[116] Gosford letter-book, 19 Dec. 1877 (PRONI, D1606/5A/4, p. 205).
[117] *Bessborough Comm., Minutes of Evidence*, pt. i, pp. 254, 324; see also Donnelly, *Land and People of Cork*, 213.

Messrs Armstrong to eject the purchaser.'[118] While trying to encourage consolidation, agents also tried to prevent subdivision. Wann would not allow tenants to sell part of their farms. 'I understand White who is living on the farm asks time to sell "part" of the land,' he wrote in 1880. 'To this I *thoroughly object*. The tenant may sell it *all* if he likes but I will not permit a partial sale.'[119] When a tenant died leaving several adult sons, agents tried to prevent them from subdividing. On the Salters' estate Spotswood usually put one son into possession and encouraged the others to leave.[120] Wann occasionally allowed the family to remain in possession as long as they did not formally divide the farm. If they attempted to subdivide, or fell out with each other, he insisted that the son who was the nominal tenant should 'pay off' his brothers and sisters. In 1867 he reported to the endowed schools commissioners that a tenant on the Dungannon estate had died leaving a family of boys and girls; the eldest, Peter McGrath, had been taken as the tenant and 'matters went smoothly on for a time' until some of the family demanded a division, which Wann 'flatly refused'. He then suggested that 'arbitrators should say what *money* Peter should pay but the others declined to accede to this'. 'I think this is a very good case to make an impression on the estate against the division of farms,' he concluded. 'A notice to quit should be served.'[121]

If all transfers of tenant right had been sales, agents' intervention might have gone no further. Tenant right, however, was bequeathed, used as a security for loans, and as a fund for providing for children and old people. Tenant right was not recognized as an asset by the courts. A tenant could bequeath his money, his stock, and his farm equipment, and if there was a dispute the courts could deal with its distribution; but they could do nothing with his tenant right. Robert Johnston, chairman of the County Down quarter sessions, told the Chelmsford committee in 1872 that before 1870 litigants had tried to have tenant right treated as an asset in legacy and debt cases, but he 'invariably' refused to recognize it, unless the landlord had given permission for its sale.[122] After the sale had taken place, there was no problem, for the purchase money became part of the tenant's estate and could be distributed among creditors and legatees.

Tenant right was a mere phantom until it was given monetary substance by the landlord, for before 1870 the tenant had no rights in the eyes of the law except to remain on his farm for the unexpired term of his tenancy. As a result, agents played a crucial role in the distribution of tenant

---

[118] Gosford letter-book, 5 Mar. 1852 (PRONI, D1606/5A/1, p. 210).
[119] Wann's letter-book, 4 Mar, 1880 (ibid. D1606/5/5, p. 325); for a similar case on the countess of Kingston's estate in County Cork, see Donnelly, *Land and People of Cork*, 214.
[120] Spotswood's letter-book, 15 July 1869 (PRONI, D1062/1/8A, pp. 82–5).
[121] Wann's letter-book, 22 Apr. 1867 (ibid. D1606/5/4, pp. 274–5).
[122] *Lords' Sel. Comm. on the Land Act, 1872*, 33; see also below, pp. 98–9.

right. Not only did they assist at its reification for disposal by the courts, but they also took over some of the functions of the courts by exercising a probate jurisdiction over tenants' property and by satisfying the claims of creditors. To some extent they did this in the interest of good feeling on their estates, for swift intervention was often necessary to prevent acrimonious disputes. One suspects, however, that they also did it because the tenants wanted them to do it and regarded them as cheap substitutes for the courts. It was, however, a difficult role. The agent had to be an amateur lawyer; he had to protect his employer's interests; he had to intervene in the tenants' most intimate affairs at a time when tempers were likely to be strained.

When tenant right was sold or otherwise transferred, agents made sure that creditors, including the landlord, were satisfied, especially when loans had actually been secured like mortgages on the tenant right. On the Gosford estate Wann wrote to purchasers, warning them not to pay over the purchase money until all claims had been established. In 1859 such a claim was taken seriously enough for Lord Gosford himself to write to James McParlin, who was about to buy Edward Cordner's farm; Cordner had borrowed money from the Revd Henry Kidd, Presbyterian minister of Drumminis, and in the estate office there was a paper signed by Cordner 'to this effect that in case of any of his land being sold, he, Edward Cordner guarantees Revd H. Kidd out of the proceeds of the sale, the payment of the debt due'. Lord Gosford concluded by asking McParlin to make sure 'that no money be paid by you to Mr Cordner until he has redeemed his pledge to the Revd H. Kidd'.[123] As part of the work of clearing up such claims, creditors were reminded that sales were about to take place—in other words, the estate office acted as a registry of deeds.

Most transfers of tenant right were made by succession or transfer within families, for sales were relatively rare. Although tenant right did not have any legal status, it was mentioned in tenants' wills. Strictly speaking such provisions were unenforceable at law. A copy of a will in Wann's correspondence directed that 'my *chattels* and land to be sold by *public auction* and the proceeds to be lodged in the Bank of Belfast with the deposit already lodged in said bank';[124] but sale by auction, or any sale, was at the agent's discretion. It seems that some wills were actually deposited in the estate office. The following will is in the Gosford papers. (Its terminology does not suggest ignorance of legal forms.)

I authorize my executors hereafter named to sell my farm which I now occupy together with all my cattle, crops, goods, and chattels to the highest and fairest

---

[123] Gosford letter-book, 31 Dec. 1859 (PRONI, D1606/5A/2, p. 203).
[124] Wann's letter-book (ibid. D1606/5/4, p. 63).

bidder and to put all the money arising therefrom to interest for the use of my beloved son, William Moore...[125]

Occasionally tenants disposed of tenant right by means other than outright sale. The sitting tenant might transfer his holding to his successor, but keep a small income from the farm for the rest of his life, or the right to live in his old house, or to have 'a place at the hearth'. The agent was informed of these arrangements. He was also expected to see that they were faithfully carried out. In 1861 Michael Lamph got William Lamph's farm; in return William got £60 and the right to use a room in his old house. The agreement was lodged in the Gosford estate office and 'it is requested by both parties that said William Wann Esq. will have the provisions of this agreement carried out'.[126]

The rules of succession varied from estate to estate, and it is not always clear how far agents acted according to the tenants' wishes. According to William Neilson Hancock, wills were not recognized unless the farm was left to only one person, either the widow or a son.[127] On some estates the widow was taken as tenant and left free to give the farm to any of her children, which 'kept up parental authority'.[128] On the Gosford estate Wann followed this practice. 'It has been the invariable practice of the estate,' he wrote to the estate solicitor in 1874, 'when a tenant dies to take the *widow* as tenant in his place and not leave her in the power of the children.'[129] On the Sanderson estate at Cloverhill, County Cavan, widows were treated less generously. A widow with a helpless family or 'without one' was 'under no circumstances' to be kept on; if there was a son of suitable age, he was to get the farm; but if the tenant had died in arrears, none of his family was to get the farm.[130] If the heir was a child, some agents insisted that the farm be sold and the money held in trust.[131] Wann was more indulgent and allowed the farm to be held in trust; on one occasion, however, he refused to do this because the child was illegitimate.[132]

In supervising transfers of tenant right, agents became involved in family affairs at difficult times. In the Gosford papers there is an account of payments from the sale of a dead tenant's farm. It realized a good price, £204. 15s.; but when debts were paid, the widow got only £12. 12s. 11d.[133]

---

[125] Gosford valuations and surveys (ibid. D1606/12/10/492).

[126] Memorandum of an agreement between William and Michael Lamph, 25 Mar. 1861 (ibid. D1606/12/12/576); see also Gosford rental (County Cavan), 1871 (ibid. D1606/7C/56, p. 2).

[127] *Report from the Select Committee on the Irish Land Act, 1870; together with the Proceedings of the Committee, Minutes of Evidence, and Appendix*, p. 17, HC 1877 (328), xii. 25.   [128] Ibid. 27.

[129] Gosford letter-book, 1 Sept. 1874 (PRONI, D1606/5A/3, p. 412).

[130] Sanderson family memoranda (NLI, MS 9492).

[131] Spotswood's letter-book, 1869 (PRONI, D1062/1/8A, pp. 86–7).

[132] Wann's letter-book, 16 Feb. 1861 (ibid. D1606/5/4, p. 113).

[133] Account of payments for the late John Marshall, Oct. 1859 (ibid. D1606/12/12).

Agents had also to face the anger of children who believed that they had been disinherited. Wann wrote to one such son, disinherited by his mother in favour of his sister who would take care 'of a delicate brother who is with her', telling him that he would not disturb this arrangement 'unless there is something more than I at present see'. He also told the son that he had letters from his mother 'dated a year or two ago not by any means favourable to the way you treated her'.[134]

The protection of orphans could drag the agent into family rows. On one occasion Wann had to evict a squatter, a brother-in-law of the late tenant and 'an idle fellow ... from another estate', who had seized a farm belonging to three orphans.[135] When a widow showed signs of marrying again, her suitors were warned that they would not get her farm. John Elliott was told by Wann in 1857 that 'it has been reported to me that it is your intention to get married to widow Davidson, and I wish to inform you that I am sure Lord Gosford will be very slow to recognize you as tenant for her farm to the prejudice of her large family.'[136] Orphans had to be watched until one of them succeeded; this, of course, started a new cycle of problems. On one farm brothers had lived 'peaceably and quietly' until the eldest married and the others would not let his wife into the house. Wann's solution was to make the eldest give 'the saying of two honest men' to his brothers to help them to emigrate.[137]

In settling tenant-right disputes the agent's ultimate argument was the notice to quit, without which he would have been powerless. It was a particularly effective way of dealing with tenants who ill-treated elderly relations from whom they had got farms. On the Hodson estate in County Cavan in 1861 the agents reported to Sir George Hodson that they 'were obliged to evict John Wallace in order to rid him from the ill-treatment he received from his son-in-law to whom he had assigned his farm'.[138] Agents, however, did not always get their way.[139] On the Hall estate the agent was willing to give a farm to the adjoining tenant; the sitting tenant, however, was determined that it would not go to his neighbour, so he came to an arrangement with another family, 'they McAteers', whose cattle were already on his land. In spite of enlisting the support of the agent ('I hope your honour will parden the liberty of which I have taken in writing to you'), the adjoining tenant got no satisfaction and 'they McAteers' were able to hold the farm during the life of the sitting tenant.[140]

An examination of the working of tenant right on individual estates shows that it led to complicated and occasionally acrimonious transactions.

---

[134] Gosford letter-book, 13 June 1873 (ibid. D1606/5A/3, pp. 361–2).
[135] Wann's letter-book, 19 Dec. 1859 (ibid. D1606/5/4, p. 81).
[136] Gosford letter-book, 29 Dec. 1857 (ibid. D1606/5A/2, p. 49).
[137] Wann's letter-book, 9 Dec. 1868 (ibid. D1606/5/4, p. 327).
[138] Hodson rentals and agents' reports, 1861 (NLI, MS 16419, p. 3).
[139] Above, pp. 39–43.
[140] Hall rent-ledger (Counties Armagh and Down), 1867–8 (PRONI, D2090/3/22, p. 12).

Agents became simultaneously referees and partisans; but estate rules and the notice to quit played a vital part in maintaining the custom; indeed, without the agent's involvement, it is hard to see how the custom could have worked smoothly. The estate rules gave the sort of quasi-legal framework that the ordinary law denied the custom until 1870; their systematic application, while it may have thwarted tenants on some occasions, gave a regularity and predictability to tenant right that enabled buyers and sellers to buy and sell with confidence. When a purchaser knew that he had been accepted by the office, or a creditor knew that his loan would be recorded and his interests protected by the agent, he could proceed in the knowledge that his chances of being cheated had been reduced. The fact that tenant-right transactions could be recorded in the office allowed tenants to make very complicated dispositions of their property and gave it much of the flexibility of ordinary landed property—with less formality and expense.

Agents were also involved in affairs that were strictly speaking none of their business. They frequently used their power to evict in the interests of orphans, widows, and creditors, whose claims were often real enough morally but insubstantial in law. In doing this they became involved in disputes that went on for years and created trouble on the estate. Negligence was as likely to lead to trouble as harshness, and not infrequently those who championed the weak incurred the enmity of the strong and acquisitive. Three conclusions about estate management and tenant right seem, however, inescapable. First, tenant right worked remarkably well, with few serious disputes, before 1870, in spite of the amount of property involved and the potential acrimony that accompanied transactions. Secondly, it is doubtful if the tenant-right custom could have worked without the power of landlords and agents to supervise it. Their power was arbitrary and flexible, which made it the more effective if only because it was often vaguely menacing. Given the dynamic nature of tenant right it is difficult to see how it could have worked without this element of arbitrary authority. The land act of 1870 was to create as many problems as it solved. Thirdly, the strange spectacle of agents managing property that was a capitalization of the rental of their employers' estates showed that symbiosis, muddle, and goodwill could make a compromise between strict economic theory and actual practice. Hence the attractiveness of tenant right as a model for reform. Whether tenant right could be turned into law and transferred to the rest of Ireland was, however, another matter.

v. The Land Act of 1870

Section 1 of the land act of 1870 legalized the tenant-right custom in the province of Ulster and section 2 legalized tenant-right customs elsewhere.

Neither attempted to define the custom, although sections 3, 4, and 7 gave rights that resembled those conferred by the custom: the right to compensation for disturbance, to compensation for improvements, and to compensation for sums paid for 'goodwill'.[141] The act was very complicated, not only because it was long (it had seventy-three sections), but because of the many distinctions that it created between different kinds of tenancies. Compensation for disturbance under section 3, which was the main refuge for tenants who could not claim under sections 1 and 2, depended on the size of the holding, its tenure, whether it was an existing tenancy or a new one, whether the tenant was in arrears, whether he had committed some tenurial misdemeanour such as sub-letting, and whether he held some special land such as a town-park or part of a demesne.[142] These were not trivial matters. The exclusion of tenants in arrears from compensation for disturbance, for example, excluded the very tenants who were likely to be evicted; the exclusion of 135,392 leaseholders from compensation for disturbance affected the prospects of about a quarter of the tenants.[143] The number of yearly holdings excluded by their valuation from compensation was not large, but their occupiers were likely to be influential and articulate. Yet too much should not be made of exceptions, for it is easy to forget, in the course of enumerating the exceptions in the act, that 'all yearly tenants, who were such on 1 August 1870, and all tenants on all lettings *subsequent* to that date, for lives, or for terms *shorter* than thirty-one years, not quitting voluntarily, may generally speaking, be considered as entitled to compensation, if evicted on notice to quit, or quitting on the termination of their leases'.[144]

The land act caused a great deal of complicated litigation. Many of its details had to be decided, in the first instance, by the chairmen of the civil bill courts, whom a judge described as 'deputy legislators'.[145] Appeals were taken to the assizes, and then to the newly established court for land cases reserved. Between 1871 and 1877 2,222 cases were resolved in the courts, including 1,420 awards of compensation and 802 dismisses.[146] During the

---

[141] 33 & 34 Vict., c. 46 (1 Aug. 1870). For the genesis and progress of the land bill see E. D. Steele, *Irish Land and British Politics: Tenant Right and Nationality, 1865–1870* (Cambridge, 1974); H. C. G. Matthew (ed.), *The Gladstone Diaries* (Oxford, 1982), vii; W. E. Vaughan, 'Ireland c. 1870', in Vaughan (ed.), *A New History of Ireland*, v. *Ireland under the Union*, I. *1801–1870* (Oxford, 1989), 746–51. For a list of land bills introduced before 1870, see below, pp. 297–9.

[142] For a summary of these distinctions, see below, App. 17.

[143] *Returns Showing the Number of Agricultural Holdings in Ireland, and the Tenure by which They are Held by the Occupiers*, pp. 16–17 [C 32], HC 1870, lvi. 752–3. See pp. 12–15 for holdings valued at £50 and more.

[144] De Moleyns, *Landowner's Guide (1872)*, 211.

[145] Lords' Sel. Comm. on the Land Act, 1872, 9.

[146] These figures and other figures on the working of the act in the courts were taken from *Judicial Statistics, Ire.*, 1871, pp. 91–3, 237, 247 [C 674], HC 1872, lxv; ibid. *1872*, pp.

same period, 250 cases were reported in *The Irish Law Times* because they raised points of procedure or law; in other words, almost an eighth of the cases raised important questions, which was a very considerable amount of law-reporting. Some of the cases gained a national celebrity and the names of the parties became household words: *Austin v. Scott, M'Noun v. Beauclerk, Friel v. Leitrim.* Some cases were straightforward. A tenant of a villa near Tramore was given nothing because the villa was not an agricultural holding;[147] a tenant in County Cork, who claimed £310, got nothing because 'he admitted having brought six or seven cows in the rainy season into the drawing room of his house'.[148] One case at least must have surprised the tenants: a sub-tenant with a house and 2 roods of land near Ennis was given £5 for disturbance and £4. 3s. for improvements because the court decided he was a tenant and not just a hired labourer (he had claimed a total of £96. 8s.).[149]

Compensation for improvements seems to have caused less trouble than compensation for disturbance: a tenant near Ballymena was not allowed to claim for two houses and a bog road because they did not add to the value of his holding;[150] a tenant near Magherabelt was not allowed to claim for a byre because it was not needed on his holding.[151] The main problem with compensation for disturbance, apart from defining those who were to be excluded, was to decide on the application of the scale of compensation. From the beginning it was made clear that it was 'a point too plain for argument' that the maximum compensation should not be given to undeserving cases.[152] (An example of an undeserving case was a tenant near Strabane who claimed five years' rent but was given three years' because he did not live on the holding.[153]) In one case there were discussions about 'sentimental loss' and the cost of getting another holding; but in the end the tenant got only the equivalent of two years' rent for disturbance and improvements.[154] The chairman of Down, Robert Johnston, however, in a case in 1872 decided that 'as a general rule he was not disposed to deviate from the scale provided by the act. . . . He therefore saw no reason why he should not give any less sum than the act gave him power to award.'[155] Town-parks caused a remarkable amount of litigation. They were clearly excluded from compensation for disturbance by section 15 of the act. The problem was to define them. They were supposed to be

---

88–90, 230 [C 851], HC 1873, lxx; ibid. 1873, pp. 84–6, 280 [C 1034], HC 1874, lxxi; ibid. 1874, pp. 79–81, 222–3 [C 1295], HC 1875, lxxxi; ibid. 1875, pp. 76–7, 224 [C 1536], HC 1876, lxxix; ibid. 1876, pp. 78–9, 224 [C 1822], HC 1877, lxxxvi; ibid. 1877, pp. 78–9, 102, 224 [C 2152], HC 1878, lxxix; ibid. 1878, pp. 68–71 [C 2389], HC 1878–9, lxxvi.
[147] *Hay v. Cooke*, ILT 5, digest, 145. [148] *Damery v. O'Callaghan*, ibid 56–7.
[149] *Molony v. Garrihy*, ibid. 15. [150] *May v. Wallace*, ibid. 101–2.
[151] *Robertson v. Bruce*, ibid. 54–6. [152] *Sloan v. Thompson*, ibid. 37.
[153] *Connolly v. Hemphill*, ibid. 144–5; see also *Kehoe v. Croker*, ibid. 56.
[154] *Darragh v. Murdock*, ibid. 38–9. [155] *Morrow v. Devling*, ibid. 6. 36.

near towns or cities; they were supposed to be let for more than an average rent; they were supposed to be held by residents in towns.[156] But what was a town? Newport, near Nenagh, was a town, according to the chairman of Tipperary: it did not have town commissioners or a corporation, but it did have six fairs annually. Portglenone, however, was not a town because it 'is little more than a village'.[157]

The greatest problems, however, were connected with the Ulster custom, which the act did not define. There were more cases under the act in Ulster than in any of the other three provinces; in 1871, 1872, and 1873, for example, over half the cases under the act were in Ulster. Ulster tenants had a choice under the act: they could claim either under section 1 or under sections 3, 4, and 7. They were therefore in a relatively privileged position, compared with tenants who could not claim under customs analogous to the Ulster custom. Yet from the beginning there were problems. First, and unexpectedly, some of the northern chairmen refused to allow simultaneous claims, insisting that tenants who came into court chose between the custom and sections 3, 4, and 7. The unease caused by this was made worse by the fact that other chairmen, notably the chairman of County Down, refused to make litigants choose their grounds, arguing that 'the whole spirit of the act was against it'.[158]

Secondly, there were problems about leases, restrictions on the custom, and the relationship between the custom and sections 9, 10, 14, and 15. These sections limited the rights of tenants to compensation: section 9, for example, excluded ejectment for non-payment of rent and sub-letting from compensation for disturbance; section 15 excluded town-parks. The judges were in some difficulty about these sections; the act did not make it clear whether they applied to section 1, which legalized the custom; but they applied to section 3, which was analogous to the custom; by extension, therefore, it seemed that they should apply to the source of the analogy. The chairman of Tyrone in June 1871 decided that town-parks were not excluded from compensation under the custom;[159] this did not settle the matter, however, for in 1872 in *Williamson v. The earl of Antrim* the chairman of Antrim, following his brother in Tyrone, decided that town-parks were under the custom; but the case was appealed to the assizes, where it was reserved for the court for land cases reserved.[160] Leasehold tenant right was probably more important. In *Austin v. Scott*, the tenant had a lease, made in 1794, that explicitly committed him to giving up his

[156] *Robert Boyd and Five Others v. Isaac Graham*, ibid. 5. 102–4.
[157] *Corbett v. Carey*, ibid. 15; *Adams v. Jones*, ibid. 74.
[158] *Fegan v. Waring*, ibid. 39. Cf. *Talbot v. Drapes*, ibid. 143–4, where the chairman disallowed a simultaneous claim under s. 3 (for disturbance) and s. 7 (for incoming payments). [159] *M'Gaughey v. Stewart*, ibid. 146–7.
[160] Robert Donnell, *Reports of One Hundred and Ninety Cases in the Irish Land Courts; with Preliminary Tenant-Right Chapters* (Dublin, 1876), 214–22; 307–13.

farm and improvements when the lease expired. The chairman of Londonderry decided that the custom could not prevail against a deed.[161] In County Down, however, in *M'Noun* v. *Beauclerk*, the chairman awarded £1,400 to a tenant whose lease had just expired.[162] Leasehold tenant right was an important matter in Ulster because there were many leaseholders (its value was put at 'between five-and-a-half and six millions sterling'[163]). Restrictions on the price of tenant right were also a matter of controversy: if a tenant had bought a farm for a limited amount was it fair to give him only that amount when he quit? *Austin* v. *Scott*, which was a sort of litigants' omnibus, also raised this problem. On this estate Major Thomas Scott had allowed only five times the rent for tenant right since 1848; the case went to the assizes and to the court for land cases reserved.[164]

A decision gratifying to the tenants was that in *Friel* v. *The earl of Leitrim*, where the chairman of Donegal awarded £250 to a tenant who had bought his farm before the third earl abolished tenant right in 1854. (The chairman decided that the 'landlord cannot by his *ipse dixit* do away with the right which attached to the estate when he entered into possession'.[165] Friel's rent was only £6, so he had got about forty years' purchase, which seemed a great victory.) Leitrim took the case to the assizes in 1872, where his appeal failed and the judge 'declined to make any alteration in the amount awarded'.[166]

In spite of these problems the Ulster tenants did well under the act. Over half of the compensation awarded between 1871–7 was paid out in Ulster and the average amount awarded was higher than the average for the whole country: about £98 between 1871 and 1877, compared with £87. They did well too because the chairmen in the north were willing to interfere with rents. In *Carraher* v. *Bond*, for example, the chairman of Down showed that the courts could fix rents under the custom. From the very beginning this case was about a rent increase: the existing rent was £15. 15s.; the landlord, J. W. MacGeough Bond, wanted to put it up to £20. 8s. 10d. 'It was a peculiar feature of the case that neither the landlord nor the tenant wanted to dissolve their mutual relations.... The issue to be decided was whether the demand of the landlord was reasonable.' The evidence was interesting for it showed how the court dealt with the problem of defining two unknown quantities. According to one of the witnesses: 'I calculated the letting value of the land at £30 and calculated the tenant's interest to be worth £9. 15s. 6d. annually. I took the Ulster tenant right at £8 an acre.' In other words he first calculated the full economic rent of the land free of tenant right (£30); then assumed that tenant right was worth £200 (25 acres at £8 an acre); allowed the tenant interest of

---

[161] Ibid. 234–6; *ILT* 5, digest, 172–3.   [162] Donnell, *Reports*, 242–6.
[163] *Lords' Sel. Comm. on the Land Act, 1872*, 270.   [164] *ILT* 5. 173–4.
[165] Ibid. 187.   [166] *Leitrim, appellant; Friel, respondent*, ibid. 6. 86.

£4 17s. 9d. per cent, which amounted to £9. 15s. 6d. on £200; and produced the new rent by subtracting that from the £30. The chairman, however, decided that 'there was not sufficient ground for the demand of £20. 8s. 10d.' and made his award accordingly, giving the tenant £300, which implied that he started from the value of the tenant right, like the valuator, but put it at a higher figure (£12 an acre).[167]

The legalization of the Ulster custom had some remarkable results. The tenant right, which before 1870 had been used by tenants as a security for debt, now became a legal asset that the courts had to recognize. Edward Gardner, a solicitor in County Down, told the Chelmsford committee in 1872 that 'I have already prepared several mortgages of the tenant right', which did not happen before 1870. The mortgages were registered now 'and that is notice to the landlord that this transaction has taken place'.[168] The civil bill courts now did what the agent did before 1870. J. C. Coffey, the chairman of Londonderry, told the same committee: 'We are obliged to ascertain the whole value of the chattel interest as if we were going through an administration suit ... and we compel the farm to be sold for the purpose of effecting justice between the parties.'[169] This took away the landlord's power of settling family disputes, which had been a characteristic of the custom before 1870.[170]

A case in County Antrim in 1871 showed what could happen. Three brothers who had lived together on a farm on the Pakenham estate disputed their father's will; the landlord tried to eject two of them, and to put in the third, John Williamson, as the tenant. The two brothers threatened with ejectment claimed £1,200 for the tenant right; the landlord appealed to section 18 of the act, which made unreasonable conduct a bar to compensation. The claimants' solicitor replied that 'if there was any unreasonable conduct, it was on the part of the landlord, who was substituting his jurisdiction for that of the constituted courts'. The chairman agreed, concluding 'it is a case of a man doing what he thought was right towards a particular tenant, and favouring him at the expense of another. In that, in my humble judgement, Mr Pakenham was doing wrong.' He gave the two brothers £600, which was fairly generous for a farm whose rent was £35. 10s. 8d. The landlord may have gained some consolation from the fact that in another court, where the probate case was heard, 'the judge and jury, although finding in favour of these two men, gave it as their opinion that, in justice and equity, this farm should have come into the possession of John Williamson.'[171]

Decisions such as this enhanced tenants' credit. According to Robert Gardner, who claimed he had lent money at 5 per cent on the security of

---

[167] Ibid. 19–20. [168] Lords' Sel. Comm. on the Land Act, 1872, 223.
[169] Ibid. 260. [170] Above, pp. 89–92.
[171] Williamson v. Pakenham, ILT 5. 118–19.

tenant right, 'already there has grown up amongst the tenantry such a sense of property since this act was passed, and such a feeling they would not be disturbed, that they regard this as reasonably good security.'[172] This was fairly predictable in Ulster, but the act seems to have had the same effects even where the custom did not prevail. Charles Uniacke Townshend described the sale of a farm in Tipperary by the court of bankruptcy, which he claimed he could have prevented before 1870 ('they could sell the interest field by field, if they deemed it wise on behalf of the creditors, to do so').[173] Creditors could now, in certain circumstances, eject debtors, insert themselves between the ejected tenant and his landlord, and make themselves eligible for compensation under sections 3, 4, and 7 of the act.[174] If decisions such as these enhanced the tenants' credit, they created new problems by allowing tenants to fall into difficulties. Whether the land act was solely responsible for the increase in credit after 1870, or whether it shared that role with the increasing deposits in the commercial banks is a nice point. In any case, credit and its corollary, debt collection, increased and became involved with the land act. 'That act,' according to William Neilson Hancock, 'taken in connexion with the abolition of imprisonment for debt, has brought the antiquated, complicated, unjust, and burdensome state of the law as to sheriff's sales into prominence.'[175]

To some extent the landlords had brought these difficulties on themselves by not making written agreements that would have taken care of predictable circumstances such as bankruptcy.[176] Another cause of dispute after 1870, arising from the same origin, was the preservation of game. In law landlords had no right to enter farms to hunt—if they had not reserved that right when the farm was let. After 1870 some tenants, especially in County Donegal, obstructed fishermen and hunters. The Marquis Conyngham's gamekeepers were turned off the mountains by his tenants; a hunting tenant on the Murray Stewart estate was forbidden to walk along a salmon river by the riparian tenants.[177] An incident on the Styles estate was recounted by several witnesses before the Chelmsford committee. The tenant who had taken the shooting was not allowed 'to fire a shot'; but the tenants told the landlord 'that as he is a good sort of fellow he may go and have a day's shooting himself sometimes'.[178] ('They did not see why he should have the letting of game which was feeding upon their crops.'[179]) Turbary also seems to have caused disputes. James Johnston, a County Donegal landlord, claimed that one of his tenants, a

---

[172] *Lords' Sel. Comm. on the Land Act, 1872*, 225.   [173] Ibid. 102.
[174] Ibid. 127–8.
[175] William Neilson Hancock, 'The Law of Judgments', *Jn. Stat. Soc. Ire.* 6: 48 (Dec. 1875), 500. For the growth of indebtedness in the 1870s, see *Cowper Comm., Minutes of Evidence*, 976–81.   [176] *Lords' Sel. Comm. on the Land Act, 1872*, 107.
[177] Ibid. 50, 233.   [178] Ibid. 48.   [179] Ibid. 233.

Scotsman, resisted his rights to cut turf and 'wrote me a very impertinent letter, as I considered, for daring to interfere with his farm'.[180] Before 1870 landlords could deal with such disputes 'on account of the tenant right having been principally in the power of the landlords'.[181]

Contemporaries complained that the act made landlord and tenant relations worse. According to Lord Ranfurly's agent, Courtenay Newton, the act caused 'a growing alienation between the landlord and the tenant'.[182] These disputes about game, turbary, leases, and town-parks were certainly a new subject for public argument. Subsection 3 of section 3, which enabled landlords to exclude new lettings from compensation for disturbance by giving leases for thirty-one years, seems to have tempted the 'good old duke of Leinster, the most liberal and generous of landlords' to become unpopular by offering leases of that length.[183] Certainly the act stirred up a considerable wave of agitation in Ulster.[184] Whether the act discouraged landlords from improving is more difficult to determine, because there is little evidence except contemporary statements. On the estates below, the picture is not a simple one.[185]

What did the land act do? It did not stop evictions; in the decade 1860-9 there were 9,671 evictions; in the decade 1870-9 there were 6,857.[186] It did not stop the service of notices to quit (21,572 were stamped between 1875 and 1880[187]); it did not reduce the number of ejectments brought on notices to quit, which seems to have increased, although it is difficult to be certain because of the defects in the judicial statistics in the late 1860s; certainly the proportion of ejectments caused by notices to quit, probably a more reliable measure, did not fall after 1870, but hovered about 30 per cent from year to year.[188] In other words, things went on much as they had done before 1870, which suggests either that the land act was ineffective or that it was not needed. It did have, however, one

---

[180] Ibid. 284.   [181] Ibid. 90.   [182] Ibid. 89.

[183] James Macaulay, *Ireland in 1872: A Tour of Observation. With Remarks on Irish Public Questions* (London, 1873), 279. For the Leinster lease, see *Bessborough Comm., Minutes of Evidence*, pt. ii, pp. 1325–33; see also pp. 1109–19. It is difficult to estimate the number of leases that were granted to take advantage of subsection 3; in 1870 there were about 135,000 leases; in the 1880s it was said that there were 150,000 leaseholders (*Cowper Comm., Minutes of Evidence*, 21); if it is assumed that 3% of 135,000 expired annually, 40,500 leases expired between 1870 and 1880; in other words, 55,500 new leases were granted in the 1870s. See also Donnelly, *Land and People of Cork*, 204–10.

[184] S. C. McElroy, *The Route Land Crusade, Being an Authentic Account of the Efforts Made to Advance Land Reform by the Route Tenants' Defence Association, the Antrim Central Tenant Right Association, and the Ulster Land Committee* (Coleraine [1909]).

[185] See below, App. 18. See also B. L. Solow, *The Land Question and the Irish Economy, 1870–1903* (Cambridge, Mass., 1971), 86.   [186] See below, App. 1.

[187] Return 'of the Number of Notices to Quit Served in the Respective Years from [16 Oct. 1875] to 1880, Inclusive, as Shown by the Stamps Issued of the Denomination Required for Such Notices According to the Provisions of the Land Act of 1870', HC 1881 (53), lxxvii. 755.   [188] Above, n. 146.

measurable advantage for the tenants: of the 3,625 families evicted between 1871 and 1876, about one-third got some form of compensation—about £86 each on average. There was, however, a tremendous gulf fixed between what the tenants claimed and what they got. In 1871 claims lodged amounted to £142,308; the gross amount awarded was only £13,664, or less than 10 per cent; in 1877 claims amounted to £255,225; but the gross amount awarded was only £15,401, which was only 6 per cent of the amount claimed.[189]

The act did not, therefore, directly affect thousands of holdings, like the land of 1881; between 1871 and 1877 just under 5,000 cases came before the courts and only a total of £123,729 was awarded, which was hardly a crippling burden to put on landlords. It did not lead to a great transfer in the ownership of land, even though the board of works offered the tenants loans to buy their farms.[190] It did not give the tenants the three Fs. It did not give tenants outside Ulster the protection of tenant right: tenant right applied to tenants in arrears, section 3 did not; the value of tenant right was enhanced by low rents, but compensation under section 3 was reduced by low rents. The act did not tie the Irish electorate to Gladstone, as the general election of 1874 was to show, although it increased his support in Ulster, where the number of Liberals returned increased in 1874 and 1880. The generous treatment of Ulster tenants under the act, who virtually got the three Fs in 1870, paid off there, if nowhere else. The negative attributes of the act might be adumbrated at even greater length; but it did have positive, if not easily measurable, effects on landlords and tenants. Sections 3, 4, and 7 between them gave bits of the three Fs: there was a sort of right of sale, consisting of improvements, compensation for disturbance, and possibly incoming payments; tenure became more secure because eviction became more expensive; rents became more difficult to increase.

The courts, except in Ulster, did not fix rents; between 1871 and 1876 there was no case where the courts certified that eviction was caused by an exorbitant rent (under section 9), which was the only power over rents conferred on courts by the act.[191] Yet the act inhibited rent increases because rents could be increased only by mutual consent or by issuing a notice to quit and bringing an ejectment against the tenant. A landlord who wanted to increase his rents would have to calculate the cost of two

---

[189] *Judicial Statistics, Ire., 1871*, p. 237 [C 674], HC 1872, lxv. 471; ibid. 1877, p. 102 [C 2152], HC 1878, lxxix. 366.

[190] Between 1870 and 1878 the board of works advanced loans of £416,802 to 702 tenants to buy 42,440 acres. For details see *Report from the Select Committee on [the] Land Act, 1870; together with the Proceedings of the Committee, Minutes of Evidence, Appendix, and Index*. pp. 340–1, HC 1878 (249), xv. 382–3.

[191] *Return in 'Tabular Form . . . of the Number of Civil Bill Ejectments, Other than Civil Bill Ejectments for Non-Payment of Rent, Entered, Tried, and Determined, in Each County in Ireland, for Each of the Three Years Ending 21 Dec. 1876'*, p. 7, HC 1878 (25), lxiii. 457.

possible penalties that might be inflicted on him or his successor. First, if his tenants refused to pay an increased rent, he might be made to pay as much as one-third of the fee simple value of his estate in compensation; secondly, having increased his rents, he increased the amount of compensation that his tenants could claim if they were disturbed. The total rental of the country, based on rents on the eleven estates in Appendix 6, went up by only £200,000 between 1870 and 1879, compared with £800,000 between 1859 and 1869.[192] Comparing actual rents with potential rents during the shorter periods of 1865-9 and 1871-5 shows that the gap between the two increased slightly after 1870. Was this caused by the land act? It is very difficult to be sure. After all, the courts in a way now offered landlords a forum for making decisions by inviting arbitration. A good case for rent increases, based on comparisons of prices, could have been made on many estates; it might even have been argued under section 18 that eviction was reasonable for such a purpose.[193] This does not seem to have happened. On a group of estates managed by Robert L. Brown, an interesting pattern of rent increases occurred in the 1870s that suggested, although it did not prove, that landlords were afraid to risk going into court.[194] The holdings on these estates fell into three groups: leaseholds that expired in the 1870s; yearly tenants whose rents had been increased in 1868; yearly tenants whose rents had not been increased for years. During the 1870s very large increases were put on the first group, who were not protected by section 3 of the land act; increases on renewed leases were large, just over 50 per cent on average; the raised rents were very high compared with the tenement valuation. There were hardly any increases on the yearly tenants, who were protected by section 3; their rents were low; just over the valuation, which was low compared with the yearly rents increased in 1868; they were low compared with even the old leasehold rents. The notes made by Brown show that he was aware of this contrast; rents that were not increased were described as 'exceedingly low', 'low', 'fair'.[195]

[192] See below, App. 9.
[193] The act forced some landlords at least to think systematically about rent increases. What Thomas Baldwin called the Portacarron lease seems to have been an attempt, amateurish but interesting, to regulate rents by using agricultural prices; eight articles were named, of which 'the average is to be struck'; but no allowance was made for labour, etc., and the articles were given equal weight. See *Bessborough Comm., Minutes of Evidence*, pt. ii, p. 999.
[194] Survey of the Westropp estate in the counties of Clare and Limerick, 1871-7, Robert L. Brown, agent (NLI, MS 5397). [195] Ibid. 21, 84, 89.

5
Estate Management

i. Ideas and Means

In June 1861 a sub-inspector of constabulary in County Donegal submitted a report to the county inspector on the management of Lord Leitrim's estate.[1] He could, he claimed, 'write for a week and tell the hardships the people on the earl of Leitrim's estate have to suffer'. He confined himself, however, to giving 'a few particulars'—running to ten pages of manuscript—of how Leitrim and his bailiffs oppressed a people 'who, if permitted to avail themselves of the rights of British subjects, are a quiet, obliging, and well disposed peasantry'. In January 1860, for example, a corn stack, belonging to a man named Gamble, was burned by accident; 'but Lord L. and his bailiffs said it was maliciously done, and valued it at £5, which sum Lord L. ordered his bailiffs to collect off the townland'. The tenants 'dare not say one word, as they would be put out if they did'. To the injury of oppression, Leitrim added the insult of wanting to appear popular. A grand illumination for his visit to Milford in May 1861 was 'got up by order of Captain Baker [the agent], who sent Alic Russell round to each tenant with an *order* that a candle was to be in each pane of glass in the front of each house'. On another occasion when Leitrim wanted signatures for a petition to the House of Lords alleging that life and property were insecure in north Donegal, he told his head bailiff

to go round and have each tenant to sign it; or for him to stand on a rent day in the agent's office, and as each tenant comes in, he (the bailiff) says 'Come Mick, the Lord wants you to sign this paper as he is going to show it to the Queen' and the poor tenant replies, 'Sure it is myself that's a bad writer. Will you do it for me?'

Eight years later in 1869, apparently in connection with inquiries being made by the government in preparation for the land bill, Richard Hamilton, the poor law inspector in County Donegal, submitted a report on Leitrim's estate that amplified that of 1861.[2] Every April 'notices to quit are served on all the tenants' and 'it appears from the rate books ... his lordship has ninety-nine farms, containing 4,995 acres and valued at £822 a year, on this estate in his own hands, from each of which it is presumed an occupier has been withdrawn.' The effect of this system of management

---

[1] Larcom papers (NLI, MS 7633, no. 94).   [2] National Archives, RP 1869/5078.

was 'to keep the people in a state of constant apprehension and to check all enterprise or improvement of any kind'. 'The system pursued by his lordship does not prevail on any other estate in this part of the north of Ireland.' Leitrim had an obsession with detail that was unusual in a great nobleman, and 'a regular system of espionage is carried out over the whole estate—even the movements of the agent being reported on'. The surviving records of the Leitrim estate show that this was true—and probably worse than Hamilton imagined. All scraps of information were purveyed to Leitrim; even if nothing happened, it was reported. Much was only gossip: the servants in Leitrim's house had given the constabulary tea and whiskey and 'sat up singing songs till one o'clock'; Robert Stewart said he had seen Robert Wilson taking the constables to Leitrim's own room and giving them whiskey.[3]

Leitrim's career from 1854 to his murder in 1878 was controversial. He was as difficult as a tenant as he was as a landlord, for he quarrelled with the board of Trinity College, Dublin, from whom he held 28,000 acres in Donegal;[4] he was removed from the commission of the peace in 1863 for insulting the lord-lieutenant, Lord Carlisle;[5] he was blamed for being the chief cause of the land act of 1870.[6] In the oral tradition of the counties of Donegal and Leitrim, his actions were long remembered: he hated goats because they nibbled the bark of newly planted trees, and their owners were ordered to kill those 'gourmandizers'; a tenant who ploughed up a pasture was ordered to put back the sods by hand; tenants, waiting to pay their rents at Lough Rynn, were kept standing bareheaded in the rain.[7]

The accumulation of such actions created the tone of an estate: rent increases, evictions, and the character of the agent and the landlord were perhaps the more definable ingredients in the mixture that made good or bad landlords. Estates were great centres of social, economic, and political power, providing employment, capital for improvements, and political patronage. The big house was a centre of hospitality, a focus of gossip, and a source of spectacle. Rents absorbed about a quarter of agricultural output and were potential reservoirs of agricultural capital. Landlords and agents were often *ex officio* poor law guardians, and as justices of the peace they dominated the petty sessions. How this power was used varied greatly, ranging from the truculent meddling of Lord Leitrim to estates such as that of Thomas Staples Irwin near Dungannon where rents were not increased, but nothing was done to help the tenants, who were

[3] Leitrim estate reports (County Donegal), 29 May 1865 (NLI, MS 13339(6)).
[4] W. J. Lowe, 'Landlord and Tenant on the Estate of Trinity College, Dublin, 1851–1903', *Hermathena*, 120 (1976), 11.
[5] Larcom papers (NLI, MS 7634, nos. 114–24).
[6] William Hart to G. V. Hart, jun. 9 Apr. 1878 (PRONI, D3077/F/6/120).
[7] David Thomson, *Woodbrook* (Harmondsworth, 1976), 196–202; and information supplied by Mrs Emily Cathcart, Bellanaleck, Co. Fermanagh.

expected to pay their rents and 'go be damned'.[8] Between these two extremes there was a variety of styles: the paternal despotism of Lord Fitzwilliam;[9] the hesitant fussiness of William Wann on the Gosford estates; the conscientious benevolence of John Hamilton of St Ernan's who, according to Fr. Doherty, went about doing good 'like his Master';[10] the sharp, energetic shrewdness of Sir John Benn-Walsh;[11] and the 'unbending integrity of Mr Joy [Lord Mountcashell's agent], and his honour and honesty, and all that'.[12]

The disapproval of Lord Leitrim expressed by the constabulary and poor law inspectors (there is a marginal note in the 1869 report that 'a more shocking state of things was never described in the management of an estate ... than appears in this') suggests that there was more to the management of an estate than the mere observance of the letter of the law and the free play of economic forces. In the day-to-day management of an estate, absolute freedom of contract, the idea that society was a *tabula rasa* and that things could be so arranged that the past was irrelevant, was a practical impossibility. Custom, inertia, and routine were more sure guides in the short term. 'The active voluntary part of man is very small', wrote Walter Bagehot in another but not unrelated context, 'and if it were not economized by the sleepy kind of habit, its results would be null. We could not do every day out of our own heads all we have to do.'[13]

The most celebrated works on estate management did not assume that the relation between landlord and tenant was that of agricultural producer and *rentier* capitalist. Robert E. Brown, Duncan George Forbes MacDonald, Henry Stephens, and J. Bailey Denton assumed that the relationship was one of mutual dependence: respect on the one hand, condescension and generosity on the other.[14] The standard Irish work on estate management, by Thomas de Moleyns,[15] was more legalistic in its approach than any of these; but on its binding were inscribed the words 'Property has its duties as well as its rights'.

---

[8] Murrough O'Brien's commonplace book, 32–3 (MS in private possession).
[9] Robert Chaloner's letter-book, 1842–53 (NLI, MS 3987); Fitzwilliam memoranda books, 1858–66 (ibid. MSS 4985–6, 4988–91, 4995–6, 4999).
[10] John Hamilton, *Sixty Years' Experience as an Irish Landlord* (London, [1894]), 350.
[11] James S. Donnelly, jun., 'The Journals of Sir John Benn-Walsh Relating to the Management of his Irish Estates, 1823–64', *Cork Hist. Soc. Jn.* 79: 230 (1974), 86–123; 80: 231 (1975), 15–42.
[12] *Devon Comm., Minutes of Evidence*, pt. i, p. 565.
[13] Walter Bagehot, *The English Constitution*, intro. by R. H. S. Crossman (London and Glasgow, 1973), 64.
[14] Robert E. Brown, *The Book of the Landed Estate* (London and Edinburgh, 1869); Duncan George Forbes MacDonald, *Estate Management* ... 10th edn. (London, 1868); Stephens, *Book of the Farm*; J. Bailey Denton, *The Farm Homesteads of England* (London, 1864).
[15] *The Landowner's and Agent's Practical Guide* (Dublin, 1860); 2nd and 3rd edns. (1860); 4th edn. (1860); 6th edn. (1872).

If these were the textbooks of estate management, the ethos that sustained them was simultaneously more complicated and pervasive. The novels of Scott and Disraeli, reinforced by Trollope's, probably had as much influence on how landlords saw themselves as books on estate management. The architecture of the mid-nineteenth century, with its battlements and banqueting halls, was as powerful a symbol of landlords' aspirations as the land act of 1860 and the free trade in land established by the encumbered estates acts. Maclise's *Christmas in the Baronial Hall* may seem to have little to do with the technicalities of land law, but it was none the less evocative in a country where gentlemen's houses were made to look like ancient Irish castles.[16] Traditional acts of respect persisted well into the nineteenth century. When Lord Lanesborough visited his estate at Newtownbutler in County Fermanagh in 1852 he was greeted with a traditional act of deference. 'The horses were withdrawn from the carriage, and the tenantry, amidst enthusiastic applause, drew him on.'[17] The third marquis of Waterford's funeral procession from Curraghmore in 1859, with its nice gradations of rank and function among the mourners, was a sign that the feudal spirit was still alive; the fact that the coffin was escorted by the marquis's own labourers 'dressed with Irish frieze and leather gaiters'[18] was as traditional as the arrangements made at Abbotsford in 1832.

Even John George Adair, who became notorious for his evictions at Derryveagh, seems to have been a romantic. He was drawn to County Donegal, he claimed, by the wild beauty of its scenery and by a desire to improve the condition of the people—a not entirely incredible claim, in spite of the disaster that followed, for his Derryveagh estate was not a good investment and was a waste of time and energy when better bargains were still available in other parts of Ireland. One of his first steps was to surround himself with Scots shepherds; if he had wished to create a Scottish idyll in the Donegal highlands by surrounding himself with 'pawky' Scots, he was badly mistaken in his men, for they would have been more serviceable in the entourage of a Highland cattle thief than in the household of a Victorian gentleman. The fact that in one of the ballads lamenting the evictions it was alleged that Adair's grandfather was a 'ploughman poor' suggests that popular prejudice was not profoundly different from the highest romantic aspirations of the day.[19]

The one characteristic of estate management that might be said to have been fashionable, in that it owed more to the commercial than to the feudal spirit, was the strictness with which accounts were kept. In the Inchiquin accounts there was an instruction that 'no bills are to be run at any shop, for everything is to be paid for at the time it is obtained or soon

[16] Jeanne Sheehy, *The Rediscovery of Ireland's Past: The Celtic Revival, 1830–1930* (London, 1980), 40. [17] *Irish Farmers' Gazette*, 21 Aug. 1852, p. 399. [18] Ibid. 9 Apr. 1859, p. 172. [19] Vaughan, *Derryveagh Evictions*, 15–16.

after as possible.... Every transaction for money to be entered in this book.' Lord Inchiquin himself inspected the accounts, and 'every morning after the men are set to work a book with the daily report of employment to be sent in to Lord Inchiquin at breakfast time, this book not to be allowed to be in arrear even if Lord Inchiquin is absent'.[20] It is impossible to generalize, for estate records, even the most rich, are not complete, but it seems that many landlords took a detailed interest in the management of their estates. The records of the guardians of Lord Powerscourt, the tenants' request book of the Farnham estate, William Wann's correspondence with Lord Gosford, and the agents' reports on Sir George Hodson's County Cavan estate, all suggest that landlords expected to be informed and consulted. The degree of supervision varied and it is doubtful if all great landlords were as strict as Lord Inchiquin. 'There is no educated human being less likely to know business than a young lord,' wrote Walter Bagehot; but Lord Dunraven, who was young and a lord, was interested in different methods of book-keeping and his papers include a letter from William Steuart Trench explaining a system of presenting accounts that was commended by the marquis of Lansdowne as 'the only clear account which he had ever yet been able to obtain of the necessities and capabilities of his Kerry property'.[21]

The landlord's personality was crucial in the management of an estate; variety, therefore, was inevitable. Not only that, but the influences on the tone of an estate were often the intangible ones of temperament—on both sides. The law enforced some regularity in management; the ethos of the landed class itself also worked towards uniformity, although Irish landlords were by no means a homogeneous class with common characteristics. Routine and custom, while adding to this variety, worked towards continuity. The power of routine was demonstrated by the fact that most landlords let their holdings by the year, instead of giving leases or making written agreements. In the absence of a written agreement the law presumed that a yearly tenancy existed; it was convenient, therefore, for landlords to let the law take its course; but leases, although their importance was exaggerated, had advantages that would have repaid the cost of making them.

They could have been used to simplify management by giving landlords more subtle sanctions than the threat of eviction to secure arrears of rent, to enforce good farming practices, and to encourage improvement. In 1856 John George Adair let 390 Irish acres at Bellegrove to two Scots farmers for twenty-one years at an annual rent of £1,564, which was a

[20] Inchiquin account-book, 1863–7 (NLI, MS 14811); see also Lindsay Proudfoot, 'The Management of a Great Estate: Patronage, Income and Expenditure on the Duke of Devonshire's Irish Property, c. 1816 to 1891', *Ir. Econ. & Soc. Hist.* 13 (1986), 38.
[21] Dunraven papers (PRONI, D3196/F/17/4).

very high rent even for good land; but if they observed 'a certain system of husbandry' the rent would be annually abated by 50 per cent to £782.[22] This was a useful device, giving the landlord a powerful sanction, while offering the tenants a generous inducement to behave responsibly—and giving them security for twenty-one years. On the Butler estate at Castle Crine, County Clare, tenants made agreements with the landlord that obliged them to lodge sums of money as security for their rents, with the unusual provision 'that should the times improve the rent can be raised in proportion'.[23] (More unusual were leases in Tipperary with a covenant 'making the lease null and void where the tenant or any of his family committed a murder'.[24])

A system of leases or agreements for terms of years would have taken much of the power from arguments in favour of security of tenure; it might not, of course, have removed the demand itself. Landlords could have moved away from even a semblance of security of tenure by virtually abolishing yearly tenancies by written agreements that would have allowed the eviction of tenants without even six months' notice to quit.[25] Few landlords seem to have bothered with leases or agreements. Leases were indeed granted; in 1870 there were about 50,000 twenty-one and thirty-one year leases in existence, about one for every ten holdings.[26] Nor is there evidence that many landlords tried to replace yearly tenancies by tenancies at will. William Scully, who so nearly came to a bad end in the 'battle' of Ballycohey, tried to do this, but he was exceptional.[27] (His long and profitable experience of managing landed prosperity in the USA may have given him the idea.)

In spite of the interest taken in estate management by landlords, the daily running of an estate devolved on the agent and his assistants, who might include on a large estate clerks, bailiffs, agriculturists, bog-rangers, and possibly a solicitor.[28] Agents varied in their closeness to their employers and in their involvement in his affairs. Most remote perhaps, were the professional firms managing estates in several counties such as Guinness, Mahon, Hardy, & Co., who managed Sir George Hodson's estate in County

[22] Registry of Deeds, 1856/6/195.
[23] Butler estate (County Clare): register of tenancy agreements, 1849–52 (NLI, MS 4253); see agreement dated 27 Oct. 1849.
[24] Beere to C. W. O'Hara, 29 Jan. 1873 (NLI, MS 20321(26)).
[25] De Moleyns, *Landowner's Guide* (1872), 60–1.
[26] *Returns Showing the Number of Agricultural Holdings in Ireland, and the Tenure by which They are Held by the Occupiers* [C 32], HC 1870, lvi. 737; for leases on County Cork estates, see Donnelly, *Land and People of Cork*, 201–4.
[27] Homer E. Socolofsky, *Landlord William Scully* (Lawrence, Kan., 1979), 52.
[28] For a full account of land agency in County Cork see Donnelly, *Land and People of Cork*, 173–87; see also Hoppen, *Elections, Politics, and Society*, 138–44; Proudfoot, 'The Management of a Great Estate', 35–6; S. M. Hussey, *The Reminiscences of an Irish Land Agent* (London, 1904).

Cavan,[29] or Samuel Hussey's firm, which collected rents annually amounting to £250,000.[30] Most close, possibly, were agents who were related to their employers, either managing the family estate or working further afield, such as the family of William Steuart Trench, who managed the Bath estate in County Monaghan, the Lansdowne estate in County Kerry, and the Digby estate in the King's County, as well as their cousin's estate in the Queen's County.[31] Some devoted themselves exclusively to one estate. The Revd John Moore told the wife of a candidate for the Annesley agency in 1845 that

> the agent is expected to devote the entire of his time to Lord Annesley's business, also to be *much* over the estate. The schools are to be looked after; in short it would be expected that the agent should do all in his power to advance the temporal and spiritual interest of the people.[32]

William Wann managed the Dungannon Royal School estate as well as Lord Gosford's estates in Armagh and Cavan; but he lived at Markethill, near Lord Gosford, and his correspondence shows that he was deeply involved in Lord Gosford's affairs, including his politics, his debts, and the needs of his family.

The management of detached portions of an estate was a problem solved in different ways. Wann managed Lord Gosford's Cavan estate as well as the Armagh estate, travelling to Arva by train to collect the rents; the Erne estates in Sligo and Mayo were managed by resident agents and not by the Fermanagh agent—the Chambers family on the Sligo estate were long resident there, but there were several changes on the Mayo estate before Captain Boycott arrived in the 1870s.[33] The great institutional landlords adopted various expedients: the London companies had resident agents such as Alexander Spotswood,[34] who managed other estates in County Londonderry; the commissioners of endowed schools had a local agent for each school's estate, although Wann was neither resident nor exclusively devoted to their service.[35]

Some agents were paid a salary, £400 a year on the Annesley estate, for example; but most received a commission on rents collected, usually 4 or 5 per cent. What is impressive about Irish estates is their cheapness of

---

[29] Hodson rentals and agents' reports, 1861 (NLI, MS 16419, p. 3).
[30] *Lords' Sel. Comm. on the 1881 Land Act, Second report*, 97; on land agency firms, including Hussey's, see Donnelly, *Land and People of Cork*, 182, 184.
[31] Trench, *Realities of Ir. Life*; *Report of the Evicted Tenants Commission*, ii. *Minutes of Evidence, Appendices, and Index*, p. 132 [C 6935-1], HC 1893-4, xxxi.
[32] Annesley letter-book, 19 Apr. 1845 (PRONI, D1854/6/5).
[33] Erne rentals (Counties Mayo and Sligo), 1847-79 (PRONI, D1939/10/1-3).
[34] Spotswood's letter-book, 1860-76 (PRONI, D1062/1/8A); see also Olive Robinson, 'The London Companies as Progressive Landlords in Nineteenth-Century Ireland', *Econ. Hist. Rev.* 2nd ser. 15: 1 (Aug. 1962), 106.
[35] *Endowed Schools Comm. 1857-8*, Appendix, 21-33.

management, about 6 per cent.³⁶ At the very least the agent was expected to collect the rents and to keep accounts; but generally he chose new tenants, supervised estate expenditure, and carried out evictions. Some agents, however, were more like rustic statesmen than mere rent collectors: they were poor law guardians and justices of the peace; they organized voters at elections; some were public figures appearing before parliamentary inquiries and writing books on the land question. William Steuart Trench did both, Samuel Hussey published his memoirs in 1904, and John Hancock gave memorable evidence to the Devon commission.³⁷

The training of agents was as varied as their functions. Some were solicitors, like John Weldon in *The Big House of Inver*; some added a knowledge of agriculture to a liberal education, like William Steuart Trench, educated at Armagh Royal School and famous for his farming at Cardtown; some were ex-soldiers, such as Captain Boycott; some were professionally trained in firms like Hussey's.³⁸ That many were 'men who have been educated at a county school, where they never got beyond compound fractions and copper plate . . . polished off by a few balls which turn up in their locality, to which everyone is admitted' may have been less true after the famine.³⁹ Some, regardless of their training, or lack of it, were competent, such as Edward Curling, Lord Devon's agent, who spoke more sense about rents in a few words than others did in books;⁴⁰ some had skills that were not taught even in the most polished schools, such as Francis Currey, the duke of Devonshire's agent, who spoke Irish.⁴¹

The Revd John Moore, when looking for an agent for his nephew, Lord Annesley, was 'anxious to the very heart to get a man who will really be of use to the property, a gentleman in every sense of the word, one who will uphold the Annesley interests and who will be a comfort to my nephew to have on his attaining his majority'.⁴² A man of business who was 'a gentleman in every sense of the word' was not easy to find: Captain Despard, a former agent of Lord Annesley, had taken away the office rentals 'from which we have suffered great inconvenience'.⁴³ There were 200 applications for the post when he left, but his successor William Hunter turned out to be unsatisfactory, although he had been warmly recommended as 'perfectly qualified for any situation connected with the

---

³⁶ See below, App. 18. ³⁷ *Devon Comm., Minutes of Evidence*, pt. i, pp. 477–89.
³⁸ Donnelly, *Land and People of Cork*, 184.
³⁹ *Remarks on Ireland; as It Is; as It Ought to Be; and as It Might Be . . . by a Native* (London, 1849), 13; see also Donnelly, *Land and People of Cork*, 183.
⁴⁰ *Sel. Comm. on Land Tenure, 1865*, 211; see also *Bessborough Comm., Minutes of Evidence*, pt. ii, p. 1263.
⁴¹ Thomas Carlyle, *Reminiscences of my Irish Journey in 1849* (London, 1882), 105.
⁴² Annesley letter-book, 31 Oct. 1846 (PRONI, D1854/6/3, p. 34); on the social standing of agents, see Donnelly, *Land and People of Cork*, 179, 183.
⁴³ Annesley letter-book, 7 Nov. 1846 (PRONI, D1854/6/3, p. 44).

superintendence of landed property'.⁴⁴ Within a short time of his appointment, Moore was grumbling that he 'would sooner act as agent, clerk, and bailiff myself than be harassed as I have been for twelve months past with the manner in which you have conducted the whole affairs of the estate'.⁴⁵

It is difficult to estimate how much contact agents had with tenants. Was it possible to know four or five hundred, even a thousand tenants? Trench, for example, could not find his way about the Shirley estate in County Monaghan without a map.⁴⁶ (It was certainly not impossible for agents to know by sight all of the tenants, even on a large estate; Daniel Holland, the Tory registration agent in Derry, knew 'by appearance and name' everyone in the city.⁴⁷) Revd John Moore, who acted as agent for a short time for his nephew, was in no doubt that he knew the tenants: in the winter of 1846, 'after *one week's work*', he knew every family, the number of stacks of grain, cows, pigs, horses, and sheep 'on all the farms on nine townlands'.⁴⁸ Sir John Benn-Walsh, who visited his Irish estates only once a year, knew his tenants. He had a sharp, appreciative eye; a good dinner, or a smart new hotel attracted his attention; he noted with approval the widow Quinlan's two daughters 'who are the belles of my estate, fine, tall, handsome girls with beautiful figures'; or that one of his tenants had 'a notable, stirring wife. They gave us a little entertainment of tea, eggs, bread, and butter. It was pleasant to see so much activity and spirit.'⁴⁹ But Sir John was a vigorous man: 'at once more exacting and more progressive than most of his fellow proprietors', he increased his rents by 41 per cent between 1847 and 1866.⁵⁰ He managed part of his estates himself and did not think agency an onerous task:

> my experience of this and my other estates convinces me that a gentleman of ordinary intelligence and business habits might manage a considerable estate, paying one or two bailiffs and accountants, far more economically than through gentleman agents and without taxing his time and attention more than would afford him a little healthy and agreeable occupation.⁵¹

It was widely believed that agents were often the cause of trouble between landlords and tenants. The marquis of Hertford's agent in County Antrim, Walter Stannus, who was alleged to have made a tenant decapitate a dog and present its severed head at the office, because he disapproved

---

[44] Ibid. 6, p. 37 (24 Sept. 1845).   [45] Ibid., p. 10 (5 Nov. 1846).
[46] Trench, *Realities of Ir. Life*, 174.
[47] Sir John Ross, *The Years of my Pilgrimage: Random Reminiscences* (London, 1924), 67.
[48] Annesley letter-book, 5 Nov. 1846 (PRONI, D1854/6/6, p. 10); Lord Hillsborough claimed that he knew all of his Edenderry tenants (Hoppen, *Elections, Politics, and Society*, 135).
[49] James S. Donnelly, jun., 'The Journals of Sir John Benn-Walsh Relating to the Management of his Irish Estates, 1823–64', *Cork Hist. Soc. Jn.* 79: 230 (1974), 109; 80: 231 (1975), 28.
[50] Ibid. 79: 88–9.   [51] Ibid. 80: 33.

of tenants 'keeping hunting dogs',[52] was matched in fiction by Valentine M'Clutchy, and Mr Pigot in *Laurence Bloomfield in Ireland*. Lord Lansdowne believed that the Trenches, whose ability for self-advertisement was matched by the amount of unwelcome attention they attracted, had stirred up trouble on one of his estates during the land war by rudeness to a tenants' delegation.[53] On the other hand, estate records show that landlords often pressed agents to act more firmly. Although Richard Hamilton, the poor law inspector, believed that 'the feeling of the country is not so much against Lord Leitrim personally, as it is against the subordinates employed by his lordship', the estate records show that Leitrim was the driving force behind them. (He employed six different agents between 1854 and 1869.)[54] Sir John Benn-Walsh congratulated himself in 1852 that he had arrived in Ireland just in time to 'spur' his agent 'to make a determined stand' in forcing the tenants to pay their rents.[55] In 1882 Lord Annesley, safely absent in Corfu, wrote to his agent, urging him 'to fight my former tenants, but present enemies, by every means in your power, assisted by my lawyer'.[56] Agents often tried to avoid trouble. Richard Beere boasted that he had kept 'the O'Hara family and their tenants out of litigation for the last forty-five years'.[57] Avoiding disputes, rather than exacerbating them, was probably the aim of most agents. Publicity, petitions to the landlord, and legal wrangling were better avoided.

Part of the business of management was choosing the bailiffs and more humble instruments of estate management. Their closeness to the tenants, their role as the office's eyes and ears, and their local ties and ambitions could lead to disputes. A dispute on Sir George Hodson's Cavan estate was caused partly by the bailiff making himself 'very unpopular by jealously performing his duties'.[58] It was as difficult to get good bailiffs as it was to get good agents. Wann tolerated for nine years a drunken agriculturist on the Gosford estate in County Armagh. Although he was threatened with dismissal he persisted in his drunkenness until finally dismissed in 1859. The qualifications that Wann looked for in his successor give an idea of the difficulties of the post. He should be 'a stern temperance man'; the tenants 'are of a class that a Church of England man would be preferred'; he should be a 'man with a conciliatory manner', so that 'he could manage to arrange in a quiet way' disputes between tenants; 'and above all things to be free *from receiving the slightest favour or bribe from any tenant and*

---

[52] Godkin, *Land War in Ire.*, 338.
[53] H. W. E. Petty-Fitzmaurice, 5th marquis of Lansdowne, *Glanerought and the Petty-Fitzmaurices* (London, 1937), 137–8. [54] National Archives, RP 1869/5078.
[55] Donnelly, 'The Journals of Sir John Benn-Walsh', 119, 121.
[56] Annesley letter-book, 13 Mar. 1882, (PRONI, D1854/6/8, p. 23).
[57] Beere to C. W. O'Hara, 7 Feb. 1865 (NLI, MS 20321(21)); see also Spotswood's letter-book, 26 Mar. 1861 (PRONI, D1062/1/8A, p. 31).
[58] Hodson rentals and agents' reports, 1861 (NLI, MS 16419, pp. 3–4).

to abstain from drinking with them'. Part of the problem of managing an estate was revealed by the reference that Wann gave his drunken agriculturist when he dismissed him. He 'was very much under my notice ... he has always acted with the strictest honesty and fidelity ... he invariably evinced a desire to act fairly and impartially'. 'He had', concluded Wann, 'my best wishes for his future welfare.'[59]

ii. Arrears and the Payment of Rents

In *The Landowner's and Agent's Practical Guide*, Thomas de Moleyns allowed himself a rare excursion into sententiousness when discussing the collection of rents. A new agent's first rent collection was his most embarrassing duty; for the tenants would 'all with one consent' begin to make excuses. The new agent may, however, 'with kindness, yet with firmness, very quickly prove that money must be had—and it will be had'.[60] Estate accounts and correspondence confirm the impression that the collection of rents and the elimination of arrears was the most pressing of an agent's duties. Even slight increases in arrears made agents concoct excuses. The agents on the Hodson estate in County Cavan, which seems to have been relatively free from arrears during the whole period, were at pains to explain an increase from £125. 4s. 4d. in 1860 to £260. 19s. 7d. in 1861. 'We made every exertion to collect the rents, and in some cases where we thought the tenants were able to pay, proceedings were taken.'[61]

It was often alleged that landlords deliberately allowed tenants to fall into arrears, so that their power over them would be increased.[62] Estate accounts, however, suggest that this was unusual after the famine; in any case, it was legally unnecessary because the notice to quit gave landlords as much power as arrears. Many agents in fact tried to get rid of the 'dead' or 'hanging' gale, as it was ominously called, by encouraging tenants to pay off their arrears, for 'when a man is paid to the day he will endeavour to keep so and not fall back again'.[63] To achieve this, arrears were cancelled or abandoned as hopelessly lost. This explains why falls in arrears were not always matched by increases in receipts, especially in the early 1850s. On the Hall estate, for example, in the early 1850s arrears of over £2,000 were struck off and in the 1860s an additional £1,500 was lost— the two sums combined exceeded a year's rent. Tenants on the Hall estate

---

[59] Gosford letter-book, 21 Sept. and 12 Oct. 1859 (PRONI, D1606/5A/2, pp. 196–7).
[60] De Moleyns, *Landowner's Guide* (1872), 382.
[61] Hodson rentals and agents' reports, 1862 (NLI, MS 16419, p. 33); see also ibid., p. 84 for a similar crisis in 1863.
[62] William Carleton, *Valentine M'Clutchy, the Irish Agent and Solomon McSlime, his Religious Attorney* 3rd edn. (Dublin, 1867), 75.
[63] Wann's letter-book, 2 May 1874 (PRONI, D1606/5/5, pp. 143–4); cf. Hoppen, *Elections, Politics, and Society*, 130.

were also given discounts if they paid punctually: in 1854 when arrears inherited from the 1840s were beginning to be cleared, a discount of 4s. in the pound was offered to those who paid punctually that year.[64] On the Deane estate in County Kildare a case of arrears was dealt with in a way that was a nice blend of sharpness and indulgence. A tenant whose rent was increased from £24 to £36 in 1854 owed arrears of £122. He did not, however, succumb to the twin burdens of arrears and a greatly increased rent, for he was still on the estate in 1871, when a note in the rental recorded that

in consequence of the large amount of his arrear, a sick wife and large, young family, and losses in cattle etc., his rent was abated to £24 a year on the terms of his paying £36 a year until the arrear was all cleared, after which he was to pay the full rent of £36 a year.

This was a strange arrangement but it worked, for after seventeen years of effort, the agent noted that the tenant 'has now cleared up to 1 May last'.[65]

Agents were remarkably successful at collecting rents. Measured against potential performance, they were more successful at collecting them than at increasing them. On nine of the twelve estates whose arrears and receipts are given below arrears were small after the early 1850s. On only three estates—the Garvagh, Hall, and Knox estates—were arrears high after the mid-1850s, and on two of these—the Hall and Knox estates—great progress had been made by the late 1860s. Only on the Garvagh estate did the 'dead half-year' survive not only the prosperity of the 1850s but the greater prosperity of the 1870s.

If receipts rather than arrears are examined, however, the performance of agents—and tenants—is revealed as even more impressive: on none of these estates did receipts fall below 90 per cent of annual rents between 1851 and 1878 (except on the Knox estate in 1852). To find years when receipts fell below 90 per cent, one must look at the immediate post-famine years, or at 1879 and its successors. In practice, of course, the success rate was rather higher than 90 per cent; the averages for each decade show that, taking one year with another between 1851 and 1879, the success rate was closer to 99 per cent than to 90 per cent. Equally remarkable was the apparently limited effects on receipts of the crises of the period—the famine, the depression of the early 1860s, and the land war. It is tempting to discern a revolution in estate management after the famine, for accounts seem to have been better kept, punctuality and regularity became more common, and the prosperity of the mid-1850s was

[64] For arrears and receipts on twelve estates, including the Hall estate, see below, Apps. 7 and 8. See also Wann's letter-book, 21 Jan. 1875 (PRONI, D1606/5/5, p. 162).
[65] Deane rental (County Kildare), 1871 (NLI, MS 14282).

carefully husbanded to liquidate the burden of famine arrears. The Erne estate in County Donegal appears to be an example of post-famine reform; for not only was the famine arrear cleared in the 1850s, but the pre-famine arrears, which had seemed endemic, were cleared, and never again reached their former level. Even the Knox and Hall estates give an impression of order being established, although this took a long time. The evidence for such a revolution, however, is too slight to be conclusive, and the changes that came about can be as easily explained by the prosperity of the 1850s and mid-1860s.

A rough comparison of Irish and British estates suggests that Irish tenants paid as punctually as the British, once the post-famine years had passed. On the Murray Stewart estate in Scotland, for example, arrears in 1858 were 5 per cent; on the County Donegal estate, in spite of all the disadvantages suffered by its tenants, arrears in the same year were only 8 per cent.[66] The archetypal English landlord, John Steadyman of Wearywork Hall, assumed that he would carry arrears of 6 per cent every year.[67] Some of the better Irish estates were as good or better than this. On the Ashtown estate receipts did not fall below 100 per cent between 1852 and 1873; on the Inchiquin estate they did not fall below 98 per cent between 1848 and 1878. The Erne, Hamilton, and Hodson estates came close to the Wearywork Hall record.[68]

The fluctuation of arrears and receipts gave landed incomes some of the flexibility that was denied to them by the payment of fixed rents. Landlords were able to cream off some of the prosperity of the good years, especially in the mid-1850s. A similar clearing of arrears allowed landlords a small share of the mid-1860s boom.[69] If landlords benefited from good years, it must be remembered that in bad years they tolerated an accumulation of arrears that were in effect interest-free loans to their tenants. Landlords such as Lord Garvagh and Roger Hall of Narrow Water gave virtually permanent loans as long as they tolerated high arrears, which they did for most of the period.

Although agents and landlords could influence the pattern of arrears and receipts on their estates, fluctuations in the value of agricultural output determined the size and incidence of arrears and receipts. Taking the twelve estates as a whole a pattern emerges: arrears were high in the late 1840s and early 1850s, in the early 1860s, and in the late 1870s. Between these crises there were periods of recovery, which were most dramatic in the mid-1850s and the mid-1860s. After 1879 a change took place on estates,

[66] Murray Stewart rentals (Wigtown, Kircubright, and Donegal), 1858 (NLI, MSS 5477, 5896).
[67] Bateman, *Great Landowners* (1883), p. xxv.   [68] See below, App. 8.
[69] See the Knox estate below, App. 7; see also Murray Stewart rentals (County Donegal), 1858–69 (NLI, MSS 5896–903).

for arrears tended to be higher in the 1880s and 1890s than in the 1860s and 1870s. The recovery that had characterized the 1850s did not recur in the 1880s. The crisis that began in 1879, therefore, was a turning-point and not just a reverse like the depression of the early 1860s. After 1879 arrears accumulated and remained high. The contrast was strong on the Inchiquin estate, where arrears had been very low before 1879 but reached over 100 per cent by the 1890s. The contrast, however, must not be exaggerated; for receipts still remained high on some estates; on others the pattern did not change much; the Garvagh estate remained more or less as it had been in the 1870s.

Although the collection of rents on all estates was influenced by forces that were common to all, there were striking differences within that fundamental pattern. First, the size of arrears and receipts varied from estate to estate, suggesting that some were more vulnerable than others. On the Knox estate in the early 1860s, for example, arrears that were already high doubled, while on other estates the effects of the depression were not so dramatic.[70] Secondly, the timing of the crises varied slightly from estate to estate. The worst year of the 1860s on the Crofton estate was 1861, but 1862 was the worst on the Erne, Hamilton, Knox, and Midleton estates. Thirdly, some estates experienced difficulties in the late 1860s that were not felt by others. The Blacker, Erne, Hall, and Midleton estates had slight increases in arrears in the late 1860s. The reasons are not obvious. The banking crisis of 1866, the high price of potatoes in 1867, and a relative fall in the value of agricultural output in 1867 compared with 1866 may have had something to do with it. But as a crisis it is barely perceptible and not to be compared with the early 1860s. Wann was sceptical about its severity. In 1869 he received a memorial from the Dungannon Royal School tenants asking for a reduction in rents; but on making enquiries from other landlords he found that rents were being punctually paid. He suggested, therefore, that no 'general or universal' reduction was required, if only because 'this affair has been got up by a few who went through the estate. Some names are to it and the parties in their graves.'[71]

What is interesting about the fluctuations of receipts and arrears is the crises that did not occur, suggesting remarkable resilience in Irish agriculture. In 1857 there was a banking crisis in Britain that made the following year 1858 'one of the worst years of the later nineteenth century'.[72] On none of the twelve estates, however, was there any sign of difficulties. One

---

[70] See below, Apps. 7 and 8; see also Murray Stewart rental (County Donegal), 1863 (NLI, MS 5899).

[71] Wann's letter-book, 18 Nov. 1869 (PRONI, D1606/5/4, pp. 357–8).

[72] Sir Albert Feavearyear, *The Pound Sterling: A History of English Money*, rev. edn. by E. V. Morgan (Oxford, 1963), 295; Philip Ollerenshaw, *Banking in Nineteenth-Century Ireland: The Belfast Banks, 1825–1914* (Manchester, 1987), 79–80.

of the few signs of strain appeared on the Gosford estate, where Wann noted in 1857 that 'markets have got a tumble with us owing to the screw having been so closely applied by the banks. Farmers will be slow in bringing out their produce and I fear we may look for *late* rent paying this season.'[73] (There was in fact a trifling increase on the County Armagh estate in 1857, but it was not more than 1 or 2 per cent.[74]) Likewise, the failure of Overend, Gurney, & Co. in 1866, described as 'the most severe while it lasted' of all the banking crises of the nineteenth century, may have had only a small effect on tenants' ability to pay.[75] What was most remarkable, however, was the almost imperceptible effects of the serious potato failure of 1872, when the yield of potatoes was the third lowest of the thirty years 1851–80 (only 1861 and 1879 were worse). The marquis of Sligo wrote despondently to Lord Dufferin in September 1872:

We have had more than our usual rains and the hay, not yet saved, lies washed in the fields while the potatoes are rotting—but no one can tell how far that rot may go. God save us from such a plague as that of twenty-five years ago.[76]

But only the Hodson and Midleton estates showed any significant increases in arrears. Arrears of 11 per cent on the former made it as bad as 1861–3. The ease with which most tenants, with some exceptions, seem to have weathered the crisis of 1872 suggests that the system could take considerable shocks. Good seasons, good prices, and careful attention by agents made the payment and collection of rents one of the most successful aspects of estate management. The resilience of landlords and tenants, however, was not strained greatly, for none of the crises between the early 1850s and the mid-1870s was protracted.

iii. Estate Expenditure

'An Irish estate is like a sponge,' wrote the marquis of Dufferin, 'and an Irish landlord is never so rich as when he is rid of property.'[77] Lord Dufferin was thinking of the expenses that were almost inseparable from the ownership of an estate. When rents had been collected, certain expenses had to be met: fixed charges such as head rents, quit rents, and tithe rent charge; taxes such as income tax, county cess, poor law rates, and succession duty; the cost of management, improvements to tenants' farms, works of charity, the upkeep of a house and demesne, portions for younger children, jointures for dowagers, and interest on encumbrances.

Lord Inchiquin had an estate of over 20,000 acres in County Clare with

[73] Gosford letter-book, 14 Nov. 1857 (PRONI, D1606/5A/2, p. 43).
[74] Gosford rental, 1857 (PRONI, D1606/7A/63).
[75] Feavearyear, *The Pound Sterling*, 301.
[76] Sligo to Dufferin, 16 Sept. 1872 (PRONI, D1071H/B/B).
[77] Dufferin to duke of Argyle, 7 May 1874 (PRONI, D1071H/B/C).

a rental of about £12,000, but taxes, the cost of management, improvements, and interest took up just over half of his receipts between the 1850s and the 1880s.[78] Some landlords seem to have been better off than Inchiquin, although the vagaries of estate accounts may account for some of the more important differences. On the Hodson estate in County Cavan taxes, management, and improvements took only 20 per cent of receipts; but on the Crofton estate in County Roscommon taxes, improvements, interest, and the upkeep of Mote Park took 84 per cent. The difference between these two was caused mainly by high interest on the Crofton estate (39 per cent) and the upkeep of Mote Park (17 per cent); but this does not mean that Sir George Hodson was an absentee without encumbrances, but simply that his Cavan estate was managed separately from his County Wicklow estate, and the upkeep of Holybrooke Park at Bray was not charged to the Cavan accounts. Similarly Lord Erne's net income was much greater than 54 per cent of his rents of his County Fermanagh estate, because the accounts on which the estimates below are based do not include the Donegal, Sligo, and Mayo estates.

The main cause of the differences between estates, assuming that most of them supported a house and demesne, was interest payments, ranging from nothing to 48 per cent, in the estates whose accounts are given below. An attempt to summarize the position of estates suggests that average net income was less than 40 per cent of receipts. Just over 60 per cent was taken by taxes (12 per cent), management (6 per cent), improvements (11 per cent), interest on encumbrances (17 per cent), and upkeep of a house (17 per cent). If a net income of only 40 per cent seems a bit low, and it is only guesswork based on a summary of the accounts below, the pattern on individual estates supports it: Lord Ranfurly had no interest payments in his accounts, but his net income was only 64 per cent; the costs of Narrow Water House were not included in the Hall accounts, but even so the net income was only 63 per cent. Most landlords were not as rich as they must have appeared to their tenants; or rather, they had less room to manœuvre than was commonly imagined. To a landlord with a net income of only 40 per cent of his rental, an abatement of 25 per cent was a serious matter.[79]

Yet there was more resilience in the system than the estate accounts suggest. For one thing the upkeep of estates was not quite as ruinous as Lord Dufferin implied. When he inherited his estates in 1847, his rental was over £18,000 and encumbrances amounted to only £29,000. By 1872, after the first stages of his political career 'had exhausted his income and most of his credit', his estate had encumbrances of £304,824. In other

---

[78] For expenditure on nine estates, including Lord Inchiquin's, see below, App. 18.
[79] For the effects of rent reductions on remittances, see also Proudfoot, 'The Management of a Great Estate', 51.

words, between 1847 and 1872, he spent at least £726,000 (that is, rents of £450,000 and borrowings of £276,000). Little of this extravagance, despite his protestations, can be traced directly to expenditure on his estate. If all the items of improvement and charity that he enumerated in an inventory of his outgoings—roads, schools, cottages, churches, fences, drains, and farm buildings—are added up, they fall just short of £80,000 during the period 1847–72.[80] This is an impressive sum, especially when it is remembered that Irish landlords were accused of spending nothing on improvements, but it falls far short of the £150,000 that he believed he had spent 'in the shape of improvements' and from which he had reaped 'no other advantage than the ameliorated condition of the farmers themselves'.[81] Improvements took up about 18 per cent of his rental, which was a substantial amount, but hardly ruinous when compared with his income and encumbrances.

What is interesting about Lord Dufferin is that he incurred heavy losses not because he was an improving landlord but because he lived extravagantly. Between 1852 and 1872 he spent £26,000 on yachts, which was more than he spent on purely agricultural improvements such as farm roads, drains, and fences. What is also interesting is the ease with which he accumulated his vast debt, for between 1847 and 1872 he borrowed on average the equivalent of £11,000 a year, or nearly two-thirds of his rental. Great flexibility was, therefore, available to landlords, especially if they were relatively free from debts to begin with. A landlord who was not hopelessly encumbered could borrow his way out of at least one crisis in a generation and face with equanimity a temporary loss of income.

The expenditure of part of the rents on charities and improvements was one of the most important weapons in the armoury of estate management. Landlords' charities, which have been included with improvements in the table below,[82] were not large, but they reveal the expectations that landlords were supposed to satisfy and the numerous points at which they touched the affairs of the community. First, they gave money to schools. Lord Erne made regular payments to the schools at Lifford and Ballindrait, and Sir George Hodson helped to build and maintain three schools on his County Cavan estate, while Lord Inchiquin paid the salary of the teacher of an 'industrial' class. Secondly, they helped local organizations and good causes. Lord Ranfurly subscribed annually to the YMCA, the Tyrone Protestant Orphan Society, the 'cricket field committee', and the choir in the parish church. Thirdly, some gave generously to the disestablished Church of Ireland: the Archdale accounts show that Clogher's equivalent of Dean

---

[80] Dufferin's schedule of expenditure (PRONI, D1071A/136/3).
[81] Dufferin to duke of Argyle, 7 May 1874 (ibid. D1071H/B/C).
[82] See below, App. 18.

Ponsonby was at work in Fermanagh in the 1870s.[83] (The buildings of the church, rather than its clergy, had been the object of generosity before 1869: Lord Dufferin spent £1,450 on 'religious buildings', and Lord Enniskillen presented the parish church in his eponymous town with a bell inscribed to 'his friends the Inniskilling Men, 1841'.[84])

Landlords were subjected to a variety of requests that were too varied to be classified, but were perhaps more revealing than the more conventional outlets for estate charity. In the St George accounts there was a note that the widow Canthill had been given £2 'in consideration of the long and expensive illness of her late husband, Nicholas Canthill deceased, late tenant on the lands of West Ashtown'.[85] The trustees of the Powerscourt estate were petitioned by Samuel Manly who wanted an 'elastic stocking', for which 6s. 6d. was given.[86] Lord Ranfurly gave 8s. in 1862 for a coffin for James Thompson.[87] The generosity of Lord Fitzwilliam, one of the richest landlords in the United Kingdom, embraced the humblest requests: in 1861 a note was made in the agent's memoranda book to the effect that 'food must be allowed for W. Thomas's pigeon—vetches etc. or damaged corn'.[88] It is probable that the estate accounts did not include all the donations of landlords; fox-hunting and all its complications, for example, seems to have been kept separate from the affairs of the estate.

It was, however, the larger item of improvements that was most important in estate management. Before 1870 the law presumed that all permanent improvements such as drains, buildings, roads, and fences, even if made by the tenants, belonged to the landlord, unless they had been made with the landlord's permission and registered under the Landed Property (Ireland) Improvement Act, 1860.[89] The smooth progress, therefore, of agricultural improvement required landlords either to make improvements themselves or to pay their tenants for doing so. There was more to improvements, however, than agricultural innovation. They were the means by which landlords justified their existence, impressed their presence on the countryside, and enhanced their prestige. According to R. O. Pringle in 1872 the effects of good landlordism were actually visible: 'There is no one

---

[83] Archdale rentals and accounts (Counties Fermanagh and Tyrone) (PRONI, D704/50, p. 17); R. B. McDowell, *The Church of Ireland, 1869–1969* (London, 1975), 67, shows that the laity contributed £2 million in the eleven years after disestablishment. For Dean Ponsonby see George Birmingham, *The Bad Times* (London, 1908).
[84] W. H. Bradshaw, *Enniskillen Long Ago* (Dublin and Enniskillen, 1878), 48.
[85] St George rental and accounts (Counties Leitrim, Roscommon, Tipperary, and Waterford), 1854 (NLI, MS 4010).
[86] Powerscourt requests-book, 1850–2 (NLI, MS 16377, no. 616).
[87] Ranfurly rental and account (County Tyrone), 1861–2 (PRONI, D1932/2/5).
[88] Fitzwilliam memoranda book, 1860 (NLI, MS 4991, p. 60).
[89] 23 & 24 Vict., c. 153 (28 Aug. 1860).

who can see the tenantry on the Erne estates without being struck with the remarkably respectable appearance they present, whether at home or abroad.'[90] (Even after a century, what could be achieved by benevolent— if despotic—landlords is still visible in Caledon in County Tyrone, in Adare in County Limerick, and in Hillsborough in County Down.)

The estate accounts that survive show that Irish landlords spent something on improvements, even if these frequently included works such as the beautifying of demesnes that were not of much use to the tenants.[91] Houses and out-offices were built, land drained, roads constructed, and fences erected as in England and Scotland. H. G. Murray Stewart spent heavily on roads, for example, on his remote estate in County Donegal in the 1850s and 1860s. Lord Dunraven borrowed £14,850 from the board of works for building and drainage between 1858 and 1871, or the equivalent of 10 per cent of his rental.[92] Lord Caledon set up a system for pumping water to Caledon, and subscribed £130 to a new chapel as well as building the 'very neat' labourers' cottages that still adorn the village.[93]

Some idea of the variety of improvements on an Irish estate can be got from the Erne accounts for the County Fermanagh estate. Money was given for street lamps in Lisnaskea, houses in Enniskillen, the courthouse in Derrylin, the 'old' forge at Teemore, the school house at Callow Hill, planting trees on an island in Killymackan lough, building three buttresses for the wall at Lisnaskea church, for half the purchase price of a bull for the tenants on the Knockninny division of the estate, and for thatching the widow McManus's house at Molly.[94] Other landlords kept pedigree stock. According to R. O. Pringle the Herefords kept by the Reynells of Killynon had improved neighbouring stock;[95] a Kilkenny landlord, Revd Waller de Montmorency, allowed each tenant the free service of two cows, and until the beginning of the land war his tenants 'seemed very anxious to take advantage of my bull'.[96]

Tenants were harangued at agricultural shows, invited to compete for prizes for good cultivation, and urged to farm better by precept and

---

[90] R. O. Pringle, 'A Review of Irish Agriculture', *Journal of the Royal Agricultural Society*, 2nd ser. 8 (1872), 36.

[91] See below, App. 18; see also *Poor Law Inspectors' Reports, 1870*; for improvements on County Cork estates, see Donnelly, *Land and People of Cork*, 165–9; see also Robert Brian MacCarthy, *The Trinity College Estates, 1800–1923: Corporate Management in an Age of Reform*, (Dundalk, 1992), 197.

[92] Dunraven papers (PRONI, D3196/F/17/8, 39); Dunraven also converted a part of the ruined Trinitarian abbey at Adare into a convent for the Sisters of Mercy (Sheehy, *Rediscovery of Ireland's Past*, 61). [93] Dunraven papers (PRONI, D3196/F/17/22).

[94] Erne accounts (County Fermanagh), 1858–98 (PRONI, D1939/9/1–3).

[95] Pringle, 'A Review of Irish Agriculture', 5.

[96] *Cowper Comm., Minutes of Evidence*, 769; for Lord Gosford's bull 'Wild Chieftain' see Gosford valuations and surveys (PRONI, D1606/12/14).

example. In the Dunraven papers, for example, there is a leaflet explaining 'how to keep a cow and pig upon an acre of land'; the cow was 'never' to be let out of its house, not one foot of land was to be kept under pasture, and the land was to be dug, not ploughed.[97] Some of the largest landlords kept agriculturists to advise tenants. R. O. Pringle described the work of the agriculturist on the Gosford estate, who 'lived amongst the tenantry, went about among them from day to day, talked to them familiarly as they worked in their fields, and discussed the operations they were engaged upon'.[98] Landlords also supplied building materials free to tenants who would do the building themselves. On the Fitzwilliam and Powerscourt estates timber and slates were provided, and Sir George Hodson gave iron gates as well as timber and slates.[99] Some landlords gave 'allowances' to tenants, that is, deductions from their rents to cover the cost of improvements they had made on their own initiative. Between 1842 and 1872 Lord Dufferin 'set off' nearly £10,000 of arrears against tenants' improvements.[100] In 1861–2 Lord Erne allowed £564. 7s. 3d. to tenants whose lands had been flooded by Lough Erne.[101] Lord Ashtown's agent allowed a tenant £3 for keeping a hotel 'to his lordship's satisfaction'.[102]

The table below[103] shows that about 11 per cent was spent on improvements and subscriptions. At first sight this is impressive, especially when it is remembered that Irish landlords were accused of spending nothing. The figure of 11 per cent, however, is probably higher than what was spent on most estates. It includes the very high figure of 27 per cent on the Murray Stewart estate; if this estate is left out, the average falls to 9 per cent. The estates in this table were large, and six of them belonged to peers; they were, in fact, the sort of estates where high expenditure on improvements was most likely to occur. On the Knox estate in County Roscommon, which was small, only trifling sums were spent on improvements or charity: 10s. in 1870, for example, to buy drinks for the tenants.[104] (It is significant that only 8 per cent was spent on the Erne estate, for Lord Erne was one of the best known 'improvers' of his day.) If these estates represent the higher rates of spending on improvements, it is certain

---

[97] Dunraven papers (ibid. D3196/F/17/27).

[98] Pringle, 'A Review of Irish Agriculture', 34; see above, pp. 112–13 for an agriculturist who was dismissed for drunkenness.

[99] See e.g. Powerscourt requests-book, 1852–6 (NLI, MS 16378, nos. 778, 782, 796, 868, 1088, 1304); see also *Poor Law Inspectors' Reports, 1870*.

[100] Dufferin's schedule of expenditure (PRONI, D1071A/136/3).

[101] Erne accounts (County Fermanagh) (ibid. D1939/9/1).

[102] Ashtown rental and account, 1865–6 (NLI, MS 1767).

[103] See below, App. 18; see also Lindsay Proudfoot, 'The Management of a Great Estate: Patronage, Income and Expenditure on the Duke of Devonshire's Irish property', *Ir. Econ. & Soc. Hist.* 13 (1986), 39, which shows that the Duke of Devonshire spent 11.6% of receipts on improvements.

[104] Knox rentals and accounts, 1870 (NLI, MS 3178).

that the average for all estates was lower—probably as low as 4 or 5 per cent.[105]

Irish landlords were often compared unfavourably with British landlords. Lord Cowper, who presided over a royal commission in 1886, believed that he could count on his fingers the number of Irish landlords who spent on improvements.[106] Between 1856 and 1875 the duke of Bedford spent almost £240,000 on repairs and permanent improvements on his Thorney estate, or 34 per cent of his rents. On his Bedfordshire and Buckinghamshire estate, the percentage was even higher—43 per cent in the same period. The dukes of Bedford were very rich; their rents from their agricultural estates were almost £80,000 a year; in addition, they owned some of the most valuable property in central London.[107] It is not realistic to compare ordinary Irish landlords with such leviathans as the duke of Bedford, the marquis of Westminster, and the duke of Devonshire. John Steadyman of Wearywork Hall, who was John Bateman's 'typical £5,000 a-year squire', spent only 14 per cent of his rents on repairs, drainage, local charities, and subscriptions to the Cidershire Foxhounds and the Boggymore Harriers.[108] (Only 8 per cent was spent on what were purely agricultural improvements.) R. J. Thompson, who was perhaps as good a guide as Bateman, put expenditure on improvements on English estates rather higher—at 27 per cent of receipts before 1881.[109] This figure might, however, be too high, for Richard Perren in a study of agricultural investment in England in the late nineteenth century implied an expenditure of about 20 per cent.[110] Whether or not Thompson's estimate is preferred to Perren's, or even to Bateman's, does not matter when comparing England and Ireland, for it is clear that much less was spent in Ireland. It is also clear that there was as much variety in England as in Ireland: the difference between the duke of Bedford and John Steadyman was as great as that between the Grocers' Company and Lord Ranfurly.[111]

[105] Cf Cormac Ó Gráda, 'The Investment Behaviour of Irish Landlords, 1850–75: Some Preliminary Findings', *Agric. Hist. Rev.* 23: 2 (1975), 151–3, where it is estimated that from 3% to 5% of income was spent on improvements; the Irish Land Committee's estimate, which implied an annual rate of 5% between 1840 and 1880, was probably modestly self-flattering (*Bessborough Comm., Minutes of Evidence*, pt. ii, p. 129).

[106] Quoted in Pomfret, *Struggle for Land in Ire.*, 28, where *Fall of Feudalism*, 240 is given as the source.

[107] H. A. Russell, 11th duke of Bedford, *A Great Agricultural Estate, being the Story of the Origin and Administration of Woburn and Thorney* (London, 1897), 220–3; David Spring, *The English Landed Estate in the Nineteenth Century: Its Administration* (Baltimore, 1963), 41.   [108] Bateman, *Great Landowners* (1883), pp. xxiv–xxv.

[109] R. J. Thompson, 'An Inquiry into the Rent of Agricultural Land in England and Wales during the Nineteenth Century', *Journal of the Royal Statistical Society*, 70 (Dec. 1907), 603.

[110] Richard Perren, 'The Landlord and Agricultural Transformation, 1870–1900', *Agric. Hist. Rev.* 18 (1970), 41–2; see also Susanna Wade Martins, *A Great Estate at Work: The Holkham Estate and its Inhabitants in the Nineteenth Century* (Cambridge, 1980).

[111] See below, App. 18; Olive Robinson, 'The London Companies as Progressive Landlords', 114.

iv. Why Did Landlords not Spend More on Improvements?

Although Irish landlords spent something on improvements, their efforts appeared perfunctory. Plans for the systematic improvement of estates existed, but they were rare. In 1853 the firm of Brassington & Gale made such a plan for the Powercourt estate, but its implementation did not appear prominently in the Powerscourt requests-book.[112] There were no signs in the correspondence of William Wann that he was following systematically the plan drawn up thirty years before by William Greig.[113] Even where a landlord was resident and enthusiastic, progress could be slow. In 1854 Lord Dunraven began keeping 'a sort of memorandum book and also journal of what occurs on the Adare estate'. In 1855 a list of 'things to be done' was made, but little was done: of thirty-six things planned, only no. 27 was finished and only nos. 15, 21, 25, and 33 were even begun. 'Such', reflected Dunraven, 'is the exceeding slowness here and difficulty of getting through any work.'[114]

There were four possible reasons why Irish landlords spent little on improvements, but while these can be described, it is difficult to quantify their individual influence or even to assess the cumulative effect of their combined influence. First, the custom of entailing estates discouraged investment by life tenants whose successors might not even be members of their immediate families; secondly, landlords' indebtedness hampered their ability to spend—even if they had been willing; thirdly, the smallness of the holdings made improvement difficult; fourthly, Irish agriculture did not provide opportunities for a large expenditure.

The first of these may be disposed of easily. The custom of modifying the effects of primogeniture by making family settlements was common in Ireland, but remedies were provided, for the land improvement acts enabled the board of works to make loans to limited owners who could charge their estates with annuities to repay the loans. The landed property improvement act of 1860 went even further and allowed limited owners to charge their successors with part of the cost of improvements—regardless of the source of the money spent—and to grant 'improvement' leases of terms up to forty-one years and building leases up to ninety-nine years.[115] The existence of family settlements, therefore, whatever its effects on the ownership of estates, cannot be blamed for the low rate of spending on improvements.

---

[112] For an example of its implementation see Brassington & Gale's valuation of the Powerscourt estate, 1853 (NLI, MS 2740, p. 7) and Powerscourt requests-book, 1852–6 (ibid. MS 16378, nos. 1058, 1146).
[113] William Greig, *General Report on the Gosford Estate in County Armagh, 1821*, ed. with intro. by F. M. L. Thompson and David Tierney (Belfast, 1976).
[114] Dunraven papers (PRONI, D3196/F/17/21).
[115] De Moleyns, *Landowner's Guide* (1872), 390–415.

The effects of indebtedness are more difficult to assess. The heavily encumbered estates in the table below,[116] such as the Crofton and Inchiquin estates, spent something on improvements, and the Crofton estate spent more than others less encumbered. Nor does it seem that Irish landlords were endemically more indebted than British landlords, in spite of their reputation for improvidence. Both were subject to the same conventions in the provision of jointures and portions, and to the same temptations: extravagant building, lavish entertainment, gambling, and political ambition. David Cannadine's calculations of encumbrances on a group of large estates in Britain shows that about 25 per cent of rents was consumed by interest payments.[117] Even taking the highest estimate of Irish landlords' indebtedness, they do not seem to have been markedly more impecunious than their British neighbours.[118] In the absence of strong evidence showing that Irish landlords were more encumbered than British, indebtedness is hardly an explanation of the different rates of spending.

The smallness of Irish holdings appears at first a more promising explanation. In 1870 holdings in Great Britain were almost three times as large, on average, as those in Ireland.[119] A comparison of individual estates makes the contrast appear even more sharply: Lord Garvagh's estate in County Londonderry had about 400 tenants; an estate in Wiltshire, yielding a slightly smaller rental, had only thirty-nine tenants.[120] There was an intellectual prejudice in favour of large farms and against small ones. Consolidation was supposed to precede investment in buildings. 'Experience points to one main principle of action,' wrote Bailey Denton, whose book on farm buildings is striking evidence of the lavishness of estate architecture in nineteenth-century Britain: *'no farm should be so small that it cannot support a house above the pretensions of a bailiff's cottage.'*[121] The plans in Denton's book make this point emphatically: Earl Spencer spent £900 on buildings on a farm of 500 acres at Boddington in Northamptonshire; the duke of Bedford spent £3,500 on a farm of 500 acres at Thorney in Cambridgeshire. (There were plans for 'small' farms, but even they were not comparable with most Irish farms: buildings for a small dairy farm of 75 acres at Broxton cost £1,430.) Irish landlords could not have built on this scale on small holdings. Spending £100 on each

---

[116] See below, App. 18.
[117] David Cannadine, 'Aristocratic Indebtedness in the Nineteenth Century: A Restatement', *Econ. Hist. Rev.* 2nd ser. 33: 4 (1980), 569–73.
[118] See below, App. 18.
[119] *Agricultural Returns of Great Britain, with Abstract Returns for the United Kingdom, British Possessions, and Foreign Countries 1870*, pp. 20–1 [C 223], HC 1870, lxviii. 382–3.
[120] Garvagh rentals (County Londonderry), 1846–81 (PRONI, D1550/20A); *Particulars of Expenditure and Outgoings on Certain Estates in Great Britain and Farm Accounts Reprinted from the Reports of the Assistant Commissioners*, pp. 24–5 [C 8125], HC 1896, xvi. 492–3. [121] Denton, *Farm Homesteads of England*, 103.

holding on the Garvagh estate would have almost equalled the fee simple value of the whole estate. Since Irish landlords could not spend on buildings without simultaneously spending ruinously, they were deprived—or relieved—of one of the most expensive forms of estate expenditure. (The board of works shared the prejudices of the time, for they refused to advance money for buildings on farms whose rents were less than £50.)[122]

The nature of Irish agricultural production also limited the amounts that could be spent, for it offered few opportunities for expensive improvements. The mild winters and luxuriant pasture in Ireland, for example, meant that the house-feeding of livestock was unusual, so there was not the same need for outbuildings as in parts of Britain. The inferior quality of livestock, the slovenly cultivation practised by Irish farmers, bad fences, ruinous gates, and filthy houses gave landlords many opportunities for haranguing their tenants. When Lord Erne visited his Mayo estate in 1850 he was 'struck with that absence of cleanliness and comfort, which [are] so necessary to health and happiness'; he warned his tenants not to keep dung outside their doors or pigs inside, and left them 'much gratified' by his advice.[123] Advice, however, was cheap.

Irish landlords' failure to invest in improvements is not easily explained. Causes can be discerned and discussed, but in the end no simple, single explanation emerges. The smallness of holdings, for example, was obviously important—if only as an excuse—but it is not a complete explanation. One of the estates with the highest level of spending was the Murray Stewart estate, which had very small holdings—about 1,500 paying a rental of only £7,000.[124] Likewise, the level of spending on the London companies' estates was high, although it was argued that the smallness of their holdings was an impediment to investment.[125] Even if small holdings were not an impediment, large holdings in Ireland were not necessarily an incentive. On the Inchiquin estate in County Clare there were many substantial holdings, but Lord Inchiquin's spending was modest. There were about 500 tenants on Inchiquin's estate, which made it different from a British estate, but £150 spent on each holding—enough to build a good house with three bedrooms—would have taken about 20 per cent of rent receipts between 1851 and 1881. No British landlord could have built houses for his tenants 'if he had had to build a few dozen houses on 200 or 300 acres';[126] but

---

[122] Samuelson, *Land and tenantry of Ire.*, 20-1.
[123] *Irish Farmers' Gazette*, 22 June 1850, p. 301; see also Hoppen, *Elections, Politics, and Society*, 132.
[124] W. E. Vaughan, 'An Assessment of the Economic Performance of Irish Landlords, 1851-81', in F. S. L. Lyons and R. A. J. Hawkins (eds.), *Ireland under the Union: Varieties of Tension. Essays in Honour of T. W. Moody* (Oxford, 1980), 193.
[125] Olive Robinson, 'The London Companies as Progressive Landlords', 115.
[126] B. L. Solow, *The Irish Land Question and the Irish Economy, 1870-1903* (Cambridge, Mass., 1971), 80; see also 77-85 for a discussion of improvements.

few Irish landlords had holdings so small; even on the Murray Stewart estate the landlord would not have had to build on this scale.

There were in fact opportunities on Irish estates that were promising. Between 1847 and 1880 only 270,000 acres were drained by means of loans from the board of works, at an average cost of £7 an acre.[127] If Irish landlords had spent £1 million a year, or less than 10 per cent of their rents between 1851 and 1880, over 4 million acres could have been drained, or 20 per cent of the whole surface of the country. (In 1870 Thomas Baldwin estimated that 6 million acres needed to be drained; this could have been done in thirty years by spending about £1.5 million a year.[128]) No Irish landlord could have built the elaborate imitations of Balmoral that were fashionable as farmhouses on some of the great estates in Britain in the 1850s; but the more humble house-building carried on in Britain would not have been impossible in Ireland, or even extravagant. Denton, for example, produced designs for houses with three bedrooms, which could be built for £150, and which were better than most farmers' houses in Ireland.[129] If landlords had spent £1 million a year, or less than 10 per cent of their rents between 1851 and 1880, they could have built 200,000 of Denton's houses, or enough for 40 per cent of their tenants. If, however, landlords had chosen to build the less commodious houses designed by Henry Stephens, which cost only £70 each, 430,000 could have been built—enough to rehouse most tenants.[130]

Any of the alternative methods of increasing rents, described below, would have produced enough extra income to have paid for the replacement of many of the houses in rural Ireland.[131] If landlords built houses that were the average of Denton's and Stephens's, rents tied to agricultural output would have provided enough extra income to have built almost 300,000; rents based on the TCD leasing powers act would have provided enough for over 600,000 new houses! (The TCD system would have produced £66.9 million of extra rent, which divided among Denton's and Stephens's houses, and drainage, would have built 148,000 of the former, 318,000 of the latter, and drained 3.1 million acres. In other words nearly every tenant in Ireland would have had a new house built by his landlord and part of his farm drained in the thirty years after the famine.) Such an expenditure would have transformed the appearance of the countryside, increased the productive capacity of much of the land, and assisted powerfully in bettering the living conditions of tenants. That landlords failed to do this can be only partly explained by the obstacles in their way.

---

[127] Cormac Ó Gráda, 'The Investment Behaviour of Irish Landlords, 1850–75: Some Preliminary Findings', *Agric. Hist. Rev.* 23: 2 (1975), 146–7.
[128] Thomas Baldwin, *Handy Book of Small Farm Management* (Dublin, [1871]), 182; above, pp. 83–4.   [129] Denton, *Farm Homesteads of England*, 113.
[130] Stephens, *Book of the Farm*, ii. 546.   [131] See below, App. 13.

Their failure can be just as plausibly traced to their inability to see the opportunities on their estates and the benefits that such a policy would bring.

They could have imitated British landlords even on estates that were very unlike British estates. But much better than imitation would have been adaptation; they should have developed a distinctive style of management to cope with small holdings and wet land. Estates were centres of social authority and reservoirs of finance; landlords could have mitigated the disadvantages of small holdings and imposed order on the confusion inherent in such a system. By financing and supervising the grading of butter, for example, they could have prevented the losses suffered by Irish butter-producers in the 1870s. By keeping teams of horses for hire, or by providing agricultural machinery, they could have helped tenants to get rid of one of the worst diseconomies of scale on small farms—the keeping of too many horses. They could, too, have advanced loans on easy terms to tenants, or at least on easier terms than the banks or shopkeepers. Most important of all, perhaps, they could have run insurance schemes for livestock, or even for securing rents in bad years. Nothing would have been more useful for small livestock producers, whose futures could be threatened by the death of a single animal, than insurance.

There were landlords who did some of these things. The Grocers' Company lent money to tenants for improvements at 5 per cent.[132] Lord Erne provided agricultural machinery for his Fermanagh tenants.[133] Edward and Charles Curling ran the Newcastle Mutual Assurance Club, which insured horses and cows for a premium of 6d. in the pound.[134] These imaginative ventures were rare: there were few agricultural machines in Ireland (only 389 steam threshing-machines in 1865);[135] loan societies, the institutional form that investment might have taken, were declining after 1850;[136] insurance schemes were very rare indeed.

Did Irish landlords miss a great opportunity? It is arguable that they were wise not to invest huge sums in their estates because the returns on agricultural investment were small; even the tenants themselves seem to have been aware 'that no ordinary agricultural improvements would yield 5 per cent in perpetuity'.[137] There were, however, reasons that should have transcended considerations of the actual return on investments. First, only landlords could do much that had to be done on farms. Drainage, farm roads, and fences, where the area of operation was larger than the individual

---

[132] Olive Robinson, 'The London Companies as Progressive Landlords', 108.
[133] *Irish Farmers' Gazette*, 2 Oct. 1858, p. 729.
[134] Dunraven papers (PRONI, D3196/F/17/35); see also PRO, HO 45/6472.
[135] *Agricultural Statistics, Ire.*, 1875, p. 10 [C 1568], HC 1876, lxxviii. 422.
[136] *Forty-Third Annual Report of the Commissioners of the Loan Fund Board of Ireland*, p. 4 [C 2898], HC 1881, xxviii. 556.
[137] Olive Robinson, 'The London Companies as Progressive Landlords', 108.

farm, often needed the force of the landlord to overcome awkward farmers. As Lord Leitrim pointed out to Dufferin, a small tenant, even if he owned his holding, 'cannot make a road up to his house, or obtain an outfall for his drains, or accomplish any one thing which should extend beyond the four corners of his holding without the assistance of some superior power'.[138] When Colonel Smith of Baltiboys in County Wicklow wanted to drain a farm to give relief in 1848, the tenant on whose farm the work was to begin 'refuses to let his farm be drained, refused [sic] to let the colonel's carts cross his fields, refuses to let our gangs of drainers set foot upon his fields to cross to Cairn's land'.[139] In the end the landlord got his way by threatening the trouble-maker with the law. Without the landlord's power, or the existence of a powerful and intrusive state, local initiative was likely to be thwarted.

Secondly, estate expenditure was a means of controlling tenants that was much less obnoxious than threats of eviction. William Wann, for example, was quite clear about the use of landlords' largesse; 'in giving the lime and seeds and such like I have always tried to assist in the *first* place the *honest industrious tenant who punctually settles his accounts*'.[140] (There is also the story in Trench's *Realities of Irish Life* of the conspirators, one of whom wanted Trench's assassination postponed until he had got the gates that Trench had promised him.[141]) The use of estate expenditure as a means of control, however, went much further than merely making one or two recalcitrants pay their rents. Estate management after the famine was dominated by one single characteristic, which was the virtual one-way flow of money from tenants to landlords. That this flow was not as great as it might have been, that it was not for the most part resisted by those who sustained it, did not alter the fact that the whole system was vulnerable. If a quarter of the rents had gone back to the tenants in the form of loans, gifts, new houses, and drained fields, the tenants would have been inextricably tied to their landlords. Money spent by landlords would have had more social effects than if it were simply left in the tenants' pockets as uncollected rent. Only estate expenditure could have improved the conditions of the smallest tenants. While they shared in the increased prices like other farmers, their incomes remained low. An annual expenditure of £2 million a year would have generated a demand for their labour, which could have been organized to occur at times of the year when work on farms was scarce. Estate expenditure would have transformed the appearance of the countryside, thatched cottages would have been replaced by

---

[138] Leitrim to Dufferin, 11 Apr. 1868 (PRONI, D1071H/B/C).
[139] David Thomson and Moyra McGusty (eds.), *The Irish Journals of Elizabeth Smith, 1840–1850* (Oxford, 1980), 183.
[140] Wann's letter-book, 24 Apr. 1863 (PRONI, D1606/5/4, p. 185).
[141] Trench, *Realities of Ir. Life*, 197.

slated houses, and weeds and rushes might have been less prevalent. A visually transformed landscape would have separated the Ireland of the 1870s from the ravages of the 1840s. Uneconomic estate spending was or should have been the tax that landed property paid for its continued existence. In a society where private property was sacred but landed privilege suspect, landed wealth was uncomfortably visible, eminently desirable, and highly concentrated. This was not only an Irish phenomenon, for criticism of landlordism was a deeply ingrained habit in Britain. High spending on improvements was, therefore, the propitiatory offering required of a class that was not only privileged, but aware of its privileges.

v. Landlords' Indebtedness

In 1876 Wann reflected sadly that 'Lord Gosford's disposition to be generous is crippled by his means.'[142] Earlier in the year he had drawn up a list of his employer's encumbrances, amounting to £155,161 and consuming £6,657, or about 40 per cent, of the rents.[143] Of the nine estates below,[144] five paid some interest. The Crofton and Inchiquin estates paid considerable sums; the Clonbrock and Murray Stewart estates paid small sums. The ruinous mansion, with its succession of gamblers and drunkards, finally brought to bankruptcy by crafty attorneys, was a familiar picture. The encumbered estates court did not solve the problem for writers of fiction, whatever it did for landlords, for Castle Rackrent was succeeded by the big house of Inver, and Attorney Quirk by old John Weldon. Irish debts were contracted with *élan* and borne with equanimity. The Dillons of Ballyhaunis, 'who had three thousand a-year, and spent six ... were a really delightful family,—three daughters and four sons, all unmarried and up to anything', seemed a permanent part of rural life.[145]

It is difficult to measure the indebtedness of Irish landlords. On the group of estates below, the amount of rent receipts spent on interest ranged from nothing to 39 per cent; on average it was about 17 per cent of rent receipts on those estates charged with interest, although it must be admitted that this is an average of doubtful import. For one thing not all interest payments were included in the estate accounts, although it was regarded as good management practice for the agent to deal with all interest payments.[146] When Lord Inchiquin died in 1900 his personal debts, which were not secured on the estate, amounted to £31,000, of which £12,112 was an 'overdraft and outstanding promissory notes' at the Provincial

---

[142] Gosford letter-book, 17 Nov. 1876 (PRONI, D1606/5A/4, p. 113).
[143] Ibid., p. 76 (memorandum of Lord Gosford's encumbrances, 1876).
[144] See below, App. 18.
[145] For English spendthrifts see David Cannadine, 'Aristocratic Indebtedness in the Nineteenth Century', *Econ. Hist. Rev.* 2nd ser. 33: 4 (1980), 569–73.
[146] De Moleyns, *Landowner's Guide* (1872), 384.

Bank.[147] If the estate accounts and other sources such as mortgages do not give the full picture of indebtedness, the rentals do not give a full picture of incomes, for rents may have been supplemented by interest from mortgages (a very high proportion of mortgagees were landlords), from farming profits, and from the terminal magic of compound interest realized through life insurances. (In the 1860s a single premium of £33. 17s. 11d., paid at the age of 20, yielded an assurance of £100.[148])

Should the figure of 17 per cent be increased? Professor L. P. Curtis in a fascinating and detailed article, based on records of over 200 estates, produced a higher figure: 27 per cent of the tenement valuation as 'the minimal state of indebtedness'.[149] Before increasing the figure of 17 per cent, however, several things must be considered. First, if Professor Curtis's figure were based on rent receipts before 1879 and not on valuation, his figure would fall, possibly as low as 23 per cent. Secondly, most of Professor Curtis's examples of indebtedness come from the period after 1879, when it is reasonable to assume that indebtedness was higher than in the period before 1879. Thirdly, Professor Curtis used the land commission's records to produce a lower estimate, 16 per cent, which gives some strength to a figure lower than 27 per cent. On the whole, therefore, while the figure of 17 per cent is low, it is doubtful if it should be increased to 27 per cent. The differences between the two figures can probably be best reconciled by splitting the difference and taking 22 per cent of rent receipts as the average of interest payments.

What were the causes of indebtedness? Dot Blake of Handicap Lodge, unlike his friend Lord Ballindine, did not need to borrow money because he did not have an estate, a mother, a pack of hounds, or a title; in any case, as he told Lord Ballindine, who suffered from all of these burdens, 'No one would lend me money, if I asked it.'[150] (More to the point, perhaps, than Dot's freedom from burdens was the fact that 'he took very good care that he was never charged a guinea, where a guinea was not necessary; and that he got a guinea's worth for every guinea laid out.') To a large extent debt was inseparable from landed property, for its accumulation was either a result of tempering primogeniture by providing for other members of the family, or an alternative to selling land.

The main family charges were jointures for widows and portions for

---

[147] List of debts of the late Rt. Hon. Edward Donogh O'Brien, Baron Inchiquin, up to and ending 8 Apr. 1900, in Inchiquin rental, 1900 (NLI, MS 14577).

[148] *Chambers's Encyclopedia* (London, 1868), v. 601.

[149] L. P. Curtis, jun, 'Incumbered Wealth: Landed Indebtedness in Post-Famine Ireland', AHR 85: 2 (Apr. 1980), 332–67. Professor Curtis relied on three sources: mortgage ledgers of the Representative Church Body, covering 120 estates, which produced an average of 27.4% (p. 344); the rentals of ten estates, which produced 27% (p. 356); the records of the land commission, which produced 16.3% (p. 350).

[150] Anthony Trollope, *The Kellys and the O'Kellys* (London, 1929), 43, 118.

younger children. On the Knox estate in County Roscommon, Mrs Knox's jointure took half the rent in the 1850s.[151] Between 1851 and 1856 the dowager Lady O'Brien received £18,252 from the Inchiquin estate, or the equivalent of 28 per cent of its rents for six years. (Her daughter-in-law, who was widowed in 1872, received only £1,000 a year.) Younger children were not so well provided for. When Lord Gosford married Lady Theodosia Brabazon in 1832, the estate was charged with £10,000 'in case there should be two or more children ... on the body of the said Lady Theodosia Brabazon ... other than and besides an eldest or only son'.[152] There were five younger children—a son and four daughters—to share the income from the £10,000, which was £400 in 1876—not a lavish provision for the younger children of an earl. (The younger son did rather better than his sisters, for he also received the income of a sum of £6,000 as well as his share of the £400.) When Lady Gosford was widowed in 1864 her jointure was £1,500, or less than 10 per cent of the rental;[153] her jointure and the portions of the younger children accounted for only 13 per cent of the rental, which was much less proportionately than John Steadyman's relations received, for his mother, two maiden aunts, four sisters, and a disreputable brother, Wildbore, took up 36 per cent of his income.[154]

Although family charges were ubiquitous, their importance should not be exaggerated. First, the largest of them, jointures, did not last for ever, in spite of the fabled longevity of dowagers. Secondly, jointures and portions were usually nicely adjusted to benefits received when a marriage contract was made: the jointure of one period was merely the delayed recognition of a dowry received earlier. The whole system was not so much a drain on landed incomes, but a carefully planned lottery that rearranged incomes within the landed class.[155]

More important as a cause of indebtedness was the extravagance that was almost intrinsically part of the ownership of land. The building and maintenance of large houses—Crom annually consumed 20 per cent of Lord Erne's Fermanagh rents—was only the most visible and impressive of the expenses associated with landed grandeur. Fox-hunting, especially keeping a pack of hounds, and the preservation of game were traditional extravagances; but the nineteenth century produced new ones, such as yachting. Lord Dufferin, who had been warned in 1858 by Sir James

---

[151] Knox rentals and accounts, 1849–86 (NLI, MS 3178).
[152] Registry of Deeds, 1832, dccclxxxix. 439; ibid. 1862/9/22.
[153] Ibid. 1864/30/68; Gosford letter-book, 1876 (PRONI, D1606/5A/4, p. 76).
[154] Bateman, *Great Landowners* (1883), p. xxiv.
[155] For a slightly different view see Curtis, 'Incumbered Wealth', 338: 'family charges, especially portions for younger children, accounted for the heaviest incumbrances on many estates. Providing capital sums for the children of landed families tied up precious assets at a time when these might have been gainfully invested in commercial or industrial enterprizes yielding 4 or 5 per cent.'

Graham that 'game, next to love and money, is the most futile source of laurels in this world', spent, as mentioned above, £26,000 in twenty years on yachts.[156] Probably the worst of the apparently respectable threats to landed wealth was a political career. In the Abercorn accounts there are records of £9,000 paid to Lord Claud John Hamilton in 1866 and 1868-9, of which £3,384 was election expenses for the Derry election of 1865, when Lord Claud polled 379 votes and won the seat.[157]

Dot Blake stayed out of debt because nobody would lend him money; but landlords seem to have had little difficulty in borrowing. The ease with which Lord Gosford ran into debt showed the ready availability of money, some of which came from other landed families and some from financial institutions and businessmen.[158] Mortgages were an attractive investment, easily enough foreclosed on, especially after 1849, and often the first step on the road to acquiring landed property. Dr Thomas Cuming, who lent Lord Gosford £8,730 in 1854 and another £10,000 in 1877,[159] was in the habit of telling Wann when they met in Armagh that he hoped his payday was far off.[160] Institutions appear among mortgagees, although less frequently than one might expect. In 1880 the Standard Life Assurance Co. lent Lord Gosford £48,000, and the Roman Catholic authorities were not unwilling to lend to landlords even in the 1880s.[161] When the Irish church, the Presbyterian church, and St Patrick's College, Maynooth, were disendowed, much of their compensation money was put into mortgages. In the 1870s the Church of Ireland advanced £3.5 million to Irish landlords, the Presbyterians £121,000, and St Patrick's £314,670.[162]

The effects of indebtedness, especially of a moderate burden taking up about 20 per cent of rent receipts, are difficult to assess. Under the encumbered estates act, a creditor could petition for a sale when encumbrances exceeded half of the estate's net rent, which was the annual rent less taxes and fixed charges.[163] The passing of old families under the burden of debt, especially in the early 1850s when so much was changing, was disturbing. A new landlord who 'knew not Joseph', as a worried tenant told the Devon commission, was a worrying prospect, even when he was not a grasping speculator. (This tenant, memorable for his nice use of biblical language, had in fact nothing to fear when Lord Mountcashell's Antrim

---

[156] Graham to Dufferin, 25 Aug. 1858 (PRONI, Mic. 22, reel 2, vol. ix); Dufferin's schedule of expenditure (ibid. D1071A/136/3).

[157] Abercorn annual accounts, 1866 (PRONI, D623/C/8/47); Walker, *Election Results, 1801-1922*, 103; see also Hoppen, *Elections, Politics, and Society*, 84.

[158] For Adair's ability to raise money see Vaughan, *Derryveagh Evictions*, 52-4.

[159] Registry of Deeds, 1854/13/160, 1877/45/140; Gosford letter-book, 9 May 1877 (PRONI, D1606/5A/4, p. 156). [160] Ibid., p. 125 (18 Jan. 1877).

[161] Registry of Deeds, 1880/34/138; Emmet Larkin, 'Economic Growth, Capital Investment, and the Roman Catholic Church in Nineteenth-Century Ireland', *AHR* 72: 3 (Apr. 1967), 869. [162] Curtis, 'Incumbered wealth', 341, 360 n. 72.

[163] 12 & 13 Vict., c. 77, s. xxii.

estate was broken up, for he was given a lease in 1846.)[164] If debts led to the breaking up of estates, it is also true that family settlements and mortgages kept estates together for much longer than might have been possible under a 'free' system of landownership. It is possible that the need to pay interest limited what was available for improvements. This, however, is not clear. On the Crofton estate in the 1850s and 1860s spending on improvements seems to have gone down as interest increased; but spending on improvements remained high, compared with estates where interest was lower.[165]

The effects of indebtedness, therefore, on relations between landlords and tenants were not predictable. One thing is clear, however, any estate expenditure that could not be reduced when rents fell made estate management difficult. On the nine estates below the average net income was about 40 per cent, and even this was probably higher than average. Lord Belmore told a select committee in 1882 that his estate was not encumbered except with his mother's jointure, that he got only a fifth of his rents into his own pocket, and that a rent reduction of 20 per cent would leave him with nothing.[166] Landlords and agents were anxious, therefore, to keep rents steady; hence, possibly, the rather conservative management of rents, the thoroughness with which rents were collected, and the fear of anything like a combination against rents. Hence too, the difficulty of giving abatements when tenants wanted them.

Wann's difficulties in the 1870s in managing Gosford's large debts show some of these problems. Part of the debt of £156,000 was inherited by the fourth earl when he succeeded in 1864: about £53,000 can be traced to the early 1830s when the Graham estate was bought; and a further £16,000 was a family charge.[167] These and other mortgages in the 1860s were not crushing, taking about 25 per cent of rents. Indeed the prospects of the estate had improved greatly in the preceding half century. In 1817 57 per cent of the rents had been taken up by interest payments,[168] but the second earl's brilliant marriage to an heiress had not only enabled £80,000 to be spent on building Gosford Castle, but had also enabled mortgages to be redeemed by the sale of her English estates.[169] Prudence would have suggested, however, that some effort should have been made to reduce the debt inherited by the fourth earl in 1864. Instead, between 1864 and 1876 £60,000 was added to the inherited debt by borrowing from the bankers Coutts & Co. The new earl went on a long tour of India and the agent

[164] National Archives: encumbered estates rentals, iii. 34; *Devon Comm., Minutes of Evidence*, pt. i, p. 565. [165] See below, App. 18.
[166] *Lords' Sel. Comm. on the 1881 Land Act, Second Report*, 49.
[167] Registry of Deeds, 1841/15/252; 1842/3/143; 1847/9/3; 1852/4/90; 14/94; 1854/13/160; 14/107; 1857/5/288; 1858/2/191; 1861/24/284; 1862/9/22; 1864/30/68; 40/49.
[168] Curtis, 'Incumbered wealth', 337 n. 19.
[169] Bence-Jones, *Ir. Country Houses*, 143; Registry of Deeds, 1864/40/49.

did not hear from him for months; he bought a yacht and took to gambling. The exalted rank of some of his gaming friends did nothing to reassure Wann, who was anxious in 1873 to deny a report 'of the prince of Wales having been successful in a gambling transaction with Lord Gosford'.[170] (Four years later Wann returned to the subject in a letter to Dr Cuming, from whom he was seeking a loan for Lord Gosford: 'the old silly reports' about Lord Gosford were revived but he was 'thoroughly satisfied there is not the shadow of foundation for it', and he denied that his employer had lost £1,000 'in a gambling transaction with a gent in this county'.[171]

Whatever the causes of Gosford's indebtedness, two things are clear from the estate correspondence: first, in nine years from 1864 to 1873 he borrowed a sum that was the equivalent of half the fee simple value of the Cavan estate; secondly, it was done not only quickly, but also with a sort of nonchalance. Wann was informed, but only perfunctorily: in 1871 Gosford wrote to say that he had just borrowed 'a few thousand pounds from Coutts & Co. and had given them security for it and this he will pay off himself by degrees'.[172]

What were the problems of managing such a debt? Wann was able to use the Ulster Bank, in which his brother was employed, to get money either for interest payments that occurred at times of the year when money was short, or for sudden demands from Gosford. In August 1872, he got £2,000 to pay off a claim 'which he did not just expect'.[173] The Ulster Bank was accommodating as long as rents came in regularly. In 1879 and 1880, however, arrears amounted to 10 per cent of rents and the overdraft grew: in August 1880 Wann's son and successor asked for £3,000, but had to ask for £4,000 a few days later. The bank, however, wanted security and suggested a life insurance policy or the title deeds of part of the estate.[174] The marquis of Huntly guaranteed the overdraft and in the following year, 1881, Gosford's father-in-law, the duke of Manchester, guaranteed a larger overdraft of £5,000.[175] Some months later another guarantor had to be found to an additional £2,500.[176] (This overdraft, moreover, was necessary in spite of the fact that Gosford had borrowed £48,000 from the Standard Life Assurance Co. in 1880.[177]) The crisis of 1879–81 was a serious one for landlords; but even a less serious crisis could have caused trouble for Gosford: When a bad harvest made arrears inevitable in 1872, Wann warned Gosford that for the first time he 'felt really uneasy as to financial

---

[170] Gosford letter-book, 6 Apr. 1873 (PRONI, D1606/5A/3, p. 356).
[171] Ibid. 4, p. 177 (16 Aug. 1877).   [172] Ibid. 3, p. 280 (8 Aug. 1871).
[173] Ibid., p. 325 (23 Aug. 1872).
[174] Wann's letter-book, 14, 19 Aug. 1880 (PRONI, D1606/5/5, p. 351).
[175] Ibid. 5, p. 355 (16 Sept. 1880); 6, p. 32 (29 July 1881).
[176] Ibid. 6, p. 36 (20 Sept. 1881).   [177] Registry of Deeds, 1880/34/138.

affairs': Lady Gosford's jointure was in arrears and 'if a limit is not made it will be perfectly impossible to go on'.[178]

Another problem was that a single creditor could cause a crisis by demanding repayment of a loan. When interest payments had passed about 40 per cent of receipts, inability to pay off even one mortgagee could precipitate a forced sale of part or even the whole of an estate in the landed estates court. In 1877 such a crisis occurred. A mortgage of £10,000 created in 1829 had passed to Robert Dundas of Arniston. Wann wrote anxiously to Lord Gosford's solicitor: 'Today a letter from Messrs Andersons, agents to Mr Dundas, which is of a startling nature, threatens to bring the Armagh estate into the market if Mr Dundas is not immediately paid his claim.'[179] Gosford was lucky on this occasion for Wann was able to transfer the mortgage from Dundas to Dr Cuming.[180] There was also the problem that as mortgages accumulated the cost of getting more seems to have increased: Coutts & Co. asked for 5 per cent on their third advance to Lord Gosford (£10,200) when they had been satisfied with 4 per cent on their first two advances (£45,000).[181] Even mortgagees of long standing might from time to time try to increase their interest rates. In 1875, for example, the holders of a mortgage of £14,000 tried to increase their rate of interest from 4 to 4½ per cent.[182] Of all the problems, however, the most intractable was the problem of controlling their cause. Lord Gosford's financial enterprise threatened on one occasion at least to go further than borrowing. In 1872 Wann warned him against 'showing all your private affairs to perhaps a stranger, and to me it *sounds odd* that he tells you *not to mention the matter to your solicitor*, a gentleman who has honourably, I have no doubt, acted for your family over fifty years and who has all your family papers'.[183]

In the mid-1870s the problem of managing Lord Gosford's debt was partially solved by the sale of the Cavan estate. Wann had suggested its sale as early as 1868, when he had hoped to get twenty-five years' purchase.[184] In 1871 he had higher hopes, thinking it might realize thirty years';[185] but when the estate was sold it brought in only twenty-three years'.[186] Selling an outlying estate made sense: its fee simple value of even twenty-three years' purchase was much more than its mortgageable capacity. The elimination of part of the debt was useful because it made a forced

---

[178] Gosford letter-book, 1 Oct. 1872 (PRONI, D1606/5A/3, p. 332).
[179] Ibid. 4, p. 169 (11 July 1877).
[180] Registry of Deeds, 1877/45/140; Gosford letter-book, 9 May 1877 (PRONI, D1606/5A/4, p. 156).
[181] Gosford letter-book, 11 Nov. 1873 (PRONI, D1606/5A/3, p. 382); see also ibid. 4, p. 76. [182] Ibid. 4, pp. 3-4 (3 and 5 Feb. 1875).
[183] Ibid. 3, p. 342 (23 Nov. 1872).
[184] Ibid., pp. 192, 198 (6 Aug. and 19 Oct. 1868). [185] Ibid., p. 302 (25 Dec. 1871).
[186] Ibid. 4, p. 49 (10 Feb. 1876).

sale by creditors less likely. At the end of the transaction Lord Gosford's net income had increased, but the problem was not solved. Even in 1877 Dundas of Arniston's threat of foreclosure caused a crisis, and the remainder of the debt was still substantial. Wann had hoped for a simpler solution, more in keeping with the traditions of landed wealth—that 'some *good* rich Princess' would marry Lord Gosford.[187] Only an enormous fortune could have saved the Cavan estate by 1875. In fact Gosford married the daughter of his neighbour, the duke of Manchester. Wann, however, may have derived some satisfaction from the fact that a *prince* was a party to the marriage settlement: His Serene Highness Prince Edward of Saxe-Weimar.[188]

[187] Ibid. 3, p. 188 (16 June 1868).
[188] Registry of Deeds, 1876/37/100.

6
Agrarian Outrages

i. 'A Bould Intrepid Gentry'

In 1852 William Wann complained that an insurance company had refused to insure his life because he was an agent.[1] The fact that Lord Gosford's tenants had just complimented him in a public address and that it was his 'natural disposition to be civil and courteous with the people' seems to have counted for little against the contemporary belief that Irish landlords and agents were often the victims of murderous attacks by their tenants. If rural societies defined themselves by the crimes they committed, the English shot pheasants and gamekeepers, and the Irish shot landlords and agents. (English tenants occasionally shot their landlords. In 1849 James Bloomfield Rush was tried at Norwich assizes for shooting his landlord, Isaac Jeremy of Stanfield Hall. Rush, who was alleged to have said that 'it would not be long before he served Jeremy with an ejectment for the other world', shot Jeremy at his door, went into the house, shot Jeremy's son, and wounded his daughter-in-law and a servant.[2])

There was much to support the idea that the Irish countryside was a violent place. The tithe war of the 1830s and the land war of 1879–82 were sensational upheavals, but they were not the only disturbances. During the famine there was a wave of crime: between 1846 and 1849 62,000 outrages, including 756 homicides, were reported by the constabulary.[3] Just as this was subsiding, a small but alarming wave of agrarian crime began in 1849 and persisted until 1852, being particularly troublesome in parts of south Armagh, south Down, Monaghan, and Louth. In February 1852 Revd Robert Henry of Jonesborough, convinced that a seismic change in the ratio of rogues to honest men had taken place around him, claimed that 'the whole country seems now to be convulsed and organized through the length and breadth of the land—threatening letters, murders, and attempts at murder seem to be the order of the day'.[4] (These incidents led to the appointment of a select committee of the House of Commons to

---

[1] Wann's letter-book, 18 June 1852 (PRONI, D1606/5/3, p. 147); for the belief that agrarian outrages were endemic in Ireland, see *Punch*, 29 July 1878 and *Stones of Venice*, ed. E. T. Cooke and Alexander Wedderburn (London, 1904), ii. 195 (I am indebted to Dr Edward McParland for this reference). [2] *Annual Register, 1849*, 378–416.
[3] National Archives, ICR, returns of outrages, 1846–9.
[4] Ibid., outrage papers, Louth, 1852/65.

investigate rural disorder in that part of Ireland.⁵ Wann's difficulty with the insurance company may have been caused by the same events.)

Even during the relatively quiet period between the immediate aftermath of the famine and the onset of the land war, there were periods of tension. Agrarian outrages increased in the early 1860s and again in 1869–70. Between 1857 and 1878 there were 113 agrarian homicides, many of which attracted considerable attention: the two murders on the Adair estate in County Donegal in 1861 and 1863, the shooting of three landlords in 1862 (in April, May, and July); the murder of a constable and a bailiff, and the wounding of William Scully at Ballycohey in 1868; the murder of several landlords and big farmers in 1869–71, when there were twenty-three agrarian homicides; and finally the murder of the third earl of Leitrim (then in his seventy-second year), his clerk, and coachman, near Milford in April 1878.⁶

It was an age when militant language often led to blows. In Galway in 1852 Fr. Edward O'Malley, the priest at Roundstone, accused the daughter of Michael McDonough of being a 'jumper', 'struck her with a loaded whip the moment she stood up, and struck her with it twice more'. As he brought his pastoral visit to a successful conclusion, he told the crowd that had gathered outside the house that 'if there was no fire nearer than Heaven, it would be God's will that the house should be burned to ashes before morning.'⁷ Violent behaviour was not only common, it was apparently not taken much notice of. In October 1879 two solicitors and a drunken shoemaker drove from Glaslough to Emyvale and 'as they drove along, amused themselves by firing shots at and into houses'. Although thirty shots were fired, some narrowly missing alarmed householders, the case against the culprits was dismissed by the magistrates.⁸

The impression of disorder was increased by law enforcement arrangements in Ireland, which differed considerably from those in the rest of the United Kingdom. First, the magistracy was reinforced not only by stipendiary magistrates, who were experienced, professional, and mobile, but also by professional prosecutors.⁹ Secondly, the constabulary was not only centralized and controlled by the government in a way that British police forces were not, it was also impressively ubiquitous and formidably accoutred. (Ireland was well policed by British standards, for it had twice as many policemen on the basis of population as Great Britain.) Thirdly, and

⁵ *Sel. Comm. on County Monaghan, 1852.*
⁶ National Archives, ICR, returns of outrages, 1857–78; Vaughan, *Derryveagh Evictions*; Homer E. Socolofsky, *Landlord William Scully* (Lawrence, Kan., 1979), 39–64; A. M. Sullivan, *New Ireland* (London, 1877), ii. 350–71.
⁷ National Archives, outrage papers, Galway, 1852/416.
⁸ Ibid. ICR, return of outrages, 1879.
⁹ See *Thom's Directory* annually for stipendiary magistrates and for crown and sessional solicitors.

perhaps most conspicuously, Ireland appeared to be governed by special criminal legislation. Between 1847 and 1875, twenty-eight coercion acts were passed by an apparently alarmed parliament.[10] These fell into two unequal classes: first those suspending habeas corpus for two periods (from 25 July 1848 to 1 September 1849 and from 7 February 1866 to 25 March 1869); secondly, those prolonging the crime and outrage act of 1847 and its descendants. Before 1871 it could be said that habeas corpus was suspended only during grave political crises and that the more pedestrian and less alarming crime and outrage acts were used to deal with rural disorder; but in 1871 the Westmeath act enabled the lord-lieutenant to detain without trial persons suspected of being Ribbonmen in Westmeath and in certain parts of Meath and the King's County.[11] During the land war habeas corpus was again suspended in certain districts, and in 1882 trial by jury was seriously modified.[12] Ironically, however, the only time between 1848 and 1881 when Ireland was not under coercive legislation of either kind was between June 1880 and March 1881, a period of great importance in the development of the land war.

The impression that a semblance of order could be maintained in Ireland only by a repressive administrative apparatus can be exaggerated. There was a remarkable improvement in the Irish crime rate in the decades after the famine.[13] When Ireland was compared with other parts of the United Kingdom, it did not appear more crime-ridden. In 1871, for example, there were fewer indictable offences in Ireland, on the basis of population, than in England and Wales. It is true that 'offences against human life' were more common in Ireland (350 compared with 301, assuming that the population of the two countries was the same); also riots and breaches of the peace were more common in Ireland (106 compared with 11), as were common assaults (377 compared with 57), and malicious offences against property (631 compared with 145). On the other hand, offences against property generally were much less frequent in Ireland, as were attempted suicides, rape, unnatural offences, perjury, child-stealing, and bigamy. On the whole, therefore, while Ireland was more violent than England and Wales, the difference between the two countries owed more to assaults than to 'offences against human life'.[14]

Too much should not be made of the coercive legislation. It is true that the suspension of habeas corpus deprived Ireland of one of the most cherished liberties of the British subject. On the other hand, the very mass of coercive legislation between 1847 and 1875 was misleading: most of the

---

[10] I. S. Leadham, *Coercive Measures in Ireland, 1830–1880* (London, [1880]), 36–7.
[11] 34 & 35 Vict., c. 25 (16 June 1871); see also Charles Townshend, *Political Violence in Ireland: Government and Resistance since 1848* (Oxford, 1983), 63–4.
[12] 44 & 45 Vict., c. 4 (2 Mar. 1881); 45 & 46 Vict., c. 25 (12 July 1883).
[13] Below, n. 112 and Appendix 19.
[14] *Judicial Statistics, Ire.*, 1871, p. 23 [C 674], HC 1872, lxv. 257.

twenty-eight acts were renewals of the acts of 1847 and 1856; the act of 1856, which was renewed until 1870, reduced the penalties in the 1847 act. The very fact that so many acts were passed shows not that Ireland was endemically disordered, but that parliament was unwilling to make either the crime and outrage act of 1847 or the peace preservation act of 1870 a permanent part of the criminal law. Their temporary character suggests not only a solicitude for the freedom of the subject, but also a curious optimism that regarded Irish disorder as recurrent rather than endemic and permanent. It is also remarkable that the government did not make fundamental changes in the ordinary procedure of the criminal law: majority verdicts for petty juries, for example, would have greatly helped the police. Changes were made in the jury laws, but not in the predictable direction: Lord O'Hagan's act of 1871 lowered jurors' property qualifications.[15]

The coercive legislation at its most severe was hardly draconian, except by the remarkably liberal standards of mid-nineteenth-century Britain. The Crime and Outrage (Ireland) Act, 1847, allowed the lord-lieutenant to 'proclaim' disorderly districts and to move extra police into them; the only major penal provision of the act was the lord-lieutenant's power to make the proclaimed districts pay for the cost of the extra police.[16] The Peace Preservation (Ireland) Act, 1870, was hardly more remarkable. It made it necessary to have a special licence to carry a revolver; justices could punish witnesses who refused to give evidence; houses could be searched for evidence of the handwriting of persons suspected of writing threatening letters; public houses could be closed by the lord-lieutenant; strangers could be arrested and made to account for themselves; newspapers containing treasonable matter could be confiscated.[17] The special legislation applied to Ireland suggests not only disorder, but also a remarkable liberality and openness in criminal procedures. A more secretive and arbitrary regime would have dealt with its *mauvais sujets* more discreetly, and a country where public houses could be closed only by a special warrant from the highest official in the land was hardly groaning under oppression.

ii. What Were Agrarian Outrages?

Agrarian outrages were the portion of all outrages that the Constabulary Office defined as agrarian. Of the 197,835 outrages reported by the constabulary in the whole country, outside the Dublin metropolitan area, between 1844 and 1880, 21,423 were agrarian.[18] They were different in

---

[15] 34 & 35 Vict., c. 65 (14 Aug. 1871); Townshend, *Political Violence in Ireland*, 61.
[16] 11 Vict., c. 2 (20 Dec. 1847).
[17] 33 & 34 Vict., c. 9 (4 Apr. 1870); Townshend, *Political Violence in Ireland*, 60.
[18] National Archives, ICR, returns of outrages, 1844–80; see below, App. 19. On the origins of the separate enumeration of agrarian outrages, see Hoppen, *Elections, Politics, and Society*, 363.

certain ways from ordinary outrages. First, they fluctuated more violently. While serious outrages declined between the 1840s and 1870s, agrarian outrages went up in the early 1850s, in the early 1860s and late 1860s, and above all in the late 1870s and early 1880s. Secondly, their composition was different. The most common agrarian outrages were threatening letters, which accounted for about 45 per cent of agrarian outrages reported between 1845 and 1880. Threatening letters accounted for only 8 per cent of ordinary outrages. Thirdly, they attracted more attention in the press and among officials than ordinary outrages.

The Returns of outrages, annually printed by the government, did not define agrarian outrages. Contemporaries, however, were in no doubt that they were caused by disputes between landlords and tenants, a definition enshrined in the *Oxford English Dictionary*; contemporaries were also convinced that their most serious manifestation was the murder of landlords and agents. But how did the officers in the Constabulary Office define them? There are several sources that make it possible to compare the workings of the constabulary's mind with public perceptions. There are short reports on all agrarian homicides from 1857 on, and on firings at the person from 1869 in the Returns of outrages;[19] there is a file on agrarian outrages from early 1871 to July 1872 in the Official Papers;[20] there is a report on crime compiled by the inspector-general, Sir Henry John Brownrigg, in the National Library of Ireland.[21]

The summaries of 113 homicides, made by the constabulary between 1857 and 1878, show that landlords were only a minority among the victims, at most a mere handful, even if small, obscure landowners are included. The number of socially prominent figures was small: Alderman Sheehy in Limerick, J. H. Fetherston Haugh, JP, in County Westmeath, George Cole Baker in County Tipperary, and the third earl of Leitrim. Even if landlords' servants are included, homicides arising out of disputes between landlords and tenants fall far short of the total of 113. The servants add considerably to the reckoning: the two stewards of Adair; Patrick Kirwan, a caretaker of Charles Clarke, JP, DL, murdered while living on an evicted farm; Patrick Mitchell, a land steward in Limerick, shot in 1873 because he had served a notice to quit on a priest. Servants accompanying their masters died in incidents where their masters were the target: Samuel Morrow with Scully in 1868; John Hyland with Patten S. Bridge in 1876; John McKim and Charles Buchanan with Lord Leitrim in 1878. Even when landlords and their servants were attacked in separate incidents, the servants seemed more likely to

[19] National Archives, ICR, returns of outrages, 1844–80.
[20] Ibid. OP 1872/85; below, p. 147.
[21] Report on the State of Ireland in 1863 by Sir Henry John Brownrigg (NLI, MS 915); below, p. 155.

die. Thomas Waters, the Revd James Crofton's process server, was shot dead after serving a notice to quit on the notorious 'Captain' Duffy; but in a separate incident Crofton escaped death, and actually pursued his attackers.

If all homicides of landlords and their servants are combined they account for only 24 per cent of agrarian homicides. What accounted for the remaining three-quarters? Four main causes can be discerned: disputes within tenants' families accounted for 32 per cent; disputes between tenants accounted for 27 per cent; disputes between tenants and sub-tenants accounted for 5 per cent; and attacks on those who took evicted land accounted for 10 per cent. As well as incidents that would have been easily recognized by Mr Punch, there were many, arising out of family feuds, that would have been familiar only to readers of Zola. In Kerry in 1875 Thomas Quilter and his sister-in-law, Honoria, were beaten to death, and their house burned, by John Quilter, Honoria's son, who had just come back from America and wanted the farm. (John may have been encouraged to commit the double murder because his uncle 'had incurred much obloquy for living with his sister-in-law as her husband'.) In Kilkenny in 1877 there was one of the most appalling murders of the whole period. James Brett, who was deaf and dumb, was murdered by his brother John and his cousin Walter Mealy, because the former was afraid that their father would leave his farm to James. The brief account of the murder has none of the insouciance that characterized attacks on landlords: James 'went to shake hands with his brother John, when the latter at once plunged a knife into his left side, neck, and right breast, assisted by Mealy, who held one of deceased's hands, kicked him in the stomach, and otherwise injured his person'. Quarrels between tenants were equally brutal. In Cavan in 1872 a small farmer, who had been at law with a neighbour about a piece of bog, was found dead, having been stabbed eighteen times with a clasp-knife.

This is a remarkable modification of the contemporary picture of agrarian homicides. Landlords were the victims of only one-quarter of them; even if attacks on those who took evicted land are added to attacks on landlords, the combined total rises to only 34 per cent. Family disputes were the biggest single cause (32 per cent) of the five causes described above; disputes between neighbours and between tenants and sub-tenants combined (32 per cent) were almost as important a cause as disputes between landlords and tenants and taking evicted land combined. The 5 per cent in which sub-tenants were the victims is small, but impressive when it is remembered that sub-tenants were not numerous; tenants and sub-tenants seem to have been less harmonious than tenants and landlords.

The typical agrarian homicide was caused by a family dispute or a row between neighbours.²² An analysis of the weapons used further dispels the contemporary picture of assassins lurking behind hedges with blunderbusses, for only 45 per cent of those killed died of gunshot wounds, while 30 per cent died of head injuries, 11 per cent of less precisely described injuries, and 7 per cent of stabs and cuts. It is remarkable that in an agricultural country, where pitchforks, spades, scythes, and billhooks were plentiful, so few homicides were committed with them. The case of Andrew McSharry in Leitrim in March 1870, who 'died from the blow of a loy', was one of the few cases where that weapon was clearly described. One of the most unusual murder weapons was that used by a man called Doherty in Donegal in 1873, who murdered his aunt, and later confessed that 'while in a state of intoxication, he committed the murder with a water[ing] can, having first emptied it'.

Most of the homicides were wild, impromptu affairs. James Shanahan in Tipperary in February 1865 was struck on the head with a stone; William O'Brien in Leitrim in October 1869 was found dead, his head having been battered with a stone. Even when other weapons were used, stones were used as supplements. In Tipperary in April 1870 one of the murderers of Pat Kirwan, a caretaker who was beaten to death, confessed that 'he struck Kirwan with a pitchfork, which knocked him down, and then smashed his skull with stones'. Other wounds were more surprising. In Donegal John Shiels bit Bryan Coyle's thumb in a row about a farm of 3 acres; within a month Coyle died from the effects of the bite. Pitchforks, stones, and teeth were not the expected weapons of cold-blooded assassins, but were most likely to be used in mad quarrels and drunken rages. They were also the weapons of intimate mayhem—between neighbours and within families.

It is true, however, that the contemporary picture of the rural assassin was accurate in that almost half of the agrarian homicides used firearms. Most of the incidents where landlords or their servants were attacked were shooting affrays. Gustavus Thiebault, a Frenchman who was also a Tipperary landlord, was shot in April 1862, as was Francis Fitzgerald a month later. About three-quarters of the homicides caused by landlord–tenant disputes were shooting incidents, and to that extent, therefore, they conformed to the contemporary picture. (It is possible to find several landlords who were shot but not by their tenants: Mrs Kelly in Westmeath in 1856 and Hugh Bradshaw in Tipperary in 1869, for example.)

Can it be assumed, on the evidence of the homicides, that only a fraction

---

²² For a discussion of family disputes see David Fitzpatrick, 'Class, Family and Rural Unrest in Nineteenth-Century Ireland', in P. J. Drudy (ed.), *Irish Studies*, 2 *Ireland: Land, Politics and People* (Cambridge, 1982), 37–75. The figures above on homicides support the argument that 'there is little reason to suppose that feuding within families became either negligible or benign after the famine' (ibid. 62).

TABLE 2. Deaths caused by gunshot wounds

Source of Dispute	% of each class caused by gunshot wounds
Within families	30
Between neighbours	40
Landlords and tenants	74

of all agrarian outrages was caused by disputes between landlords and tenants? It is possible that landlords were under-represented among the homicides, for they were not as accessible as tenants. Table 2 shows that the more socially remote the attacker was from his victim, the more likely it was for firearms to be used. Because firearms were more likely to be used in disputes between landlords and tenants than in domestic quarrels, landlords and their servants were less likely to be killed. Attacks with firearms, which required planning and opportunity, were likely to be abandoned for lack of either. The firearms used, old blunderbusses loaded with scrap metal and poorly charged, were neither accurate nor particularly lethal. Of eighty-nine attacks with firearms between 1869 and 1878, only twenty-six were mortal. Even when actually wounded the victim had a chance of recovery, for the projectiles were sterilized by the blast; on the other hand, a tenant stabbed in the abdomen with a pitchfork had little chance of recovery.

Although the firearms used by rural murderers improved during the nineteenth century, with revolvers replacing blunderbusses, it is doubtful if it made much difference. Peter Barrett, a London postman whose father was evicted in County Galway, hired a revolver from a surgical-instrument maker in the Tottenham Court Road, came over to Ireland, and fired at his father's landlord, Captain Eyre Lambert. Five shots were fired, four took effect, one lodging in Lambert's temple, but he lived to testify against his attacker and seems to have suffered nothing worse than a bad shock. (Barrett was a better shot than many of his contemporaries, but he had hired a revolver that was too light—a strange mistake for a man who served in the Middlesex Volunteers.)[23] It seems too that assassins fired less accurately at landlords than at their friends and relations. Over half of the tenants, neighbours, and close relations fired at were killed; only one-fifth of the landlords fired at were killed. In other words it seems that landlords may have been under-represented in the ranks of death for technical reasons. It is probable, therefore, that attacks on landlords accounted for more than 24 per cent of all agrarian outrages. When firings during the

[23] National Archives, ICR, return of outrages, 1869; ibid. CCS 1870/197.

TABLE 3. Firings at the person, 1869–1878

Source of dispute	% of total
Landlords and tenants	54 [24]
Taking evicted land	6 [10]
Family	10 [32]
Neighbours	19 [27]
Tenants and sub-tenants	10 [5]
Others	1 [2]

Note: The figures in square brackets give the % for homicides at p. 143 above.

decade 1869–78 were analysed in Table 3, in the same way as homicides, this was found to be so. The most striking difference between firings and homicides was the greater proportion of the former involving landlords and the taking of evicted land: 60 as compared with 34 per cent. Family disputes showed the most reduced proportion: 10 as against 32 per cent, but disputes between neighbours and tenants and sub-tenants, when combined, hardly changed.

It is plausible to see firings as the most characteristic attack made on landlords; certainly, they fit the contemporary view of agrarian outrages better than homicides. First, firings at landlords were more frequent than homicides; in 1869, for example, there were only two homicides of landlords and their servants, but eleven firings. Secondly, county grandees were rather more common among the victims of firings than among homicides: two JPs, a high sheriff, and a rector in 1869–70, for example, compared with a Scots farmer and a 'gentleman' among the homicides. Thirdly, firings were often associated with an eccentric casualness that seemed peculiarly Irish. Patten S. Bridge was fired at twice—in March 1875 and March 1876—but escaped; in September 1860 Lord Leitrim was fired at by a publican in Mohill, who believed himself to be king of Ireland and prime minister of England.[24] Yet the significance of even firings can be exaggerated. Not many Irish landlords were fired at; few were fired at more than once. Between the famine and the land war only two landlords of the first rank were assassinated: Lord Leitrim in County Donegal in 1878 and the earl of Mayo in 1872; but the latter was assassinated far from his native Meath. Firing was not even predominantly agrarian in its provenance, like threatening letters, for agrarian firings accounted for only 17 per cent of all firings in the decade 1861–70, while agrarian threatening letters accounted for 46 per cent of all threatening letters. If tenants were

[24] For Leitrim and James Murphy, see Larcom papers (NLI, MS 7634).

TABLE 4. Agrarian outrages, 1871

Source of dispute	% of total
Landlords and tenants	25 [39]
Taking evicted land	5 [8]
Family	16 [21]
Neighbours	29 [23]
Tenants and sub-tenants	6 [8]
Others	19 [1]

Note: The figures in square brackets give average % for homicides and firings based on Table 3.

as likely to shoot each other as to shoot their landlords, they were also, in disputes with their landlords, more likely to use the instruments provided by the commissioners of national education and Anthony Trollope than those provided by Messrs Colt, Armstrong, and Whitworth.

A further insight into the constabulary's definition of agrarian outrages can be obtained by using a file kept in the Official Papers in the Chief Secretary's Office.[25] Table 4, based on a sample of over a hundred cases, changes slightly the picture based on homicides and firings. Disputes between landlords and tenants have lost some of the prominence that homicides and firings gave them; family quarrels have also gone down, but rows between neighbours have gone up. It is also interesting that a substantial number of outrages in the Official Papers file cannot be classified because they did not have the apparent simplicity of motive that characterized homicides and firings. These included a farmer in County Cork who set fire to his own premises, a farmer in Cavan who was attacked because of a dispute between Protestants and Catholics, and a county surveyor who was threatened by road contractors. Why these were classified as agrarian outrages at all is not clear; nor is it clear why the letter sent to Captain McTernan, RM and 'evidently written by an admirer of Mr Broderick, an attorney' should have been classified as agrarian.

It is hard to resist the conclusion that agrarian outrage was a convenient taxonomical receptacle for all disputes that were remotely connected with land. Thomas Cully's house, for example, was fired into in July 1871 and his dog wounded. The cause was that he had sided with a Mrs Anne Tucker in a dispute with her brother, Dr Phillips, and had been '*advised* to mind himself'. The dispute between Mrs Tucker and Dr Phillips may have been about land, but that is not clear from the report. Likewise, the

[25] National Archives, OP 1872/85; see below, p. 155 for an analysis of threatening letters based on Report on the State of Ireland in 1863 by Sir Henry John Brownrigg (NLI, MS 915).

threatening letter received by Lord Castlemaine and his cousin, Miss Handcock, in June 1871, may have had its origin in a dispute about land, for it appeared that Castlemaine had driven out a tenant whom he suspected of writing threatening letters. Since, however, the constabulary believed that 'Miss H.' had written these, and had 'induced' Castlemaine to blame the tenant, the case was hardly a typical landlord–tenant dispute.[26]

Even if the cause of the outrage was not connected with the management of an estate, the constabulary seem to have classified as agrarian any crime that affected landlords. A Kildare landlord who received a threatening letter from a discharged groom was returned as a victim of an agrarian outrage. Likewise, when the Hon. Reginald Temple Harris Temple of Waterstown, County Westmeath, received a threatening letter, it was classified as agrarian; the fact that it was classified at all was remarkable because it was 'nearly illegible and quite incoherent'. Having classified one incident as agrarian, the constabulary tended to lump together all incidents that were superficially similar. It was easy to see why a threatening letter to a Protestant blacksmith in County Tyrone, who was trying to buy a farm that belonged to a Catholic, should have been agrarian. It was not, however, easy to see why the notice posted on the gate of Knockbride chapel in County Cavan was agrarian, for it was done 'with [the] design of causing the RC inhabitants to assemble for defence of [the] chapel and so come into collision with [the] Orange party who were to assemble on 12 July near the chapel.'[27]

The constabulary's vagaries may be excused, however, by the fact that they faced considerable taxonomical problems. In September 1871 in County Mayo, for example, 'a low sized man wearing a dark coat and an old soft hat which covered his face' called on a herd of Lord Lucan, and warned him to get out. There were, according to the constabulary, three possible motives for this warning: first, the herd had impounded trespassing sheep; secondly, the people thought that if herds could be intimidated, the lands they looked after would be broken up and let in small farms. The third motive, however, transformed this agrarian outrage into something more complicated, for the constabulary thought that it was done to prevent the closing of the local constabulary station by creating a panic about agrarian crime.[28]

Not only did the constabulary inflate agrarian outrages by including outrages that were only remotely agrarian, they also inflated their numbers. Between April and August 1871, the Official Papers file included 104 reports, but in the same period the Returns of outrages recorded 154 outrages. This seems to have been explained by the continuation into 1871

---

[26] National Archives, Op 1872/85, nos. 3, 24, 32, 39, 60, 74, 81, 84, 120).
[27] Ibid., nos. 49, 63, 102, 113.   [28] Ibid., nos. 57, 126.

TABLE 5. Agrarian outrages, 1848–1880

Source of disputes	%	no.
Landlords and tenants	35	5,803
Taking evicted land	12	1,990
Family	15	2,487
Neighbours	24	3,979
Tenants and sub-tenants	8	1,326
Others	6	994
TOTAL	100	16,579

Note: This table was constructed by combining as equally weighted components the four analyses in Tables 3, 4, and 7. The number of outrages was taken from the Return of outrages, 1848–80.

and 1872 of the practice used in 1869–70 of returning as separate offences incidents that were not in fact discrete.[29] In May 1871, for example, forty-three tenants in County Leitrim were visited by armed men who made them swear they would not pay more than 1s. bog money and would do no duty work. This was included in the Returns of outrages as forty-three outrages.[30] (Since the constabulary thought that the tenants had arranged the affair themselves, it was hardly reasonable to allow this incident to inflate the Returns of outrages.)

Agrarian outrages were, therefore, a catch-all in the taxonomy of total crime, for they included not only outrages caused by disputes between landlords and tenants, but all crimes caused by disputes about land. Some outrages against landlords, even if they were unconnected with the tenure of land, also seem to have been included. The composition of agrarian outrage changes significantly, depending on whether homicides, firings, or outrages in 1871 are taken as a guide.[31] The combination of these three with an analysis of threatening letters in Table 5 gives an informed but hardly definitive answer to the question of what agrarian outrage was.

Table 5 shows that disputes between landlords and tenants were the largest cause of agrarian outrages, for they accounted for just over one-third of them. If disputes caused by tenants taking evicted holdings are added, the combined total comes to just under half of all agrarian outrages, which rather modifies the idea that all agrarian outrages were caused by disputes between landlords and tenants. The most striking thing about this table, however, is the smallness of the figures; 5,803 agrarian outrages were caused by disputes between landlords and tenants in just over thirty years; it sounds a lot, even when it is remembered that just under half of

[29] *Returns 'of Outrages Reported to the Royal Irish Constabulary Office from 1 Jan. 1844 to 31 Dec. 1880'*, p. 15 [2756], HC 1881, lxxvii. 901.
[30] National Archives, OP 1872/85, no. 53.   [31] See below, App. 19.

these were probably threatening letters. In the same period, however, the constabulary reported 150,072 outrages of all kinds, including agrarian outrages; 5,803 was just under 4 per cent of this figure.

iii. Threatening Letters

Threatening letters, with their crude drawings of coffins,[32] laconic warnings, and pseudonyms, were a nuisance to the constabulary, a pretext for bravado in landlords and agents, and a source of quiet satisfaction to the semi-literate practisers of what must have been a solitary vice. They were also the most common agrarian outrage, accounting for just under half of all agrarian outrages.[33] The genre, which the romantically inclined might be tempted to see as the popular riposte to the notice to quit, reveals a hidden Ireland; what they tell about landlordism is not, perhaps, their most important revelation.[34]

According to the constabulary they became more frequent after agrarian murders, 'the public mind being then in a state of agitation, and more easily influenced by attempts at intimidation'.[35] The letters' frequent references to murders and attempted murders certainly suggest that outrages, still fresh in the public mind, were the bullion reserve that gave this paper currency its liquidity. In March 1869 William Ormsby of Enniscrone, County Sligo, was warned to 'remember William Scully'.[36] Occasionally the writer claimed that he was an assassin. John Carr, agent of the Achill mission, got a letter in August 1871, postmarked Preston, and purporting to be from James Hunter's assassin, 'to the effect, that the writer would not eat his Christmas supper until after he had lodged a ball in his [Carr's] old carcase'.[37] Victims who had been threatened with the death of an earlier victim became in their turn epistolary scarecrows. Captain Rowland Tarleton, shot in April 1869, had received a letter in the previous November (which he had kept 'a strict secret') threatening him with the fate of 'Fetterson of Mullingar or Scully of tiperary'. Almost a year later one of his successors was warned that 'you will be treated as Tarlynton was.'[38]

In 1862 threatening letters clearly followed the pattern suggested by the constabulary, responding dramatically to the assassination of three landlords

---

[32] *Sel. Comm. on County Monaghan, 1852*, 185–7.   [33] See below, App. 19.

[34] Just over 5,500 threatening letters were recorded by the constabulary between 1850 and 1879; they were outnumbered by evictions (below, pp. 230–1); they were vastly outnumbered by notices to quit (above, p. 24). The remarkable restraint of the Irish is shown by the fact that between 1940 and 1944 at least 3 million poison-pen letters were written in France (Eugene Weber, 'The Occupiers and the Occupied' in *TLS*, 12 Aug. 1983, p. 850).

[35] Sir Henry John Brownrigg, *Examination of Some Recent Allegations Concerning the Constabulary Force in Ireland, in a Report to his Excellency the Lord-Lieutenant* (Dublin, 1864), 71; Report on the State of Ireland in 1863 by Sir Henry John Brownrigg (NLI, MS 915, p. 5).   [36] National Archives, RP 1869/4468; see also ibid. 1870/3528, 5163.

[37] Ibid. 1871/16234.   [38] Ibid. 1869/7395; 1870/5113.

in that year. Normally letters followed a seasonal pattern, which was the same as that of agrarian outrages as a whole. They were at their lowest in the late summer and early autumn, rose during the winter, reached a peak in March, and began to fall in April and May. The year 1862 began like any other year in the decade 1856–65 and was normal until May, when threatening letters increased, instead of beginning the descent that would have been their normal route.[39] The letters were apparently responding to the murder of two landlords: Gustavus Thiebault in April and Francis Fitzgerald in May. It is worth noting, however, that the peak was reached in May and that the murder of Walter Braddel in July did not cause another sharp increase. (It is possible, although unprovable, that the failure of Braddel's murder to start another epidemic was due to the fact that Francis Fitzgerald's murderer, Thomas Beckham, was hanged at Limerick in July.) The tendency of threatening letters to increase after an assassination was demonstrated in 1862, but it did not repeat itself in 1868, when there were three assassinations involving landlords; even after the 'battle' of Ballycohey, which was a most startling incident, threatening letters did not increase dramatically. The wave of threatening letters that did come in the late 1860s came a year later, between October 1869 and May 1870. It is true, of course, that the murders of 1868 were referred to in threatening letters in 1869–70. In April 1869, for example, Bevan Slator of Clinan House, Mullingar, was warned that he would get 'a Fetherstone touch', and in December a large farmer was warned that he would be sent 'where Fetherson[sic] is gone'.[40] (The assassination of the third earl of Leitrim in April 1878 did not cause a startling increase in threatening letters, although in timing and notoriety it resembled the Fitzgerald case in 1862.)

The sanction threatened in the letters was usually death. A tenant on the Henry estate in Tipperary was warned that he would be 'treated with a bullet';[41] a herd was threatened with a 'a hot breakfast'.[42] One of the most unusual threats was that made to 'a sort of a gamekeeper' who was warned: 'I will leave you a dead nigger for your wife.'[43] Frequently the letters were adorned with sketches of coffins, pistols, and in one case, a harp with a crown lying beside it. Sometimes the threats were oblique. A caretaker in County Westmeath in 1869 was told 'to recollect the year 1827'—when his father and uncle were hanged for incendiarism.[44] Owen Colgan, who received three threatening letters in 1869–70, was warned that his assailant would 'do shurer work than the lad that fired at old Mickey' (Colgan's

---

[39] Ibid. ICR, return of outrages, 1862.
[40] Ibid. RP 1871/9364; 1870/471. J. H. Fetherston Haugh, JP, DL was murdered in April 1868. [41] Ibid., outrage papers, Tipperary, 1852/657.
[42] Ibid. RP 1870/21611. [43] Ibid. 1869/16344. [44] Ibid. 19022.

uncle who had been fired at and missed years before).[45] Threats were occasionally more elaborate than simple death. The Messrs. Perry of Ballinagore were threatened with post-mortem decapitation 'to make the greatest parable of them that ever was made in Ireland'.[46] (Hugh Bradshaw, a Tipperary landlord, who was shot in 1868, had been threatened with post-mortem castration, but since the constabulary thought that the author of this letter was his wife, the case was hardly a typical one.[47]) Insults were added to threats. Thomas Cormack of Rathcormack was told he had an 'unnatural semi-masculine daughter' and Revd J. Brabazon Grant was told to get rid of his Protestant servants and to 'banish this old Orange hoore and her daughter'.[48]

It was significant that the threats were nearly always directed against the recipient and not against his family. The favourite means of delivery through the post office left the victim free to keep the letter a secret from his family and friends. There were, of course, exceptions. Miss Counsel, daughter of Lawrence Counsel, who had taken Creggan House after Captain Tarleton's murder, was accosted on the road by a man who touched his hat and said, 'Miss, beware, I will be at your father's wake before this week is out.'[49] The pseudonyms adopted by writers varied throughout the period. Molly Maguire, who threatened Revd T. W. Green in Longford in 1852, or 'Mary Ane Mugire' of Cloon Grove, who threatened a tenant in the same county, probably appeared more frequently in the early 1850s.[50] Her successor in the 1870s as a ubiquitous righter of wrongs was Rory of the Hill. In 1869–70 Rory appeared in a variety of forms: 'Roary of the Hill' near Westport and again at Swineford;[51] George Hope was threatened by his 'loveing friend R. of the Hill';[52] on Achill the spelling was 'Rorey'.[53] In Westmeath he appeared as 'roedy of the hill', 'Roary Mountainneer', 'R. H.', and 'rory of the green', as well as in his classical and accepted form.[54] Even in 1869–70, however, Rory did not have it all his own way, for an unpopular constable was warned not to 'think that Molly Maguire and her children is dead.'[55] In 1869–70, however, Rory was so extravagantly invoked that his name lost some of its magic. In December 1870, after his most luxuriant efflorescence, Rory wrote to a herd in County Westmeath, protesting 'I am still alive.'[56] Neither Rory nor Molly Maguire had a monopoly of invocation. In the early 1850s the latter had to compete with 'Captain Rock' and 'Daniel Blacknight, captain'.[57] None of these, however, had the historical pretensions of the writer who ended a letter to a

---

[45] Ibid. 1870/960.   [46] Ibid. 1871/2021.   [47] Ibid. 1869/11937.
[48] Ibid. 1870/14290, 15541.   [49] Ibid. 8139.
[50] Ibid., outrage papers, Longford, 1852/131.   [51] Ibid. RP 1870/3606, 5140.
[52] Ibid. 1871/5163.   [53] Ibid. 9521.
[54] Ibid. 1870/17216; 1869/18428; 1870/471; 1869/17058.   [55] Ibid. 1869/14944.
[56] Ibid. 1870/21611.
[57] Ibid., outrage papers, Limerick, 1852/403; Kilkenny, 1852/180.

tenant in County Monaghan with 'signed by order of the Irish parlimint'.[58] In the late 1860s Rory was rivalled by 'Captain buck shot', 'enemies to oppression', 'a lover of pace and fareplay', 'A. W. Meath boy', 'one of the executive', 'Captain Maguire', 'O'Donnell the Boo', 'Captain fare not', and 'anonymous'.[59]

It is not easy to assess the importance of these pseudonyms. They were obviously an attempt to frighten by assuming titles such as captain, or by implying a connection with an organization by using words such as 'executive'. One writer, for example, simply claimed 'i am a soger', showing that he at least believed that the pen was not mightier than the sword.[60] The writers also valued the ubiquity conferred by well-known pseudonyms such as Rory of the Hill, which gave a certain authority to the letters. It is possible to spot pseudonyms that may have been collective in that several letters emanated from a group of letter-writers. The 'enemies to oppression' who threatened James Seery of Archerstown may have been the same 'enemies to oppression' who warned land jobbers in the same district not to take land.[61] Other literary usages showed that writers valued the strength that an appearance of collective support gave their letters. Some used the nominative singular of the first personal pronoun; but many used 'we'; even Rory, who was a collective phenomenon though grammatically singular, would occasionally enhance his collective persona not only by assuming the royal 'we', but also by taking advice from his council. A tenant near Swineford who had a dispute with a neighbour, for example, received a letter that was 'signed in council by orders Rory of the Hill'.[62] Writers also tried to assume a collective identity by referring to comrades: 'i am a man that is bound by the bonds of loyalty to ritify such cases', claimed the 'Captain buck shot' who wrote to G. J. Hornidge, JP, of Calverstown, County Westmeath;[63] also, the second letter received by Bevan Slator in May 1870 was 'signed by order of the committee'.[64]

Why did the aggrieved send threatening letters? To some extent because it was cheap and easy, and there was little chance of being caught. Before the passage of the Peace Preservation (Ireland) Act, 1870, the constabulary could not search a house for writing materials. The ferocity with which the courts treated those convicted of writing threatening letters was a sign of the difficulty of detecting them. At the spring assizes at Clonmel in 1870, for example, Mr Justice Morris sentenced a bailiff to five years' penal servitude for writing a threatening letter to his agent and to himself under

---

[58] Ibid., Monaghan, 1852/44.
[59] Ibid. RP 1868/2105; 1869/2273, 7395, 16344; 1870/5113, 22231; 1871/9364; OP 1872/3/7; RP 1869/4912. [60] Ibid. RP 1869/17058.
[61] Ibid. 1869/3866, 16642; for a similar coincidence see ibid. 1869/7395, 15349.
[62] Ibid. 1870/5140; see also 1869/2273, 14944. [63] Ibid. 1868/2105.
[64] Ibid. 1871/9364.

TABLE 6. Recipients of threatening letters, 1863

Recipients	% of total
Landlords and agents	33
Bailiffs	7
Tenants	51
Others	9

the pseudonym Rory of the Hill.[65] Writing was in itself the gratifying exercise of a skill that had been acquired with difficulty. Many of the letters were obviously written by the semi-literate and were written with difficulty; some were of course written by the highly literate who wished to appear illiterate (the 'Captain buck shot' referred to at the end of the previous paragraph seems to be in this category); some were quite polished and written with zest. A shopkeeper in Moate was ordered to get out by a correspondent who said he was 'hoping to find you in good health as this leaves me at present'.[66] Edward Golding, Lord Templetown's agent in Monaghan, received a letter that was thought to have been written by the brother of a Presbyterian minister, which showed strongly the influence of King James's bible. The agent was accused of behaving as 'proud Pharaoh wrought with the Israelites in the land of Egypt'.[67]

The actual cause of individual letters is in many cases easy enough to discover. In 1863 Sir Henry John Brownrigg, the inspector-general of constabulary, made detailed returns of agrarian outrages, which make it possible not only to analyse the kind of disputes that caused threatening letters, but also to identify the status of their victims.[68] Table 6 shows, in fact, that tenants were more likely to send threatening letters to each other than to landlords. (It is interesting that bailiffs did not appear more prominently.)

It is not unreasonable to expect similarities between threatening letters and cases of firing at the person, for letters were essentially projectiles that could be used against the socially remote as well as against neighbours and relations. The evidence of Brownrigg's report, when analysed by sources of dispute in Table 7, supports this. In descending order, the victims of threatening letters were landlords, tenants who took evicted holdings, neighbours, and sub-tenants. Threatening letters were infrequently used in family disputes, which supports the idea that they were projectiles; but

[65] *Ballinrobe Chronicle*, 19 Mar. 1870. [66] National Archives, RP 1870/21872.
[67] Ibid., outrage papers, Monaghan, 1852/166.
[68] Report on the State of Ireland in 1863 by Sir Henry John Brownrigg (NLI, MS 915).

TABLE 7. Threatening letters, 1863

Source of dispute	% of total	
Landlords and tenants	38	[54]
Taking evicted land	26	[6]
Family	2	[10]
Neighbours	20	[19]
Tenants and sub-tenants	9	[10]
Others	5	[1]

Note: The figures in square brackets give the equivalent % for firings in Table 3.

their rareness is surprising, considering that in family disputes the writers of threatening letters enjoyed a ring-side seat. The most important difference between threatening letters and firings was in attacks on tenants who took evicted land. The figure of 26 per cent is much higher than in the three analyses discussed in the preceding section, which on average suggested that only 7 per cent of outrages were caused by tenants taking evicted land.

Most letters were laconic, containing few intellectual flourishes, and apart from showing that a grievance existed, often tell little or nothing of its circumstances. In the early 1850s there were a few references to 'tyranny' and 'justice'; by 1869–70 the ideas were more complicated, reflecting probably the greater penetration of rural consciousness by radical ideas. A notice posted in County Mayo was headed 'The land for the people'.[69] Equally interesting was the letter in the same county that claimed 'We wish to have everybody in his own place in [the] course of time.'[70] In 1871 the bailiff of William Pike on Achill was warned to 'let the poor man live'.[71] In County Westmeath the same theme was touched on: 'the poor man as well as the rich man' must have a chance of getting grass, and a farmer who had just taken grass was warned 'to have nothing to do whatever in the taking of any grass farm which must be left to the public'.[72] The interests of the public were again touched on in a letter to Marcus G. Russell, who was accused of wanting to increase his sheepwalk and 'to destroy the public at large'.[73] Some letters claimed that a new era had dawned. Richard Fetherston Haugh of Rockview, County Westmeath, was warned to dismiss his steward: 'for the time was when he could persecute labouring men but that time is gone by'.[74] The new era implied the restitution of what had been 'lost' earlier. Russell, referred to above,

---

[69] National Archives, RP 1870/3528.   [70] Ibid. 5140.   [71] Ibid. 1871/9521.
[72] Ibid. 1869/3866.   [73] Ibid. 18428.   [74] Ibid. 1869/18259.

was told that his farm should go to the adjoining tenants, 'now they were able and willing to hold where their four fathers lived'. Another farmer was warned by Rory to give up a farm he got twenty-two years before, for 'I am going round through the country recalling all the lands lost by injustice.'[75]

In some letters there were attempts to imitate official forms: there were references to committees, executives, councils, and parliaments. 'These are the Irish laws at present,' claimed one writer, 'which will be carried out effectively as sure as you rise each morning.'[76] A tenant who was contesting a brother's will was warned: 'You are violating a law that I as a member of a certain society am bound on my oath to keep down.'[77] What was particularly remarkable in 1869–70 was the attitude to rents revealed, for the word 'valuation' appears frequently, and the government valuation was presented as a standard. In October 1869, for example, a notice on Moate chapel addressed the 'slaves of the soil' and urged them to withhold their rents 'until ample justice is done you by giving you land at a fair valuation'.[78]

iv. What Caused Agrarian Outrages?

Fr. Lavelle had no doubt about the answer. Landlords and tenants lived in a state of war, produced by the injustice of conquest.[79] In reality, agrarian outrages responded to a variety of causes, not only to disputes between landlords and tenants, but to family disputes, and disputes between tenants as well. They fluctuated from year to year, being most frequent in 1849–52, 1862–4, 1869–70, and 1879–82; the year 1850, for example, which was the worst year of that particular outbreak, was about five times as bad as any of the quiet years of the 1850s; the contrast between the land war and the quiet years of the 1870s was even more striking, with rates about twelve times as high.[80] Agrarian outrages fluctuated within individual years: they were highest in the autumn and winter and lowest in the spring and summer. This seasonal pattern was remarkably stable from year to year.[81] Even sharp increases in numbers did not upset it: during the land war, when rates reached unprecedented levels, the seasonal pattern persisted. Agrarian outrages varied from county to county. In the early 1850s the worst county, Tipperary, had eighteen times the rate of the best county, Dublin. During the land war Kerry, the worst county, had twenty-seven times the rate of Antrim, the best county.[82]

Fluctuations in agrarian outrages can be related to other fluctuations in

---

[75] Ibid. 1870/1748.   [76] Ibid. 1869/7104.
[77] Ibid. 1870/14290.   [78] Ibid. 1869/16105.
[79] Lavelle, *The Irish Landlord since the Revolution* (Dublin, 1870), 280.
[80] See below, App. 19; National Archives, ICR, returns of outrages, 1848–82.
[81] For 1862, which was exceptional, see above, p. 151.   [82] See below, App. 22.

the countryside. The outbreaks of the early 1850s, early 1860s, and late 1870s coincided with agricultural crises that caused increases in arrears and evictions. Yet the effect of arrears and evictions was not so clear in 1869–70 because the incidence of arrears was limited and evictions did not increase sharply. The seasonal fluctuations are not easily explained. Were they caused by the long winter nights? or the idleness of the winter months? or the settling of accounts that took place after the harvest? The differences between counties are even more difficult to explain. It is arguable that they were even more important than annual fluctuations. The difference between the best and worst counties in 1879–82, for example, was greater than that between the good years of the 1870s and the bad years of 1879–82. By using statistical techniques that measure patterns of coincidence, leaving causal connections to be inferred, it is possible to suggest some relationships. There was, for example, a positive relationship between evictions and agrarian outrages; it was quite strong in the 1870s, slightly less strong in the 1860s, and weak, indeed not necessarily positive at all, in the 1850s; it was stronger in 1879–82 and 1862–4 than in 1848–52 and 1869–70.[83] In the 1870s, for example, Antrim, Down, and Londonderry had few evictions and few agrarian outrages; the opposite was true at the other end of the scale, in Galway, Kerry, and Longford. A few counties, however, did not fit into the pattern, even in the 1870s when the relationship was strongest; the King's County, for example, was one of the worst for outrages, but not for evictions; Fermanagh was the opposite, being the second most peaceful county, but about average for evictions.[84]

There was a tendency for agrarian crime to persist in some counties, suggesting that once the habit got a grip, it persisted. Counties that were bad in 1848–52 tended to be bad again in 1862–4; the connection persisted but became weaker in 1869–70 and 1879–82; by 1879–82, the relationship with 1849–52 was very weak.[85] Some counties, however, had a record of heroic consistency. Tipperary was the worst county in 1848–52, almost the worst in 1862–4 and 1879–82, and bad in 1869–70; Dublin and Antrim, on the other hand, were always among the best.[86] It would, however, have been difficult to have predicted the distribution of agrarian outrages in 1879–82 from their distribution in 1848–52; Mayo and Galway, for example, moved from being among the most peaceful counties to being the leaders of disturbance at certain periods of the land war.

Ordinary outrages changed less from place to place than agrarian outrages. The worst counties in the 1850s were the worst in the 1860s and among the worst in the 1870s.[87] Also ordinary outrages did not fluctuate violently from one period to the next, but declined gradually after the late

---

[83] See below, App. 23. [84] See below, App. 21. [85] See below, App. 23.
[86] See below, App. 22. [87] See below, App. 20.

TABLE 8. Causes of agrarian outrages, 1848–1880

Cause of dispute	%	nos.
Evictions and 'grabbing'	30	4,974
Rents	8	1,326
Succession to farms	8	1,326
Competition for farms	18	2,984
Trespass, grazing, etc.	5	829
Sub-tenants	8	1,326
Other	23	3,814
TOTAL	100	16,579

Note: This table is based on information about the causes of outrages in National Archives, ICR, returns of outrages, 1857-78, OP 1872/85, and in Report on the State of Ireland in 1863 by Sir Henry John Brownrigg (NLI, MS 915).

1840s. The difference in range between ordinary outrages and agrarian outrages was different: in 1851–60 the worst county for ordinary outrages had six times as many as the best; the worst county for agrarian outrages had twelve times as many as the best. In spite of these differences, however, there was a positive relationship between agrarian and ordinary outrages, especially in the 1860s and 1870s, suggesting that the former might have been an epiphenomenon of the latter. This relationship was stronger than that between agrarian outrages and evictions and that between agrarian outrages in different periods. The possibility that ordinary and agrarian outrages were related was strengthened by their tendency to increase simultaneously in times of crisis such as 1862, 1868–70, 1879–82, 1885–6, although ordinary outrages did not increase as dramatically as agrarian outrages.

It is possible to look more closely at the causes of agrarian outrages by using the sources that were used above.[88] Table 8 shows that evictions and 'grabbing' were the largest single cause of outrages and much larger than any other. The large number of outrages classified as 'other' partially reflects the constabulary's habit of putting all sorts of crimes in the agrarian category. It is remarkable that rents caused so few outrages, less than competition for farms, and the same as disputes about succession to farms and disputes between tenants and sub-tenants. Sub-tenants seem to have caused trouble out of all proportion to their numbers, suggesting that tenants were not very happy as small landlords. A major reform of the law of landlord and tenant would not have abolished agrarian outrages; for

[88] Above, pp. 142–3, 147, 154–5.

one thing, 23 per cent of them were so miscellaneous that neither the three Fs nor peasant proprietary would have affected them. Competition for farms, trespassing, disputes about succession, and disputes with sub-tenants, which accounted for 39 per cent, would have continued. At most the three Fs would have made some inroads into the 38 per cent caused by evictions and rents; but again the three Fs would not have abolished them. It is clear, however, that any legislation that wanted to reduce agrarian outrages would achieve more by concentrating on evictions rather than on rents.

At least four of these causes could increase quickly in importance when agricultural output fell: evictions, rents, competition for farms, and sub-tenants, amounting to 64 per cent in all. But what about the other causes of disputes? Between 1879 and 1882 landlords and their servants attracted more attacks, both relatively and absolutely, than they did before 1879. Between 1857 and 1878 they were the victims of 24 per cent of agrarian homicides; during the land war they were the victims of 36 per cent. Yet the increased attacks on landlords and their servants did not account for all of the increase in homicides. Measured against homicides in the 1870s, there were forty-two extra homicides between 1879 and 1882; only eighteen of these, however, were caused by attacks on landlords and their servants. A further ten were caused by tenants taking evicted land, which leaves fourteen 'extra' homicides, caused by disputes between tenants and within families, ten being caused by the former and four by the latter.[89] In fact all of the components of agrarian crime increased during the land war; those caused by taking evicted land increased most, those caused by disputes with landlords were next, followed by disputes between tenants; finally came family homicides, which increased by one-third compared with the pre-1879 rate.

The cause of outrages, therefore, during crises was not simple. The usual causes of friction between landlords and tenants were multiplied when rents were hard to collect, when evictions increased, and when farms changed hands, which is simple enough. At the same time, however, disputes within the tenantry seem to have increased, which is not so simple. There were also differences between the crises. First, the amount of crime generated in the early 1850s and early 1860s, compared with evictions and threats of eviction, was small compared with 1879–82. Secondly, the crisis of 1869–70 did not coincide with an agricultural depression. Arrears on some estates had increased slightly in the late 1860s;[90] also there were problems in parts of the west;[91] but there were no sharp increases in evictions, not even in Mayo and Westmeath, where the trouble was worst.

[89] National Archives, ICR, returns of outrages, 1879–82; for family disputes see Fitzpatrick, 'Class, Family and Rural Unrest in Nineteenth-Century Ireland', 37–75.
[90] See below, App. 7.   [91] Larcom papers (NLI, MS 7612, between nos. 4 & 5).

The only economic explanation that fits the 1869–70 outbreak is that the profits of grazing lands reached a peak in the season 1868–9, possibly causing fierce competition for any land that was available in the following year.[92] It is difficult to demonstrate, but it is also possible that the crisis was exogenous, growing out of the agitation connected with the land bill. First, the main wave of disorder coincided with the period of speech-making between the passing of the church act and the introduction of the land bill.[93] Secondly, many of the outrages were directed against rents: tenants trying either to reduce existing rents, or to prevent landlords increasing them.[94] (The connection between evictions and agrarian outrages was weaker in this crisis than in 1848–52, 1862–4, or 1879–82.[95]) There is no convincing evidence that rents were more difficult to pay in 1869–70: there was no large increase in arrears on the estates below;[96] there was no increase in civil bill ejectment processes in 1869;[97] there was no unusual withdrawal of funds from the commercial banks. It is possible that both landlords and tenants were trying to anticipate the land bill: the landlords were trying to increase rents before it became impossible to do so; the tenants were struggling to prevent the approaching cup from being dashed from their lips.

The crisis of 1869–70, which it is tempting but wrong to dismiss as a taxonomical illusion created by a moral panic in Dublin Castle, helps to explain why the land war generated more crime than the crises of the early 1850s and early 1860s.[98] Those crises suggested that the land system was insulated, responding mainly to internal pressures, and offering opportunities for agitation only when arrears and evictions were high. It is tempting to see the land system as a great but rigid machine, creating and distributing wealth, but generating friction even in the best years. When the flow of payments was interrupted, the machine worked less smoothly, and friction increased. The crisis of 1869–70, however, suggests that the friction could be increased from outside, without the aid of internal pressure. Great open-air meetings, discussion in the newspapers, and the prospect of legislative change stimulated excitement. For many tenants attendance at tenant-right meetings or voting Liberal was enough; for others threatening letters and more direct efforts seemed appropriate. The crisis of 1879–80 was a combination of the economic dislocation that

---

[92] W. E. Vaughan, 'Farmer, Grazier and Gentleman: Edward Delany of Woodtown, 1851–99', *Ir. Econ. & Soc. Hist.* 9 (1982), 60; *Sel. Comm. on Westmeath, 1871*, 71; A. C. Murray, 'Agrarian Violence and Nationalism in Nineteenth-Century Ireland: The Myth of Ribbonism', *Ir. Econ. & Soc. Hist.* 13 (1986), 59.
[93] Thornley, *Isaac Butt*, 69–79; Comerford, *Fenians*, 175–81.
[94] See e.g. National Archives, RP 1870/6970 and 1871/14028.
[95] See below, App. 23. [96] See below, App. 7.
[97] See below, App. 2. [98] See below, App. 19.

caused the crises of the early 1850s and early 1860s with the excitement of 1869–70.

v. The Importance of Agrarian Outrages

Agrarian outrages were not so numerous as to justify extreme views of their significance. Landlords as a group, however, did attract a lot of crime. They were a small group, even when agents and bailiffs are added, certainly less than 5 per cent of the tenants in numbers, yet they attracted 35 per cent of agrarian outrages.[99] This may have been a small fraction of total outrages, but it was a lot for a small group. This reflects the fact that landlords formed the pivot for a large number of transactions, which accounts for the disproportion on a mere *per capita* basis. The average tenant was involved in only one transaction likely to lead to crime: the succession to his farm. The average landlord, on the other hand, over a thirty-year period was involved in thousands of transactions that could provoke crime.

One reason why agrarian outrage received so much attention was the moral entrepreneurship of those who discussed it. Both landlords and tenants had axes to grind: the former argued that sterner government would restore order; the latter argued that land reform would remove the causes of outrages. The *Galway Vindicator*, in a leader in May 1862, discussing the murder of landlords, argued that a good land bill would do more to prevent the perpetration of such crimes than the hanging of 'every suspected person in the country'.[100] (The facts changed quickly of course when coercive legislation was discussed. 'Never was a country so free from crime of every sort as Ireland is at the present day,' wrote John Blunden in a pamphlet in 1873, criticizing the peace preservation act and the Westmeath act.[101])

Did agrarian outrage frighten landlords? Did it slow up the operation of estate management? When J. H. Fetherston Haugh was murdered in 1868, it was believed that the cause of his death was his attempt to increase rents. After his death, 'those managing the late Mr Fetherston's property have warned the tenants on the estate to pay *the old* rent'—in other words, they gave up the proposed increases.[102] Other examples of landlords' pusillanimity can be found. In March 1869 G. J. Hornidge resigned as agent for estates in Westmeath because he was afraid that a 'reign of terror is setting in'.[103] In 1872 Dr Samuel Edge refused to serve the office of sheriff of the Queen's County because he had been 'repeatedly' attacked, never

---

[99] Above, p. 149.
[100] *Galway Vindicator*, 21 May 1862; see also *The Nation*, 24 May 1862, Larcom papers (NLI, MS 7637), and National Archives, outrage papers, Tyrone, 1852/100.
[101] John Blunden, *The Coercion Acts (Ireland): A Speech Delivered before a Meeting of the Home Government Association, 24 June 1873* (Dublin, 1873), 4.
[102] National Archives, RP 1868/14733.   [103] Ibid. 1869/11971.

told his servants where he was going, and was 'afraid of having public appointments to keep'.[104] Even William Steuart Trench, for all his high words, could temper bravado with prudence. Having disturbed the barony of Farney by refusing an abatement in 1851, he left the district, and from a safe distance offered an abatement of 25 per cent. In County Monaghan as a whole, one RM thought that the cowardice of certain landlords encouraged crime: one landlord gave an abatement after being fired at; Lord Blayney refused an abatement, but gave 25 per cent after Thomas Bateson was murdered.[105]

On the other hand, threats made some landlords more stubborn. Richard Fetherston Haugh of Rockview, undeterred by his kinsman's murder in 1868, threatened to dismiss his thirty-six labourers when his steward got a threatening letter in November 1869.[106] Captain George Cole Baker was shot dead by one of his tenants, probably Thomas Dwyer, on whom he had served a notice to quit for quarrelling with a neighbour about a right of way. Baker's death put a stop to the ejectment for a year, and proceedings against the Dwyers had to begin again. Baker was survived by his father, Revd William Baker, who decided to get rid of the Dwyers. The constabulary warned him that his life was in danger; his solicitor threw up the case in spite of 'learning the use of the newest pattern of revolver'; but old Baker was 'a singularly incautious man, frequently giving utterance to very strong language, and determined and jealous to a degree'. He got a new solicitor; the Dwyers enlisted the support of their neighbours in the Glen of Aherlow, some of whom were overheard discussing the right time to murder old Baker; but on 29 August 1870, the sub-sheriff, protected by forty-five constables, evicted Thomas Dwyer. Having got Dwyer's farm, Baker 'compelled all his tenants to attend and take part in the destruction of Dwyer's house'.[107] Fear of attack may have restrained some landlords, but probably had the opposite effect on others. Evictions did not stop in Monaghan in the early 1850s, or in Westmeath in 1869–71, or in County Mayo in 1869. Most remarkable of all was the great wave of evictions that began in late 1881 and continued into 1882, in spite of high rates of agrarian outrage.

Reports of agrarian outrages revealed the nature of rural society. None of the sources gives a more intimate picture of rural relationships than the constabulary reports: Charlotte Hinds, the Cavan landlord murdered in 1854, giving an old lame man a lift home from Ballyconnell;[108] Hugh Bradshaw carousing in his kitchen with his tenants;[109] the conversation between Mrs Neill and the man who procured her murder;[110] the strange

[104] Ibid. OP 1873/16. [105] Ibid., outrage papers, Monaghan, 1851/243.
[106] Ibid. RP 1869/18259; see also ibid. 1870/17270. [107] Ibid. 17097.
[108] Ibid., convict reference files, 1856/D/26. [109] Ibid. RP 1869/11937.
[110] Ibid. OP 1872/3/15.

machinations of landlords and tenants manœuvring for position by using the law for their own ends, as in the Davis and Slator cases.[111] The constabulary reports show, although they scarcely mention explicitly, the progress of a revolution in rural Ireland. First, the countryside became less violent between the famine and the land war. Secondly, relations between landlords and tenants were deeply influenced by the operation of a police force that was numerous, centrally controlled, worked within a carefully administered system of law, and had its own *esprit de corps*. It is a simplification, but not a gross one, to say that by the 1870s rural society was dominated by three groups, police, priests, and landed proprietors, and that the third of these was by no means the most powerful. All three were involved in the law enforcement revolution that took place after the famine; indeed, it is arguable that the most important contribution to rural society made by landlords was as magistrates. It is also arguable that the constabulary, working under a centralized government, helped to weaken the landlords before 1879: the land war merely demonstrated what had already happened—landlords had lost control of their tenants.

The decline of serious crime between 1847 and 1876, from 20,968 to 2,048 outrages reported, was remarkable. Admittedly 1847 was a very bad year, when almost as many outrages were recorded as in the whole four-year period 1879–82. Even comparing 1876, however, with pre-famine years, when over 5,000 outrages were recorded, or with the 'normal' post-famine years, when over 4,000 were recorded, the fall appears remarkable.[112] The decline in outrages accompanied other changes: greater prosperity,

---

[111] Ibid. RP 1871/9364, 14028.

[112] See below, App. 19. Dr Hoppen does not think that rural crime declined after the famine: 'it is a mistake to imagine that rural Ireland was in every sense a more peaceful place in the decades immediately after the famine than it had been in the 1830s and 1840s' (Hoppen, *Elections, Politics, and Society*, 356); 'those supposedly decisive reductions in serious crime and violence which have so often been identified as a particular feature of immediately post-famine society seem, on closer examination, ... to have been far from immediate and only haltingly decisive' (ibid. 366). If the numbers of outrages, including agrarian outrages, before, during, and after the famine are compared the contrast is striking: between 1837 and 1844, an average of about 5,600 outrages a year were reported; between 1845 and 1852 the numbers were much greater, being on average about 12,000 a year; but in 1853 the number fell below the pre-famine average, which was not exceeded again until 1880, when 5,669 outrages were reported. If, however, outrages are related to population the change is not so striking nor does it come so early in the 1850s; in 1837–44 there were annually 70 outrages per 100,000 of estimated mid-year population; the post-famine rate did not fall below 70 per 100,000 until 1855; it remained just under 70 per 100,000 in 1856 and 1857, and fell to just under 60 per 100,000 in 1858. After 1858 it rose above the pre-famine rate only in 1862, 1870, 1880, 1881, and 1882. Outrage rates certainly suggest that the post-famine change was not immediate because it did not begin until 1858 and it was 'halting' because it was interrupted in the early 1860s. Whether the five high years between 1858 and 1882, however, render it 'indecisive' is not so clear. If the *trends* of the outrage rates are calculated, they show falls for the periods 1837–69, 1837–79, or 1837–89. Such calculations may not resolve the problem, but they certainly cover 'the decades immediately after the famine'.

uninterrupted emigration, greater literacy, and greater punctuality in paying rents.[113] There was, however, an ancillary revolution hardly noticed by contemporaries: from the 1850s on laws were passed transforming the public behaviour of country people in ways that were not suggested by traditional Christian morality.

In 1851 the summary jurisdiction act set new standards of behaviour on the roads. It became illegal to leave a cart unharnessed on a public road; to leave stones, timber, dung, or turf 'so as to cause danger'; to have dogs unmuzzled or unlogged within 50 yards of a road; to carry loads that projected more than 2 feet beyond the wheels of carts; to allow pigs to wander on the roads; to sell beasts on a road, or to fly a kite from a road. Finally, continuing a process of labelling that had begun with the census, the ordnance survey, and the tenement valuation, all carts had to display their owners' names 'in legible letters not less than an inch in height'.[114] This was hardly a draconian statute, but the trend continued and culminated in the public health act of 1878, which was intrusive. It became illegal to keep pigs in a house 'so as to be a nuisance to any person'; to have a wake for anyone who died of a dangerous, infectious disease; not to remove manure when ordered to do so by a justice; not to disinfect a house whose inhabitants had infectious diseases. Most remarkable of all was section 147, making vaccination compulsory for children under 14, if ordered by a justice.[115] (Another act in 1879 made vaccination compulsory for all children within 3 months of birth.[116]) These acts were, however, only part of a process that included more than carts and vaccination. Between the 1850s and the early 1880s the constabulary were given the power to search poachers on the public road;[117] the compulsory registration of births, deaths, and marriages was established in 1864;[118] dogs had to be licensed;[119] the opening hours of public houses were further restricted,[120] and Sunday closing was introduced;[121] it became an offence to sell liquor to children under 16;[122] railway companies were forbidden to put on special trains for prize fights.[123]

Landlords acting as magistrates were deeply involved in the enforcement of this legislation. From the early 1850s more and more people appeared before the petty sessions, charged with offences that had not existed a

---

[113] See also Fitzpatrick, 'Class, Family and Rural Unrest in Nineteenth-Century Ireland', 62, for a discussion of the effects of changes in family size and the decline of sub-letting on rural crime. [114] 14 & 15 Vict., c. 92 (7 Aug. 1851).
[115] 41 & 42 Vict., c. 52 (8 Aug. 1878). [116] 42 & 43 Vict., c. 70 (15 Aug. 1879).
[117] 25 & 26 Vict., c. 114 (7 Aug. 1862).
[118] 26 & 27 Vict., c. 11 (20 Apr. 1863); 26 & 27 Vict., c. 90 (28 July 1863).
[119] 28 & 29 Vict., c. 50 (19 June 1865).
[120] 35 & 36 Vict., c. 94 (10 Aug. 1872). (I am indebted to Dr Elizabeth Malcolm for information on the licensing laws.) [121] 41 & 42 Vict., c. 72 (16 Aug. 1878).
[122] 35 & 36 Vict., c. 94 (10 Aug. 1872).
[123] 31 & 32 Vict., c. 119, sect. 21 (31 July 1868).

generation earlier. At Clonbur petty sessions in November 1869, for example, two men were fined 1s. each for not having their dogs licensed—almost a day's wages for a relatively new offence.[124] In 1840 there were 146,000 summary convictions at the petty sessions; in 1880 there were 194,371.[125] Most of those convicted in the 1870s were first offenders; most were men; a very large proportion of the male population, therefore, must have passed through the courts in a single decade. The petty sessions came to impinge on the lives of ordinary people as much, if not as frequently and persistently, as the confessional and the national school.

What effects did this have on relations between landlords and tenants? The countryside became more orderly and less exasperating for those who lived there. A letter to the *Evening Mail* in 1868 from 'An English-Irish landlord' made this point with an anecdote. Before the famine a certain landlord, who could not collect his rents, was approached by 'Old B.', the leader of a faction, who offered to collect the rents if he were made agent. His methods were simple and effective: he threatened to quarter his faction on the defaulters. Recently, however, 'Old B.', having undergone the usual transformation from rogue to venerable figure, whipped a boy whom he had caught stealing his gooseberries, but he had to give the boy £1 to avoid prosecution for assault.[126]

Of all the groups effected by these changes, probably the gentry changed most. From being practically the only law enforcement agency in the eighteenth century, they became merely an ancillary of the nineteenth-century constabulary and heavily dependent on a force they did not control. When agrarian outrages happened there were high words in Tory newspapers about lynch law. The reality, however, was less exciting. At the first sign of danger the landlords usually turned to the constabulary for protection. Landlord-inspired violence was almost negligible; in 1871 in Londonderry Revd Mitchell Smyth's servant struck a tenant and a labourer with a hatchet in a row about timber;[127] a tenant in Kilkenny in 1849 who went to execute a writ of replevin was met 'by a large body of men, armed by the landlord and his agent with guns, pistols, and bayonets, and other deadly weapons', and one of his servants was shot dead.[128] Landlords rarely responded to personal attacks with that intrepidity that was so necessary in the eighteenth century. They rarely returned the fire of their attackers. Some cases did occur, but they were rare. In September 1879 Sydney Smyth, the son of a Mayo agent, shot and killed one of his father's attackers;

---

[124] *Ballinrobe Chronicle*, 27 Nov. 1869.
[125] National Archives, ICR, return of outrages, 1850; *Judicial Statistics, Ire., 1880*, p. 28 [C 3028], HC 1881, xcv. 270. (The figures relate to the whole country exclusive of the Dublin metropolitan area.) [126] Newscutting in the Larcom papers (NLI, MS 7613).
[127] National Archives, OP 1872/85, no. 57.
[128] Ibid., outrage papers, Kilkenny, 1849/246.

in December 1880 Miss Louisa Martha Ellard, who was fired at near Oola station, fired three shots from a small revolver at her attackers.[129]

By 1870 it is doubtful if many landlords wanted to go back to the eighteenth century; few would have agreed with William Steuart Trench, who in 1852 told Lord Rossmore that he had armed himself and his 'people'; for 'I have long thought and have acted on it throughout that if we are not able to hold the country (except in the case of actual insurrection) with our own aid, we are not fit to have it'.[130] It is doubtful if even the northern gentry, who were relatively confident of their power in the countryside, wanted to go back to the state of affairs brought to an end by the party processions act in 1850, when magistrates had to use all their resources of influence, bluff, and boldness to keep Ribbonmen from attacking Orangemen on 12 July, and vice versa on St Patrick's day.[131] Nor did the southern gentry find it worth their while to encourage faction fights, confident 'that factions would serve the same purpose as the stone thrown by Cadmus among the earth-born warriors of Thebes, that of turning the violence of the combatants... upon one another'.[132] By the 1850s the gentry were at least two generations away from the conditions that prevailed in the contemporary *antebellum* south: they could not have coped with lynchings, *charivari*, or a countryside without police and prisons. When the trouble began in 1879 pens rather than pistols were the gentry's first resource; extra police, paid for by the Treasury, rather than their own armed servants, was what they wanted.

The landlords' position in the new law enforcement hierarchy was not, from their point of view, a comfortable one. On the one hand, they were still formally responsible for the good order of their counties; twice a year as grand jurors they waited on the assize judges to be lectured on the state of their counties; they were given lavish marks of respect by the constabulary—JPs were saluted and arms were presented to the lieutenant of the county and the deputy lieutenants. On the other hand, they did not control the constabulary: neither promotions nor postings were greatly influenced by the lay magistrates; the numbers and distribution of the force as a whole were determined by the government, and paid for by the Treasury. They were not completely independent as magistrates; for not only did the supervision of the court of queen's bench persist, but stipendiary magistrates and the constabulary kept an eye on them, and were quick to report their shortcomings to the Castle.

---

[129] Ibid. ICR, returns of outrages, 1879–80.
[130] Ibid., outrage papers, Monaghan, 1852/39.
[131] *Papers Relating to an Investigation Held at Castlewellan into the Occurrences at Dolly's Brae on 12 July 1849*, p. 41 [1143], HC 1850, li. 371.
[132] George Cornewall Lewis, *On Local Disturbances in Ireland and on the Irish Church Question* (London, 1836), 289.

The restraints on lay magistrates were not merely formal, for several were removed from the commission, or threatened with removal. Thomas Weldon Trench, Lord Digby's agent in the Queen's County, having been asked by the people of Geashill to protect them from tramps, who were going about 'levying large contributions upon them', imprisoned Alice Delin, who died in prison on Christmas Eve 1861. After a great public outcry, including the publication of a parliamentary paper[133] and a pamphlet,[134] the lord chancellor decided not to remove Trench from the commission, but merely to rebuke him. 'The whole proceeding', Trench was told, 'was hasty and irregular; it had the appearance of great and unnecessary harshness, and the conviction and committal were both illegal.... The lord chancellor hopes he may, without peril to the administration of justice, refrain from taking the extra step of removing you from the commission of the peace.'[135] The gentry had to share their traditional power and prestige with *fonctionnaires*; but it was all the more galling that stipendiaries and constabulary assumed existing positions of prestige. The constabulary assumed the uniforms, military bearing, and airs and graces that were the prerogative of the army and militia. The stipendiaries were even more insidious. At first they were just JPs who were paid; gradually they were given extra powers denied to ordinary magistrates; eventually they became known as resident magistrates, appropriating to themselves the very title that the gentry had formerly used to differentiate themselves from the stipendiaries. Uneasily lodged in a system they did not control, acting as petty judges under constant scrutiny, the gentry were forced to administer a system of law where discretion, flexibility, and bargaining were not valued. They were also forced to administer a penal code that was gradually extending itself beyond its traditional limits and creating new causes of annoyance that had nothing to do with their interests as landlords.

Did this weaken the landlords? There is no overwhelming evidence that they were unpopular as magistrates. A Meath magistrate was fired at in 1870 because he had committed for trial a man who had a sheepskin for which he could not account.[136] Dr Samuel Edge, a magistrate in the Queen's County, was unpopular as a magistrate and landlord.[137] But such cases seem to have been rare. There was some envy of their wide powers. Bishop Nulty, for example, thought that they should not have the power of granting licences to publicans.[138] Much of the odium of enforcing the new legislation fell not on the landlords acting as magistrates but on the

---

[133] Copies 'of the Deposition Taken at a Coroner's Inquest Held at Tullamore in the King's County, 3 January 1862, on the Body of Alice Delin...' HC 1862 (377), xliv. 639.
[134] The Case of the Old and Respected Poor Alice Delin: 'Done to Death' on Christmas Eve, in the Barony of Geashill.... No beggar! (Dublin, 1862).
[135] Larcom papers (NLI, MS 7639).
[136] Sel. Comm. on Westmeath, 1871, 169.
[137] National Archives, OP 1873/16.
[138] Sel. Comm. on Westmeath, 1871, 114.

constabulary, especially in connection with the summary jurisdiction act and the dog regulation act. According to William O'Hara, RM, 'the employment of the constabulary in cases of road nuisances makes them unnecessarily unpopular'. Another RM, Benjamin Hill, was more specific: 'nothing tends more to prevent the constabulary from gaining information from country people than ... prosecuting them for the trespass of their pig or cow, and when they see the police coming they always suspect it is for that purpose.'[139] (Sir Francis Head found that in the west of Ireland the logging of dogs was blamed on 'the aristocricy [sic] of England'.[140])

There were, however, losses as well as gains for the landlords. First, the new police gave them too much power in some respects, and not enough in others; secondly, the new law enforcement system gave magistrates few opportunities to do favours to those who fell foul of it; thirdly, the very efficiency of the constabulary meant that landlords no longer needed to keep in touch with local realities—with trouble-makers, men of influence, factions, and family connections. From being the governors of the countryside, they became merely rich men who happened to live there, taking a prominent and ornate rather than an indispensable part in its affairs. They could now employ as bailiffs, not the local, natural NCOs, but Scotsmen and agriculturists. When the agriculturist on Lord Gosford's estate was dismissed for drunkenness, the agent wanted a successor who would abstain from drinking with the tenants.[141] If the agent had really wanted to keep in touch with the tenants, conviviality would have been a necessary qualification, and not a disqualification, for the post. On the other hand, the constabulary enabled landlords to carry out evictions with relative ease; without such a ready instrument, evictions would have been slower and more dependent on bargaining. Yet the whole legal system was not made to conform to the new constabulary system: the civil law was still heavily dependent on the sub-sheriff and his civilian assistants, and on litigants themselves. If the constabulary had done everything necessary at evictions, such as serving processes, landlords would have had an even more powerful instrument at their service.

By the 1870s landlords had ceased to make themselves useful by providing law and order as they had done in the eighteenth century. The new system that employed them did not give them the obvious alternative role—to mediate between their dependents and the encroachments of an expanding bureaucracy—for it was not arbitrary enough to give many opportunities for mediation. At most the magistrates restrained the constabulary. Westmeath magistrates, for example, were reluctant to convict under section 23 of the peace preservation act, which made it an offence

[139] National Archives, RP 1870/2757.
[140] Sir Francis B. Head, bt., *A Fortnight in Ireland* (London, 1852), 225.
[141] Above, pp. 112–13.

to be out at night without a good reason. In early 1871, after a number of murders, the constabulary were inclined to arrest servant boys or 'noted' Ribbonmen if they had no better reason for being out at night 'than ... that they had been spending the evening with a friend, or playing the flute at a Sunday night dance, or card playing in a cabin'. The magistrates, however, dismissed such cases. 'The view taken by the magistrates completely nullifies the action of the police,' complained Sub-Inspector Harcourt.

They stated that any person (no matter how bad his character) had a perfect right to be out, at any hour of night, for business or pleasure; and that if a man gave any such reason, as before mentioned, when found by the police, that the latter should not arrest him—unless they could prove that his excuse was untrue.[142]

The liberality of the lay magistrates was not shared by Captain Talbot, RM, who believed that 'a man of bad character known to the police is not on his legitimate business sauntering from public house to public house no matter what trifling excuse he may allege.'[143]

Magistrates occasionally thwarted the constabulary. William Evans of Gilliardstown House, Killucan, an extensive land agent in County Westmeath, who was also a JP, fired at two men whom he saw lurking in his garden. The men, who 'came to the pleasure ground after work to meet one of the servant maids', were wounded by the falling shot, but refused to give evidence against Evans, who was 'very popular among the people'. The constabulary had pressed the case, and at first the men were willing enough to prosecute; but their ardour cooled when Evans gave them a *douceur* of £120. The lay magistrates on the bench understood what was going on and dismissed the case; but the RM protested, insisted that his protest be recorded, and complained formally to the under-secretary.[144] Private justice had advantages. It offered some prospect of reparation, which official justice usually did not. In 1851 three men broke into the house of Michael McVeagh, near Drumlish, County Longford, and stole £56. One of the thieves was recognized by a man called Kenny, and turned approver. A reward of £30 had been offered, and it was divided between the approver, the victim, and Kenny, who had identified the thief. Its division showed the wretched inequality of official justice: Kenny got £5; the approver got £15 (and presumably his share of the plunder); the unfortunate McVeagh got £10 'in consideration of the loss he sustained', a poor recompense for the £56 he had lost, 'which he had acquired by hard industry, and close application to business for the past forty years'.[145]

Examples of magistrates helping tenants in difficulties come to light occasionally. The rector of Drumkeeran, Revd Edward Semple, discovered

---

[142] National Archives, RP 1871/4466; see also ibid., outrage papers, Monaghan, 1852/31.
[143] Ibid. RP 1871/3349.   [144] Ibid. 1869/2947.
[145] Ibid., outrage papers, Longford, 1852/110.

irregularities in the management of the Vaughan Charity at Kesh, County Fermanagh; when he received two threatening letters in November 1851, the constabulary arrested Mrs Anne Acheson of Kesh; but she was released when William Archdall, JP, whose family owned 33,000 acres in Fermanagh, offered to act as her surety.[146] When Charles Crotty was fired at and later seriously wounded in Mayo in March 1870, the district where he lived was subjected not only to a police tax but also to a levy of 4s. in the £ of valuation to pay compensation to Crotty. Part of the district appealed against the levy, led by Fr. James Browne, and a memorial was sent to the lord-lieutenant on behalf of 'a quiet, peaceable people of primitive habits'. The memorial was signed mainly by priests, but also by three laymen, all JPs: Valentine Blake, Captain Maurice Blake, and Robert Tighe. The RM concerned was not impressed: Maurice Blake (who was Valentine's son) was 'a certain candidate for the representation of the county at the next general election', and his 'great supporter' among the clergy was Fr. Browne, the leader of the agitation; Tighe was 'a most excellent old gentleman', whose son Thomas was 'somewhat of a leading politician in Mayo', and also spoken of as a candidate at the next election. (Thomas was 'an extensive grocer, brewer, manure merchant, and agricultural seedsman', whose business transactions *connect him most closely with the people*'.)[147]

It is not clear how often landlords tried to keep their tenants out of court. 'It is a common practice for poor persons to come to the head constable to settle any little pecuniary disagreement between them';[148] did they go to their landlord to save them from being fined for having an unlicensed dog? Given the intimate, personal nature of rural Ireland, it is highly improbable that every transgression found its way into the courts.[149] Normally, of course, it is safe to assume that the legal system dealt with only a fraction of all the offences committed; but so many petty crimes found their way into the courts, that it is hard to believe that they were merely the exposed tip of a submerged mass.[150] It is difficult, therefore, to resist the conclusion that landlords did not mediate between their tenants and the acerbities of an enthusiastic constabulary.

The fines and terms of imprisonment imposed by the petty sessions, over 150,000 fines a year, could have formed a fund at the disposal of magistrates, to be redistributed, abated, or increased, as it suited their interests—if the legal system had been less thoroughly supervised, and less machine-like in its operation. An idea of the symbiosis that could have been created by a more arbitrary and personal system of law can be got from the cases that were created under the Westmeath act. The essence of the act was its

---

[146] Ibid., Fermanagh, 1852/71.   [147] Ibid. RP 1872/3472.
[148] Head, *A Fortnight in Ireland*, 204.
[149] Erne accounts (Co. Fermanagh), 1858–78 (PRONI, D1939/9/1, p. 81).
[150] *Judicial Statistics, Ire.*, 1871, p. 22 [C 674], HC 1872, lxv. 256.

arbitrariness: suspected Ribbonmen could be imprisoned without trial. Less than twenty suspects were imprisoned, although the constabulary kept an eye on about sixty more in Westmeath and the neighbouring districts of Meath and the King's County.[151] The lord-lieutenant's arbitrary power gave the constabulary a means to bargain with suspects who were beyond the reach of the ordinary law. While the suspects were in gaol the government and constabulary appear to have kept three objects in view: to persuade some to emigrate in return for their release; to keep some in gaol until it was clear that their confederates outside had learnt to behave themselves; to patch up some kind of reconciliation between victims and suspects, using the prospect of liberation as a bait.

The obvious candidates for emigration were the riff-raff of the conspiracy, employed by the leaders. Patrick Murray, a labourer 'capable of committing any crime for money or drink', declared in April 1872, during a drunken spree in Kells, that he would shoot J. A. Nicholson of Balrath ('I'd rather than all I earned I could get a shot at him'). Since Nicholson had already been fired at, Murray was immediately put in gaol, but was released in August, on condition that he emigrated. The RM William Byrne suggested this, pointing out that Murray was so dissipated that he would never save enough money to come home again. The actual business of raising the passage money, however, revealed some of the unexpected assumptions of rural life. Murray and his family expected Nicholson to pay; but he refused, saying he was not afraid of Murray. According to the RM, this refusal 'will make Murray a more bitter enemy'. Eventually when Murray's mother approached Nicholson a second time, he agreed to pay half the passage money; the constabulary suggested that the RM should pay the other half, which he did, although protesting.

The most prominent suspect to emigrate was James Mealia, a hotel-keeper in Mullingar and one of the leaders of the conspiracy. Mealia had been present at the murder of Thomas Waters and Thomas Anketell; he had emigrated to Buenos Aires in the early 1860s, having been publicly excommunicated for Ribbonism. The constabulary were not anxious to arrest him, for as soon as the Westmeath act became imminent he sold his hotel and prepared for flight. He was, however, arrested in June 1871, but released very quickly and allowed to emigrate. In other cases the state of Westmeath was considered when releases were discussed. William Barry, RM, for example, was in favour of releasing James Hynds only eight months after his arrest because the district he had came from was 'satisfactory'; but the constabulary objected, claiming that 'unmistakeable terrorism prevails'.

The case of William Malowney showed how suspects, victims, and the

[151] National Archives, OP /1872/3/1–15; the cases cited below are easily located under the suspects' names.

authorities could be bound together in a series of implicit bargains. Malowney was described as 'an exceedingly bad man... almost American but without the nasal twang. Has a sharp fox-like expression. Respectable looking.' He had been dismissed from the Messrs. Perrys' mill for misconduct in 1868; afterwards he not only wrote several threatening letters, but appears to have got his successor at the mill, Francis Dowling, murdered in November 1870. As soon as the Westmeath act passed he fled, which suited the authorities. In February 1874, however, one of the Perrys called on the RM, asking him to allow Malowney to come back, without fear of arrest, to visit his wife, who had typhus. The authorities refused, but a few months later in June Henry Perry, 'who is a tender-hearted man, wished to run the chance of any personal risk that William Malowney's return might bring to him, rather than that his wife should die in his absence'. He tried again within a few days, arguing that Malowney had been punished enough by an enforced absence of two and a half years and that he 'may turn over a new leaf'. Finally in July 1874 the government agreed to allow him to return and the under-secretary gave instructions that Malowney's family were to be told that his return was due to Perry's intercession.

The most dramatic example of bargaining was the case of 'Captain' Duffy, who was a leader of the conspiracy. He had been involved in the murder of Thomas Waters and the attempted murders of G. J. Hornidge, a tenant called Keelaghan, and Revd James Crofton, his landlord. He was arrested in October 1872 and after a year in gaol he had a most unexpected visitor: Revd James Crofton, whom he had tried to murder. What they said to each other was not recorded, but it is tempting to see their meeting as a parochial rehearsal of the famous meetings that took place in Kilmainham nine years later. Within a week Crofton wrote to the lord-lieutenant asking for Duffy's release, claiming that Duffy had promised not to meddle in any disturbances if released. 'I know all Duffy is accused of,' said Crofton, 'but I think he has a sort of savage honour and kindness might do more with him than severity.' His release would 'be a graceful compliment to the County Westmeath, which is now perfectly quiet'. William Morris Reade, RM, to whom the case was referred, was sceptical and claimed that after meeting Duffy, Crofton had met his tenants, whose rents he had tried to increase, and offered them a choice. Either they paid the increased rents and took leases or he would sell the estate to the highest bidder. Reade suspected that Crofton and Duffy had made a bargain. 'It savours strongly of his feeling his way with Duffy before going to the country,' wrote Reade. 'Should it however seem that any treaty has been come to between Mr Crofton and Captain Duffy, I would say let him stay where he is for the present.' The government, however, were not as squeamish about making a treaty between Crofton and Duffy, for Duffy was released within a month of the Kilmainham meeting. Reade seems to have had his way in only one respect. When Duffy was released he was told that his release was 'the act of his excellency alone, entirely independent of any application to him from any source', which doubtless convinced Duffy that he owed his enlargement to Crofton.

The initiative did not always come from landlords like Crofton, but from the suspects and their friends, who were confident that the word of a magistrate would help them. James Hynds appealed to Samuel Winter, JP and to Lt.-Col. Nugent, JP (whose servant he had threatened) for a character before his release in July 1873. Patrick Dunne, a small farmer and brick-maker, suspected of procuring the murder of J. H. Fetherston Haugh, had prominent friends: G. J. N. D'Arcy of Hyde Park, Killucan, 'considers him quiet and peaceable', and Fulke Greville, MP for Westmeath, took up his case. (Dunne's stepfather, Michael Cavanagh, appealed to Gladstone, 'whose fame for justice and generosity has reached even our humble cottage'.)

The Westmeath act pacified Westmeath. Between 1872 and 1877 there were no agrarian homicides and only one firing in the county. The act worked in a way that was contrary to the principles of the ordinary legal system: the punishment bore no relation to the crime; suspects were encouraged to abscond; serious crimes, such as the murder of Francis Dowling, were conveniently forgotten in order to patch up the quarrel between Malowney and the Perrys; imprisonment was not for a fixed term, but held *in terrorem*. The Westmeath act did not show that Ireland could have been better governed by *lettres de cachet*; but it did show that pacifying connections between rogues and their victims could be established by an arbitrary legal system that played on mutual parasitism. Some landlords were quick to see the possibilities of the act. Joseph Tuite, who had an estate of 7,000 acres in Westmeath, recommended the arrest of James Kenny whom he was about to evict for non-payment; but Captain Barry, RM did not agree, for Tuite, 'like others in this district, would wish to make recent exceptional legislation auxiliary in the eviction of a tenant'.

If landlords found the legal system unresponsive to pressure, they found the constabulary confident and assertive. When a magistrate accused the constabulary in Enniskillen of negligence and insolence, the county inspector protested that his subordinate 'had too much the feelings of a gentleman to *intentionally* give offence, or neglect the duties of his office'.[152] In practice the constabulary was a bureaucratic institution, with its own procedures. Paper was its most characteristic *matériel* and words its most commonly used weapon. William Beers, a County Down magistrate, complained at a meeting of magistrates that a sub-inspector had referred to him in a report, not by his name, but as 'this magistrate'. The sub-inspector

---

[152] Ibid., outrage papers, Fermanagh, 1849/154.

explained his usage with a fluency that must have dismayed the other magistrates present. 'The phrase "this magistrate" was merely used', he said, 'to avoid tautology and to commence a sentence without useless repetition of his name.' When the magistrates, unimpressed and probably uncomprehending, asked him to withdraw the phrase, he refused, appealing to his 'position as an officer and a gentleman'.[153]

The constabulary had the ear of the government. There was probably nowhere in Ireland, not even in the offices of *The Nation* newspaper, where landlords were treated with such objectivity as in Dublin Castle, for the constabulary and the RMs successfully interposed themselves between the government and the gentry. They had an impressive record of fairness—occasionally they would take the side of landlords, occasionally not. By the 1860s the RMs had established as a dogma that lay magistrates were not as conscientious as they should have been. In 1870 in reports on the state of the country RMs spoke freely of 'the pusillanimous and timid conduct of some landlords and magistrates, [which] has been the cause of serious evil'.[154] Hints of landlords' culpable selfishness were freely dropped: 'resident country gentlemen are not infrequently influenced in similar cases by the same weakness of *disinterested* kindness and charity,' wrote A. J. R. Stritch, RM, who was shocked when Sir George O'Donnell and Captain Kingscote were parties to a memorial asking the lord-lieutenant to lift the police tax that he had imposed after the 'foul murder' of James Hunter.[155] There were complaints about lay magistrates' bad attendance at the petty sessions. During the disturbances in County Monaghan in 1851 Patrick Howley, RM, asked eight magistrates to meet him, but only two came, for 'now that there is a stipendiary magistrate in the district the whole responsibility and onus is thrown on him'.[156]

It would be an exaggeration to say that the 'aristocracy of Ireland ... had no hand, act, or part in the government of the country ... for the last twenty years',[157] but it is true that between 1846 and 1874 the Tories were out of office for most of the time. The constabulary reports, which even after the lapse of a century seem open-minded and impartial, if a little prim, must have had a cumulative effect on those who read them, whether lords-lieutenant, chief secretaries, under-secretaries, or law officers. The constabulary also emerged in the late 1860s not only as the heroes of the Fenian fiasco, but vindicated after the criticism of the early 1860s. 'Who would govern Ireland', reflected Sir Thomas Larcom, contemplating changes

[153] Ibid., Down, 1849/27.   [154] Ibid. RP 1870/2757, report of D. G. Bodkin.
[155] Ibid. 1871/20698.
[156] Ibid., outrage papers, Monaghan, 1851/20; see also RP 1871/9868; for surveys of magistrates' performance see RP 1879/14981 (7628); 1880/13911. (I am indebted to Richard Hawkins for these last two references.)
[157] [Robert Maunsell,] *Recollections of Ireland: Collected from Fifty Years' Practice and Residence in the Country* (Windsor, 1865), 272.

in the constabulary's prestige, 'must have much patience, with a wholesome disregard to cuckoos and parrots, whether in parliament or the press.'[158]

The constabulary, RMs, and the Castle set a practical limit to the landlords' power. According to Lord Carlisle in 1864 (lord-lieutenant 1855–8, 1859–64), 'there has always been a disposition among some remnants of the old ascendancy party to recover what they formerly lost,' that is, control of the constabulary established in 1836.[159] By the late 1860s it is doubtful if there was even a small risk that the constabulary would pass out of the control of the government. Consequently, the constabulary, the RMs, and the Castle added a formality and inflexibility to law enforcement that did not suit the exigencies of estate management. It was not only that the constabulary were cumbersome, punctilious, fussy about legal niceties and their own regulations, and always reporting to the Castle; nor was it that they were well prepared for the wrong crisis and more concerned about form than substance; but they also operated only on the fringes of the civil law, merely protecting sub-sheriffs and bailiffs and leaving the real work to be done by litigants.

A dispute in County Tipperary in 1850 between a sub-inspector and a rate collector who was trying to seize the goods of defaulting tenants, a predicament different only in form from that which faced many landlords and agents at that time, shows some of the problems of using the constabulary to protect those who enforced the civil law. Patrick Horan, the rate collector, had failed to make a seizure, for 'the people commenced shouting as is constantly the practice in such cases. . . . *Persons, to the amount of three hundred*, gathered about us, made use of the most awful threats'. On making another attempt, he had a constabulary escort under the command of Sub-Inspector Brew, who either misunderstood his instructions or arrived late. The rate collector, meanwhile, seeing a grey horse being smuggled from one farm, and a grey mare and a foal from another, seized them, although he lost sight of them 'in consequence of a turn in the lane'. Technically he should not have seized animals that he had lost sight of, but he followed them, broke into the house where they were hidden, and seized them, also taking a few carts just to make sure he had enough.

Afterwards Horan and Brew blamed each other for what had happened. The rate collector accused the constabulary of arriving too late; the sub-inspector accused the rate collector of leaving too early. The rate collector claimed that the constabulary were useless even when they had arrived. 'In one instance', he claimed, 'I was nearly knocked down by a man named Pat Davigan and his wife in presence of a constable and about

---

[158] Larcom papers (NLI, MS 7619, no. 1).   [159] Ibid., no. 18.

seven sub-constables not one of whom interfered.' The sub-inspector had his answer ready: the rate collector had broken the law and acted recklessly, for having lost sight of the horses, he had no right to break into an outhouse to seize them. He thought 'he was right because he was successful'; 'that his conduct ought to be pardoned because he merely broke the law against those who resisted it'. In short, the rate collector 'was more ignorant of the law it was his duty to enforce than the simplest peasant in the country'. The sub-inspector was also sceptical about the resistance offered: women, he said, 'always scold under such circumstances and I confess that I know no way of stopping them, the difficulty of restraining a woman's tongue is proverbial'.

It is clear that the rate collector was not unduly worried about niceties. It is doubtful, however, if he regarded himself as above the law. He would have seen the law as accommodating opposing rights, which could be invoked or waived at discretion. Sub-Inspector Brew, however, did not see the law as discretionary, but as a series of rules that governed all actions. The row between them had started earlier than the failed rendezvous. When asked to provide and escort, the sub-inspector had put forward a plan that would have turned the seizure into an elaborate operation. 'Mr Brew', complained the rate collector, 'offered his opinion and proposed how those townlands should be surrounded . . . to which I objected *in toto*, I considering that Mr Brew was only bound to protect me.' Having failed to turn a prosaic debt-collection into a minor military expedition, Brew gave himself the last word. 'Mr Horan', he wrote, 'was an active, determined, and useful man, and with a little wholesome restraint upon him would be an excellent officer.'[160]

The constabulary and RMs were not inevitable; in different political circumstances Ireland might have had a different police system. There might have been county forces, in which officers and men would have been dependent on the gentry for promotion. They would have shared local values, and local ties of kinship, and would have been less machine-like in their operation. There might have been no police except a gendarmerie that would have been engaged only when major disturbances occurred, or when the public revenue was not paid. In both cases the gentry would have been more powerful, if less well protected; they would have been kept in touch with local problems, they would have had to conciliate and intimidate trouble-makers, they could have bargained with legal penalties; on the other hand, they would have been more likely to have been the victims of attacks, and could not have carried out evictions with such ease.

[160] National Archives, outrage papers, Tipperary, 1850/912.

7
Resistance to Landlordism

i. Principles of Aggregation

Landlords were greatly outnumbered by tenants. It was unlikely that landlords could mobilize more than 20,000 able-bodied followers to confront well over half a million tenants. Not only were landlords numerically weak, but they suffered from weaknesses that made them vulnerable to tenants' resistance. They extracted money in a peculiarly visible way; they lived ostentatiously among their tenants; they were easy to get at; their property, in spite of demesne walls, was vulnerable; they were dependent on the operation of legal procedures, whose application was objective, public, and ultimately dependent on the constabulary for enforcement. A rent strike would have crippled the landlords: their burdens were fixed, foreclosure by creditors was not improbable, and unlike industrialists faced by striking workers, a rent strike would bring them no compensation in the form of reduced costs.

The tenants, on the other hand, were numerous, they knew each other, and they had much in common. Their ability to organize themselves, to find what Bishop Nulty called 'principles of aggregation', was crucial to the history of landlord–tenant relations.[1] The development of a trade union among them would have greatly modified the management of estates even without the land acts of 1870 and 1881. Organized resistance, both legal and illegal, between 1879 and 1882 played an important part in changing landlordism. How much organized resistance was there before 1879? Few of the tactics adopted between 1879 and 1882 were new, for tenants had combined to oppose their landlords, encouraged by politicians and others, in 1849–52 and 1869–70.[2]

In 1852, which was by no means the worst of the troubled years after the famine, not only did the tenant league persuade voters to support candidates pledged to land reform, but there was local resistance to the collection of rents and evictions. In County Longford, for example, a bailiff who had served ejectment processes was visited by thirty men, 'some of them with pistols, more with swords', who put him on his knees

---

[1] *Sel. Comm. on Westmeath, 1871*, 116.
[2] For resistance to rents and evictions, see above, pp. 34–9, 63–6; see also Charles Townshend, *Political Violence in Ireland: Government and Resistance since 1848* (Oxford, 1983), 115–16.

to shoot him; but in the end they did not, and merely 'robed' him of his gun.³ In County Tipperary horses and cows seized for arrears were forcibly rescued 'by a number of persons some of whom were armed with spades, sticks, and heavy pieces of wood'.⁴ The ingenious obstruction of legal procedures also occurred. During 1849 and 1850 tenants discovered a loophole in the law allowing them to rescue goods seized for rent. In County Tipperary in September 1850 a party of 200 assembled on a Saturday night, cut the growing corn on a farm of 300 acres, and most remarkably, assembled 'upwards of seventy carts' on the following day and carried away the whole crop.⁵

In 1869–70 there was a wave of crime that coincided with the public meetings organized by a revivified tenant league.⁶ According to an RM in County Mayo, much of the criminal activity, mainly threatening letters and gangs 'visiting' houses, was 'for a general object—the reduction of rents in some shape or form, and not for any immediately personal advantage'.⁷ In March 1870, for example, a party of twenty or thirty visited six houses near Claremorris, warning the tenants not to pay more than the tenement valuation.⁸ Nor was this activity confined to Mayo, although it was probably most frequent there. In February 1870 in County Westmeath the constabulary intercepted a similar party, arrested four of them, and seized a revolver 'of excellent manufacture'.⁹ Altogether in 1869–70 there were probably as many as 100 incidents like these.¹⁰ There was a case of passive resistance in Tipperary in 1870 when 300 people attended a sheriff's sale of the goods of an insolvent tenant, but not a single bid was made.¹¹

Even the organization of local associations, connected with each other through a central body, was not new, for the tenant league of 1850 not only grew out of the tenant protection societies but in its turn encouraged the formation of more local societies. In County Cork in 1852, for example, Fr. David Walsh, the curate of Kildoney, asked his congregation to subscribe to the tenant league and a collector was appointed for each townland in the parish.¹² Nor was social ostracism new, except in its eponymous debt to Captain Boycott; the league in 1851 discussed the possibility of making tenants who took evicted farms 'unworthy to associate with honest

---

³ National Archives, outrage papers, Longford, 1852/105.
⁴ Ibid., Tipperary, 1852/112; see also ibid., Armagh, 1852/18 and Queen's County, 1852/177.   ⁵ Ibid., outrage papers, Tipperary, 1850/1251.
⁶ Thornley, *Isaac Butt*, 69–79; Comerford, *Fenians*, 175–81; above, pp. 160–1.
⁷ National Archives, RP 1871/14028.
⁸ Ibid. 1870/6970. See also 1870/16261 for a visit by a party of 40 in Aug. 1870, which was well after the outbreak of disorder in the winter of 1869–70.
⁹ Ibid. 1870/7126.
¹⁰ Ibid. ICR, returns of outrages, 1869–70. See also Return 'of Outrages Reported to the Royal Irish Constabulary Office from 1 Jan. 1844 to 31 Dec. 1880', p. 15 [C 2756], HC 1881, lxxvii. 901.   ¹¹ *Ballinrobe Chronicle*, 29 Jan. 1870.
¹² National Archives, outrage papers, Cork, 1852/79.

men'.¹³ In Fermoy in 1852 there was a case of incitement to boycott: Fr. William McCarthy went to John Buckley's public house and harangued a crowd of thirty or forty, warning them 'to shun Buckley's house and not to go near him anymore', because he had 'declined to vote for Mr Scully'.¹⁴

It is difficult, however, to quantify the amount of organized resistance to landlords before 1879. Large numbers of tenants attended meetings in the two years before the general election of 1852; large numbers attended meetings in 1869–70; many voted for Liberal candidates in 1852 and 1868; many contributed to the funds of the tenant league in the 1850s; many attended amnesty meetings in 1869. Yet even if the most generous estimates are made, less than a majority of tenants took part in meetings or voted for tenant-right candidates. Fewer joined the branches of the tenant league in the 1850s, or the farmers' clubs of the 1870s. Even if the number of known clubs was only one-half of those that actually existed, their membership could not have included more than 10 per cent of the tenants.¹⁵ There was nothing except the farmers' clubs resembling the formal organization of trade unions. Agrarian outrage reports show a collective element in many outrages. The tendency of threatening letters to lay claim to a collective persona has already been noted.¹⁶ If agrarian homicides between 1858 and 1878 are examined, almost three-quarters had a discernible, if frequently exiguous, collective element—either because more than one person was involved, or because the crime arose out of a common predicament. Too much should not be made of this, however, because the collective element was often slight. Outrages caused by rents or evictions could be seen as collective, but only in the sense that all tenants paid rents and many were threatened with eviction. Closer investigation often shows that the circumstances were peculiar. Furthermore, even if all agrarian outrages directed against landlords had a collective element, which is highly unlikely, it is still not impressive in amount or even degree of co-operation.¹⁷

The tenants were not, however, an unarticulated mass of discrete families. Certainly agents and constabulary were aware of the dangers of concerted opposition, the former at gale-days, and the latter because of the strain put on their resources at evictions. The constabulary could concentrate

---

¹³ Charles Gavan Duffy, *The League of North and South: An Episode in Irish History, 1850–1854* (London, 1886), 41–2.

¹⁴ National Archives, outrage papers, Cork, 1852/184; see also James O'Shea, *Priest, Politics and Society in Post-Famine Ireland: A Study of County Tipperary, 1850–1891* (Dublin and Atlantic Highlands, NJ, 1983), 57.

¹⁵ See Samuel Clark, *Social Origins of the Irish Land War* (Princeton, NJ, 1979), 219, where thirty clubs are mentioned; see also Hoppen, *Elections, Politics, and Society*, 469, where a further eleven are added to Clark's thirty. Even assuming an average membership of 500, only a small percentage of farmers were involved. For the geography of popular movements, including the tenant league and amnesty meetings, see Hoppen, *Elections, Politics, and Society*, 480; for Fenians in the mid-1860s and in 1879 see Comerford, *Fenians*, 208, 222.

¹⁶ Above, p. 153. ¹⁷ Above, p. 149.

their forces only by denuding other areas of policemen; to gather enough constables to carry out major evictions, the reserves in several counties would be used. Agents worried about trivial incidents. William Wann was worried in 1855 about a combination against the crane-master in Arva.[18] The fact, however, that the estate endured nothing worse was for him a matter of self-congratulation when it was offered for sale. 'The estate', he said, 'is nicely balanced as regards the religious character—one half Orange and the other half Roman Catholic. I have looked on this perhaps as a fortunate matter, as such classes *don't combine* to resist landlords and agents.'[19]

Kinship was, of course, one of the most powerful 'principles of aggregation' in the countryside. Three men arrested for the murder of James Howard Fetherston Haugh in 1868 were 'all first cousins to each other'.[20] The formidable 'Captain' Duffy and William Malowney, the leading Ribbonmen in Westmeath, were cousins.[21] It was the relations of Patrick McCooey and James Kirk (hanged for the attempted murder of James Eastwood) who planned to take away their bodies, after their execution in Dundalk in July 1852, and lay them in front of the door of Michael Lawless, who had given evidence against them.[22] 'There is no family but has plenty of people belonging to them,' said a threatening letter in 1869, obviously expecting such a statement to carry weight.[23]

The constabulary were aware of other connections in the countryside. There were, for example, remnants of factions in the 1850s and 1860s. In the early 1860s the inspector-general of constabulary mentioned the Dergs and the Mahers in the King's County, the Duffys and MacNaboos in County Longford, the 'three-year-olds' and 'four-year-olds' in County Cork, and the Whigs and Tories in County Leitrim.[24] The factions were not very important, for the constabulary had almost completely suppressed the fighting that was their main activity. They were not, however, extinct, for one of the men suspected of murdering Francis Fitzgerald in Limerick in 1862 was supposed to have been sheltered by the 'four-year-olds'.[25] The constabulary also spoke of 'connections': the railway workers dismissed by the station-master of Mullingar, who was murdered in 1869, 'had a large and bad connection in the railway';[26] a man accused of murder and

---

[18] Gosford letter-book, 13 Aug. 1855 (PRONI, D1606/5A/1, p. 386).
[19] Ibid. 3, p. 198 (19 Oct. 1868); cf. Wann's reaction to Orange exuberance, below, p. 205.
[20] National Archives, RP 1868/14733.   [21] Ibid. OP 1872/3/9.
[22] Ibid., outrage papers, Louth, 1852/187.   [23] Ibid. RP 1869/15512.
[24] Report on the State of Ireland in 1863 by Sir Henry John Brownrigg (NLI, MS 915, pp. 66–7).
[25] Larcom papers (NLI, MS 7637, no. 42); for factions in 1879 see National Archives, RP 1879/2909 (Sligo), 5930 (Limerick). (I am indebted to Richard Hawkins for these last two references.)   [26] National Archives, RP 1869/11971.

acquitted, although he had admitted his guilt, was one of a numerous family 'who stood in a particular position in the locality, and commanded more influence than his humble rank would lead one to suppose'.[27] The constabulary also believed that hurling matches, races, and patterns were blinds for serious trouble-making. In County Limerick George Fosberry, JP, of Adare, struck a responsive chord when he claimed that hurling matches 'were only got up to prevent notice being taken of strangers from different directions meeting'.[28] The authorities were also suspicious of lonely public houses, remote from constabulary stations; for usually the public house 'affords the police the best means of watching and observing the conduct of the disorderly and suspected of a district'.[29]

Some forms of collective action were created by the government itself through the imposition of penal taxes on disturbed districts, where the inhabitants were forced to combine to defend their interests. After James Hunter's assassination in County Mayo in 1869 a tax of about one-third of the tenement valuation was imposed on his neighbours, forcing them to go about the county begging for money to pay it. They did not, however, stop at begging: three memorials were presented to the lord-lieutenant, including one signed by Sir George O'Donnell, JP, DL and Captain Kingscote, JP.[30] Another interesting response to official action was the often complicated and laborious efforts made to arrange petitions on behalf of convicts lying under sentence of death. The inhabitants of Cavan who pleaded for the life of Thomas Dunne, sentenced to death for the murder of Miss Hinds near Ballyconnell, were typical of such movements.[31] The equally unsuccessful, but even more vigorous efforts made to save John Holden, who had murdered one of his comrades in the constabulary in Dungannon, showed the capacity of local leadership to extend over wide areas when emotions were roused.[32]

All this did not add up to much. Small groups of kinsmen, remnants of factions, tenants annoyed by penal taxes, and little knots of secretive topers were no doubt capable of being formidable, if only in flashes, but they were not likely to work together for long periods. Some of these 'principles of aggregation' were as likely to impede as to facilitate opposition to landlords.[33] Family feuds, faction fights, parish rivalries in sport were divisive; also the solidarities that they represented could work in unexpected ways. Peter Lavelle, the bailiff of an estate in County Mayo, got a threatening

---

[27] *First, Second, and Special Reports from the Select Committee on Juries (Ireland); together with the Proceedings of the Committee, Minutes of Evidence, and Appendix*, p. 177, HC 1873 (283), xv. 581.   [28] National Archives, outrage papers, Limerick, 1852/182.
[29] Ibid. RP 1871/4430.   [30] Ibid. 1871/20698.
[31] Ibid., convict reference files, 1856/D/26.   [32] Ibid. 1860/H/26.
[33] David Fitzpatrick, 'Class, Family and Rural Unrest in Nineteenth-Century Ireland', in P. J. Drudy (ed.), *Irish Studies, 2. Ireland: Land, People and Politics* (Cambridge, 1982), 58–9.

notice in April 1871, after he had met twenty tenants to tell them that the rent of their mountain grazing would be increased. He was, however, unworried by the notice, for 'the greater number of the inhabitants are his friends and relatives and... he does not feel as much apprehensive of danger as he would had they been other than his relatives'.[34] Collective action did not invariably work against landlords. In 1869 during the disturbances in Mayo and Westmeath a fire broke out at Lord Kilmaine's house near Ballinrobe. It was not a malicious fire and 'the tenants were present in large numbers and made every effort to suppress the flames and save the mansion.'[35]

In 1870, also in Mayo, Balla petty sessions heard a case whose significance could easily have been misunderstood. Captain Browne of Brownehall prosecuted two men who had tried to prevent him hunting with the South Mayo Harriers by getting in his way and threatening him with a pistol. They were part of a large crowd that pursued him, shouting 'Skin him alive.' On the face of it, this seemed to anticipate the obstruction of hunting that happened during the land war ten years later.[36] The evidence heard at the petty sessions, however, showed that the two men prosecuted by Browne were supporting their own landlord, Sir Robert Lynch Blosse of Athavallie, who was quarrelling with Browne. Athavallie and Brownehall were contiguous, and Sir Robert and Browne had grown up together; but they had quarrelled about pheasants: Sir Robert had bought and preserved them; Browne had lured them into his land and shot them. Sir Robert had forbidden Browne to enter his lands. The men who had threatened Browne, therefore, were merely showing that they shared Sir Robert's detestation of Browne's unsportsmanlike behaviour.[37]

It must also be remembered that large areas of the country were not only relatively peaceful, orderly, and responsible, but were admitted by the authorities to be so. When Thomas Bateson was murdered in County Monaghan in December 1851, a meeting was held in Derry to express indignation at his death and to subscribe £3,000 as a reward for the arrest of his murderers.[38] In County Down in 1849, after several cases of arson, special constables were appointed at a large meeting in Castlereagh, chaired by the marquis of Downshire.[39] (In County Down, according to the clerk of Holywood petty sessions, 'the humbler classes are generally respectful to the laws and not actuated by any bad feeling towards the higher classes,

---

[34] National Archives, RP 1871/9521.   [35] *Mayo Constitution*, 26 Oct. 1869.
[36] L. P. Curtis, jun., 'Stopping the Hunt, 1881-2: An Aspect of the Irish Land War', in C. H. E. Philpin (ed.), *Nationalism and Popular Protest in Ireland* (Cambridge, 1987), 349-402.   [37] *Mayo Constitution*, 26 Feb. 1870.
[38] National Archives, outrage papers, Monaghan, 1851/244.
[39] Ibid., Down, 1849/9.

and the wealthy are generally very friendly and considerate to the poor'.[40]) Nor was this exemplary behaviour confined to the north. In 1848 George McDonald of Parsonstown memorialized the lord-lieutenant for financial assistance. His business had been ruined because he had chased and arrested two men who had attacked Lord Rosse's agent. According to the crown solicitor, however, McDonald's financial difficulties were not caused by commercial ostracism, for 'in a town so orderly and peaceable as this is, I think conduct so creditable to be rather serviceable than injurious to him.'[41]

Combinations—certainly those of a criminal kind—against landlords were sporadic, localized, and rarely involved more than groups of neighbours or kinsmen. Occasionally something more was established, as in County Westmeath in the 1860s. A tradition of resistance might be built up by several struggles. The tenants of Kilcoosh, who resisted the sheriff in 1853, had put up an impressive struggle in the previous year (over a turf bank) in which two men had been wounded.[42] The effects of such struggles on landlords were not negligible; they were, nevertheless, not likely to be permanent, for the tenants lacked formal organization and the ability to formulate abstract, permanent principles. Even making the most of what opposition there was, there was in fact nothing in rural Ireland before 1879 to compare in effectiveness and sophistication with the agricultural labourers' unions that were organized in England in the 1870s. Alfred Simmons's Kent and Sussex Labourers' Union, for example, had at the end of its first year 130 branches and 8,000 members, in spite of farmers sacking and evicting its members, and strike-breaking by soldiers and coastguards.[43]

In some respects Simmons faced more formidable problems than Davitt and Daly in 1879: agricultural labourers were poorer, more dependent than most small farmers; also, those who employed them had to be opposed without being destroyed, which was not a consideration that bothered the land league. It could be argued, of course, that farmers were more difficult to organize than labourers; but the farmers of Aberdeen set an excellent example of self-help, or as Gladstone preferred to call it, home rule, during the outbreak of foot-and-mouth disease in the 1860s.[44] There were two exceptions to the apparent failure of country people to organize effectively, one of which was positive and the other negative: the conspiracy known as Ribbonism and the ability of tenants to shield criminals from the law.

[40] Ibid. 1849/26.   [41] Ibid., Tipperary, 1851/378.
[42] Ibid., Galway, 1852/197; above, p. 20.
[43] Rollo Arnold, 'The "Revolt of the Field" in Kent, 1872-9', *Past & Present*, no. 64 (Aug. 1974), 71-95.   [44] John Vincent, *Gladstone and Ireland* (London, 1977), 233.

ii. The Concealment of Criminals

When James Howard Fetherston Haugh was shot near Killucan in April 1868, his driver 'was refused all assistance and told by [a] woman that for £300 she would not give it'.[45] Constabulary reports contain many examples of witnesses afraid to give evidence, juries that refused to convict on the clearest evidence, and even victims who refused to prosecute their assailants. The coercive legislation passed between 1847 and 1875 was intended to put pressure on communities that concealed evidence: a communal fine in the form of the police tax, the levying of compensation for agrarian murder, and punishment of those who would not give evidence were attempts to deal with localities where normal judicial processes would not work.[46] The authorities believed that agrarian crime was more likely to evoke sympathy than ordinary crime. In a report on the state of Tipperary in 1870 S. F. Carew, RM argued in favour of the suspension of habeas corpus. Although the detection of crime by the constabulary was more frequent 'than is generally supposed', he claimed that it was unlikely that juries would convict 'in cases of agrarianism'.[47] Another RM went further:

The detection of crime and the procuring of any reliable evidence will always be extremely difficult, as long as the people are dissatisfied with the laws, especially those relating to land. Should a law be passed, giving tenants a legal remedy against arbitrary evictions and excessive rents, the government might hope for a large diminution in crime.[48]

According to the chairman of County Meath, 'in all instances of ordinary crime such as private murders and assaults, casual riots, larcenies, etc., which are all unconnected with the dangerous confederacies in Ireland, the crimes are made amenable to justice.'[49] Even illicit distillation was easier to detect than agrarian crime, according to Arthur Mitchell, RM, who had to deal with the disturbances in County Mayo in 1870, because rewards persuaded the poteen-makers to betray each other.[50]

An example of how the constabulary were frustrated occurred near Mullingar in 1851 when 'an agrarian outrage of a very desperate character was perpetrated'. A family called Hussey, who had taken a farm from which another family had been evicted, were attacked in their house by six men. One of the sons, Matthew, was wounded in the head; his father, Thomas, jumped out of bed, threatened the intruders with a pistol that misfired; 'at the same time one of the fellows outside presented a blunderbuss at him, which went off', wounding Hussey's cousin, James Carey, as

---

[45] National Archives, RP 1868/14733. [46] Above, pp. 140–1.
[47] National Archives, RP 1870/2757. [48] Ibid., report of J. C. Rutherford.
[49] Larcom papers (NLI, MS 7619, no. 21). [50] National Archives, RP 1871/14028.

he was getting out of bed. Carey died, one of the Husseys identified the man with the blunderbuss as James Kenny, and a coroner's jury brought in a verdict of wilful murder against him. So far the constabulary had reason to congratulate themselves on clearing up a crime 'concocted by the principal landholders in the neighbourhood', who were related to the Husseys' evicted predecessor.

The constabulary suffered a setback, however, when their principal witness, Christopher Hussey (who had identified Kenny) absconded to the USA. A year later, in July 1852, the constabulary traced him to New Haven, where he was staying with his sister and brother-in-law. A constabulary agent arrived with a plausible ruse to lure Christopher back to Ireland: a fictitious letter, concocted by the constabulary but purporting to have been written by his father, claiming he would be evicted if Christopher did not come home to give evidence against Kenny. Christopher's sister not only refused to persuade him to return, but told the constable that she wished 'more power to Kenny's steady hand. He has shot four and has about four more to shoot as soon as he gets out of gaol.' As for her father, she prayed to God that Kenny might 'shoot the head off the old rascal, her father, for daring to send for Christy to prosecute him'. The constable was also surprised to find that the Irish in New York knew of his mission before he arrived; only treachery in his own police station at Dysart could have explained such a leak.[51]

This case, with its conspiracy hatched by neighbours, family feuding, and American ramifications shows the problems faced by the constabulary. Such a case made credible the statement of the RM who in 1870, in a report to the government, told of a man 'who by way of recommending himself to a farmer's daughter that he was anxious to marry, she having a good fortune, announced himself as the person who shot a gentleman's steward'.[52] It was not only small farmers and labourers who had such attitudes. On the morning that Thomas Bateson was murdered in County Monaghan, the rector of the parish, Revd Alexander Hurst, was told by his steward that a man was being attacked on the road. The steward wanted to rescue him, but the rector told him 'to mind his own business and not to interfere'. When the rector was told that Bateson had been murdered near his gates, he excused himself by saying that 'he thought it was a drunken quarrel'.[53]

The constabulary had some remarkable failures in the decades after the famine. The Derryveagh case was not cleared up; William Scully's attackers were not even identified; Lord Leitrim's murderers were not convicted; Captain Lambert's attacker was arrested, after some fine work by the

---

[51] Ibid., outrage papers, Westmeath, 1852/175; see also ibid., Tipperary, 1852/324; ibid. 1849/2462; ibid. RP 1870/733.   [52] Ibid. RP 1870/2757, report of J. G. Jones.
[53] Ibid., outrage papers, Monaghan, 1852/222.

constabulary, but was eventually released. All those involved in five dramatic murders of landlords in 1868 escaped, including those involved in the strange Bradshaw case in County Tipperary.[54] Failure to get evidence was, however, only one of the constabulary's problems. For one thing many witnesses were prepared to give evidence in the hope of getting a reward. According to William Kemmis, the crown solicitor of County Tipperary, writing in 1849, 'in the present state of general destitution and consequent demoralization... a feeling generally exists that a conviction ensures a witness engaged in the prosecution a rich recompense.'[55] Often the conspirators turned on each other. In October 1849 three keepers, put on Redmond Brien's farm because he had not paid £4 of poor law rates, were murdered. Nine suspects were arrested, including Brien; three immediately offered themselves as approvers, including Brien, who was probably the instigator of the murders. The RM in charge of the case was apparently not surprised when the approvers petitioned the lord-lieutenant for compensation for giving evidence.[56]

Witnesses occasionally came forward because their consciences were troubled. The Eastwood case in County Louth was partly resolved by the evidence of Alice Campbell, who lived near Castletown, Eastwood's house. At first she would not name the men she had seen on the morning of the attack, 'being terrified by threats of several persons'; but in the end, having 'been uneasy in [her] mind at not having told the truth', she named Kirk and McCooey, who were hanged in July 1852.[57] A case on the Kingston estate in County Limerick showed the strange workings of conscience and family feuding. Part of the Kingston estate had been bought by a tenant's son, Patrick Dwyer, who had returned from America where he had become rich 'by hard labour, industry, intelligence, and thrift'. When draining his lands, he was opposed by the former bailiff, Patrick Gorman, who feared eviction because he was quarrelling with the new owner's relations. Gorman 'put himself prominently forward on the part of the tenants, intermeddling in matters with which he had no concern'. He decided, however, to supplement these efforts by persuading Michael Long to shoot the new landlord, offering to get him a gun and an 'old loose coat', and to help him to emigrate. Long refused because he had a sister who would help him to emigrate anyway. He did not tell the constabulary, but he told Tom Lyons, who was related to the new landlord; Tom Lyons told his wife, who told Mary Hanlon, who told the first mover of the plot, Patrick Gorman. When Gorman tried to frighten the reluctant assassin, threatening to have him 'taken on account of it', Long decided in self-defence to tell the landlord.

[54] Ibid. RP 1869/11937.
[55] Ibid., outrage papers, Tipperary, 1849/2494; see Fitzpatrick, 'Class, Family and Rural Unrest', 47.   [56] National Archives, outrage papers, Tipperary, 1849/1658.
[57] Ibid., Louth, 1852/146.

'I got up the next morning when it was duskish and took my shoes in my hand and [went] to Flemingstown to tell Mr Dwyer.' In spite of the fact that the people on this part of the Kingston estate were 'the most reckless and demoralized peasantry' in Ireland, the constabulary not only got wind of the plot, but sworn information as well.[58]

For serious crime as a whole, the constabulary had a detection rate that was comparable with that of the English and Welsh forces.[59] They probably suffered as much from forensic backwardness as from obstruction by the public. The importance of footprints was understood, but the use of fingerprints lay in the future; ballistic analysis was hardly even considered, and bloodstains could barely be identified as human. The rules of evidence, especially in capital cases, were strictly applied. In November 1872 in County Clare, for example, an agent who was about to evict a tenant was fired at; the evicted tenant's son, Brian Kearney, was arrested and charged. The evidence against him seemed incontrovertible: the blunderbuss had exploded, blowing off the assassin's hand; the constabulary found a forefinger at the scene of the crime; Brian Kearney had recently lost his hand. At the assizes, however, Kearney was acquitted, not because the jury was corrupt, but because the crown failed to prove that the blunderbuss was lethally loaded.[60]

Occasionally the law provoked a concerted obstruction that had nothing to do with the original crime. In January 1872, Humphrey Davis, a bailiff on the McDermott estate near Ballina, was shot while lying in his bed. There was little doubt that he had been fired at from outside: there were no powder marks on the bedclothes; his own gun had not been discharged; pieces of glass were found in the room. At first his neighbours professed 'a great anxiety to assist the investigation', but a coroner's jury brought in a verdict of accidental death. This was almost inevitable, because the peace preservation act of 1870 had provided that the victims of agrarian attacks should be compensated at the expense of the locality where the crime was perpetrated.[61] Davis's neighbours had to pay £530, a sum equivalent to a rent increase of 25 per cent. They did not pay willingly. Having failed to stop proceedings under the peace preservation act by using the coroner's jury, they retained counsel to put their case before the grand jury. When that failed, they tried to have the head constable disciplined for incompetence. Finally the lord-lieutenant was anonymously petitioned to remove Arthur Mitchell, the RM in charge of the case: 'They would deem it a

---

[58] Ibid., Limerick, 1852/76.
[59] See e.g. *Judicial Statistics, Ire., 1871*, pp. 23, 35–6 [C 674], HC 1872, lxv. 257, 269–70; see also Charles Townshend, *Political Violence in Ireland*, 82–4.
[60] National Archives, ICR, returns of outrages, 1872; *First, Second, and Special Reports from the Select Committee on Juries (Ireland)*, p. 38, HC 1873 (283), xv. 442.
[61] 33 & 34 Vict., c. 9 (4 Apr. 1870).

blessing if the scene of his labour were transferred to some other place.' The case against Mitchell was interesting: his brother, a man 'who at any time will drink with the meanest of the people', had given away the identity of a constabulary detective, who was working as a gardener in McDermott's employment. The aim of all this was presumably to impugn the evidence collected by Mitchell and the constabulary, on which the penal tax was based. The interesting point, however, was that the people were apparently genuinely convinced that Davis's death was not an agrarian murder, for a detective reported that 'all agree he was shot accidentally with his own gun.'[62]

Whether agrarian crime was more difficult to solve than ordinary crime is not clear. Threatening letters, the largest component of agrarian crime, were inherently difficult to clear up. The statistics in the Returns of outrages give little help, because committals and convictions for agrarian crimes were not given separately. What is clear, however, is that before the late 1860s the constabulary were successful in getting convictions in cases where landlords and their servants were attacked. Simply measured in terms of the number of assassins who were hanged, the record is grimly impressive. There were four hangings in County Tipperary in 1848 for agrarian outrages: Terence Corboy for murdering a process server in 1846; John Daly and William Carty for conspiring to murder J. U. Bayly, the marquis of Ormond's agent; Martin Ryan for shooting at a landlord named Lloyd.[63]

Most notable of all was the number of hangings in connection with troubles in the counties of Armagh, Louth, and Monaghan in 1849–52: in 1852 Kirk and McCooey were hanged for attacking Eastwood,[64] and Francis Berry for attacking Merideth Chambré;[65] in 1853 two men were hanged for conspiring to murder William Steuart Trench; in 1854 three were hanged for Thomas Bateson's murder, which had taken place three years before.[66] Although it would be exaggerating to say that this record of effectiveness continued, it remained impressive: two men were hanged in 1856 for Charlotte Hinds's murder near Ballyconnell;[67] in 1857 the two Cormack brothers were hanged for the murder of an agent in County Tipperary.[68] In 1858 and 1859, however, the constabulary had some notable failures, and in 1862 the prospect for landlords appeared bleak when three landlords, including Francis Fitzgerald, were shot in quick succession.[69] The constabulary and the judiciary, however, retrieved some of their

---

[62] National Archives, RP 1871/14028.
[63] Ibid., convict reference files, 1848/C/21, 96; R/36.
[64] Ibid., outrage papers, Louth, 1852/20; convict reference files, 1862/B/28.
[65] Ibid. 1852/B/33.   [66] Ibid. 1853/H/42; 1854/G/7.   [67] Ibid. 1856/D/26.
[68] Ibid. RP 1920/8218.   [69] Ibid. ICR, return of outrages, 1862.

reputation in 1862 by the speed with which Thomas Beckham, Francis Fitzgerald's assassin, was brought to justice: the murder, arrest, trial, and hanging took place within a nine-week period.[70]

The only real breakdown in order that took place between the famine and 1879 occurred between 1868 and 1871, when a number of murders and shootings were perpetrated with impunity: the murders in 1868 of James Fetherston Haugh, Samuel Morrow, Darby Gorman, and George Cole Baker; the murders in 1870 and 1871 of two bailiffs, a process server, and a caretaker. Just as alarming were the firings: sixteen directed between 1869 and 1871 at landlords or their servants, including some socially prominent victims: J. A. Nicholson, JP, County Meath; Richard Warburton, JP and high sheriff of the Queen's County; Captain T. E. Lambert, JP, County Galway; Miss Gardiner and Charles Crotty in County Mayo; Revd James Crofton, rector of Dunleer, in County Westmeath.[71]

This particular wave of disorder broke only when habeas corpus was suspended in 1871. Between 1871 and 1879 the constabulary's record improved, for the only two major attacks on landlords were quickly dealt with: one man was hanged for the attack on Patten Smith Bridge in 1876 and arrests quickly followed Lord Leitrim's murder in 1878. Looking at the period as a whole it would be difficult to argue that tenants did not occasionally combine to shield murderers—the attack on Scully in 1868 and Lord Leitrim's murder are the two obvious examples. On the other hand, the constabulary's failure in many cases owed nothing to widespread obstruction by tenants. Indeed, considering the number of rural assassins who were hanged between 1848 and 1878 only an assassin with a poor grasp of actuarial reality would have believed it possible to attack a landlord with impunity.[72]

iii. Ribbonism

In February 1852 the constabulary at Tinahely arrested a tramp who called himself Charles Harris. In the days after his arrest Harris amazed the constabulary with elaborate accounts of an extensive Ribbon conspiracy, stretching from Armagh in the north to Limerick in the south, in which Harris played the humble but important part of hired assassin. Having come to County Wicklow with a party of six from Westmeath, Harris's first target was William Owen, Lord Downshire's agent. They could not find Owen, went to Carlow, but came back to Tinahely 'to go up to Mr Fenton's place in the glen to be revenged of him by shooting him'. ('Our

---

[70] Ibid., convict reference files, 1863/D/15; Larcom papers (NLI, MS 7637).
[71] National Archives, ICR, returns of outrages, 1868–71.
[72] Cf. Hoppen, *Elections, Politics, and Society*, 423, where agrarian violence is described as 'predominantly practical, realistic, and (metaphorically as well as physically) hard-headed'.

object in meeting them was what we call to settle accounts.') What interested the constabulary most, however, were his references to the north, where an agent, Thomas Bateson, had been murdered just two months before.

Harris did not rush into his revelations, but with the relish of an implacable raconteur he prevaricated. 'The prisoner states that he has a strong objection to [saying] anything about *Armagh* or *Monaghan* . . . and states he will have no objection to state more in a few days.' Later, having admitted that he spent twenty-six days in Armagh, he '*will* not tell *anything* or any of the houses or places he was in the County Armagh—[he] disremembers them all'. Eventually, and with apparent reluctance, he revealed that an Armagh farmer, James 'Flower Pot' Jenkins, got up a gang of twelve, including Harris and 'Foxey' Tom Tobin, 'for the purpose of civilising those tyrannical tyrants who were getting too much of their own way in the counties of Armagh and Monaghan'. There were meetings in 'the big barn', a couple of men were waylaid, and a house 'visited'.

Sub-Inspector Donoghue, who arrested Harris, was credulous but uneasy. 'I fear the Ribbon system is spreading into this county,' he wrote to the inspector-general; 'I had not indeed an idea that this was the case and much as I do know of crime now after a long service, I had not a notion the Ribbon system was so extensive.' The lay magistrates were less cautious and insisted on letting Harris make a sworn statement a week after his arrest. There were aspects of his revelations that should have aroused suspicion. He was obsessed with food and drink. During his missions, he claimed, he got 'the best of eating and drinking, pancakes and whiskey'; during the attempt on Fenton, he had been promised 'plenty of whiskey, bacon, and cabbage'; in County Tipperary his employer had 'procured the best of eating and drinking for those men and myself'; during a 'visit' in Monaghan, after the terrified mistress of the house had recovered from a fainting fit, she offered Harris and his accomplices 'cold beef or anything we choosed or liked'. There were other problems with his evidence, apart from an obsession with food. He was, he claimed, a Protestant; his employer in County Armagh, 'Flower Pot' Jenkins, was 'in the Methodist way of thinking'. Yet Ribbonism was generally supposed to be a Catholic conspiracy. Also it is interesting that Harris called himself a Whiteboy. In the end, Harris turned out to be an impostor who went around constabulary stations, giving himself up as a deserter. Doubts, however, remained. The RM, Captain Warburton, was not convinced that Harris was merely an impostor but 'a most diabolical character and a most dangerous person to be set at large'.[73]

The Harris case sums up the difficulties of defining Ribbonism in the years after the famine. First, much of the evidence came from disreputable

[73] National Archives, outrage papers, Wicklow, 1852.

but shrewd rascals like Harris, who told the constabulary what they wanted to hear. Secondly, a widespread, tightly organized conspiracy, directed against landlords, was revealed. Thirdly, there was the characteristic confusion about nomenclature: Harris called himself a Whiteboy, but the constabulary called him a Ribbonman. Finally, the inconclusive end of the whole affair was not untypical: vast networks of conspiracy frequently turned from steel to gossamer after a little investigation. Tom Garvin's study of Ribbonism showed

that a fairly well-institutionalized form of agitation established itself in the counties of north Leinster, north Connacht and south Ulster during the last decades of the eighteenth century and that it persisted throughout the first half of the nineteenth century. It also appears that after the 1860s this network, like many of the local agrarian groups with which it was so often confused, was assimilated into the later organizations of fenianism, the land league, Parnell's Irish national league and in particular, Hibernianism.[74]

After the famine the constabulary occasionally discovered cases that implied the existence of widespread, ramified secret societies. In 1861, for example, Head Constable Byrne raided a public house in Letterkenny and arrested Denis MacMenemin, who tried to destroy some papers before he was arrested. When the papers were pieced together they revealed passwords and the names of Ribbon leaders in Sligo, Enniskillen, Cootehill, Belfast, Castlewellan, Clough, and Newcastle-upon-Tyne.[75] When defining Ribbonism after the famine, the constabulary tended to mix in varying proportions three separate ingredients: the memory of a pre-famine movement; quite recent cases involving passwords, oaths, and secret meetings; actual conspiracies against landlords and agents.

The public, however, had little appetite for the refinements of police evidence, and readily accepted vivid, even lurid, descriptions of Ribbonism. The description of the Ribbon lodge in Allingham's *Laurence Bloomfield in Ireland*, for example, was in the tradition established by Carleton for the pre-famine period, with its parish master ('spoilt priest, attorney's extra clerk, and then sub-tax-collector, handy with his pen').[76] Another

---

[74] Tom Garvin, 'Defenders, Ribbonmen and Others: Underground Political Networks in Pre-Famine Ireland', in C. H. E. Philpin (ed.), *Nationalism and Popular Protest in Ireland* (Cambridge, 1987), 227–8; for pre-famine Ribbonism see also M. R. Beames, 'The Ribbon Societies: Lower-Class Nationalism in Pre-Famine Ireland', ibid. 245–63; for a general account of Ribbonism, see Townshend, *Political Violence in Ireland*, 14–24. (According to Townshend, 'In the 1850s . . . a dramatic decline set in, and lasted (with the equally dramatic exception of the 1870–1 Westmeath disturbances) for something like a quarter of a century' (p. 16).) See also S. Pollard, 'The Ethics of the Sheffield Outrages', *Transactions of the Hunter Archaeological Society*, 7: 3 (1953–4), 118–39 for an account of violent combinations among the Sheffield saw-grinders in the 1860s.
[75] Vaughan, *Derryveagh Evictions*, 31–2.
[76] William Allingham, *Laurence Bloomfield in Ireland: A Modern Poem* (London and Cambridge, 1864), 155–75.

contemporary account of Ribbonism was the trial scene in Trench's *Realities of Irish Life*. Trench was a remarkable man, a novelist *manqué*, whose other published work was *Ierne, a Tale*.[77] For many like Trench, Ribbonism was ubiquitous, one of the 'realities' of Irish life; Trench also helped to create the impression that Ribbonism was aimed mainly at landlords, or agents like himself. When he was an agent in Farney in the early 1850s he complained that the barony was '*swarming*' with Ribbonmen;[78] when he moved to the barony of Geashill in the King's County in 1860, it was infested with Ribbonmen.[79] Trench had information that was not available to the constabulary, who did not believe in the existence of Ribbonism in Geashill. His source was 'a girl [in Tullamore] who knew a great deal about what was going on in the barony of Geashill', which she would not tell the constabulary.[80] Trench was not the only contemporary who had clear, vivid ideas about Ribbonism. While the constabulary were tentative about the location of Ribbonism's headquarters, William Johnston of Ballykilbeg had no doubt that 'its native place is Rome'. Johnston, who saw Ribbonism as something more than an anti-landlord conspiracy, may have been closer to the truth than Trench.[81]

The Victorians were fascinated by the esoteric, and especially by secret societies. The *carbonari* in Italy, the Ku-Klux-Klan, the beginnings of trade unionism, the ritual of friendly societies, and the complex federation of the freemasons not only created an atmosphere of credulity, but actually gave some observers personal experience of secret societies.[82] Edward Cardwell, chief secretary from 1859 to 1861, for example, visited Oxford in 1861 to attend the annual festival of the 59th Lodge of the Ancient Order of Druids.[83] When magistrates and police concocted elaborate descriptions of Ribbonism they may have been projecting into inchoate rural combinations their own experience of freemasonry.

How important was Ribbonism? Was it, as Sir Francis Head claimed, the cause of 'a bloody and barbarous civil warfare, such as exists within the limits of no country on the surface of the globe'?[84] Only two major outbreaks of conspiratorial disorder between the famine and the land war are well documented: the murders in south Armagh, Monaghan, and Louth in 1849–52, and the disorder in County Westmeath in the late 1860s and

[77] Trench, *Realities of Ir. Life*, 188–9. *Ierne, a Tale* was published in London in 1871.
[78] National Archives, outrage papers, Monaghan, 1852/43.
[79] Larcom papers (NLI, MS 7639, no. 97). [80] Ibid., no. 90.
[81] William Johnston, *Ribbonism, and its Remedy: A Letter Addressed to the Rt. Hon. the Earl of Derby, First Lord of the Treasury* (Dublin, 1858), 3; see also Garvin, 'Defenders, Ribbonmen and Others', 244, where the tendency of social and economic historians to play down Ribbonism's 'political and nationalist aspects' is deplored.
[82] C. W. Heckethorn, *The Secret Societies of All Ages and Countries* (2 vols.; London, 1875); see also Benjamin Disraeli, *Sybil or the Two Nations* (Harmondsworth, 1980), 268–71.
[83] Newscutting from *The Times*, 2 Jan. 1861, in Larcom papers (NLI, MS 7603).
[84] Sir Francis B. Head, *A Fortnight in Ireland* (London, 1852), 240.

early 1870s.[85] The number of cases of Ribbonism in the Returns of outrages was not impressive. There were none before 1850 (Whiteboyism seems to have been the favoured generic term between 1837 and 1850); between 1850 and 1862 there were fifty-one cases, and only one in the period 1863–93 (in Westmeath in 1869).[86] Ribbonism seems to have been confined to certain counties, mainly in north Leinster, Connacht, and south and west Ulster.[87] Of these, three counties (Donegal, Leitrim, and Longford) accounted for almost half the cases. According to Sir Thomas Larcom in 1860, Ribbonism was a thing of the past, like the vendetta in southern Europe.[88] Sir Henry Brownrigg, the inspector-general of constabulary, was not so dismissive in a report in 1863, but he confined Ribbonism to the whole of five counties[89] and to parts of twelve.[90] In a report in the early 1880s only eleven counties were returned as affected by Ribbonism.[91]

Not one of the fifty-two cases referred to in the Returns of outrages was returned as agrarian, which is puzzling if Ribbonism was an anti-landlord conspiracy. It is also strange that Westmeath, which was the scene of a formidable anti-landlord conspiracy in the late 1860s and early 1870s, produced only one case of Ribbonism. A special return of outrages in Westmeath, covering the years 1862–9, recorded 142 Ribbon outrages, which makes the single case in the Returns of outrages in 1869 even more puzzling.[92] (This special return also classified Ribbon cases separately from agrarian outrages.) The difference between the one case in the Returns of outrages and the 142 outrages in the special return can be explained by the fact that in the Returns of outrages the constabulary seem to have classified as Ribbonism only acts that arose exclusively from membership of a secret society, such as having passwords or documents, or being present at a Ribbon meeting. Crimes arising out of Ribbonism, such as assaults, threatening letters, and homicides, were returned as such, and not as Ribbon cases. This seems to explain why 142 Ribbon outrages, including two homicides, one firing, twenty-nine serious assaults, sixty-one threatening letters, and seventeen attacks on houses, were represented by only one case in the Returns of outrages.

---

[85] *Sel. Comm. on County Monaghan, 1852; Sel. Comm. on Westmeath, 1871.*
[86] National Archives, ICR, returns of outrages, 1850–93; in another summary table, however, only thirteen cases were recorded for 1850–63.
[87] Antrim, Armagh, Cavan, Donegal, Down, and Londonderry; Longford, Louth, Meath, and Westmeath; Leitrim, Mayo, Roscommon, and Sligo; Limerick. See also Garvin, 'Defenders, Ribbonmen and Others', 226–7. [88] Larcom papers (NLI, MS 7603, p. 59).
[89] Report on the State of Ireland in 1863 by Sir Henry John Brownrigg (NLI, MS 915, pp. 50–7): Donegal, Leitrim, Longford, Monaghan, and Westmeath.
[90] Antrim, Armagh, Cavan, Down, Fermanagh, Londonderry, and Tyrone; King's County, Louth, and Meath; Roscommon, Sligo.
[91] National Archives, Crime Dept. 'B' files, no. 134: Armagh, Cavan, Donegal, Fermanagh, Monaghan, and Tyrone; Longford, Louth, Meath, and Westmeath; Leitrim.
[92] National Archives, RP 1869/19348; ICR, returns of outrages, 1862–9.

The constabulary's reluctance to return Ribbon cases as agrarian outrages may have been caused by their awareness of Ribbonism as something more than an agrarian secret society, directed against landlords or tenants who took evicted farms. 'It must not be supposed that the operation of Ribbonism is confined to disagreements about land,' wrote Sir Henry John Brownrigg, the inspector-general. 'Its influence, wherever it exists, goes to prevent the exercise of any private legal right whatever, which may not comport with the will of the confederacy.'[93] The murder of the stationmaster of Mullingar, Thomas Anketell, in 1869, for example, was defined as a Ribbon outrage, although it had nothing to do with land, and arose out of 'the utterly disorganized state of the officials connected with the Midland Railway'.[94] Information collected by the constabulary about the occupations of Ribbon suspects does not suggest that it was overwhelmingly a farmers' organization. During the disturbances in Westmeath in the early 1870s a list of over fifty suspects was drawn up by the constabulary in connection with the Westmeath act. Farmers were not the biggest group: farm labourers were the biggest group (33 per cent), farmers' sons were next (24 per cent), and farmers came third (22 per cent); the remainder (21 per cent) were in trades not engaged directly in farming—publicans, hotelkeepers, masons, and butchers.[95]

Two cases reported by the constabulary in Westmeath in the late 1860s show how Ribbonism could embrace personal quarrels unconnected with landlordism. In April 1870 two men came to Michael Brennan's house in Cloneyhaigue and ordered him to bring back his son-in-law from America and give him the farm; three months later, one of Brennan's labourers was warned to leave his work; a month later in August another labourer was threatened with death while cutting oats. The cause of this persecution was Joseph Nugent, Brennan's son-in-law, who after his wife's death, wanted not only to marry again, but also to have his father-in-law's farm, in spite of Brennan's 'well known intention being to leave it to Nugent's youngest son'. Nugent was 'a prominent party man', whose interests, during his absence in America, had been looked after by three families, all associated with the Ribbon society and all related to him.[96] The second case occurred in December 1870 when Thomas Oakes, the petty sessions clerk in Tyrrelspass, got a threatening letter because his son had taken the post of clerk with the firm of Messrs. Perry, Ballinagore. The letter, the constabulary believed, was written by William Malowney, who had been dismissed two years before from the same post, and whose successor, Francis Dowling,

---

[93] Report on the State of Ireland in 1863 by Sir Henry John Brownrigg (NLI, MS 915, p. 50).   [94] National Archives, RP 1869/11971.
[95] Ibid. OP 1872/3; cf. Crime Dept. 'B' files, no. 134, where 56% of the Ribbon suspects were farmers.   [96] National Archives, RP 1870/17355.

had been murdered. Malowney was one of the leading Ribbonmen in Westmeath, who later fled to escape arrest when habeas corpus was suspended in 1871.[97]

Ribbonism, therefore, was difficult to quantify because it was difficult to classify. In the special return for Westmeath, 21 per cent of ordinary crime was ascribed to Ribbonism; but it is highly unlikely that the same percentage of all ordinary crime throughout the rest of the country was caused by Ribbonism. Such a large volume would have made Ribbonism more important than agrarian crime. Between 1850 and 1869 80,000 ordinary outrages were reported by the constabulary; 21 per cent of these would have been 16,800, probably generating about 400 homicides.[98] In such circumstances the constabulary's efforts to combat Ribbonism would have been greater; more specifically Ribbon cases—passwords, secret meetings, etc.—would have come to light than the fifty-two recorded in the Returns of outrages. The number of Ribbonmen identified by the constabulary could not plausibly have been held responsible for so many outrages. In the early 1880s in the 'B' file report on Ribbonism only 120 Ribbonmen, in eleven counties, were identified. In County Fermanagh, for example, Ribbonmen were outnumbered by the county's titled nobility.[99] The number of Ribbonmen in County Westmeath, however, was less implausible: the fifty considered for arrest in 1871 could possibly have committed the 142 outrages ascribed to them between 1862 and 1869.

The constabulary may have been more discerning than the public, but they were deceptively ready with definitions of Ribbonism that connected it with agrarian conspiracies—whether before select committees in 1852 and 1871, or in confidential reports. In a report written in the 1880s Ribbonism was described as a secret society, with passwords, signs, and a formidable initiation oath. It was hierarchical, consisting of five orders: county delegates, parish masters, body masters, committee men, and ordinary Ribbonmen. The first order implied an organization that extended over a number of counties; the fact that there were four layers of membership in each parish implied a numerous local membership. The society's *modus operandi* was equally clear, according to the constabulary. At quarterly meetings the county delegates discussed 'their own wrongs and grievances, or those of their neighbours'. Obnoxious landlords, agents, and bailiffs were placed on trial, and 'if pronounced guilty, sentenced by a majority of votes to such punishment, involving death, or the destruction of property, as the case may seem to them to merit'. The sentence was carried out by men brought from remote districts so that they could not be identified, or connected with the crime. Afterwards they were helped to emigrate, or if

[97] Ibid. 1870/22231; OP 1872/3/9; above, pp. 171–2.
[98] National Archives, RP 1869/19348; ICR, returns of outrages, 1850–69; see below, App. 19.
[99] Ibid., Crime Dept. 'B' files, no. 134.

caught, funds were provided for their defence. Each order had a particular function: assassins were chosen from the committee men; the parish masters and body masters were the links between the members and the county delegates; the ordinary Ribbonmen were probationers.[100] To this hierarchy was added a headquarters that was variously located in Belfast, Dublin, Liverpool, Glasgow, and Manchester.[101]

The constabulary remained faithful for a long time to this hierarchical version of Ribbonism. In 1852 the inspector-general mentioned county delegates and parish masters in his evidence to the select committee on County Monaghan;[102] in 1871 the select committee on Westmeath heard of a headquarters, five orders, and a variety of oaths, all sanguinary.[103] The evidence given in 1871 seems to have shaped official thinking for the next ten years, for the 'B' file document closely resembles Stephen Seed's evidence to the select committee.[104] Although such an elaborate hierarchy implies that the constabulary knew Ribbonism well, their description arouses some suspicions. The hierarchy was too complex to fit the number of conspirators identified by the constabulary. Even allowing for the fact that two or three times as many more were not identified, Ribbonism was an army of generals, certainly by the 1880s. Also it is strange that the constabulary rarely placed suspects in the hierarchy. This is remarkable in the Westmeath cases, because ascription of status would have strengthened the case for arresting a suspect.[105] The same vagueness characterized constabulary reports on Ribbonmen in Monaghan, Louth, and Armagh in the early 1850s. The constabulary were sure that Barney Quin of Glasdrummond had 'arranged all the murders committed in Armagh, Louth, and Monaghan for the past ten years'; they were also sure that he had given James Finnegan a case of pistols to shoot James Eastwood, telling him 'to get a couple of smart fellows to aid him'.[106] But the constabulary did not place Quin, or Finnegan, or Kirk and McCooey, hanged for the attempted murder of Eastwood, in the Ribbon hierarchy.

Similarly the constabulary's description of Ribbonism's *modus operandi* was more theoretical than practical. The reason for having a hierarchy of officers, with decisions to assassinate coming down from the county delegates, was presumably to separate motive and opportunity by putting intermediaries between the aggrieved party and the actual murderers. The reality seems to have been different. Conspirators engaged wild characters

---

[100] Ibid.   [101] *Sel. Comm. on County Monaghan*, 1852, 127.   [102] Ibid.
[103] *Sel. Comm. on Westmeath*, 1871, 92–3, 107.   [104] Ibid. 89–97, 162–3.
[105] National Archives, OP 1872/3; see A. C. Murray, 'Agrarian Violence and Nationalism in Nineteenth-Century Ireland: The Myth of Ribbonism', *Ir. Econ. & Soc. Hist.* 13 (1986), 66, for one suspect described as a parish master.
[106] National Archives, outrage papers, Louth, 1852/209; see also ibid., Monaghan, 1852/42.

who were not averse to leaving the country, although none wanted to leave by the rapid vertical transit system operated by the sheriffs. 'Culloville' Thornton, whose evidence hanged his two accomplices and provided Trench with his most vivid copy, was a restless, wandering character. He had deserted his wife, was living with Margaret Meehan, worked on the Dundalk–Enniskillen railway and sometimes in north Dublin during the harvest, and went to chapel when he was 'in the way of it'. He was, however, 'never an idler and would spend the money courageously'.[107]

The organization of assassinations was more makeshift than the constabulary description implied, for it involved a crude personal sponsorship that was anything but typical of a secret society divided into separate compartments. In the Eastwood case James Finnegan claimed that he had originally been asked to kill Eastwood by Barney Quin of Glasdrummond in Rafferty's public house in Dundalk in December 1851. Having agreed, he was then approached by Neddy McGuinness (threatened with eviction by Eastwood) who promised him £5 when the murder was committed. He was also approached by Pat Mooney who gave him 2s. 6d. towards his expenses 'till the job was done'. Finnegan was not an accomplished assassin: he eventually got out when McCooey, whom he had recruited in Barney McEntaggart's barn, failed to show up. (McCooey was jittery as well as unpunctual, for 'he was afraid of Mr Eastwood's big dog'.)[108]

The disclosures made during the trials of Hodgens, Breen, and Corrigan, accused of attempting to murder Trench's bailiffs, Patrick McArdle and Patrick McMahon, also showed a system of *ad hoc* sponsorship that left all parties vulnerable to betrayal. The organizers were Corrigan and a man called Curtis, who promised the assassins £20 each for shooting Trench, and £10 each for McMahon. Corrigan was to collect the money for Hodgens (later hanged) and Curtis for Thornton (who turned approver); they were to send 'to Pat Boyle who had the money that was collected'. Other overtures were made to the assassins: a tenant on the Bath estate, called Trainor, offered them £5 for Trench and £2 for McMahon, because Trench wanted 'to take the best part of his land from him'. Another tenant extended the operation by offering £10 for McArdle. Throughout the approver's evidence there were frequent references to small sums changing hands: 6d. was spent on whiskey to steady their nerves for the attack on McArdle; 'we bought bread and tea, eels and other fish,' Thornton recalled. On one occasion he was offered whiskey, 'but I would not drink, having a sore leg'.[109] All this was far removed from the expected movements of a hierarchical secret society. It was not, for one thing, very secret; there was

[107] Ibid., convict reference files, 1853/H/42.
[108] Ibid., outrage papers, Louth, 1852/209; convict reference files, 1862/B/28.
[109] Ibid. 1853/H/42.

no attempt to separate those who initiated from those who perpetrated the crime.

There were some who were sceptical about the very existence of the Ribbon society. Bishop Nulty of Meath told the Westmeath committee that two-thirds of his priests did not believe in its existence, and the rest 'had no positive or direct knowledge of it, and only argued its existence from circumstances'. There was not, he said, 'a regular organized confederacy, having passwords, being bound by an oath, and acknowledging a common executive authority'. Nulty did not completely disagree with the RMs who testified to the existence of Ribbonism in his diocese. There were, he admitted, secret societies consisting of 'small cliques of vagabonds here and there ... who formerly belonged to the regular Ribbon confederacy'; 'their principle of aggregation' was their common evil purpose and their personal knowledge of each other.[110] (According to Dr Murray the connections between the small cliques in Westmeath were tenuous: 'only in one instance ... was mention made of any link between a Ribbonman of one district and a leader from another.'[111])

There is no doubt that Ribbonism was used generically and carelessly to describe behaviour that seemed to result from conspiracies. The constabulary tended to use words like Ribbonism, Whiteboyism, and Rockism indiscriminately for the same actions. An RM in County Fermanagh, for example, reported that Ribbonism was extensive 'amongst some of the lower class'; but in the same county, another RM spoke of Whiteboyism.[112] There was also the problem of confusing Ribbonism with benefit societies. In County Louth in 1852 a fiddler was arrested for having Ribbon documents, which he claimed were the membership card of the 'Buffaloes', issued in Liverpool, and 'the paper with the figure of St Patrick' he had got in a chapel in Armagh 'from a boy'.[113] The confusion between benefit societies and more sinister groups was shown in County Louth when three men were committed for assault, 'known to be active and leading members of the Ribbon confederacy' and possibly involved in a murderous conspiracy. A printed document was found on one of them, entitled 'General Regulations for the Patriotic Association or Sons of the Shamrock'. On the face of it, the document was not sinister. There were references to 'bodies', parish masters, county delegates, and committee men; but the main preoccupation was that records should be kept jointly by the 'master' and by one committee man, 'and by that means no defraud can be committed'.[114] A society that kept records of its membership, worried about peculation,

---

[110] Sel. Comm. on Westmeath, 1871, 109, 113–14, 116; for an explanation of why Nulty condemned a secret society in whose existence he did not believe, see Murray, 'Agrarian Violence and Nationalism in Nineteenth-Century Ireland', 64. [111] Ibid. 66.
[112] National Archives, outrage papers, Fermanagh, 1852/24, 51.
[113] Ibid., Louth, 1852/71. [114] Ibid., 1849/200.

and actually *printed* its rules could have been a benefit society, albeit an illegal one.

It seems plausible that at some point crude societies such as this moved towards respectability. James J. Bergin's *History of the Ancient Order of Hibernians* traces the Hibernians from Rory O'More and the 1641 rising, through the Defenders, the Whiteboys, and the Ribbonmen, to the Hibernia Funeral Society and St Patrick's Fraternal Society. The rules of the Hibernians, given by Bergin, are those of a benefit society, whose aim was to 'promote Friendship, Unity, and True Christian Charity'.[115] The confusion between what may have been harmless societies and those that were not was shown in the report on the 1857 riots in Belfast, when the 'Rules of the Belfast Hibernian Benevolent Society' were presented as the rules of the Ribbon society. Yet this society had aspirations to legality, for one of its rules laid down that the clerk of the peace was to be informed of its meeting-place. The only thing about it that might have aroused suspicion was its exclusion from membership of members of the constabulary, militia, or police; but the reason for this was prudence rather than disloyalty, for the society also excluded any member of 'any trade, calling, or profession, which may subject him to hurt'.[116]

At different times Ribbonism meant murderous conspiracies among tenants, unregistered benefit societies of dubious antecedents, and the Catholic equivalent of the Orange order.[117] It is also clear that the constabulary built up a composite picture of Ribbonism, elements of which were taken from different periods and different places. This seems to have happened to George Talbot, RM, who came to Westmeath in 1863, having previously served in the counties of Galway and Mayo, where there was no Ribbonism, and crime was 'of the ordinary kind, principally assaults and petit larceny'. In Westmeath, however, he found a 'totally different state of society'. When cases of an agrarian kind came before him, he found that 'a number of persons who had no connection whatever with the case were present and seemed deeply interested in the proceedings'. Eventually he became familiar with their faces and learnt their names, 'so that by their presence I could easily know the nature of the case I had to try'.

The Walsh case, a dispute about the purchase of the goodwill of a farm, showed him how the society worked: the men who attacked Walsh were brought from outside, entertained, and supplied with arms while the constabulary's movements were watched.[118] Talbot, having like Bishop Nulty

[115] James J. Bergin, *History of the Ancient Order of Hibernians* (Dublin, [1910]), 29–31; see also Murray, 'Agrarian Violence and Nationalism in Nineteenth-Century Ireland', 57, 70–1, and Garvin, 'Defenders, Ribbonmen and Others', 244.

[116] *Report of the Commissioners of Inquiry into the Origin and Character of the Riots in Belfast in July and December 1857*, pp. 267–9 [2309], HC 1857–8, xxvi. 269–71.

[117] National Archives, outrage papers, Tyrone, 1849/164; ibid., Down, 1849/315; ibid. 1850/113.   [118] Ibid. OP 1870/10.

no direct knowledge of Ribbonism, 'argued its existence from circumstances', and went on to crown his efforts by adding county delegates, parish and body masters, a code of laws, passwords and signs, and regular meetings. His evidence for this conspiratorial superstructure did not come from Westmeath, but from a trial that had taken place in County Longford in 1864.[119] It is interesting that Talbot went to Longford for his evidence when there was evidence just as useful—and dubious—nearer home. In February 1859 the constabulary near Mullingar arrested Martin Fallon for being drunk. Fallon, who had just come back from the USA, was found to have Ribbon documents, including passwords ('The Irish brigade is in the advance') and 'Regulations & Constitution of the Shamrock Society of New York'. Normally the constabulary could not have prosecuted Fallon, for it was not illegal to be a member of a secret society outside Ireland. Unfortunately for Fallon, however, his arrest coincided with a Ribbon case in Belfast, and one of the Belfast approvers was able to testify that Fallon's passwords were those of the Irish Ribbon society.[120] So a connection between Belfast, Mullingar, and New York was established.

Talbot was a busy, worried magistrate, absorbed in a desperate struggle to restore order in Westmeath. It is hardly surprising that he clutched at any clue that made sense of what he faced. It is doubtful, however, if Talbot's picture of Ribbonism was as influential as William Steuart Trench's, published in 1868. How genuine were Trench's revelations, especially his description of the Ribbon trial? His main source was the approver Thornton, whose revelations were made not in court, but in gaol just before he was spirited away by the authorities to begin a new life. There is no way of checking Thornton's story; nor is it possible to prove that Trench invented it. What throws doubt on Trench's account is his story of the attempt to get a reprieve for Hodgens, who was sentenced to death. According to Trench, Thornton told him that Hodgens knew the Ribbonmen's secrets and would reveal all if promised his life. Trench, however, had a problem. Hodgens's chance of getting a reprieve depended on the value of his information; for its value to be assessed he would have to betray his confederates, but with no guarantee of a reprieve. If his information turned out to be useless, he would have betrayed his confederates for nothing. Trench, with the sensibilities of a gentleman, understood Hodgens's dilemma, rushed to Dublin, sought an audience of the lord-lieutenant, and got the promise of a reprieve. Whether the reprieve took effect, however, depended solely on Trench's judgement: if Hodgens's information was worth having, he was to be reprieved; if not, not. In other words Hodgens was to have the luxury of privately confessing to Trench, of betraying his

---

[119] Ibid. RP 1869/19348, p. 15; for the case in Longford see convict reference files, 1869/M/2; for more on Talbot, see Murray, 'Agrarian Violence and Nationalism in Nineteenth-Century Ireland', 57–8, 62, 63. [120] Larcom papers (NLI, MS 7722).

friends on spec, but with the confidence that his treachery would not take effect if it did not secure his reprieve. At first Hodgens was attracted by the offer and willing to talk; but after a visit from his priest, he refused to tell anything, saying he was content to die for his country.[121]

This is one of the most extraordinary stories in *Realities*. It seems improbable that a lord-lieutenant would have delegated so irresponsibly the prerogative of mercy to a magistrate, even to one as officious as Trench. Also, Hodgens's information, given in return for a reprieve, would not have been much use in court. As private information it might have been useful, but hardly as useful as the salutary effects of his execution. In fact the file on Hodgens's case, put together for the lord-lieutenant, shows Trench's story to be suspect, to put it mildly. There was no mention of Trench's efforts on Hodgens's behalf; and most damaging to Trench's credibility, Hodgens made a statement to the authorities after he was sentenced. On 16 July 1853 Charles Hunt, RM wrote to the under-secretary:

> Patrick Hodgens has intimated a desire to make disclosures and I have received directions from the attorney general to visit him in gaol, to inform him that no hope can be held out to him whatever, and if after he is so informed, he persists in making any statement, I am to commit such to paper.

A week later the trial judge, J. D. Jackson, wrote to Larcom that 'the prisoner Hodgens after his conviction made a statement in writing... implicating a bailiff on the Bath estate'.[122] Either Trench forgot that he was acting with others, or he got the whole affair seriously wrong. In either case this incident throws doubt on the rest of his story.

The word Ribbonism had different uses, which showed different perceptions of rural organization, but they do not establish the fact of a great confederacy directed against landlords. Conspiracies that were local and sporadic were made to appear ubiquitous and continuous by their connection with pre-famine Ribbonism and its post-famine survivals. The constabulary rushed into public houses, seized papers, arrested topers incongruously possessed of prayer books, and collected sanguinary oaths; but what those arrested had in common, beyond the fact of their arrest, was not clear. Whether most of them had anything to do with disputes with landlords was not clear either. If the constabulary had been as assiduous in noting the conspirators' ideas as in constructing shadowy confederations, the connection between Captain Duffy's followers 'and the better-known militant organizations' of the late nineteenth century might have been clearer.[123] Dr Murray suggests that the Westmeath conspirators did not even call themselves Ribbonmen; in threatening letters written

---

[121] Trench, *Realities of Ir. Life*, 269–75.
[122] National Archives, convict reference files, 1853/H/42.
[123] Garvin, 'Defenders, Ribbonmen and Others', 244.

during the crisis in Westmeath, there was not 'a single reference to Ribbonism, the Ribbon society or Ribbonmen'.[124] (This lack of self-awareness was not so great in the early 1850s; when Patrick McCooey made his dying speech on the gallows on 31 July 1852 he warned his 'dear beloved fellow Christians' of Dundalk 'in the name of Jesus Christ to have nothing to do with Party or Ribbonism'.[125])

While the constabulary were often too anxious to establish the existence of Ribbonism, they often recognized the possibility of *ad hoc* conspiracies that were not Ribbonism. Neither the Scully case,[126] nor the murder of George Cole Baker,[127] for example, seem to have been regarded as Ribbon outrages. The disorder in County Mayo in 1869–70 attracted the attention of the authorities just as much as Westmeath did (but obviously did not interest the public, for Mayo was hardly mentioned before the select committee in 1871). The Mayo outbreaks, however, were not described as Ribbonism. William Morris Reade, an experienced Westmeath RM, was sent to Mayo in early 1870, but did not fall into the temptation of superimposing his Westmeath experience on what he found. The crowds, ranging from twenty to 200, that roamed the countryside in the winter of 1869–70, he described as 'Rory' detachments, or as 'agrarianism'.[128] RMs with experience of Mayo produced their own definitions of what was happening. According to A. J. R. Stritch, 'agrarianism is not an organized conspiracy at all'; it was widespread but intangible, operating within no particular limits, and with no known centres or strongholds. It was 'not even organized as was the Ribbonism of the past'; its outrages were traceable to local causes, and often the work of individuals and not of groups.[129] Another Mayo RM, however, encountered something different at Ballina, where there was 'a widespread organization known to be such by the peasantry'; the crimes committed between December 1869 and May 1870 were 'attributable to organized system and cannot be ascribed to individual or unpreconcerted effort'.[130]

iv. Why Was There No Mass Movement against Landlordism before 1879?

It was difficult to organize something analogous to a trade union among a tenantry that had no corporate traditions, institutions, and leadership. There were no communes in the countryside, no communal land to be managed, no communal taxes to be paid, no headmen, and no *maires*; there

---

[124] Murray, 'Agrarian Violence and Nationalism in Nineteenth-Century Ireland', 60; see above, p. 156 for a reference to 'a certain society' in a threatening letter written in Westmeath; this seems to be, however, the exception that proves the rule.
[125] National Archives, outrage papers, Louth, 1852/187.   [126] Ibid. RP 1869/5522.
[127] Ibid. 1870/17097.   [128] Ibid. 1870/5330.   [129] Ibid. 2757.
[130] Ibid. 1871/14028.

was no school, therefore, for teaching the rudimentary arts of government. The parliamentary franchise, which was wider after 1850, was exercised by less than one-third of the tenants until 1885; parliamentary elections did inspire a good deal of organized action, even among non-voters, but they occurred infrequently (there were only seven between 1852 and 1880).[131] Poor law elections were more frequent, the electorate larger, and the poor law guardians had considerable prestige, if the use of the abbreviation 'PLG' in petitions and newspaper reports is an indication of social prestige.[132] The poor law unions, nevertheless, were remote, and highly specialized in their functions. The relieving officers and the chairman of the board were probably not as remote as the prefect of a French department, but they were hardly intimate figures. Above all, the poor law imposed no communal burdens that had to be redistributed by local negotiation. The judicial system did not impose any corporate burdens or responsibilities, except when police taxes were imposed on disturbed localities. Service on juries was limited to leaseholders before 1871;[133] service on coroners' juries was apparently the only burden that might be imposed on most tenants.[134] Occasionally tenants might be sworn in as special constables, but that was rare and carefully controlled.

Likewise, for most tenants, religion did little to inculcate those arts of management that are necessary for voluntary organizations. The Roman Catholic church did at least offer focal points of local organization in a society that was often ramified rather than nucleated; but the church did not have an elected system of government, like the select vestries and kirk sessions of the Church of Ireland and the Presbyterian church, whose existence in the Ulster countryside probably had more to do with its political and social life than was appreciated by many contemporaries. Indeed, the whole question of rural organization can be simplified to the single proposition that until the tenants could run a select vestry they could not run a trade union. For the great bulk of the tenants, therefore, religion was not the training-ground for the formal and institutional behaviour that was necessary to modify the tendencies of a rural and familial society.

The absence of formal corporate traditions was not mitigated by the organization of farming, which did not encourage local organization. Farms were worked as separate units, farmers prospered or failed as individuals, and lived scattered through the countryside. Where there was co-operation, it was informal or customary, taking the form of swapping, either of horses, machinery, or time. Occasionally it took place between equals, but

[131] Walker, *Election Results, 1801–1922*, 193.
[132] See e.g. National Archives, convict reference files, 1856/D/26.
[133] *First, Second, and Special Reports from the Select Committee on Juries (Ireland)*, p. 63, HC 1873 (283), xv. 467.
[134] For an example see National Archives, RP 1875/17226, and above, p. 38.

frequently big farmers lent to smaller ones. Such practices, based on a tradition of neighbourliness, were far removed from formal, concerted action: there were no organizing committees, no written rules, no sense of a group as opposed to individual neighbours, and no question of pooling resources for a common end. In any case, neighbourliness was as likely to include as to exclude landlords and agents.

It is unlikely that the tenants saw themselves as members of a group with clearly defined economic characteristics. If anything they had a hierarchical view of society. No two farms, for example, were exactly the same in valuation, rent, acreage, buildings, and amenities. There were psychological obstacles to organization: small farmers, whatever their circumstances, were their own masters over a whole range of important matters. It is easy to understand that farm labourers, who worked under discipline for long hours with little initiative in deciding what they did, might find some compensating sense of control over their lives by joining a trade union and attending lectures.[135] Farmers did not need a similar outlet, for they were self-sufficient, self-absorbed, and self-propelled.

As well as the difficulty of organizing tenants, there were external obstacles: the constabulary, priests, and the landlords themselves. The constabulary were a powerful obstacle to crowd protests; they were not at their best as detectives, being too big, too martial in their bearing to be effective *mouchards*, but they could control mobs, even when the mobs were armed with sticks and stones. In September 1852 in County Mayo, for example, fifty constables escorted the bailiffs of the Bingham estate who were distraining for rent, and the people 'seeing the police force on the ground' paid their rents. 'The people', according to the RM who reported the incident, 'now clearly see that violence is useless when opposed by the constituted authorities and successfully resisted.'[136] The fact that so many evictions took place peacefully was largely due to the presence of the constabulary; in fact the preliminaries of eviction, the serving of notices to quit and ejectment processes when the constabulary were not present, were the most dangerous part of the whole operation. Both of William Scully's disasters took place when he was serving ejectment processes.[137]

In their struggle against disorder the constabulary had powerful allies among the Roman Catholic clergy. The clergy of the diocese of Armagh, for example, refused to admit Ribbonmen to the sacrament;[138] Bishop Nulty issued a pastoral letter denouncing Ribbonism.[139] After a violent incident

---

[135] For agricultural labourers' unions in Ireland see Pamela L. R. Horn, 'The National Agricultural Labourers' Union in Ireland, 1873–9', *IHS* 17: 67 (Mar. 1971), 340–52.
[136] National Archives, outrage papers, Mayo, 1852/328.   [137] Above, pp. 34–5.
[138] *Sel. Comm. on County Monaghan, 1852*, 324.
[139] *Sel. Comm. on Westmeath, 1871*, 114.

RMs often noted with approval the support they had received from the clergy. In County Westmeath in 1862, after a fight at a funeral, caused by a Ribbon dispute, J. L. Cronin, RM praised 'the *active* sympathy (with the authorities) of the RC clergy in this district, in putting down crime (particularly when of a Riband complexion)'.[140] After the attack on James Eastwood the parish priest made the most important crown witness give evidence.[141] Landlords and agents also appreciated the priests' support. William Wann was annoyed when an Orange flag was flown on the church opposite the presbytery.[142] The marquis of Sligo, when lamenting the decline of deference in County Mayo in the 1870s, saw landlords and priests as suffering equally. 'The people here', he told Lord Dufferin, 'are getting idle, unwilling to work, independent as they think, not only of the priest and landlord but also of the necessity to labour.'[143]

An interesting case in County Westmeath, unconnected with Ribbonism, showed nicely the complexity of the relationship between constabulary, landlords, and priests, and their capacity to settle disputes. Fr. Kearney, the parish priest of Moate, took a lease of 6 acres from Lord Castlemaine for twenty-one years at the exorbitant rent of £50 a year. His plan was to collect market tolls on behalf of Castlemaine, which 'would be devoted to the completion of a Roman Catholic chapel which Mr Kearney is building in Moate'. The tolls had not been collected for years, had caused rows even then, and the RM feared that riots would take place on the next market day. 'Which is to be protected, the public against any mob that may be there to support Mr Kearney's claims?', asked the RM, 'or Mr Kearney against the public unwilling to pay the tolls?' In the end the government, the constabulary, the people of Moate, and the farmers and gentry who would have come to the market were rescued from an embarrassing predicament by Bishop Nulty, who forbade Fr. Kearney to go on with his plan.[144]

Landlords also played a part in discouraging organized opposition. By avoiding regular rounds of rent increases, by keeping rents low, and by their inertia in times of rising prices, they vitiated resistance. By tolerating all kinds of apparent inequalities in the levels of rents, they encouraged grumbling but postponed concerted action by banishing uniformity. To some extent the landlords were lucky rather than shrewd: most years from the early 1850s to the late 1870s were prosperous; also, they were not offered tempting or dangerous opportunities, except possibly in the early

[140] Larcom papers (NLI, MS 7639, no. 56).
[141] National Archives, outrage papers, Louth, 1852/146.
[142] Wann's letter-book, 1 July 1870 (PRONI, D1606/5/5, p. 6); see above, p. 180, for Wann's appreciation of denominational differences.
[143] Sligo to Dufferin, 16 Sept. 1872 (ibid. D1071H/B/B).
[144] National Archives, RP 1869/5425; for an example of conflict between the constabulary and a priest see ibid. RP 1869/1783.

1850s when there was a vogue for large farms. It is also arguable that landlords had little real choice after 1870, for the land act made rent increases difficult at a time when prosperity should have made them easy.[145]

Other external factors played a part in retarding tenants' organization. First, Irish public opinion was preoccupied with a legislative solution to the land question. Even after 1870, more effort went into criticizing the shortcomings of the land act than into organizing resistance to the routine working of landlordism. Secondly, there were powerful competing demands made on those who might have organized rural trade unions: the churches, education, and the Fenians attracted men who might have been good rural leaders; also, of course, the empire attracted many Irishmen: Charles Gavan Duffy, one of the few politicians who might have built up local organizations, did not become the Alfred Simmons of Ireland, but prime minister of Victoria.

The absence of formal organization among the tenants had certain consequences for landlord–tenant relations. Opposition based on family ties, or on groups of neighbours, might be prolonged, tedious, and even lethal, but it was not permanent and did not involve more than a dozen townlands or a parish. Such opposition would for the most part respond only to the extremes of landlord behaviour, or be led by extremely aggressive tenants. The ordinary transactions of estate management passed unnoticed and unregulated. Finally such combinations had only a limited range of weapons with which to attack landlords; for in the absence of formal organization there was not much that tenants could do that was not criminal.

What could tenants faced with a harsh landlord do?[146] Obviously the obstruction of legal procedures was one possibility. Eventually, however, in the absence of fierce resistance, ejectment processes could be served and evictions carried out. In the case of distraint, however, resistance was successful, for it seems to have become rare after the early 1850s, when it appears to have been common, although frequently resisted. Trench found, for example, when he set out to seize cattle, that men were stationed on the hills to give warning of his approach.[147] Part of the reason why distraint fell into disuse was the constabulary's reluctance to assist, since it was a private procedure and not the execution of a decree given by a court. Tenants had other resources. They could present memorials, often well and eloquently written. On the Hodson estate in County Cavan in 1861 an agitation against the closing of the Skea school was got up by the former schoolmaster. 'A very unpleasant series of letters, chiefly anonymous, were written,' and then a circular was issued, calling a meeting 'for the purpose of considering a memorial to Sir George Hodson, bt., to

---

[145] See below, App. 9.   [146] Above, pp. 34–9, 63–6.
[147] Trench, *Realities of Ir. Life*, 83.

reopen Skea school and other grievances connected with the manor'.[148] The tenants of the Castledaly estate near Moate presented a memorial to their landlord in 1869 complaining that their rents were a third above the tenement valuation and asking for a reduction to be assessed by 'any just man of knowledge'. The memorial was drafted by a lawyer in Moate, was signed by twelve tenants (seven were marksmen), and was dignified, in a rather pathetic way ('we work hard, we live poor, we spend nothing').

The blurred distinction between legal deferential protests and lawlessness was shown by the fact that, as this memorial was presented, the bailiff of the estate, Tim Daly, got two threatening letters. A notice was posted throughout the district threatening tenants who paid the unabated rent with 'the death of Tarlenten', and warning that 'the balles is made for Tim Daly'. The constabulary suspected that one of the memorialists, James Murphy, had written the threatening letters, because Tim Daly had 'indiscreetly knocked down this very James Murphy for impertinence and bravado about a fortnight ago'. (James Murphy was a man who knew his rights: when the constabulary searched his house for a sample of his handwriting, he challenged their right to do so.)[149]

Apart from writing memorials, perpetrating outrages, and resisting legal process, the tenants could apply a few indirect pressures: indignation meetings, publicity, and the withdrawal of customary marks of respect. The first warning that Stephen Butler, the home-ruler landlord in *The Bad Times*, got of the impending crisis was men turning their backs to him in Dhulough.[150] Old Mr Baker of Ballydavid, father of George Cole Baker who was murdered in 1868, was hooted at as he drove through the streets of Bansha, because he persisted in carrying out the evictions planned by his son.[151] Some tenants were ingenious enough to find a compromise between the seriously illegal and the ineffectively deferential. In December 1869 when threatening letters signed by Rory of the Hill were being written with the profuseness that was supposed to be an attribute of notices to quit, the tenants of the Costello estate near Moate were terrified when a man armed with a long gun called at their houses, announcing that he was Rory of the Hill and warning them not to pay more than 24s. for land currently let at 36s. The RM in Moate, however, was unsympathetic when the tenants came to him for protection, for he suspected 'that Rory came to their own order' to enable them to make a better case for a rent reduction. He told them that if Rory came a second time, the district would be filled with extra police.[152]

If tenants had been formally organized their position would have been

[148] Hodson rentals and agents' reports, 1861 (NLI, MS 16419, p. 3).
[149] National Archives, RP 1869/18678.
[150] George A. Birmingham, *The Bad Times*, 4th edn. (London, 1914), 180.
[151] National Archives, RP 1870/17097.   [152] Ibid. 1869/19298.

much stronger. First, they could have concentrated greater resources at points of tension; secondly, they could have responded to a wider range of grievances, and not just to the more extreme; thirdly, they would have had a more varied armoury, including rent strikes, effective resistance to ejectments in the courts, the obstruction of the courts by creating fictitious legal business, the buying-up of mortgages on encumbered estates, and even deals with anxious mortgagees would not have been beyond their resources. The collective weakness of the tenants, however, was not entirely to the landlords' advantage, certainly not in the long run, for landlords and tenants could not effectively bargain with each other. The pressures they put on each other were limited, crude, and often disproportionate to the issues at stake. Eviction, threats of eviction, and penal rents on the one hand; flattery, insult, threatening letters, and assassination on the other.

The pressures were not nicely graduated, except possibly in the case of ejectments; they did not escalate predictably, but ran precipitately to extremes, leading to sharp and violent breaks in the relationship between the parties. The relationship between landlords and tenants lacked that reciprocity of pressures that exists when one party's capacity to hurt the other is limited by the damage it inflicts on itself. Factory workers, for example, could damage their masters by going on strike, but their capacity to do so was limited by their loss of wages. The inability of landlords and tenants to bargain with each other weakened the land system in several ways. First, by permitting great acts of landlord tyranny the impression was created that there was a fundamental and irreconcilable conflict. Secondly, by allowing minor disputes to become envenomed, an exaggerated impression of disorder was created. Thirdly, the land system was left open to the incursion of outside forces, especially during agricultural crises.

v. What Caused the Land War?

The land war was not predictable in the mid-1870s. According to J. S. Donnelly, 'the relations between landlords and tenants in County Cork at the beginning of 1877 appeared so calm that the violent land war which erupted within less than three years could only have been foreseen by a great leap of the imagination.'[153] The land system had weaknesses in the 1870s, which have already been discussed, but they were not such that a great explosion seemed likely. There was little prospect that landlords would cause a crisis by trying to reorganize their estate management, even under the stimulus of the land act of 1870. The Portacarron lease, for example, showed the intellectual limitations of Irish gentlemen, 'who had certain theories but no practical knowledge'.[154] If the land war had not

[153] Donnelly, *Land and People of Cork*, 251.
[154] *Bessborough Comm., Minutes of Evidence*, pt. ii, p. 999.

broken out, landlords and tenants might have gone on as they were for another generation or two, a survival that would have affected the course of Irish history.[155] Yet the land war broke out; 11,215 families were evicted between 1879 and 1882; 11,320 agrarian outrages, of which 7,035 were threatening letters, were recorded in the same period;[156] the land act of 1881 was passed, and between 1881 and 1891 £1.2 million was struck off the rents of 277,160 holdings;[157] arrears of £1.8 million were extinguished under section 1 of the arrears act;[158] land purchase was begun in earnest by the Ashbourne act in 1885;[159] above all, Parnell and his followers came out of the land war masters of most of the Irish electorate, a mastery that was to endure until 1918.

Predatory landlordism was useful as an explanation of the land war. Take away rackrents, evictions, and fear, and it is not easy to explain why such a powerful anti-landlord movement began in the late 1870s. (If oppression caused mass movements the figures on the eviction of town tenants below suggest that a rising against urban landlords was what should have happened in the late 1870s.[160]) Explanations that cope with this problem have been put forward. J. S. Donnelly argued that the land war was caused by 'rising expectations' created by prosperity; he began by rejecting the argument 'that the storm which broke around the land question in late 1879 and 1880 acquired almost its entire force from the agricultural crisis which immediately preceded it'. He was impressed by the fact that the agricultural depression of the early 1860s, 'which was every bit as serious as the one of 1877–9', had not caused a mass movement. The crucial difference between the two crises was the duration of the prosperity that preceded them: 'little enough progress had been achieved' before the reversal of the early 1860s; 'by the late 1870s, however, progress and prosperity had given the rural community much more to defend against mutilation or erosion'.[161] Samuel Clark argued that agricultural depressions did not in themselves explain outbreaks of resistance because at most they caused only anger among the tenants, and anger without organization was not enough. In 1879, however, leadership and organization were provided by townsmen—shopkeepers, journalists, and publicans—who were over-represented among the active members of the land league. The alliance of townsmen and tenants was made possible by a number of developments before 1879: credit and ties of kinship bound together shopkeepers and farmers; the gradual decline in the numbers of agricultural labourers

---

[155] Comerford, *Fenians*, 224.   [156] See below, Apps. 1 and 19.

[157] *Report of the Irish Land Commissioners for the Period from 22 Aug. 1890 to 22 Aug. 1891*, p. 44 [C 6510], HC 1890–1, xxv. 424.

[158] 45 & 46 Vict., c. 47 (18 Aug. 1882); *Return of Payments Made to Landlords by the Irish Land Commission Pursuant to the First and Sixteenth Sections of the Act . . .* p. iv [C 4059], HC 1884, lxiv. 100.   [159] 48 & 49 Vict., c. 73 (14 Aug. 1885).

[160] See below, App. 5.   [161] Donnelly, *Land and People of Cork*, 249–50.

reduced the conflicts between them and the tenants and left the tenants free to engage their landlords. The land war, therefore, was a struggle between two groups of creditors, both of whom were trying to recover their debts: the landlords who wanted their rents and shopkeepers who wanted their bills paid.[162]

Both of these explanations are important because they concentrate on important aspects of the land war: the idea that prosperity, which suffered a sudden check, was the cause of the land war was a nice inversion of what had gone before; Clark's idea about organization and leadership added a fascinating dimension to the understanding of nineteenth-century Ireland; it drew attention to an important group beneath the national leaders and above the rank and file. Before Clark it was tempting to regard nineteenth-century Ireland as a sort of volcano, seething with discontent; all that was needed was an ingenious troublemaker to find and open a fissure. There are, however, problems associated with both explanations. Clark is weak on timing, for example; if shopkeepers, credit, and crisis are the ingredients necessary, why was there not a widespread movement in the early 1860s in those counties that were relatively well endowed with townsmen? If the land war was essentially a struggle between two groups of creditors, how did the townsmen's leadership coexist with the fact that they issued an enormous number of civil bills between 1879 and 1882? The figures below show that ejectment processes were vastly outnumbered by ordinary civil bill processes (there were 9,703 of the former in 1879 and 347,909 of the latter);[163] the same figures also show that ordinary civil bill processes declined in 1880 while ejectments increased, but they still remained very high, 289,358 compared with 10,633. How could the townsmen appear to take the side of the tenants against the landlords and issue 877,633 civil bill processes in the three years 1879–81? The complexity of the shopkeepers' position was revealed by William L. Feingold's study of the Tralee poor law guardian elections in 1881, when he found that the land league enjoyed the support of the majority of the shopkeepers in Tralee 'but it was perhaps not so large as the rhetoric of land league leaders would suggest. When neutral votes are included, it is clear that almost half the Tralee shopkeepers were not ready to throw their weight behind the league.'[164]

---

[162] Samuel Clark, *Social Origins of the Irish Land War* (Princeton, NJ, 1979). See also id., 'The Social Composition of the Land League', *IHS* 17: 68 (Sept. 1971), 447–69; id., 'The Political Mobilization of Irish Farmers', *Canadian Review of Sociology and Anthropology*, 22: 4, pt. 2 (Nov. 1975), 483–99; and id., 'The Importance of Agrarian Classes: Agrarian Class Structure and Collective Action in Nineteenth-Century Ireland', in P. J. Drudy (ed.), *Irish Studies*, 2. *Ireland: Land, Politics and People* (Cambridge, 1982), 11–36.

[163] See below, App. 2.

[164] William L. Feingold, 'Land League Power: The Tralee Poor-Law Election of 1881', in Samuel Clark and James S. Donnelly, *Irish Peasants: Violence and Political Unrest, 1780–1914* (Manchester, 1983), 304.

The difficulty with rising expectations is the narrowness of the margin between the period of prosperity that preceded the depression of the early 1860s and the prosperity that preceded the depression of the late 1870s. Was the difference between seven years (1853 to 1859) and thirteen years (1864 to 1876) important? It is easy to presume the presence of rising expectations but not easy to verify their presence. Were expectations rising? How can something so subjective be proved? The tenants' growing indebtedness certainly supports Professor Donnelly's argument, if indebtedness can be accepted as a measure of rising expectations.[165] The relationship between improvements in housing and agrarian outrages during the land war also supports Professor Donnelly: Kerry and Galway, for example, were among the counties whose housing improved most between 1851 and 1881; they were also among the counties that had the most agrarian crime between 1879 and 1882.[166] A body of evidence that assists Professor Donnelly's argument, although it must be admitted that it is not an ideal body of evidence, is the returns on lunacy in the census of 1881, when an inquiry was made into the 'mental and moral' causes of lunacy. Eleven mental and moral causes were listed, including terror, grief, love, jealousy, religious excitement, study, anxiety, and pride; but most importantly 'disappointment' and 'reverse of fortune', which at least can be related to expectations, even non-rising ones, were also included.[167] The effects of all mental and moral causes increased dramatically between 1871 and 1881, but 'disappointment' increased more than any other cause; 'reverse of fortune', however, which was closer to expectations than the rather vague 'disappointment', increased at about an average rate, coming behind 'terror', 'religious excitement', 'ill-treatment', and 'pride'.

In one sense everything that happened between the famine and the late 1870s caused the land war. If the land war is seen as the culmination of this period, its teleological force will draw everything into its ambit. The land league was a mass movement, drawing its membership and leadership from many groups in rural Ireland; every group that the land league encompassed can be drawn into a causal relationship with the land war. Shopkeepers were among land league organizers, so shopkeepers are important; Fenians were among the organizers, so Fenians are important. Literacy increased before the 1870s; labourers declined; emigration slowed down in the 1870s;[168] for many there was prosperity; for many there was just an unremitting struggle. Literacy, emigration, prosperity, and poverty, therefore, are important. To these might be added the Irish constabulary, which might seem paradoxical until it is remembered that they played a part in weakening the landlords.

[165] *Cowper Comm., Minutes of Evidence*, 976–81.   [166] See below, Apps. 15 and 22.
[167] *Census Ire., 1881, General Report*, pp. 302–3 [C 3365], HC 1882, lxxvi. 726–7. I am indebted to Edith Mary Dunlop for drawing my attention to this table.
[168] Fitzpatrick, 'Class, Family and Rural Unrest', 48.

Andrew W. Orridge has approached the causes of the land war on a broad front by examining the statistical connection between eight putative causes of the land war and the incidence of land meetings in 1879 and 1880 and of agrarian outrages in each of the four years 1879–82.[169] His conclusions are not reassuring, if one is looking for one simple explanation for the outbreak and progress of the land war. First, his results question the arguments that the land war was caused by 'a wave of change sweeping across Ireland in the later nineteenth century encompassing market relationships, rising incomes, demographic and structural change, and new élites'. Secondly, 'the explanations that have fared best deal with the immediate suroundings of the land league and land war.' These include the difficulties of small farmers in the south and west; the tendency of counties 'with the fewest labourers and the greatest number of modest holdings' to be most militant; the tendency of counties with the smallest towns, with the poorest land, and with the most Catholics to be most militant. Thirdly, he attaches considerable but limited importance to evictions: evictions between 1856 and 1875 'display a consistent and noticeable positive relationship with agrarian discontent', and evictions and agrarian outrages in 1882 are strongly connected. Finally, the land war was 'an economically provoked movement of the poorest groups which gradually spread to much of the island, although it was always strongest in less prosperous areas, and which, after the demise of the league, became a straightforward matter of resistance to evictions'.[170]

Dr Orridge does not offer one, simple explanation of the causes of the land war; but he does draw attention to the importance of the agricultural depression of the late 1870s and its effects on the small tenants of the west. Dr Orridge, having eliminated all other factors, can say that the one which remains must be the truth. The three main explanations of the land war, therefore, have naturally enough the agricultural depression of the late 1870s as their preoccupation. Agricultural depression made the payment of rents difficult; it led to evictions; it caused agrarian outrages to increase; it created discontent that could be harnessed by politicians. There were three periods of agricultural depression between the famine and the land war: in the late 1840s and early 1850s, in the early 1860s, and in the late 1870s. The first produced a tenant movement that was weak compared with that of 1879–82; the second produced no movement at all; the third produced the land league. Why did the agricultural depression that began

[169] Andrew W. Orridge, 'Who Supported the Land War? An Aggregate-Data Analysis of Irish Agrarian Discontent, 1879–82', *Economic and Social Review*, 12: 3 (Apr. 1981), 203–33.
[170] Ibid. 227–8; see also 217–18, 220, 221; see below, App. 23 for the very high correlation between agrarian outrages 1879–82 and evictions as a proportion of the decline in the number of rural houses between 1851 and 1881.

in 1877 produce the land league? There were three things that made the late 1870s different from the two earlier crises: first, indebtedness had increased; secondly, the land act of 1870 had increased the tenants' security without providing any remedies, except in Ulster, for those evicted for non-payment of rent; thirdly, there was the new departure.

The first two of these are relatively straightforward. Credit, and therefore, indebtedness, seems to have increased from the early 1860s. 'Until 1863 the branch banks were managed by old, experienced, and cautious officers, whose general policy discouraged rather than invited applications for advances from the farming classes'; but after 1863, 'owing to the rapid increase in the number of offices, the branch managers were younger and less experienced men, and were tempted to lend too freely...'.[171] Civil bills increased sharply between the mid-1860s and the mid-1870s; civil bill ejectments also increased.[172] Even before the crisis began in 1877 tenants were more likely to appear in court than they did in the mid-1860s. The land act of 1870 increased the tenants' credit, but it also inserted non-landlord creditors into a sort of tenurial crevice between the tenants and their landlords.[173] Whatever else happened the crisis in the late 1870s would have been more complicated than its predecessors. The tenants were more likely to be caught between two sets of creditors, and the landlords were more likely to have rivals in their attempts to collect their rents. In a contest between landlords and shopkeepers, the former suffered from disadvantages. Their estates were large enough to enable tenants to form a constituency among themselves; they were awkwardly visible; their methods of debt collection were akin to 'calling the huntsman and hounds into the garden to kill the hare'. The shopkeepers were small, diverse, and not so visible; their customers could not so easily form a constituency among themselves; their methods of debt collection were not so abrupt. In law both parties had given away their property and could retrieve it only by legal means; in practice, however, there was a difference: shopkeepers' credit was flexible if restricted and it could be stretched, extended, or just withheld; but land was either retained or given up *in toto*. The shopkeepers could switch the current on or off, but the landlords had temporarily given away their generators.

---

[171] *Cowper Comm., Minutes of Evidence*, 976–7; Philip Ollerenshaw, *Banking in Nineteenth-Century Ireland: The Belfast Banks, 1825–1914* (Manchester, 1987), 102–5, 114–22.

[172] See below, App. 2; see also App. 5. In the five years 1856–60, 326,689 civil bills were entered and 175,560 decrees were granted; in 1874 110,630 civil bills were entered and 65,229 decrees were granted. (*Returns 'from the Clerks of the Peace of the Several Counties and Counties of Cities in Ireland, of the Number of Civil Bill Ejectments Entered for Hearing in the Courts of the Assistant Barristers, or Chairmen, for Five Years Previous to 1 Jan. 1851... [and] for Five Years Previous to 1 Jan. 1861... Distinguishing the Number of Same Decreed, Dismissed, and Nilled in Each Respective Year'*, pp. 3–11, HC 1861 (552), li. 679–87; *Judicial statistics, Ire.*, 1874, p. 221 [C 1295], HC 1875, lxxxi. 479).

[173] Above, p. 99.

The land act had other results, in addition to its effects on indebtedness. It gave the tenants a measure of security, but only if they paid their rents; it did not, therefore, offer a substantial remedy for those who fell into arrears after 1877. If section 3 had included compensation for those evicted for non-payment, or even some provision for temporary relief in bad years, it might have been more effective; if it had included arrangements for the compulsory insurance of rents, it might have prevented the land war.[174] At the same time the act had increased the expectation of political relief; it had been conferred on the tenants by parliament and it was not unreasonable to expect further relief, such as Gladstone's proposed bill in 1880.[175] In a crisis, therefore, the invocation of parliament was as likely as agrarian outrage; what was not likely was a determined rent strike, or complicated negotiations about prices, costs, and rents. If there was to be a war, it was more likely to be fought with howitzers than with bayonets.

The land act and indebtedness together would have made the crisis of the late 1870s different from that of the early 1860s; what made it strikingly different, however, was the new departure, which made possible not only the leadership of Parnell and Davitt, but the participation of many Fenians and the winning of American-Irish support. The negotiations between Davitt, Parnell, and Devoy have been described in detail by the late T. W. Moody.[176] The change in the location and orientation of Fenianism between the 1860s and 1870s has been described by Professor Comerford: 'the geographical bias of Fenian strength had altered dramatically since the mid-1860s with the focus moving from the areas of (by Irish standards) relatively advanced urbanization to the region of north Connacht and south Ulster—more or less the old "ribbon" territory.... The IRB was now very strong in Mayo where Ribbonism had not been widespread.'[177] The one clear fact about 1879 that does not suffer from statistical complexity was that it was the only year of severe agricultural depression that found a united, flexible, and potentially powerful political leadership ready to exploit agrarian discontent. In the early 1860s the O'Donoghue and George Henry Moore were not interested in a land agitation; the Fenians were not closely connected with the tenants, especially with those most vulnerable in the west of Ireland. In the early 1850s the tenant league was only part of the movement that developed and it is debatable whether land was as important as

---

[174] Arrears of £1.8 million were extinguished under the arrears act; £250,000 a year would have comfortably discharged even the most elaborate claims under the land act of 1870 (see above, p. 101); a system of compulsory insurance for rents would have had, therefore, to raise just under £0.5 million a year in the 1870s—or about 4% of annual rents.

[175] Comerford, *Fenians*, 215, 223–4; see also *A Bill to Make Temporary Provision with Respect to Compensation for Disturbance in Certain Cases of Ejectment for Non-Payment of Rent in Parts of Ireland*, HC 1880 [bill 232], i. 427.

[176] *Davitt and Irish Revolution, 1846–82* (Oxford, 1981).

[177] Comerford, *Fenians*, 213–16, 222.

the ecclesiastical titles act in the general election of 1852. The quality of Parnell and Davitt as leaders was impressive. Parnell had one considerable advantage that he shared with many of his fellow landlords: he had no consistent, carefully thought-out ideas about the land question. Davitt had the great advantage of being known to the public without being embroiled in party politics. They were a formidable combination compared with Lucas, Gavan Duffy, and MacKnight, their predecessors in the 1850s; their potential predecessors in the 1860s, Stephens, the O'Donoghue, and John Francis Maguire, were not in the same class.

The timing of the new departure was important: it laid the foundations of the alliance before the winter of 1879, which was the worst period of the agricultural depression that began in 1877. In the 1850s the tenant league reached its zenith of political strength in 1852 just as things were getting better. Davitt and Parnell built barriers against a powerful, incoming tide, which had given plenty of warning of its approach; the tenant league built against what turned out to be a receding tide. If the new departure had occurred earlier or later than it did, it might not have achieved so much: if earlier, the protagonists might have seen through each other sooner; if later, other leaders, more closely connected with the tenants, might have organized a different kind of movement. The land question had a potentially greater share of political attention in 1879 than it had ever had before. In the early 1850s there were many grievances in the countryside as well as rents and evictions: poor law rates, for example; the Durham letter and the ecclesiastical titles act were also powerful rivals. In the 1860s the distractions were even stronger: the Fenians, the American civil war, and the apparent imminent collapse of the papal states. By the 1870s the political landscape had changed: Gladstone had dismantled the Irish church; he had laid out the lines of a new political path by passing the land act of 1870; the Pope had passed beyond mere political concerns by becoming infallible and popular; home rule was superficially an obstacle to the new departure, but its most powerful leader was prepared, temporarily at least, to take up the land question.

While the new departure, debt, and the land act of 1870 were important in making the agricultural depression of the 1870s different from its predecessor in the early 1860s, it must also be remembered that tenants rebelled against their landlords because they were allowed to rebel. The landlords in Pomfret's *Struggle for Land in Ireland* were men of power; they could do virtually what they liked: they could evict, rackrent, and change the law to serve their own ends. Power was indeed the key to landlordism; but not, as Pomfret imagined, because the landlords were powerful. They were not as powerful as he thought: they were bound by the law; their main sanctions were based on law; they had been supplanted by the constabulary as enforcers of the law. They did not dominate the constituencies or parliament; their role in local government, while still very considerable, certainly had not expanded in the 1850s and 1860s. They had failed to build up reservoirs of informal power that would have been completely under their control; they did not possess sanctions that could be applied gradually and flexibly.

8
Conclusion

Much had changed between 1848 and 1876. The law of landlord and tenant had moved towards freedom of contract, and then towards restricting it. The countryside had become more peaceful; rents in the 1870s were paid with a punctuality that would have impressed agents in the early 1850s. Housing was better absolutely and relatively; small farmers were holding their own; the land system had stood up to a number of shocks without falling into anarchy; famine was not impossible, but the use of Indian meal meant that another great famine was unlikely. Emigration maintained the existing structure of land occupation by permitting the relatively smooth removal of surplus children.

Much, however, had not changed. Poor areas such as County Mayo had shared in the prosperity, but their predicament had not been transformed. The land question had not gone away: an intellectual apparatus, sustained by rich administrative sources, had been built up, directing thought and criticism into well-worn paths. The land act of 1870 was not the inadequate measure that many of its critics imagined; but it did not solve the land question. If anything, it increased the tendency to argue in tenurial terms, confining discussion to narrow channels. The land question had not advanced intellectually. The need to cope with crises caused by accidents, bad harvests, or depressions was given little thought—debt moratoria, public works, or reserve funds for tenants in difficulties were not often discussed. Neither estate management nor the tenants' capacity for organizing themselves had apparently changed. Landlords were just as visible, just as contentious as they had been in the 1850s: they still operated a public system of law, open to scrutiny, and unassimilated by the state bureaucracy. The tenants had not organized themselves into anything that even remotely resembled trade unions, either in numbers or in effectiveness. Many of the land question's political rivals had vanished: the poor law, agricultural protection, the Irish church, the papal states, and even the Fenians had subsided or disappeared as public issues. As each problem receded the starkness of the land question appeared greater independently of any changes in relations between landlords and tenants.

What had the landlords achieved between 1848 and 1878? The landlords, with the exception of those who had discovered that Henrietta Street was the *via dolorosa* of landed wealth, had survived. They had continued to extract a large surplus from agriculture, about £340 million between 1850 and 1879, a sum far greater than that collected by any other agency in Ireland.[1] They had remained politically powerful, although not by any means dominant, playing a part in general elections, providing many MPs from their ranks, and dominating local government and the petty sessions, where they made what was probably their most important contribution to rural life. Admittedly the 1874 general election had been a reverse. Yet landlords had a foothold in the home rule movement and retained their influence in many of the non-home-rule constituencies. There was no reason to assume, therefore, that the defeat of 1874 was irreversible; in any case, defeat in Ireland had coincided with a Tory victory in the United Kingdom and the return to power of the first firmly based Tory government since 1841, which was some consolation.

The landlords had not received any great blow since the encumbered estates acts. The land act of 1870 was an impediment to estate management, but the possibility of more vigorous management was not eliminated; sections 3 and 4 were annoying, but were probably a small price to pay if they prevented a recurrence of Derryveagh and Ballycohey. No great irreconcilable conflict had occurred: there were no technical or economic changes that offered landlords great profits if they got rid of their tenants. There was, for example, no great, tempting increase in wool prices.

It would, however, be difficult to argue that landlords were vigorous or constructive after the famine. They had not fully exploited their estates, either by extracting full economic rents, or consolidating holdings, or by investment. Measured by benign standards of efficiency they took only about 80 per cent of available rents; more rigorous standards might have reduced their success rate to an even lower figure.[2] They had not consolidated holdings. Between 1849 and 1880, assuming that every eviction redistributed 10 acres, only 700,000 acres, or 3.5 per cent of the land, was distributed. It was, however, in investment that they performed worst, investing only 4 or 5 per cent of rents annually, when 20 per cent would have made an enormous impact.[3] Far from seeing landlords as central to the land system, it is difficult not to see them as peripheral. The most important changes came from outside: changes in the law, increases in prices, the railways, new fertilizers, and new sources of food.

Irish landlords were not masters of their fate. In a general sense no European landed élite crowed without challenge on its own dunghill. As agriculture became more specialized, producing more for sale, as new areas of the world began exporting food, fluctuations in prices became inevitable. As technology was applied to agriculture, changes beneficial to some were pushed ahead at the expense of others. In a particular sense

[1] See below, App. 13.   [2] Above, pp. 61–3.   [3] Above, pp. 127–8.

Irish landlords were less in control than others; Prussian junkers, for example, who could keep up the price of food in Germany, were better off.[4] Irish landlords did not control, or even perhaps influence the British state after 1846; Liberals were in power for most of the period from 1846 to 1874, and whatever else they disagreed about, they were committed to free trade; Irish landlords had some influence in parliament, but it was a power to resist rather than to innovate. They could not do much about routine administration: the constabulary were controlled by the government; the government had in Sir Thomas Larcom and his successor, servants of remarkable ability and independence.

Like many groups in British society, including churchmen of all denominations, landlords were exposed to the vagaries of a remarkably open society, which was deeply committed to free competition in ideas as well as in production. Above all, they had to live in a state where law was dominant, the rights of the subject highly regarded, and administration remarkably thorough and honest, if limited in its scope. Landlords might complain that they were not protected by the state; they might talk loudly of lynch law; but they knew what would happen to them if they were convicted of a serious crime. The British state was not an oppressive one: taxes were, with one or two exceptions, tactfully extracted; there was no conscription; there were no vexatious monopolies; citizens were not obliged to carry identity papers, or to report to the police when they moved from place to place. Consequently landlords did not have the protection of a tough state, versed in the ways of bullying peasants; nor could they make a profession of siding with tenants against officials.

Irish landlords suffered other consequences of the union. They were a less important vested interest in a rapidly expanding empire than they would have been in an Irish polity. (Even in Ireland itself, capital invested in government and India stock in 1870 was about one-seventh of Irish land's capital value.[5]) Taking British assets as whole, Irish land was a small proportion of the whole by the 1870s: in 1873 foreign investments alone were worth £1,000 million, which was about four times the value of Irish land.[6] The union also spawned many peculiar administrative practices, representing a compromise between Irish and English traditions, or perhaps more accurately a compromise between what O'Connell would take and the Whigs would give; the constabulary, the poor law, and the resident

---

[4] Fritz Stein, 'Prussia', in David Spring (ed.), *European Landed Élites in the Nineteenth Century* (Baltimore and London, 1977), 59.

[5] *Report on Certain Statistics of Banking in Ireland and Investments in Government and India Stock, on Which Dividends are Payable at the Bank of Ireland*, p. 15 [C 4681], HC 1886, lxxxi. 155; Cowper Comm., Minutes of Evidence, 1014.

[6] E. J. Hobsbawm, *Pelican Economic History of Britain*, iii. *From 1850 to the Present Day: Industry and Empire* (Harmondsworth, 1969), 139.

magistracy were perhaps the most important examples. It is very difficult to believe that any of these would have evolved in exactly the same way under an Irish parliament.

Landlords had to contend with local interests that they found difficult to control, most notably Catholic priests, Presbyterian ministers, shopkeepers, journalists, and solicitors. Neither the Catholic church nor the Protestant churches, other than the Church of Ireland, offered landlords a place in their government: the Presbyterian church was closed to a largely episcopalian gentry, and the Catholic church did not incorporate laymen, not even Catholic landlords, in its government. Pieces of benevolence were possible: land for chapels and meeting-houses, the odd gift for repairs; but these created spasms of gratitude rather than habitual dependence. The opportunity created by the reorganization of the Irish church after 1871 was, however, eagerly seized by landlords, who played a part in its government at all levels from select vestries up to the general synod, which was the largest regular gathering of Irish gentry in Dublin since 1800. Their generosity to the Church of Ireland, whether re-endowing the diocese of Clogher, or subscribing annually to parish funds, probably contributed to their political longevity in Ulster after 1885.

The landlords should have been well placed to deal with other groups in rural society that were capable of challenging their power: shopkeepers, journalists, and solicitors. Even after paying taxes and interest on mortgages, landlords were still, as a group, enormously rich. As patrons of shopkeepers, journalists, and solicitors, however, they suffered from certain weaknesses. For one thing they could not employ, in the nature of things, all of the solicitors and journalists. The legal business of an estate was considerable, but it could not conveniently be shared among several practitioners; similarly, with newspapers, the most they could do was to support one local paper, for their numbers were too small and their demands for advertising too limited to diffuse their influence.

The problem with shopkeepers was only slightly different: many shops were too small to satisfy landlords' luxurious tastes. A. J. R. Stritch, RM, for example, thought that small shopkeepers were unwilling to convict in agrarian cases, because their existence depended exclusively on small farmers: 'They have no other customers; the gentry make their purchases in Dublin or England.'[7] When Lord Inchiquin died in 1900 his debts included almost 250 items supplied by tradesmen—seeds, coal, china, saddles, 'fish and ice'—amounting to £11,000; but the suppliers were not concentrated in County Clare, or even in Limerick, but distributed through London, Dublin, Norwich, Redditch, Leeds, and Nottingham.[8] Although

[7] National Archives, RP 1870/2757.
[8] List of debts of the late Rt. Hon. Edward Donogh O'Brien, Baron Inchiquin, up to and ending 8 Apr. 1900, in Inchiquin rental, 1900 (NLI, MS 14577).

estates were big they were not usually big enough for landlords to give favoured shopkeepers a monopoly. Lord George Hill was able to enforce a monopoly for his shop at Gweedore by threatening rivals with eviction; but few landlords had such a command of territory. Many towns were beyond the control of one landlord, often being owned by several; in any case towns were often tenurial honeycombs, with leases and sub-tenancies that gave defiant bakers and butchers footholds from which to defy monopolists. The landlords did not control those vital ancillary services that might have given them control of rural trade: the banks and the railways. If, however, they had spent generously on the improvement of their estates, they might have had enough influence, through wages, orders for slates, timber, and fertilizers, to keep some shopkeepers at least in a deferential state.

It is one of the ironies of the Irish landlords' predicament that they were most successful in subaltern roles: as unpaid magistrates enforcing new laws; as a respectable audience at the general synod of the Church of Ireland; as partners of Belfast businessmen in Ulster unionism; as colonial governors. They occupied the positions that came naturally to them: the magistracy, lieutenancies of counties, the Order of St Patrick; but they were not prominent in cabinets, and did not monopolize even the lord-lieutenancy and the chief secretaryship. Irish landlords' failure went deeper than their inability to manage their estates efficiently, or to appropriate new sources of power. These were important, but only as symptoms, rather than causes. Irish landlords failed to be a real aristocracy; essentially the great estates that they inherited were sources of power, as well as of wealth; conversely, the great estates' maintenance depended on power and leadership. Territorial power could not simply be allowed to decline into *rentier* wealth: it was too visible, too cumbersome, and too decorated with the fripperies of an earlier age to allow its owners to subside into being merely rich men who lived in the country. Sir Bernard Burke might argue that the Irish peerage was not a real aristocracy, because it included so few descendants of the old Irish families, who with few exceptions were found among the untitled gentry, or roosting on titular perches outside the peerage, like the knights of Glin and the princes of Coolavin. Aristocracy, however, was not founded on Norman blood, Gaelic ancestry, or even on simple faith, but on the ability to rule.

In *Sybil* Disraeli discovered an aristocracy among the locksmiths and brass-founders of Wodgate, where there were no landlords, magistrates, clergy, or schools. The master workmen, however, who oppressed their apprentices 'as the Mamlouks treated the Egyptians', were a real aristocracy:

It is privileged, but it does something for its privileges. It is distinguished from the main body not merely by name. It is the most knowing class at Wodgate; it possesses indeed in its way complete knowledge; and it imparts in its manner a certain quantity of it to those whom it guides. Thus it is an aristocracy that leads, and therefore a fact.[9]

By any of these criteria Irish landlords had ceased to be an aristocracy. They were not the most knowing class in society: all around them were groups with greater knowledge: lawyers, policemen, and priests. Even in farming they failed to give more than a fitful lead; and their estate management showed that they did not possess complete knowledge: that agriculture would suffer periodic shocks and that landed wealth needed a new *raison d'être*. Nor did they do much for their privileges: they neither invested, provided entrepreneurial skill, nor maintained the agricultural interest in the state; they did not sustain the religious life of their communities, unlike the 'bishop' of Wodgate; they did not protect their people from the vicissitudes of the outside world. Disraeli shrewdly saw that neither brutality nor inequality necessarily subverted a social system; conversely, their absence did not maintain it. Rule by the few is maintained by the possession of rare skills: by the entrepreneurial skills of an industrialist like Lord Pirie; by leadership that involves more than average sacrifices, like that of junior officers and NCOs in an army; but one thing is essential, those who are led must need their leaders more than they resent their privileges.

Within the limits imposed on them by the law, the government, and other groups in the countryside the landlords could have done more to sustain their power. First, they could have persisted in the consolidation of holdings, imposing high rents, and creating a consciously entrepreneurial class of farmers. Secondly, they could have become a proper *rentier* class, concealing their wealth behind trustee and mortgage companies, keeping their country houses and seats on the magisterial bench, but, like Mr Maule of Maule Abbey, dealing not 'with reluctant and hard-tasked tenants, but with punctual, though inimical trustees, who paid to him with charming regularity that portion of his rents which he was allowed to spend'.[10] Thirdly, they could have organized their estates more efficiently.

The state itself offered a model. As JPs the gentry probably did more potentially unpopular acts than they did as landlords, yet they were rarely attacked as magistrates. Why not? As magistrates they acted according to rules that they did not make themselves or change on the spur of the moment; they did not act alone; they had a variety of penalties, most of which stopped short of ruining those who came before them. This could have been applied to estate management; William Blacker on one occasion, for example, invited his tenants to act as a jury and decide for themselves what rent they should pay him.[11] As Charles Gavan Duffy said, 'the tenant

---

[9] Disraeli, *Sybil or the Two Nations* (Harmondsworth, 1980), 204.
[10] Anthony Trollope, *Phineas Redux* (St Alban's, 1973), 181.
[11] Undated newscutting pasted in Blacker rental (Co. Armagh), 1847–56 (PRONI, D959/2/2).

only asks to put upon the private landlord (insatiable in the pursuit of his own interest) that restraint which the state puts upon itself.'[12] The landlords threw away many of their advantages. The great virtue of the rental system was its flexibility. Under a purchase system farmers tie up capital in land, and land once bought has to service a fixed burden of repayments, regardless of the fortunes of agriculture. Rents, on the other hand, could fall in a crisis, giving a breathing-space to farmers; but landlords failed to institutionalize this advantage. Many landlords committed themselves to *laissez-faire* economics; but a system of thought that assumed a social *tabula rasa* was not a conservative force, yet if landlords had a chance of survival it was to pose as conservatives in rural society and to shelter tenants from the disruptions of a market economy. They should have appeared as the champions of the old-world values; they should have appealed to old ties and old ways. They did not introduce the new ways with any thoroughness. Their incomes reflected an easy-going world; their ideas a world of cheap mousetraps and Lancashire cotton. The past was captured by their opponents, moreover, and used against them.

That landlords could command their neighbours' sympathy was shown in Cahir in 1850 when the coroner tried to execute a writ of *fieri facias* on Lord Glengall for the sum of £1,062, 10s. 6d. When five bailiffs arrived at Cahir Castle, they were let in, but 'one was nearly choked by the hall porter and another man'. Another escaped to Cahir to bring the constabulary, who refused to interfere; when he got back to the castle, 'Lord Glengall had arrived, and upon being informed that this bailiff was one of those who had made the seizure, his lordship hit him on the head with a cane stick'. Lord Glengall then ordered his servants to drive away the bailiffs, and 'this direction was immediately carried into effect, the bailiffs were assaulted, severely beaten, and driven a considerable distance from the house.' When they got to Cahir, their troubles began again. The postmaster and Lord Glengall's solicitor had gathered a crowd 'to beat and hunt the ruffians out of the town'. Three of the bailiffs were 'knocked down, repeatedly jumped upon whilst down, and severely cut in the head'; 'one . . . clung to a policeman and asked for protection for his life, but was refused and exposed to the violence of the mob.' The constabulary later exonerated the postmaster and the solicitor, but blamed 'a noted scold named Mary Myers, an applewoman'. In the end, in spite of constabulary support and the threat of military intervention, Lord Glengall's creditor ('who is a timid old man') surrendered his suit for a mere £150 interest.

The ferocity of Lord Glengall's servants was predictable, if reprehensible; but why did the people of Cahir join in? Lord Glengall was in debt, but Lady Glengall had a large income of her own. 'Her ladyship is extremely

---

[12] Charles Gavan Duffy, *The League of North and South: An Episode in Irish History, 1850–1854* (London, 1886), 39.

charitable and benevolent,' reported the sub-inspector. 'She spends a quantity of money amongst the shopkeepers, and gives a great deal of employment to the tradespeople and labourers, so that when she is resident in the town, the affairs of the humble classes are in quite a thriving and flourishing condition.' The people of Cahir were afraid that the bailiffs' visit would be so offensive to Lady Glengall that she would leave the country. 'They determined therefore to evince their gratitude and attachment to her ladyship in the way they fancied they could best make them manifest, by driving from the town the men who they believed intruded upon her.'[13]

Between the famine and the land war, landlords received about £340 million in rents, making them in a very real sense Ireland's most precious possession. Was the cost of landlordism confined to the extraction of money? If the land system had been radically changed in the early 1850s it is doubtful if most tenants would have been much better off. Anything less than the complete expropriation of the landlords would have transferred little to the tenants: if rent fixing had been established, rents might even have been higher in the long run; if state-assisted land purchase had taken place, it is possible that interest and amortization would have cost more than the rents. If the landlords had been dispossessed by revolution, the largest part of the rental would have gone to the big tenants: £6 million out of a rental of about £11 million would have gone to tenants with more than 50 acres. The new owners, however, would have had to carry the whole burden of local and national taxation, a burden that would probably have increased. For one thing some of the gentry's functions would have had to be discharged by professional civil servants, especially their work as magistrates; secondly, a revolution would almost certainly have added to the burden of taxation.

If the gentry had been driven from their demesnes as well as from their tenanted land, there would have been about 3 million acres for redistribution. This would have been enough to give landless families a few acres each, assuming that it all went to poor landless families, which is not a very realistic assumption when it is remembered that even the most godless revolutions tend to obey the divine precept in Matthew 25: 29. It is unlikely, however, that employment would have been found for all who worked on demesnes and in the great houses, even if the revolutionaries had set up as country gentlemen. It is doubtful if big farmers, freed from the need to pay rent, would have employed more labour; indeed, it is probable that the opposite would have occurred. The landlords' expropriation would not have solved the two major problems of rural society: the tendency of small farms to be become unviable as living standards rose and the problem of accommodating a growing population on a limited

[13] National Archives, outrage papers, Tipperary, 1851/3.

amount of land. It is also true that while a particular class of landlords could be expropriated, landlordism as a form of landownership could not be so easily done away with: sub-letting and subdivision would have created new tenurial problems, possibly more difficult to solve than those they replaced.

The cost of the land question was not confined to the millions absorbed by rents. There were less obvious costs. The tenurial aspect came to dominate the land question almost to the exclusion of all else. Gradually the three Fs and land purchase were seen as almost magical remedies that would transform the countryside. Where discussion should have been dull, technical, and sensible, it was high-flown, running to fundamentals, and corrupted by *folie de grandeur*. Hay and turnips were much less interesting than evictions; but it was one of the failings of landlords that they did not stick to hay and turnips. The settlement that came out of the land war grew out of a process of thought that was at least thirty years old. It was not an ideal solution. First, no provision was made for labourers, except permissive legislation allowing local authorities to build cottages; secondly, no provision was made for tenants who could not pay their rents in bad years, except the unique arrears act of 1882, which was by far the most original and sensible piece of land legislation passed; thirdly, the problem of sub-tenancy was ignored, and modern Ireland has found it difficult to devise any useful tenancy to complement peasant proprietary. Finally, there was no provision for the public interest. Nineteenth-century agriculture yielded a large disposable surplus, equal to the whole cost of running both central and local government. After land purchase that surplus was represented only by terminable annuities, local government rates, and a little income tax. Eventually the annuities were eroded by inflation; then they expired; local government became more and more dependent on subventions from the central government; farmers became the recipients of subsidies.

It has been argued that the British state was replaced by an Irish state between 1879 and 1886. The reality was that both states lost control of the country's most valuable asset, an agricultural surplus of at least £10 million a year, which was eventually dissipated among the new landowners. The new landowners were indeed numerous, for the undoing of the conquest at least multiplied the heirs of the Cromwellians; but their very numbers gave them an electoral power comparable with that of the eighteenth-century borough-mongers. A remarkably private system of landownership was perpetuated: there were no great state forests, no extensive common lands, no great institutions drawing their revenues from land; even stretches of beach became private property. Landlords and tenants' great achievement was to create the impression that they were the only parties to the land question.

What did the land war achieve? The role of the land war in destroying landlordism was limited. It must share the credit with the First World War, the War of Independence, and the Civil War. In fact the crisis of landlordism may be said to have preceded the land war, for the gap between rents and output was great in the mid-1870s. The effects of the land act of 1881 were not catastrophic; it did not prevent evictions, for they were more numerous in the year after its enactment than in any of the previous twenty-nine years; it did not radically distribute incomes, for in the ten years 1881–91 only £1.2 million was transferred to the tenants, or 10 per cent of the rental of the country.[14] It is arguable that the land act worked in the landlords' favour, because it stabilized falling rents. If rents had followed output, they should have fallen by almost 40 per cent between 1876 and 1886. Irish landlords did not do worse than English and Scottish landlords in the great agricultural depression: on some English and Scottish estates rents fell by as much as 20 per cent between 1881 and 1891.[15] (R. J. Thompson estimated that agricultural rent in Great Britain fell by 22 per cent between the mid-1870s and the early 1890s.[16])

The land act of 1881 on its own would not have destroyed landlordism; indeed, in certain circumstances it might have strengthened it by giving it a new institutional base. It has been argued that the land war destroyed tenants' deference for landlords and that tenants stopped lifting their hats to landlords.[17] This is a large claim; for one thing, habits of respect may be interrupted but not permanently destroyed by conflict, for deference, like hope, springs eternal. There is no evidence about hat-lifting: the constabulary compiled no statistics of its incidence. There is some evidence, however, of changes in marks of deference before the land war. Pat and Thomas McMahon, a father and son who were tenants of Lord Inchiquin, wrote to the agent, asking to have Pat's farm transferred to Thomas. The father began his letter 'Honoured Sir'; the son began 'Dear Sir'.[18] What is remarkable, though, is the continued functioning of the petty sessions during the land war; the routine trial of 670,000 petty malefactors between 1879 and 1882 by alleged social vampires hardly suggests that the bonds of society were irretrievably dissolved.[19]

It is possible that the land war might have been only an incident in the

---

[14] *Report of the Irish Land Commissioners for the Period 22 Aug. 1890 to 22 Aug. 1891*, p. 44 [C 6510], HC 1890–1, xxv. 424.

[15] *Particulars of the Expenditure and Outgoings on Certain Estates in Great Britain and Farm Accounts*... [C 8125], HC 1896, xvi. 469.

[16] R. J. Thompson, 'An Inquiry into the Rent of Agricultural Land in England and Wales during the Nineteenth Century', *Journal of the Royal Statistical Society*, 70 (Dec. 1907), 595.

[17] Joseph Lee, *The Modernization of Irish Society, 1848–1918* (Dublin, 1978), 89.

[18] Inchiquin rent-ledger (Co. Clare), 1861 (NLI, MS 14801, p. 100).

[19] Excluding Dublin and Belfast; see *Judicial Statistics, Ire.*, 1879, pp. 92–3 [C 2698], HC 1880, lxvii. 342–3; ibid. *1880*, 92–3 [C 3028], HC 1881, xcv. 334–5; ibid. *1881*, 92–3 [C 3355], HC 1882, lxxv. 334–5; ibid. *1882*, 64–5 [C 3808], HC 1883, lxxvii. 306–7.

history of landlord–tenant relations, if it had not coincided with a decisive turning-point in agricultural incomes. The agricultural crisis that began in the late 1870s was not a mere aberration or pause in a period of prosperity, like that of the early 1860s. It was in fact the beginning of a long period of economic difficulty, for some agricultural prices never again reached their 1876 level until 1914. The crisis that began in the 1870s was not short and sharp, but protracted, until a deeper crisis developed in the mid-1880s. If agricultural prices had picked up again in the early 1880s and continued their upward movement landlordism would have revived. Rents might actually have been increased by the land courts; in any case the 1881 land act gave landlords the right to have the pre-emption value of tenant right fixed by the courts for fifteen years, which was a powerful weapon for bargaining with tenants, but only in a rising market.[20]

The decline of landlordism obviously implied the decline of the gentry, but their disappearance was not inevitable; indeed, land purchase offered them inducements to keep on their houses and demesnes. Before 1914 the landlord who sold his tenanted land, but kept his demesne, was still a wealthy man, at the apex of rural society. If the world had continued as it was before 1914, landlords' descendants would have had a bright enough future, even in a home rule Ireland. (In fact a self-governing Ireland, dominated by farmers, would not have been hostile to landowners as such.) Why did so many disappear? The obvious explanations are the casualties of the First World War, the bitterness of the War of Independence and the Civil War when many country houses were burnt, and the political character of the new southern state. None of these should be exaggerated: only about seventy country houses were burnt in the early 1920s;[21] the loss of sons during the First World War was the mere speeding-up of what usually happened on the hunting-field. The effects of Free State politics are more difficult to assess; certainly many families stayed on quite amicably through all the changes of the 1920s and 1930s.

Factors other than these, however, seem equally important. First, land purchase made no provision for the recruitment of landed families: land purchase bonds did not tie families to a particular locality, and their sale did not bring new families in. The gentry's depletion after 1914 was to some extent a continuation of what had always happened to landed families, with the difference that no new families appeared. Secondly, the abolition of the lay magistracy in the Free State took away not only the gentry's status, but their main occupation as well. Thirdly, the great erosion of money that took place after 1914, and again with renewed speed after

[20] K. Buckley, 'The Fixing of Rents by Agreement in Co. Galway, 1881–5', *IHS* 7: 27 (Mar. 1951), 155–6.   [21] Bence-Jones, *Ir. Country Houses*, p. xxvii.

1945, reduced drastically the value of land bonds; so the gentry were, with some exceptions, forced to keep up large houses on the profits of demesne farming.

Landlordism's decline, therefore, was more protracted and more complicated than the reverses suffered during the land war. It is worth noting, too, that the decline of landlordism was not exclusively an Irish phenomenon. British landlords, for all their political skills, declined: Brideshead was much grander than the big house of Inver or Woodbrook, but it was a house in decline even before the Second World War. The great-grandsons of those who proclaimed the German emperor at Versailles in January 1871 were less secure than the great-grandsons of Irish landlords, who had been forced, not to proclaim an emperor, but to swallow the disestablishment of the Irish church and the land act. The fate of the great estates has been varied; all have lost their tenanted land, many demesnes have been broken up, and great houses have been demolished. Some houses have survived, but transformed in use and dignity: Tandragee Castle, the Irish seat of the duke of Manchester, became a potato-crisp factory; Dungiven Castle became a dance hall, Drum Manor a sanctuary for butterflies, and Dromoland a hotel. There are some remarkable survivals: the duke of Abercorn still lives at Baronscourt, the earl of Rosse at Birr, and the marquis of Sligo at Westport. The gate at Markree that inspired Mrs Alexander to coin the most hackneyed image of wealth and poverty in the English-speaking countries survives.[22]

The most abiding consequence of the land war, and of the land question, was the victory of home rule at the general election in 1885. The agricultural depression of the late 1870s could have been disastrous for home rule. Without the new departure, the home rulers might have missed the opportunity provided by the depression; or they might have been pulled in different directions: some to farming politics, and some back to the Liberals after 1880. (The one disaster not suffered by Butt's party in 1874 was the temptations usually held out to Irish Liberals by a Liberal government.) If the home rulers had not taken up the tenants' cause in 1880, it is hard to see how they could have done it in 1885. For one thing, agricultural grievances would have come to the fore anyway, reducing home rule to just another demand. The extension of the franchise in 1885 created a complicated electorate in the countryside, with farmers and labourers as potentially antagonistic groups. If the primacy of home rule had not been established in the early 1880s, it is difficult to see how a broadly based national movement, extending beyond a few idealists, could have developed.

[22] Ibid. 202; for the number of farms in Ireland in 1881 and 1971 see *Census Ire., 1881*, pt. ii, *General Report*, pp. 112, 199 [C 3365], HC 1882, lxxvi; *Census Ire., 1971* (Dublin, 1975, Prl. 4925), v. 2; *Census, NI, 1971, Economic Activity Tables* (Belfast, 1977), 2.

APPENDIX 1

Eviction Statistics, 1849–1887

In their standing orders the constabulary were instructed to report all 'evictions'; the only exceptions were 'when parties surrender on the termination of their lease or agreement, or when parties voluntarily surrender without any previous process of law, but as a matter of agreement'. If tenants left at the mere request of their landlord that was not an eviction; but tenants, served with notice to quit, who left before the case came into court, or when the case came into court, were considered to have been evicted.[1] It is possible that the constabulary underestimated the number of evictions; in 1869, for example, they reported 309 actual evictions (372 evictions minus 63 readmissions), but the judicial statistics recorded 950 executions of civil bill ejectment decrees and writs of habere, 206 cottier warrants, and 2,423 warrants for the removal of town tenants, which altogether amounted to 3,579.[2] William Neilson Hancock in a memorandum prepared for Gladstone in 1870 stated that the constabulary did not include the evictions of cottiers and town tenants, which helps to explain part of the difference between the constabulary returns and the judicial statistics.[3] A discrepancy remains, however, between the 950 civil bill ejectment decrees and haberes executed and the 309 evictions returned in 1869. If the constabulary reported only 30 per cent of evictions, which is what this discrepancy implies, the number of tenants evicted would be much greater than the figures below suggest; in 1850–79, for example, there would have been 174,000 evictions instead of the 52,318 reported by the constabulary.

Occasionally the constabulary failed to report evictions adequately;[4] occasionally they exaggerated their numbers.[5] There are good reasons, however, for believing that their returns were reliable. The constabulary knew the countryside well; they knew of impending evictions because they attended the courts as a matter of routine; they were experienced in the collection of statistics, such as the agricultural statistics; the Chief Secretary's Office took their mistakes seriously enough to accumulate files on the subject. The constabulary's figures do not, however, have to be taken entirely on trust. First, the figure of 174,000 evictions is improbable

---

[1] Henry John Brownrigg, *Standing Rules and Regulations for the Government and Guidance of the Constabulary Force in Ireland*, rev. edn. (Dublin, 1860), 92.

[2] *Judicial Statistics, Ire.*, 1869, pp. 215, 224 [C 227], HC 1870, lxiii. 967, 976; see below, App. 5.

[3] Hoppen, *Elections, Politics, and Society*, 127 n. 1, which is based on BL, Gladstone papers, Add. MS 44613, fos. 102–3. Evictions in towns were reported in the early 1850s (National Archives, RP 1850/16482, C187; OP 1851/28; RP 1852 C268; RP 1853/11351); the differences between the totals in these files and the totals in RP 1874/685 may, however, be explained by the omission of town tenants from the latter.

[4] National Archives, RP 1860/13818; ibid. RP 1860/19990.

[5] Cf. the 753 evictions recorded on the Cahirciveen estate of Trinity College, Dublin in National Archives, OP 1851/28 with TCD, MUN/V/76/7, p. 116.

when compared with other figures; the number of agricultural holdings, for example, fell by about 70,000 between 1850 and 1880. Secondly, cases under the land act of 1870 are a useful source of comparison. Between 1871 and 1876 the courts issued decrees or dismisses in 1,923 cases, in the same period the constabulary reported 3,625 evictions, of which 1,846 were for reasons other than the non-payment of rent. The act protected mainly tenants who were evicted for reasons other than the non-payment of rent and the coincidence between the two figures is striking.[6] It is probable, therefore, that the difference between the judicial statistics and the constabulary returns is explained by the diminishing rate of implementation that characterized the early stages of ejectments.[7]

Families evicted and readmitted, and houses levelled, 1846–1887

Year	Families evicted	Readmitted	Actual evictions	Houses levelled
1846			3,500	1,539
1847			8,140	3,580
1848			12,452	5,477
1849	16,473	3,279	13,194	5,804
1846–9			37,286	16,400
1850	19,658	5,322	14,336	5,285
1851	12,925	4,290	8,635	3,325
1852	8,183	1,971	6,212	2,182
1853	4,719	1,402	3,317	867
1854	2,142	325	1,817	347
1855	1,870	522	1,348	346
1856	1,093	224	869	210
1857	1,110	207	903	162
1858	947	235	712	127
1859	832	342	490	75
1850–9	53,479	14,840	38,639	12,926
1860	683	68	615	125
1861	1,075	269	806	151
1862	1,121	243	878	118
1863	1,704	182	1,522	180
1864	1,865	275	1,590	115
1865	905	161	744	70

[6] See above, Ch. 4 n. 146; *Return in 'Tabular Form ... of the Number of Civil Bill Ejectments, Other than Civil Bill Ejectments for Non-Payment of Rent, Entered, Tried, and Determined, in Each County in Ireland, for Each of the Three Years Ending 31 Dec. 1876'*, p. 6, HC 1878 (25), lxiii. 456.

[7] The constabulary may themselves have exaggerated the number of actual evictions by underestimating the number of readmissions; see *Return of the Number of Evictions from Agricultural Holdings Which have Come to the Knowledge of the Constabulary ...* [for the Quarter Ended 30 Sept. 1892], p. 3 [C 6872], HC 1893, lxxiv pt. 2, p. 453; see also n. 5 above.

Year	Families evicted	Readmitted	Actual evictions	Houses levelled
1866	782	186	596	55
1867	547	89	458	75
1868	617	124	493	38
1869	372	63	309	31
1860–9	9,671	1,660	8,011	958
1870	551	106	445	20
1871	482	114	368	28
1872	526	118	408	23
1873	671	152	519	26
1874	726	200	526	
1875	667	71	596	
1876	553	85	468	
1877	463	57	406	
1878	980	146	834	
1879	1,238	140	1,098	
1870–9	6,857	1,189	5,668	
1880	2,110	217	1,893	
1881	3,415	194	3,221	
1882	5,201	198	5,003	
1883	3,643	226	3,417	
1884	3,978	223	3,755	
1885	3,127	120	3,007	
1886	3,781	181	3,600	
1887	3,869	110	3,759	
1880–7	29,124	1,469	27,655	

Sources: National Archives, RP 1874/685 (for 1849–73); *Return of Evictions, 1849–80* (for 1874–80). For the years 1881–7, see below, p. 304.

The figures for 1846–8 were calculated by using the figures for ejectments in Returns 'from the Courts of Queen's Bench, Common Pleas, and Exchequer in Ireland, of the Number of Ejectments Brought in Those Courts Respectively, for the Last Three Years, Beginning with Hilary Term 1846, and Ending with Hilary Term 1849; ... and, from the Assistant Barristers' Court of Each County of Ireland, of the Number of Civil Bill Ejectments...' HC 1849 (315), xlix. 235; Returns 'of the Number of Actions of Ejectment Brought in the Court of Queen's Bench [including actions in the courts of common pleas and exchequer, and in the civil bill courts during the years 1847, 1848, and 1849]...' HC 1851 (172), l. 629.

APPENDIX 2
Civil Bill Ejectments and Ordinary Civil Bills, 1866–1886

Year	Civil bill ejectments		Ordinary civil bills	
	Processes	Executions	Processes	Executions
1866	3,281	597	193,142	
1867	3,781	542	227,564	
1868	3,940	993	218,220	
1869	3,232	683	226,581	
1870	3,588	990	223,890	
1871	4,678	926	240,090	
1872	4,983	861	243,336	17,927
1873	6,334	1,435	282,722	19,691
1874	6,534	1,707	312,531	25,165
1875	6,646	1,680	290,335	21,909
1876	6,502	1,469	277,790	19,136
1877	6,738	1,562	300,564	20,309
1878	8,381	1,995	309,634	21,678
1879	9,703	2,670	347,909	35,091
1880	10,633	2,407	289,358	20,548
1881	13,621	3,177	240,366	16,321
1882	19,035	5,190	220,943	20,078
1883	22,706	3,924	231,762	17,527
1884	22,528	4,983	236,594	18,529
1885	18,592	3,843	226,153	17,967
1886	21,064	4,175	214,823	21,104

Source: *Judicial statistics*, 1866–86; for full references, see below, pp. 304–5.

APPENDIX 3
Counties Ranked According to Evictions, 1851–1880

The counties are ranked according to the number of families evicted, excluding those readmitted, per 1,000 agricultural holdings; the counties with the lowest rates are ranked first; the counties with the highest are ranked thirty-second. The provinces are ranked from first to fourth, in the same way.

Counties	1851–60	1861–70	1871–80
PROVINCE OF LEINSTER			
Carlow	23	22 =	21
Dublin	11	7	17
Kildare	12	17	7
Kilkenny	20	18	16
King's	29	21	13
Longford	24	31	29
Louth	14	11	8
Meath	28	22 =	31
Queen's	22	19	18
Westmeath	17	20	25
Wexford	19	9	12
Wicklow	15	13	10
PROVINCE OF MUNSTER			
Clare	25	27	15
Cork	13	10	23
Kerry	30	24	32
Limerick	26	12	27
Tipperary	31	30	19
Waterford	16	16	28
PROVINCE OF ULSTER			
Antrim	5	3	1
Armagh	4	6	5
Cavan	9	8	20
Donegal	8	25	22
Down	10	2	2
Fermanagh	2	15	14
Londonderry	3	1	3
Monaghan	6	5	4
Tyrone	1	4	6

Counties	1851–60	1861–70	1871–80
	PROVINCE OF CONNACHT		
Galway	27	28	30
Leitrim	18	32	26
Mayo	32	29	24
Roscommon	21	26	9
Sligo	7	14	11
	SUMMARY BY PROVINCES		
Leinster	2	2	2
Munster	3	3	4
Ulster	1	1	1
Connacht	4	4	3

Sources: National Archives, RP 1874/685; *Return of Evictions, 1849–80*.

APPENDIX 4

Counties Ranked According to Evictions during Four Periods, 1849–1882

The counties are ranked according to the number of families evicted, excluding those readmitted, per 1,000 agricultural holdings; the counties with the lowest rates are ranked first and the counties with the highest are ranked thirty-second. The provinces are ranked from first to fourth, in the same way.

Counties	1849–53	1861–4	1869–70	1879–82
		PROVINCE OF LEINSTER		
Carlow	19	9	32	17
Dublin	4	4	22	7
Kildare	9	24	26	5
Kilkenny	20	21 =	19 =	11
King's	27	21 =	13 =	13
Longford	23	31	28 =	32
Louth	10	17	9 =	3
Meath	21	15 =	12	28
Queen's	22	25	19 =	20 =
Westmeath	18	15 =	24	14
Wexford	15	12	13 =	8 =
Wicklow	16	10	31	8 =
		PROVINCE OF MUNSTER		
Clare	31	30	18	12
Cork	14	18	2 =	24
Kerry	29	28	23	31
Limerick	30	13 =	13 =	29
Tipperary	32	26	30	20 =
Waterford	17	13 =	19 =	18
		PROVINCE OF ULSTER		
Antrim	8	5	4	2
Armagh	6	7	11	8 =
Cavan	13	8	1	22
Donegal	7	11	28 =	26
Down	5	1	5	1
Fermanagh	1	23	16 =	6
Londonderry	3	2	8	4
Monaghan	11	6	2 =	15
Tyrone	2	3	6 =	23 =

Counties	1849–53	1861–4	1869–70	1879–82
PROVINCE OF CONNACHT				
Galway	26	19	25	23 =
Leitrim	25	32	27	30
Mayo	28	27	16 =	19
Roscommon	24	29	6 =	27
Sligo	12	20	9 =	16
SUMMARY BY PROVINCES				
Leinster	2	2	4	2
Munster	4	3	2	4
Ulster	1	1	1	1
Connacht	3	4	3	3

Sources: see above, p. 234.

APPENDIX 5

Fieris, Haberes, and Warrants Issued to Special Bailiffs for the Ejectment of Cottiers and Town Tenants, 1863–1886

Year	Fieris issued	Haberes granted	Haberes executed	Cottier warrants	Town tenants
1863	3,301	601			
1864	2,928	518			
1865	2,625	416			
1866	2,534	405	97	285	
1867	2,774	422	97	274	3,228
1868	2,083	327	162	255	3,012
1869	2,544	319	267	206	2,423
1870	2,593	422	311	243	4,408
1871	2,827	399	362	314	4,836
1872	3,016	374	312	335	4,752
1873	4,386	668	342	322	5,459
1874	4,876	550	463	334	5,758
1875	4,750	470	439	383	6,105
1876	4,483	509	370	371	6,135
1877	4,811	467	389	381	7,685
1878	6,442	535	522	459	8,403
1879	9,020	979	856	527	10,022
1880	7,223	1,372	905	633	13,205
1881	9,180	1,815	1,351	1,240	11,835
1882	10,188	1,770	1,407	886	12,485
1883	6,787	1,225	986	919	12,148
1884	6,749	1,111	862	771	12,944
1885	7,027	864	671	767	12,762
1886	7,759	1,056	931	886	14,701

Source: *Judicial Statistics*, 1863–86; for full references, see below, pp. 304–5.

APPENDIX 6
The Movement of Rents on Eleven Estates

APPENDIX 6

100 = rents due in 1850 or the year nearest to 1850.

For an index based on these eleven estates, see below, pp. 249, 265–6.

— indicates a year missing in a series.

Year	Ashtown	Blacker	Clonbrock	Crofton	Erne	Garvagh	Hall	Hamilton	Hodson	Knox	Midleton
1845		100			99	102					
1846		100			99	104			100		
1847		101			97	—			99		
1848		100			98	—			—		
1849		100	100		98	—			—		
1850		100	100		100				100		
1851		100	102		100				92		
1852	100	100	104	100	100				98	80	
1853	100	100	106	—	100	100	100	100	102	100	
1854	100	100	107	—	103	100	99	95	103	103	100
1855	100	—	—	106	103	99	99	93	104	107	101
1856	100	100	—	—	103	99	101	93	107	84	101
1857	103	100	—	—	103	99	101	95	109	82	101
1858	103	100	—	—	105	101	105	96	111	—	101
1859	104	101	111	—	108	101	107	99	—	98	101
1860	105	101	113	—	111	—	106	100	—	98	101
1861	105	101	109	—	111	—	105	102	122	110	101
1862	107	—	114	129	112	—	107	104	122	110	101
1863	109	101	114	129	113	—	110	99	120	110	101
1864	110	101	115	132	114	—	115	99	119	110	100
1865	111	101	116	130	113	—	120	101	120	110	103
1866	113	101	118	130	114	—	123	103	122	110	103
1867	114	101	119	128	114	—	124	103	122	110	103
1868	115	101	118	128	114	—	124	99	122	110	103
1869	116	101	118	128	114	—	124	103	122	110	103

APPENDIX 6

Year	Ashtown	Blacker	Clonbrock	Crofton	Erne	Garvagh	Hall	Hamilton	Hodson	Knox	Midleton
1870	117	101	—	—	115	—	130	103	122	117	103
1871	122	101	—	130	115	121	—	103	122	117	103
1872	123	101	—	130	115	123	—	103	122	117	103
1873	124	101	—	129	115	123	131	103	122	117	101
1874		101	—	—	115	124	132	103	122	117	104
1875		101	—	—	115	123	—	103	122	117	105
1876		101	—	129	115	124	—	103	122	117	107
1877		101	—	129	115	125	—	103	122	117	
1878			—	128	115	125	—	103	122	117	
1879			—	128	115	125	—	99	122	118	
1880			124	—	115	125	—	95	120	119	
1881			124	127	115	125	—	93	120	120	
1882			124	128	115	121	—	93	120	120	
1883			123	126	115	118	—	—	117	117	
1884			125	128	115	117	—	95	115	117	
1885			125	—	114	117	—			117	
1886			126	125	113	116	—			117	
1887			122	124	113	116	—			112	
1888			121	117		115	—				
1889			120	114		115	—				
1890			123	110		115	126				
1891			120	109		114					
1892			122			114					
1893						114					
1894						114					
1895						116					

Sources: Ashtown rentals (NLI, MSS 1765–9); Blacker, Co. Armagh (PRONI, D959/2/1–3); Clonbrock, Co. Galway (NLI, MSS 19617–45); Crofton, Co. Roscommon (NLI, MSS 4074–94, 5632–3); Erne, Co. Donegal (PRONI, D1939/8/1–3; National Archives, ID 6 181–2); Garvagh, Co. Londonderry (PRONI, D1550/20A/22, 23/25); Hall, Narrow Water, Co. Down (PRONI, D2090/3/7–30); Hamilton, Co. Cork (National Archives, M 5571, 1–34); Hodson, Co. Cavan (NLI, MSS 16404–6, 16419, 16438–70); Knox, Co. Roscommon (NLI, MS 3178); Midleton, Co. Cork (National Archives 978/1/1).

APPENDIX 7
Arrears on Twelve Estates

APPENDIX 7

Arrears are given as percentages of the annual rents due.
Arrears on the Inchiquin estate for 1845–9 were based on rents in 1850.
— indicates a year missing in a series.

Year	Ashtown	Blacker	Clonbrock	Crofton	Erne	Garvagh	Hall	Hamilton	Hodson	Inchiquin	Knox	Midleton
1845		8			74	75			23	17		
1846		29			75	—			40	27		
1847		29	27		87	—			—	41		
1848		7	22		85	—			—	35		
1849		13			83	—			43	28	54	
1850		14	17		79	—			37	26	50	
1851	53	5	12	29	71	—			41	19	54	
1852	4	11	14	31	66	124	250	54	19	19	68	21
1853	3	0	9	—	40	131	231	9	15	14	68	21
1854	2	0	7	21	40	118	177	5	7	12	58	14
1855	2	—	—	23	31	99	149	9	4	9	—	11
1856	0	0	—	—	17	91	141	13	8	8	57	11
1857	0	2	—	—	10	66	137	3	7	5	56	13
1858	0	0	0	—	11	59	121	3	3	4	50	13
1859	0	2	1	—	7	58	116	3	—	5	—	12
1860	0	2	0	—	10	—	116	3	5	4	100	13
1861	0	2	—	15	5	—	117	4	10	5	104	19
1862	0	11	4	4	11	—	111	9	8	7	75	8
1863	0	7	5	5	5	—	100	1	10	8	85	9
1864	0	4	6	5	2	—	82	1	13	6	86	8
1865	0	5	3	3	1	—	23	2	11	6	86	15
1866	0	5	4	4	1	—	21	1	8	6	86	17
1867	0	4	3	4	4	—	20	0	3	5	32	21
1868	0	4	3	4	4	—	24	0	3	5	25	21
1869	0	10	3	6	7	—	25	0	2	6		24

APPENDIX 7

Year	Ashtown	Blacker	Clonbrock	Crofton	Erne	Garvagh	Hall	Hamilton	Hodson	Inchiquin	Knox	Midleton
1870	0	7	—	5	7	49	32	2	3	6	1	12
1871	0	2	—	3	7	52	—	0	0	5	1	8
1872	0	5	—	3	7	48	23	1	11	6	0	12
1873	0	2	—	3	4	47	27	0	2	4	1	7
1874		2	—	—	4	47	30	0	0	3	0	6
1875		6	—	2	4	42	—	0	0	3	0	5
1876		3	—	2	2	40	—	2	0	3	0	
1877		3	—	3	1	41	—	4	0	3	0	
1878			—	3	3	41	—	3	2	2	1	
1879			9	18	4	54	—	9	17	11	5	
1880			14	31	9	54	—	10	23	22	14	
1881			20	32	11	57	—	13	30	24	57	
1882			19	13	14	77	—	10	13	13	42	
1883			11	10	16	49	—	14	13	14	39	
1884			13	13	19	41	—	26	15	10	42	
1885			16	21	21	44	—			21	50	
1886			23	23	18	44	—			25	22	
1887			30	39	19	48	—			36		
1888			30	42		49	—			42		
1889			34	48		50	—			46		
1890			40	46		50	23			51		
1891			39	39		45				52		
1892			43			41				92		
1893						36				97		
1894						23				94		
1895						21				103		
1896						19				106		
1897						18				102		
1898						19				105		

APPENDIX 8
Rent Receipts on Twelve Estates

APPENDIX 8

Receipts are given as a percentage of annual rents due.
— indicates a year missing in a series.

Year	Ashtown	Blacker	Clonbrock	Crofton	Erne	Garvagh	Hall	Hamilton	Hodson	Inchiquin	Knox	Midleton
1845		99								98		
1846		78								93		
1847		94								90		
1848		101								104		
1849		94	105							105		
1850		90	105		100				83	101		
1851		96	104		89				—	106		
1852	149	87	98	98	94				—	99		
1853	101	103	104	—	102		93		87	105	61	—
1854	101	92	102	—	107	93	102	123	93	101	98	102
1855	100	—	—	100	100	106	98	102	113	102	93	109
1856	101	91	—	—	104	118	102	96	101	101	—	105
1857	100	95	—	—	126	108	104	96	108	102	—	102
1858	100	98	—	—	97	123	103	96	102	101	120	99
1859	100	96	100	—	109	106	103	100	94	102	101	101
1860	100	98	101	—	107	100	103	100	101	101	100	103
1861	100	97	—	—	107	—	101	100	103	99	—	100
1862	100	—	97	98	98	—	98	98	—	100	100	93
1863	100	101	99	99	102	—	95	96	95	99	96	112
1864	100	102	99	100	96	—	103	103	102	98	129	92
1865	100	96	103	102	94	—	105	100	96	100	90	102
1866	100	98	99	99	106	—	110	99	96	102	99	92
1867	100	99	101	100	103	—	113	101	102	99	100	93
1868	100	97	99	100	101	—	102	100	103	101	100	98
1869	100	92	101	99	100	—	100	100	105	101	—	96
	100				96		97	100	100	100	107	98
					97		100	100	101	100		

APPENDIX 8

Year	Ashtown	Blacker	Clonbrock	Crofton	Erne	Garvagh	Hall	Hamilton	Hodson	Inchiquin	Knox	Midleton
1870	100	101	—	—	100	—	92	100	99	100	122	94
1871	100	103	—	100	100	97	—	102	103	101	100	93
1872	100	96	—	100	100	104	—	100	100	99	101	93
1873	100	97	—	100	103	102	96	101	98	102	99	100
1874		98	—	—	100	101	97	100	102	100	101	100
1875		93	—	—	99	105	—	100	100	100	100	100
1876		101	—	100	102	101	—	98	100	101	100	99
1877		98	—	99	102	98	—	98	100	100	99	
1878			—	99	97	100	—	101	98	101	99	
1879			—	79	97	88	—	93	85	92	96	
1880			95	84	94	100	—	91	94	89	91	
1881			94	103	98	97	—	98	92	98	56	
1882			101	106	95	82	—	103	111	112	115	
1883			98	101	98	116	—	—	99	99	103	
1884			98	97	96	108	—	88	98	105	97	
1885			97	92	97	98	—			89	92	
1886			92	97	103	100	—			97	110	
1887			94	84	99	96	—			91		
1888			99	99		99	—			94		
1889			96	93		100	—			96		
1890			93	97		100	100			97		
1891			101	108		104				99		
1892			95			105				62		
1893						105				98		
1894						112				105		
1895						102				96		
1896						102				97		
1897										104		
1898						99				98		
1899						98				93		
1900										101		

APPENDIX 9

Agricultural Output, Rents, Potatoes, and the Cost of Labour, 1850–1886

Agricultural output was calculated by using the quantities in the agricultural statistics and the price series published in the Cowper commission.[1] Total production (the quantity enumerated multiplied by the market price) was changed into output by using Thomas Butler's proportions in the 1908 census of agricultural production, except in the case of oats and potatoes.[2] In other words, Butler's figures for output in 1908 were adjusted upwards and downwards as prices, quantities, and livestock numbers in the years 1850–86 rose or fell above those in 1908. This method, which is different from other estimates of output, has the advantage of being simple and arbitrary.[3] Its disadvantage is that it does not produce a satisfactory way of calculating the value of oats and potatoes, especially in the 1850s. These have been calculated by assuming that $1^1/_2$ cwt. of oats and 12 cwt. of potatoes per statute acre were used as seeds;[4] that each pig ate 15 cwt. of potatoes;[5] that each horse, kept for agricultural purposes, ate 1 ton of oats.[6] The balance of oats left was multiplied by the price of oats; the balance of potatoes was multiplied by the price of potatoes on the Barrington farm at Fassaroe, reduced by 40 per cent.[7]

---

[1] See below, pp. 308–9 for the agricultural statistics; *Cowper Comm., Minutes of Evidence*, 960–7. (The price series, published in the Cowper commission, was first published in the *Irish Farmers' Gazette*, 1 Nov. 1879, p. 375.)

[2] *The Agricultural Output of Ireland, 1908: Report and Tables Prepared in Connection with the Census of Production Act, 1906* (London, 1912).

[3] See B. L. Solow, *The Land Question and the Irish Economy, 1870–1903* (Cambridge, Mass., 1971), 213–17, where similar methods are used; see also Vaughan, 'Agricultural Output, Rents and Wages in Ireland, 1850–80', in L. M. Cullen and F. Furet (eds.), *Ireland and France, 17–20th Centuries: Towards a Comparative Study of Rural History* (Paris, 1980), 85–97; Cormac Ó Gráda, 'Agricultural Head Rents, Pre-Famine and Post-Famine', *Economic and Social Review*, 5: 3 (Apr. 1974), 390–1; id., 'Irish Agricultural Output before and after the Famine', *Journal of European Economic History*, 13: 1 (Spring 1984), 149–65; Michael Turner, 'Towards an Agricultural Prices Index for Ireland, 1850–1914', *Economic and Social Review*, 18: 2 (Jan. 1987), 123–36; id., 'Output and Productivity in Irish Agriculture from the Famine to the Great War', *Ir. Econ. & Soc. Hist.* 17 (1990), 62–78.

[4] James F. V. Fitzgerald, *A Practical Guide to the Valuation of Rent in Ireland; with an Appendix Containing Some Extracts from the Instructions Issued to Valuators in 1853*, by the Late Sir R[ichard] Griffith, bt. (Dublin, 1881), 50.

[5] Department of Agriculture and Technical Instruction for Ireland, *Departmental Committee on the Irish Pig-Breeding Industry; Minutes of Evidence, Appendices, and Index*, pp. 15, 91 [Cd. 8004], HC 1914–16, vi. 899, 975.

[6] Inchiquin farm account books (NLI, MSS 14810–11).

[7] This gives a higher figure for oats, especially in the 1850s, than that in Vaughan, 'Agricultural Output, Rents and Wages in Ireland, 1850–80', 94–5, where it was assumed that only one-third of oats was output; it also gives higher figures for oats and potatoes than

When the quantity of potatoes produced fell short of the amount needed for seeds and the feeding of pigs, the deficiency's cost was calculated by assuming that 1 ton of potatoes was replaced by 5 cwt. of Indian meal and that Indian meal was worth £8 per ton.[8]

Other problems associated with the calculation of output should be kept in mind. First, the prices in the Cowper commission, being mainly Dublin prices, are probably higher, for part of the period at least, than provincial market prices.[9] Secondly, the number of milch cows has to be estimated for the years 1850-3. Thirdly, the method of calculating crop yields changed in 1856, which means that either yields recorded before 1856 should be reduced, or those recorded after 1856 should be increased; the former seems to be the more likely.[10] Fourthly, the method of enumerating livestock changed in 1853 and 1856. In 1853 livestock was enumerated eight weeks earlier than in 1852, which created the impression that a large increase took place between 1852 and 1853; 'In drawing attention to the great increase in the quantity of stock in Ireland, between 1852 and 1853,' warned the introduction to the 1853 statistics, 'it is necessary to observe... that during the months of August and September (the period referred to) in 1853, a large reduction took place in the quantity of stock, owing to the ordinary consumption, and the exportation to England; we ought, therefore, to know what that reduction was, in order satisfactorily to adjust the comparison between the stock at the respective periods.'[11] (Much the same effect was achieved in 1856 when the enumeration was made in early June instead of mid-July, as in 1855. This change also affected pigs, but in the opposite direction: 'with regard to the decrease in pigs, the large number littered during the six weeks referred to is not given in the returns—as the farmers so manage their stock that the young pigs usually make their appearance about the middle of July, and are thus sufficiently old to consume the small potatoes, which are abundant in October.'[12])

The cost of labour was calculated by using the acreages of crops in the agricultural statistics and the estimates of the amount of manual labour used on the Barrington farm at Fassaroe, County Wicklow in the cultivation of wheat, oats, barley, potatoes, and turnips;[13] the amount of labour used in the cultivation of flax

---

that in Vaughan, *Landlords and Tenants in Ireland, 1848-1904* (Studies in Irish Economic and Social History, 2; Dundalk, 1984), 22, where the value of oats and potatoes was calculated by adjusting their values on the basis of Butler's 1908 estimates. See also Vaughan, 'Potatoes and Agricultural Output', *Ir. Econ. & Soc. Hist.* 17 (1990), 79-92.

[8] Peter Solar, 'The Great Famine was No Ordinary Subsistence Crisis', in E. Margaret Crawford, *Famine: The Irish Experience, 900-1900: Subsistence Crises and Famines in Ireland* (Edinburgh, 1989), 133; the figure of £8 a ton was based on contract prices in Kilkenny gaol; for Indian meal prices in the mid-19th cent. see E. Margaret Crawford, 'Indian Meal and Pellagra in Nineteenth-Century Ireland', in J. M. Goldstrom and L. A. Clarkson (eds.), *Irish Population, Economy, and Society: Essays in Honour of the Late K. H. Connell* (Oxford, 1981), 118-19.   [9] See TCD, MUN/V/98/14 for interesting comparisons.

[10] William Neilson Hancock, *Report on the Supposed Progressive Decline of Irish Prosperity* (Dublin, 1863), 37-8.

[11] *Agricultural Statistics, 1853*, pp. xxi-xxii [1865], HC 1854-5, xlvii.

[12] Ibid. *1856*, p. viii [2289], HC 1857-8, lvi.

[13] Richard M. Barrington, 'The Prices of Some Agricultural Produce and Cost of Farm Labour for the Past Fifty Years', *Jn. Stat. Soc. Ire.* 9 (1886-7), 147, 149.

APPENDIX 9

Agricultural output, rents, potatoes, and the cost of labour, 1850–1886 (£ million)

Year	Labour	Potato deficiency	Rent	Balance	Agricultural output
1850	9.9	—	10.3	9.9	30.1
1851	10.0	—	10.3	11.3	31.6
1852	10.0	—	10.2	11.4	31.6
1853	10.3	—	10.2	24.8	45.3
1854	10.4	—	10.2	27.8	48.4
1855	11.3	—	10.3	30.2	51.8
1856	11.9	—	10.5	20.3	42.7
1857	12.1	—	10.6	18.4	41.1
1858	12.6	—	10.7	17.1	40.4
1859	12.8	—	11.0	18.1	41.9
1860	13.1	—	11.3	15.9	40.3
1861	12.8	1.0	11.3	10.5	35.6
1862	12.3	0.4	11.4	8.0	32.1
1863	12.0	—	11.4	13.0	36.4
1864	12.4	—	11.5	16.4	40.3
1865	12.4	—	11.6	20.6	44.6
1866	12.8	—	11.8	21.0	45.6
1867	12.9	—	11.8	14.7	39.4
1868	13.0	—	11.8	22.4	47.2
1869	13.4	—	11.8	18.9	44.1
1870	13.9	—	12.0	20.0	45.9
1871	14.0	0.6	12.1	17.7	44.4
1872	14.0	1.8	12.1	16.2	44.1
1873	13.6	—	12.1	19.4	45.1
1874	13.4	—	12.1	25.8	51.3
1875	13.7	—	12.1	26.0	51.8
1876	14.1	—	12.2	27.0	53.3
1877	14.2	2.0	12.2	16.6	45.0
1878	14.0	—	12.2	17.8	44.0
1879	13.9	2.0	12.2	10.6	38.7
1880	13.8	—	12.1	17.7	43.6
1881	14.0	—	12.1	17.0	43.1
1882	14.1	1.2	12.0	15.9	43.2
1883	14.2	—	11.9	18.3	44.4
1884	13.9	—	11.9	15.0	40.8
1885	14.2	—	11.8	12.3	38.3
1886	14.7	0.1	11.8	7.2	33.8

and hay and the labour costs of livestock production were calculated by using the estimates in Griffith's *Instructions*.[14] The wages were taken from *Second Report by Mr Wilson Fox on the Wages, Earnings, and Conditions of Employment of Agricultural Labourers in the United Kingdom*, p. 137 [Cd. 2376], HC 1905, xcvii. The figures were then increased by 30 per cent to make an allowance for the additional labour not directly caused by the main crops and the keeping of livestock.[15]

The rent was calculated by assuming (a) the total rental was £10.3 million in 1850 and (b) that the rental increased according to an index based on the rents on the eleven estates in Appendix 6. The starting rent of £10.3 million was calculated by assuming that the rental in 1850 was 13 per cent above the tenement valuation of land, excluding buildings (£9.1 million).[16] The figure of 13 per cent was got by comparing rents and the tenement valuation on over fifty estates and adjusting the result by means of the rent index, already referred to.[17]

The balance is agricultural output minus labour, potato deficiency, and rent.

[14] Griffith, *Instructions*, 28, 32, 33.
[15] For the effects of making a larger allowance for extra labour see Vaughan, *Landlords and Tenants in Ireland, 1848–1904*, 22.   [16] Below, p. 251.
[17] W. E. Vaughan, 'A Study of Landlord and Tenant Relations in Ireland between the Famine and the Land War, 1850–78' (Ph.D. thesis, Dublin University, 1974), 53. See Solow, *The Land Question and the Irish Economy*, 69, where a slightly higher figure for 1880 (just over £12.5 million) than the one in this table (£12.1 million) is given. The tenement valuation of land, farmhouses, and agricultural buildings was £10.1 million in 1881 (*Census Ire., 1881, General Report*, p. 166 [C 3365], HC 1882, lxxvi. 590). Rents reduced under the land act of 1881 in its first ten years were 28% above the valuation (*Report of the Irish Land Commissioners for the Period from 22 Aug. 1890 to 22 Aug. 1891*, p. 44 [C 6510], HC 1890–1, xxv. 424); if all rents were as high as those reduced under the act, which is unlikely, the total rental in 1880 would have been £12.9 million. On the other hand, rents on the estates surveyed by the Irish Land Committee were 13% above the valuation (Solow, *The Land Question and the Irish Economy*, 75); if the Irish Land Committee was a reliable guide, which is not completely credible, the total rental in 1880 would have been only £11.4 million. The average of the two estimates is £12.2 million, which is a corroboration of the estimate of £12.1 million, produced by using rentals and the tenement valuation to cover the 30-year period from 1850 to 1880.

APPENDIX 10

The Tenement Valuation

The tenement valuation, carried out in the 1850s and 1860s under Sir Richard Griffith, estimated the valuation of every farm in the country as a basis for local taxation. Land and buildings were valued separately: land on its own came to £9.1 million, which did not change after the valuation was made; buildings connected with agricultural land were worth about £1 million by the 1870s. As new buildings were assessed, their valuation was added, which partly explains why different figures appear in different places. For the sake of clarity, however, when the valuation is referred to here, it means the valuation of land, excluding buildings. The agricultural prices used by Griffith were those collected in the three years 1849–51 and adjusted for the 1852 act.[1] Griffith produced other figures in his *Instructions*: for the cost of production and for commodities that were not mentioned in the act. The calculations in the *Instructions* seem to represent the high points of the scale that the valuators were supposed to use.

Was £9.1 million a payable rent in the early 1850s? This question can be answered by using Griffith's specimen calculations in the *Instructions*, combined with the figures for crops and livestock in the agricultural statistics, to calculate the total value of agricultural production.[2] Griffith's calculations have the advantage of allowing the calculations to be made without much guesswork; the value of arable production, for example, is a straightforward multiplication of Griffith's prices and the acreages and yields in the agricultural statistics. Livestock is a bit more complicated: pigs, calves, and cattle are straightforward; but milch cows and sheep require some manipulation; poultry and wool, unfortunately, are not included in Griffith's calculations.

The problem with milch cows is that Griffith assumes that each cow produced almost 2 cwt. of butter, which would give a very high figure if applied to all milch cows. An average production of 1 cwt. has been assumed here, and expenses have been reduced accordingly. Sheep are rather more puzzling: the table at p. 32 of the *Instructions* appears to contain at least one typographical error and one error of computation; the purchase price of sheep is not given, nor their ages. The problem has been solved by assuming that each fattened sheep sold for £2.51 and that they were 3 years old. The agricultural prices were those used in the valuation act and in Griffith's *Instructions*; the cost of production was calculated by multiplying

---

[1] *Report from the Select Committee on the General Valuation etc. (Ireland); Together with the Proceedings of the Committee, Minutes of Evidence, and Appendix*, pp. 213–19, HC 1868–9 (362), ix. 225–31; *Return, 'Showing the Amount of Average Prices of Agricultural Produce (Arranged in Provinces) of Forty Towns in Ireland, during the Years 1849, 1850, 1851'*, HC 1852, xlvii (307). 1; see also W. E. Vaughan, 'Richard Griffith and the Tenement Valuation', in G. L. Herries Davies and R. Charles Mollan (eds.), *Richard Griffith, 1784–1878* (Dublin, 1980), 103–22. [2] Griffith, *Instructions*, 28, 29, 32, 33.

Griffith's estimates by the acreages of tillage in the agricultural statistics and by using his estimates of the expenses associated with livestock, such as contingencies, commission, cooperage, and labour. The figures for acreages, yields, and livestock were taken from *Agricultural Statistics, 1852*, pp. xxx, xxxi, xxxiii [1714], HC 1854, lvii. 30, 31, 33.

Production and production costs in 1852 (£ thousand)

Product	Value of production	Cost of production
Wheat	2,196	1,220
Oats	10,924	8,461
Barley	1,468	733
Flax	1,588	1,014
Potatoes	8,415	7,451
Hay	4,683	1,874
Turnips	2,269	2,498
Crops	31,543	23,251
Milch cows	4,345	1,774
Cattle	5,258	570
Sheep	2,187	229
Pigs	3,432	1,073
Livestock	15,222	3,646
TOTAL	46,765	26,897

If Griffith had valued the whole country as a single farm in the early 1850s, these are the figures on which he would have based his valuation. The figure for total production is much higher than the figures for output in the early 1850s.[3] This is explained by the fact that the whole of the oat and potato crops has been included, that no reduction was made for seeds, and that the problem of double-counting was solved by calculating the costs of production.

The table has certain weaknesses as a complete inventory of agricultural production and its costs. First, the expense of producing pigs seems small; a very high proportion of the potato crop was fed to pigs, certainly one-third, possibly one-half; to prevent double-counting, therefore, it should be kept in mind that several million pounds should be taken from the figure of £46,765,000. Secondly, Griffith's estimates of production costs are, to put it mildly, generous to the producers. According to J. F. V. Fitzgerald they were as high as Bayldon's 1876 figures;[4] they are also high compared with Barrington's figures for the

---

[3] See above, App. 9.
[4] James F. V. Fitzgerald, *A Practical Guide to the Valuation of Rent in Ireland; with an Appendix Containing Some Extracts from the Instructions Issued to Valuators in 1853, by the Late Sir R[ichard] Griffith, bt.* (Dublin, 1881), 51-2

APPENDIX 10

1850s.[5] The figure of £26,897,000 certainly seems high for agricultural wages, seeds, and the upkeep of horses. (If the aim is to do justice to the tenants, however, this generosity is a strength rather than a weakness.) Thirdly, no estimate of the slaughter-value of milch cows has been included, which might add as much as £2 million to livestock. Fourthly, some allowance should be made on the production side of the account for grass consumed by horses, to balance the cost of production. Fifthly, as already mentioned, the table does not include wool and poultry; nor, of course, does it include timber, horses, and turf. It is not improbable that the potatoes fed to pigs were more than matched by the omission of these other items and that the figures may be taken as they are.

How should the £19,868,000 balance between the value of production and its cost be divided between landlord and tenant? There is no simple answer. 'The object of a correct valuation', according to Lanktree, 'is ... not to assume a certain fanciful proportion between rent and produce, but to ascertain by calculation what surplus each variety of soil is capable of affording.'[6] Griffith himself falls into his habitual obscurity on this subject. He is clear and dogmatic about production costs and prices, but how he divided 'the nett annual ... produce' is not clear; from this receptacle came rent, poor law rates, and the farmer's reward for enterprise. How Griffith proceeded from this figure to the actual scale used by his valuators is tantalizing.[7] Apart from the fact that the landlord got a bigger share of livestock production than of tillage, it is hard to see what he was doing. One thing, however, is clear: he allowed the tenant more than the 5 per cent he inserted into the first stage of his calculations. The following, which is a summary of his calculations for an acre of tillage, shows what he did:[8]

	£
Value of production	5.93
Cost of cultivation	3.25
Wear and tear of implements	0.10
5% on £5 capital	0.25
Net annual value	2.33

From the 'net annual value' £2.33 came £1.30 for rent;[9] Griffith also seems to have allowed 8s. in the £ (£0.52 in this case) for insurance, repairs, and poor law rates, which he admitted was 'liberal';[10] the balance, £0.51, gave 10 per cent on the capital of £5, in addition to the 5 per cent included in the preliminary calculation. A valuation that left the tenants 15 per cent was reasonable enough by contemporary standards.[11]

---

[5] Richard M. Barrington, 'The Prices of Some Agricultural Produce and Cost of Farm Labour for the Past Fifty Years', *Jn. Stat. Soc. Ire.* 9 (1886–7), 147, 149.

[6] John Lanktree, *The Elements of Land Valuation, with Copious Instructions as to the Qualifications and Duties of Valuators* (Dublin and Edinburgh, 1853), 28.

[7] Cf. net annual value at Griffith, *Instructions*, 29, 32, 33, with the scales at pp. 27, 30.

[8] Based on the calculations at ibid. 29.

[9] According to Griffith the best arable land, valued at between 30s. and 26s., produced 9 barrels of wheat an acre on average (p. 27); the land in the arable calculations at p. 29 produced 8 barrels; 26s., therefore, has been adopted as its valuation.

[10] Griffith to Sir Denham Norreys, 28 Jan. 1851 (National Archives, OL2/13, p. 71).

[11] John Bayldon, *Bayldon's Art of Valuing Rents and Tillages, and the Tenant's Right on Entering and Quitting Farms ...* corrected and revised by John Donaldson, 6th edn. (London, 1844), 46–9.

In practice Griffith's valuation divided the balance of £19.9 million into two almost equal parts: £9.1 million for rent and £10.8 for the tenants' gross profits. Was this fair? The answer depends on virtual imponderables such as the amount of capital employed, the entrepreneurial skill of the tenants, and the degree of risk involved. If tenants' capital is assumed to be about £55 million, which is based on Griffith's figures,[12] £10.8 million was a return of 19 per cent, which was generous. If Griffith is to be followed, however, some deduction must be made for insurance, repairs, and poor law rates; even a generous allowance for these, however, would not bring the figure of 19 per cent to below 14 per cent.

Although valuators deplored the idea of calculating rent by taking fixed proportions of produce, proportions were used in practice. In a work on the predecessor of the tenement valuation Griffith found that rents fixed by his valuators ranged from one-eighth of the gross produce of inferior arable land to one-half of the produce of pasture.[13] (By discussing the use of fractions Griffith was not ignoring good valuation practice: he did not start with fractions, but came to them by experience. 'I found it necessary', he said, 'to relieve the minds of the valuators from all care relative to the act prices.'[14]) Taking the lowest fractions that Griffith mentioned (one-eighth for arable and one-third for inferior and mountain pasture), arable in the table above would yield £3.9 million and pasture £5.1 million, which comes to £9 million—or comfortably close to the £9.1 million of the tenement valuation.

The tenement valuation of land was not revised in the nineteenth century, but in 1877 the valuation office produced a bill proposing a new valuation based on prices in the mid-1870s, which allows a rough comparison to be made with the early 1850s. The construction of a table based on the prices in the 1877 valuation bill was not as simple as that based on the 1852 prices. Unfortunately there was no handbook such as Griffith's *Instructions* because the bill did not become law.[15] There were, therefore, no production costs, and no prices for potatoes, hay, or turnips. The price of hay and turnips had to be constructed by increasing the 1852 prices by amounts fixed by other prices series; the cost of production was fixed by increasing the 1852 prices by 50 per cent, which is generous;[16] Griffith's price for potatoes, £2 a ton, was retained; the value of cattle and sheep was fixed by increasing the 1852 prices by the percentage that beef and mutton increased between

---

[12] Griffith allowed £5 an acre for arable and £10 for an Irish acre of 'superior finishing land' (pp. 29, 32); the figure of £55 million assumes capital of £5 an acre for 5 million acres of arable and £3 an acre for 10 million acres of pasture. A much lower figure would be more realistic: in 1851 total livestock, including horses, was valued at £27.3 million by the census commissioners (*Agricultural statistics, 1857*, p. xiv [2461], HC 1859, sess. 1, xxvi. 71); the cost of agricultural labour in 1852 (see above, App. 9) was about £10 million.

[13] Richard Griffith, *Outline of the System according to Which the General Valuation of Ireland under 6 & 7 Wm IV, cap. 84 is Carried into Effect* (Dublin, 1844), 4.

[14] Ibid. 1.

[15] *A Bill to Amend the Law Relating to the Valuation of Rateable Property in Ireland*, p. 5, HC 1877 (bill 102), vii. 429; see also *A Bill to Provide for the Taking and Regulating Returns of the Average Prices of Agricultural Produce in Ireland*, HC 1854 (bill 101), i. 21.

[16] The cost of agricultural labour increased by about 40% between 1852 and 1877 (see above, App. 9); the cost of oats increased by nearly 60%; but see Fitzgerald, *A Practical Guide*, 51–2, where much lower costs of production are given.

the 1852 act and the 1877 bill. Acreages, yields, and livestock numbers were taken from *Agricultural Statistics, 1877*, pp. 48, 53, 61 [C 1938], HC 1878, lxxvii. 558, 563, 571; an arbitrary yield of 3.5 tons of potatoes was used, instead of the actual yield of 2 tons.

Production and production costs, 1877 (£ thousand)

Product	Value of production	Cost of production
Wheat	1,137	721
Oats	9,018	7,861
Barley	1,718	1,052
Flax	1,333	1,370
Potatoes	6,111	11,135
Hay	15,540	4,259
Turnips	2,505	3,511
Crops	37,362	29,909
Milch cows	9,238	3,320
Cattle	14,528	1,464
Sheep	6,024	601
Pigs	6,340	1,976
Livestock	36,130	7,361
TOTAL	73,492	37,270

This table shows that the value of production increased by 57 per cent between the early 1850s and 1877; the balance between production and its costs, however, increased by 82 per cent, from £19,868,000 to £36,222,000. If this were divided roughly in the same way as in the early 1850s, the new valuation of land would have been over £16 million. (If the total actual rental was £12.5 million in the late 1870s, the tenants' share, even allowing a generous amount for taxes, insurance, and repairs, would have been about £20 million.) A higher price for potatoes, or a lower estimate of the cost of production, would have caused the balance to increase by even more than 80 per cent.

APPENDIX 11

The Trinity College, Dublin Leasing Powers Act (14 & 15 Vict., c. cxxviii (1 Aug. 1851))

The Trinity College, Dublin leasing powers act made arrangements for increasing the rents paid to the college by its tenants, who were mainly, but not exclusively, large middlemen like the earl of Leitrim, Sir James Stronge, and Charles Maxwell Close, some of whom owned considerable estates in addition to those they held from the college. Rents were to move with the prices of five commodities: wheat, oats, beef, mutton, and butter. The commodities were given different weights: oats, which had the greatest weight, were to govern five-elevenths of the rent; butter and beef were smaller, governing only two-elevenths each; wheat and mutton accounted for the remainder with one-eleventh each. Constructing the movable part of the machine, however, was not the end of the job, for two bases had also to be established: first, five 'standard' commodity prices that subsequent price increases could be measured against were needed to start the calculation; secondly, corresponding to the standard prices, there had to be a starting rent or valuation that could move with the commodities' prices. The act took prices based on average prices in thirty-nine Irish towns in 1849 and 1850 as its 'standard' prices; wheat, for example, was 8s. 4d. and oats 5s. 6d.[1] The starting rent, arrived at after considerable negotiation, was the 'townland' or 'government' valuation, excluding buildings, and reduced by 3 per cent.

Any attempt to regulate rents, whether by act of parliament or by an individual landlord, would have proceeded in this manner. As a model for adjusting rents the act has considerable authority. For one thing it was arranged by two parties acting freely; secondly, Richard Griffith was involved, directly and indirectly, just as he would have been if the government had decided to bring in a bill to regulate rents; thirdly, the act was more explicit, more detailed, and easier to follow than the rent-fixing provisions of the land act of 1881. The act was a bundle of compromises put together by the board of the college, the Irish government, and the lessees' representatives. The negotiations are an interesting example of landlord and tenant negotiations in the years after the famine, if only because each stage was carefully recorded by the registrar in the board's minutes. The protagonists were oddly assorted. On the 'tenant' side were substantial, resident landlords, represented by the Hon. Charles Clements (Liberal MP for Leitrim and son of the second earl of Leitrim), Thomas Lefroy (son of the Rt. Hon. Thomas Lefroy, a college tenant and fourth baron of the exchequer), and St John Thomas Blacker, a Kerry lessee. On

---

[1] *Copy of a Letter Addressed by the Commissioner for Valuation to the Lord-Lieutenant of Ireland, with Reference to the Present State and Progress of the General Valuation of Ireland*, p. 5, HC 1851 (4), l.909. See Robert Brian MacCarthy, *The Trinity College Estates, 1800–1923: Corporate Management in an Age of Reform* (Dundalk, 1992), 27–32 for a full account of the genesis of the leasing powers bill.

the 'landlord' side were the provost and seven senior fellows of the college, all middle-aged or elderly clergymen, but possessed of a better than average grasp of arithmetic, and tenaciously pursuing their own interests and those of the college.

In the middle, or perhaps more accurately, rather nearer to the lessees than to the college, was the Irish government, represented by the attorney-general, James Henry Monahan. (Monahan's promotion to be chief justice of the common pleas in October 1850 may have helped the college, for his impatience with the board verged on hostility. The fact that Clements was a Liberal may not have been irrelevant to Lord Clarendon's administration.) Also involved were the university's MPs (Joseph Napier and G. A. Hamilton), Mountifort Longfield, Primate Beresford, and Lord Redesdale, the chairman of the lords committee on private bills. (Later it was recalled that Lord Redesdale 'would never have given his consent to the perpetuity act without the provision for raising the rents'.)

The protagonists were under pressure to come to an agreement, once the idea of an act of parliament was suggested; both had something to lose and something to gain at each stage, but refusal to negotiate might have been far more damaging than being worsted over even important details. The relationship between the college and its lessees was symbiotic rather than mutually predatory. The board was in an exquisitely ambiguous predicament: their own emoluments as well as the college's income were at stake. The lessees were also in an ambiguous position. They were middlemen at a time when middlemen were regarded as parasites; they were, however, rather better connected than most middlemen; many of them had land other than what they held from the college. Their strength was, initially at least, the fact that the government seemed disposed to take their side against the college.

From the beginning the foundations of the settlement were revealed: the middlemen, or at any rate most of them, would stay, and stay with greater security of tenure; the senior fellows would enjoy a fixed, stable income in place of the renewal fines that had been their great emolument in the past. (Primate Beresford was uneasy about giving the senior fellows fixed incomes from the college; the public, he said, had no security that the college's estate would be as well managed as a private one; he wondered 'whether such security could be afforded by making the income of the senior fellows fluctuate at least in part with the rents'.[2]) Eventually, the superstructure of rent-fixing was added to the foundations and the leasing powers act was passed as a private act of parliament. The negotiations between the board, the attorney-general, and the middlemen were often concerned with matters peculiar to the college and its tenants. Apart from these, however, the negotiations were about matters common to all landlords and tenants and were the very stuff of any attempt, legislative or otherwise, to regulate rents: the form of the sliding scale, the 'standard' prices, and the starting rent were all discussed in detail.[3]

---

[2] TCD, MUN/V/5/9, p. 158.

[3] Cf. 50 & 51 Vict., c. 33, sect. 29 (23 Aug. 1887), where standard prices and starting rent were defined, but the sliding scale was not. [4] TCD, MUN/V/5/9, p. 190.

[5] Ibid. 234; the church temporalities act (3 & 4 Will. IV, c. 37 (14 Aug. 1833)) made arrangements 'to have the average price of wheat or oats for seven years preceding inquired of and ascertained in order that the annual rent reserved ... may be varied or increased or diminished for the ensuing seven years ... '.

The five commodities whose prices would determine the movement of future rents were gradually defined and accepted. In February 1850 the attorney-general's reply to the board's proposals mentioned five commodities (wheat, oats, butcher's meat, butter, and wool).[4] In May the board suggested that rents might 'vary as in the church temporalities act'.[5] By June the board had moved to six commodities (the attorney-general's five with mutton added); shortly after that five commodities were again mentioned.[6] Although these five were to survive to be enshrined in the act, the tenants objected to them in March 1851 because some of them were not produced on the college's estates.[7] At first there seems to have been no discussion about weighting the commodities, although by April 1851 the tenants were arguing that the weight assigned to wheat and oats should be increased, and beef, mutton, and butter reduced. They suggested 'that the following would be an equitable scale of quantities to adopt viz.: wheat 112 lb, oats 224 lb, beef 14 lb, mutton 14 lb, and butter 14 lb'.[8] The board decided to wait on Griffith 'and request his opinion as to the proportions in which the five articles of produce mentioned ... might be considered as elements of value in determining the amount of rent'.[9] Griffith received the board's representatives and solved their problem: 'that wheat being presented by unity, oats were as five, beef as two, mutton as one and butter as two'; in Kerry, however, oats should be counted as four, butter as three, with the others remaining the same; in Donegal and Armagh 'the numbers might be considered as for the rest of Ireland'.[10] This statement was the basis of the elevenths used in the act. As was not unusual, Griffith's oracular dogmatism prevailed.

Selecting the standard prices and the starting rent was more complicated because the advantages to either party were immediately obvious. It was in the board's interest to make the standard prices as low as possible and the starting rent as high as possible. In June 1850 when many other details had been settled the board suggested that the standard prices should be the average prices of wheat, oats, beef, mutton, and wool taken from the *Dublin Gazette*.[11] This was eventually abandoned because the gazette did not have the prices of beef, butter, and mutton; in any case the tenants did not like the gazette prices, for they 'are not to be relied on', and suggested arbitration.[12] Eventually, both sides were rescued by the valuation office's publication of prices in thirty-nine towns in Ireland in the years 1848, 1849, and 1850.[13] The board, however, objected to including 1848 'as its prices were affected by the great distress of the year 1847'.[14] The tenants acquiesced and the average prices for 1849 and 1850 were incorporated in the act.

The fixing of the starting rent was more difficult. The first proposal came from the attorney-general, who suggested 'the full value to be the rent which a solvent tenant would pay for the premises'.[15] The board suggested Griffith's valuation: 'This valuation is *professedly* 25 per cent *below* the full value of the lands at the time it was made, and as the present depreciation in the value of agricultural produce in Ireland is probably about the same in amount, it may, perhaps be considered,

---

[6] TCD, MUN/V/5/9, pp. 260, 270.   [7] Ibid. 361.   [8] Ibid. 371-2.
[9] Ibid. 370.   [10] Ibid. 374.   [11] Ibid. 260.   [12] Ibid. 349.
[13] *Copy of a Letter Addressed by the Commissioner for Valuation to the Lord-Lieutenant of Ireland, with Reference to the Present State and Progress of the General Valuation of Ireland*, p. 5, HC 1851 (4), l.909.
[14] TCD, MUN/V/5/9, p. 376.   [15] Ibid. 190.

as a fair representation of the *present actual value*.'[16] Later they returned to this argument: 'The letting value of the land at the time of Mr Griffith's valuation is obtained by adding one-third to the amount set forth in that valuation; and the present letting value is thence deduced by altering it in the proportion of the standard prices of agricultural produce at the time the valuation was made, to the present prices of the same.... Let this be the principle of valuation in the proposed bill.'[17]

The board's haggling gave 'great offence' to the attorney-general who threatened to proceed to legislate 'without further communication with the board'. Eventually, however, the attorney and the board came to terms and by June 1850 the government valuation was accepted as the starting rent.[18] In March 1851, however, the tenants objected to it: 'the difference between the sum of the average prices of the five articles ... does not and could not fairly represent the relative letting value of land at those two periods', because such a difference was only one element in the value of land and because land had been subjected to 'increased burdens' since the making of Griffith's valuation.[19] They were prepared to accept Griffith's valuation 'subject to such modifications as Mr Griffith shall declare to be reasonable in order fairly to meet the depreciation which has taken place in the letting value of land'; or if that did not please the board, the depreciation could be measured by the arrangements in the church temporalities act.[20] Whether Griffith gave his opinion or not is not clear, but in the end the board suggested that the valuation, minus buildings, and reduced by 3 per cent, should be the starting rent. The tenants accepted this, 'though we are far from thinking a reduction of 3 per cent from Mr Griffith's valuation as equal to the depreciation now produced by various circumstances of the present time'.[21]

There were still some loose ends, but the essential parts of the bill were agreed by June 1851. The college would give the tenants perpetuity leases; the new rents were to be based on Griffith's valuation, excluding buildings and reduced by 3 per cent; every ten years the rents could be increased; the increase would be measured by comparing the standard prices with average prices during the ten-year period, weighted according to the formula laid down in the act. In real terms the college did quite well, although the leasing powers act was not the only cause. In 1852 rents due on the old Crown estate were about £22,000; by the mid-1870s they were about £40,000.[22] The negotiations between the board, the government, and the tenants were, on the whole, gentlemanly; there were no threatening letters, and no blunderbusses were discharged in the college park. The part played by Griffith was fundamental: his valuation, his prices, and his *ex cathedra* weighting of the five commodities were the three props that held up the act. The most interesting aspect of the negotiations was the acceptance of Griffith's valuation as the starting rent. Leaving out buildings was fair enough, considering that the tenants had built

[16] Ibid. 233.   [17] Ibid. 240–1.   [18] Ibid. 240, 265.
[19] Ibid. 360; presumably the two periods referred to were the early 1850s and the period represented by the prices in 6 & 7 Will. IV, c. 84.
[20] TCD, MUN/V/5/9, p. 361; for the church temporalities act, see above, n. 5.
[21] TCD, MUN/5/9, p. 371.
[22] See W. J. Lowe, 'Landlord and Tenant on the Estate of Trinity College, Dublin, 1851–1903', *Hermathena*, 120 (1976), 5–24 for an illuminating discussion on many aspects of the college's estates.

them. As early as April 1850 the board had accepted a deduction of one-tenth for tenants' improvements, so the 'concession' of 3 per cent was not wrung from them by force of circumstances.[23] What is surprising is the tenants' acceptance of the valuation reduced by 3 per cent. They could have pointed with truth to high poor law rates, to farms lying vacant, to high arrears, to farmers' incapacity to pay existing rents due to low prices in 1849 and 1850, and to the virtually permanent loss of the potato crop.

The leasing powers act did not permanently solve the problems of the college and its tenants, for in the 1880s serious disputes broke out. The tenants wanted to change the act, arguing that the land act of 1881 had put rents on a new foundation; the college resisted, arguing that it had not pressed its claims to the full in the 1860s and 1870s. There was little argument about the actual details of the act, although as early as 1876 William Neilson Hancock, in a report to the board, pointed to one of the weaknesses of the rent-fixing provisions of the act:

> The college perpetuity act of 1851 by making rent to depend on the price of commodities alone without making any allowance for the increase of wages does not lay down a perfect theory of rent which the college tenants can apply to the occupiers as a county court judge in estimating a reasonable rent under the land act of 1870 would have to take into account the rise of wages which an occupier would have to pay and at which he is entitled to measure the wages of himself and his family.[24]

The failure to consider wages, however, did not matter much as long as prices and wages rose together. When prices began to fall in the late 1870s, however, wages did not fall. Satisfactory rent reductions, therefore, should have been slightly greater than the fall in prices—if tenants were to be helped through the bad years. Another weakness of the act that would have had to be sorted out on individual estates was its failure to make allowances for crop failures.

[23] TCD, MUN/V/5/9, p. 210.
[24] Ibid. MUN/P/22/204, p. 26. See also MacCarthy, *The Trinity College Estates*, 30, 35.

APPENDIX 12

Rents Based on the TCD Leasing Powers Act

This table is based on the assumption that the total rental of Ireland fluctuated annually according to the principles laid down in the TCD leasing powers act (14 & 15 Vict., c. cxxviii (1 Aug. 1851)). It shows the results obtained by using two different price series and two different starting prices.

The starting prices, against which subsequent prices were measured, were the 'standard prices' in the act and the prices in the 1852 valuation act. The starting rent was assumed to be the total tenement valuation of land, excluding buildings (£9.1 million), reduced by 3 per cent (to £8.8 million); the starting rent fluctuated with the prices of the commodities in the act; the weights applied to each commodity were those in the act (wheat 1/11, oats 5/11, beef 2/11, mutton 1/11, and butter 2/11).

The figures are £ million.

Year	Standard prices		1852 act prices		Average
	TCD prices	Other prices	TCD prices	Other prices	
1851–2		9.4		10.6	10.0
1852–3	9.8	10.4	10.9	11.7	10.7
1853–4	12.4	13.4	13.8	15.0	13.7
1854–5	13.5	13.5	15.0	15.0	14.3
1855–6	13.6	13.3	15.2	14.8	14.2
1856–7	12.8	13.1	14.3	14.4	13.7
1857–8	12.9	12.6	14.2	14.2	13.5
1858–9	12.1	11.9	13.6	13.2	12.7
1859–60	12.5	13.0	13.9	14.3	13.4
1860–1	13.4	12.8	15.0	14.2	13.9
1861–2	12.3	12.7	13.6	14.0	13.2
1862–3	11.9	11.7	13.2	13.0	12.5
1863–4	11.4	10.7	12.6	11.8	11.6
1864–5	11.7	12.0	13.0	13.3	12.5
1865–6	13.2	13.5	14.5	15.0	14.1
1866–7	13.7	14.2	15.1	15.8	14.7
1867–8	13.8	14.2	15.4	15.6	14.8
1868–9	14.4	13.7	15.9	15.4	14.9
1869–70	13.1	13.4	14.7	14.9	14.0

APPENDIX 12

Year	Standard prices		1852 act prices		Average
	TCD prices	Other prices	TCD prices	Other prices	
1870–1	12.8	13.7	14.2	15.4	14.0
1871–2	13.7	13.6	15.0	15.0	14.3
1872–3	13.8	14.0	15.2	15.7	14.7
1873–4	15.6	15.6	17.2	17.4	16.5
1874–5	14.8	14.9	16.5	16.5	15.7
1875		13.7		15.3	14.5
1876		14.4		16.1	15.3
1877		13.7		15.3	14.5
1878		12.2		13.6	12.9
1879		12.6		14.1	13.4
1880		12.1		13.5	12.8
1881		12.1		13.4	12.8
1882		13.1		14.6	13.9
1883		12.8		14.3	13.6
1884		11.9		13.4	12.7
1885		9.8		10.9	10.4
1886		9.2		10.3	9.8

Sources: the TCD prices were those for Dublin and Derry in TCD, MUN/V/98/14 and MUN/P/22. 'Other prices' were: the price of wheat at Fassaroe, County Wicklow and the price of oats in the *Dublin Gazette* (from Richard M. Barrington, 'The Prices of Some Agricultural Produce and Cost of Farm Labour for the Past Fifty Years', *Jn. Stat. Soc. Ire.* 9 (1886–7), 149); the price of beef and mutton in *Cowper Comm., Appendices*, pp. 960–7; the price of butter in *Royal Commission on Market Rights and Tolls. Minutes of Evidence ... since 6 July 1888*, vol. vii, *with Appendices*, pp. 111–12 [C 6286–I], HC 1890–1, xxxvii. 361–2.

APPENDIX 13
Alternative Methods of Increasing Rents, 1850–1886

The table in this appendix is based on the assumption that landlords or a special commission established by parliament attempted to adjust rents annually according to clearly defined principles, using market prices and the figures produced annually in the agricultural statistics. The figures below refer to the whole country, which is treated as one large farm; in practice, of course, any system of adjusting rents would have had to be based on small areas such as poor law unions, baronies, or even parishes.

The TCD rents are the average of the methods in Appendix 12 above. The 'profit' rents are more speculative and assume that landlords and tenants divided the balance of agricultural output (what was left after the cost of labour and the cost of potato deficiencies had been deducted), with 55 per cent going to the tenants and 45 per cent to the landlords. Rents based on output assume that £8.8 million (the tenement valuation of land (£9.1 million), reduced by 3 per cent), was a fair starting point in 1850 and that rents then fluctuated annually with the value of agricultural output.

The main problem with linking rents to agricultural output, however, is to find a base in the early 1850s for comparisons with subsequent years. The three years, 1850–2, were low; then in 1853 there was an enormous increase, followed by two very prosperous years coinciding with the Crimean war; then there was a relatively stable period, but with prices much higher than those in the early 1850s. Where were the 'normal' years? Several solutions are possible.[1] One thing is clear: the war years 1854–5 are not a good basis for comparison; nor is 1853, because that was in practice a year of war, because prices began to rise in the autumn and winter as the Russians advanced into the Danubian principalities.[2]

---

[1] See Vaughan, 'Agricultural Output, Rents and Wages in Ireland, 1850–1880', in L. M. Cullen and F. Furet (eds.), *Ireland and France, 17th–20th centuries: Towards a Comparative Study of Rural History* (Paris, 1980), 97, where average prices for 1852–4 and 1872–4 were used; see also below, p. 265, where a low estimate of rent was used as a starting-point for the early 1850s.

[2] Cf. Cormac Ó Gráda, 'Agricultural Head Rents, Pre-Famine and Post-Famine', *Economic and Social Review*, 5: 3 (Apr. 1974), 390, where it is argued that the landlords' 'share of total agricultural value added was greater in the early 1870s than in the early 1850s'; the basis of this calculation was that agricultural output of £51.1 million in 1852–4 paid a rent of £8.5 million. The rent may have been appropriate in 1850 and 1851, although it seems low, but it was hardly appropriate to put it alongside high output figures based on war prices. Any calculations of agricultural output that are highly influenced by the years of the Crimean war will make even prosperous years in the 1860s and 1870s look dull; historians' work would have been easier if Britain had gone to war with Russia in 1877. See also Ó Gráda, 'Irish Agricultural Output before and after the Famine', *Journal of European Economic History*, 13: 1 (Spring 1984), 149–65, where 1854 is used for comparisons of agriculture before and after the famine.

The years 1850 and 1851 were not good years: most prices were lower than in 1840;[3] bank balances remained steady in 1851, having increased in 1850;[4] in a report on the state of Ireland for the lord-lieutenant it was noted that 'there is little or no improvement whatever arising from the operation of the crop of 1850, and all that can be said is that there is a dawn of better things just perceptible, by reason of diminished expenditure.'[5] On the other hand rents were fairly well paid in 1850 and 1851;[6] the report just referred to noted that rents were being paid, although abatements were general; in County Cork, Benn-Walsh noted the improved conditions on his estate in 1851.[7] The year 1852 was puzzling, at first sight: output seemed to remain at its 1850-1 level; but bank balances increased sharply;[8] Benn-Walsh was even more pleased with 1852 than he was with 1851;[9] rent receipts on the Ashtown estate suggest prosperity.[10] The output figures for 1852 may need revision, because Griffith's valuation prices, based on the years 1849-51, are used for the main commodities.[11] Calculations using different prices suggest that output actually rose in 1852 to about £35 million, a figure that makes the increase of 1853 seem less dramatic and suggests some improvement a year before the threat of war caused prices to increase. In these three years, therefore, most rents were being paid; but there were signs of strain: abatements were common; some rents were not being paid; although evictions were falling rapidly, they were still high.[12] The total rental of about £10 million was probably too high, certainly in 1850 and 1851; if output had remained at these levels, it is doubtful if nominal rents due could have been maintained at £10 million. How much should rents be reduced to provided a 'fair' starting-point for rents linked to agricultural output? The tenement valuation of land, excluding buildings, was £9.1 million, which might seem fair enough for 1850 and 1851; a rental of £10 million linked to output of £35 million, which is the revised figure for 1852, is probably not unreasonable; but to be on the safe side, £8.8 million (the starting rent in the TCD calculations), was used.[13]

The alternative methods of increasing rents are benign: the starting-point for rents is lower than Griffith's valuation; the return given to the tenants is the sort of return that Griffith gave them. (For the effects of rather less benign, but not extortionate, methods, see W. E. Vaughan, 'An Assessment of the Economic

[3] Thomas Barrington, 'A Review of Irish Agriculture Prices', *Jn. Stat. Soc. Ire.* pt. 101 [1925-7], 251.
[4] William Neilson Hancock, *Report on the Supposed Progressive Decline of Irish Prosperity* (Dublin, 1863), 50-1.
[5] Larcom papers (NLI, MS 7562).   [6] See above, App. 8.
[7] James S. Donnelly, 'The Journals of Sir John Benn-Walsh Relating to the Management of his Irish Estates, 1823-64', *Cork Hist. Soc. Jn.* 79: 230 (July-Dec. 1974), 117; see also id., 'Production, Prices, and Exports, 1846-51', in W. E. Vaughan (ed.), *A New History of Ireland*, v. *Ireland under the Union*, I. *1801-70* (Oxford, 1989), 293, where 1851 is taken as the end of the post-famine depression ('the worst was nearly over by the end of 1851').
[8] Hancock, *Report*, 48, 50-1; balances increased by £2.5 million; on the other hand government stock fell by £1.9 million; see Philip Ollerenshaw, *Banking in Nineteenth-Century Ireland: The Belfast Banks, 1825-1914* (Manchester, 1987), 115-20, on the shortcomings of bank deposits as a guide to agricultural prosperity.
[9] Donnelly, 'The Journals of Sir John Benn-Walsh ...' 119, 121.
[10] See above, App. 8.   [11] *Cowper Comm., Minutes of Evidence*, 961.
[12] See above, App. 1.   [13] See above, App. 12.

Performance of Irish landlords, 1851-81', in F. S. L. Lyons and R. A. J. Hawkins (eds.), *Ireland under the Union: Varieties of Tension. Essays in Honour of T. W. Moody* (Oxford, 1980), 184.) The alternative methods' disadvantage for the tenants was that they paid high rents in good years; the advantage was that they got automatic relief in bad years. The difficulty for both parties was that it was very difficult to devise any method for coping with agricultural disasters, such as those of the early 1860s, or the late 1870s, because of their complexity and erratic incidence. The TCD system, for example, while it gave substantial relief in 1877 and 1878 would not have been very popular with tenants in 1879. The different methods used here gave the following total rentals for 1850-79. (The figures are £ million and the figures in square brackets give the percentages by which the alternative rents exceeded actual rents; if rents had remained unchanged at their early 1850s level, the total rental for 1850-79 would have been £309 million):

actual rents	341.3	
output rents	373.7	[9]
'profit' rents	400.1	[17]
TCD rents	408.2	[20]

Landlords might have argued that the starting rent in the output method was too low because tenants were able to pay over £10 million in the early 1850s before prices began to increase; if £10 million had been adopted, over £30 million would have been added to the total in thirty years. They might also have argued that 45 per cent of the balance of agricultural output was too small; under this method their land, which was much more valuable than the tenants' capital, was now subject to the same risks; that both parties were equally entrepreneurs; that land should get much more than 45 per cent. (They might also have argued later that the increase in livestock production entitled them to a larger share of the balance.) Under the TCD system landlords might have argued, not only for a higher starting rent, but for heavier weights to be given to butter, beef, and mutton, and lower weights to wheat and oats.

It is worth noting that the alternative methods of adjusting rents would have given substantial reductions between 1876 and 1886: the output and TCD methods would have given 36 per cent and the 'profit' method 51 per cent. (No allowances have been made in the actual rents for abatements in the early 1860s or late 1870s and early 1880s; the figures in square brackets give the percentages by which the alternative rents exceeded actual rents.)

Alternative rents, 1850-1886

Year	Actual rents	Output rents	'Profit' rents	TCD rents
1850	10.3	8.8	9.1	10.0
1851	10.3	9.3	9.7	10.0
1852	10.2	9.3	9.7	10.7
1853	10.2	13.3	15.8	13.7
1854	10.2	14.2	17.1	14.3

APPENDIX 13

Year	Actual rents	Output rents	'Profit' rents	TCD rents
1855	10.3	15.2	18.2	14.2
1856	10.5	12.5	13.9	13.7
1857	10.6	12.1	13.1	13.5
1858	10.7	11.9	12.5	12.7
1859	11.0	12.3	13.1	13.4
1850–9	104.3	118.9 [14%]	132.2 [27%]	126.2 [21%]
1860	11.3	11.8	12.2	13.9
1861	11.3	10.4	9.8	13.2
1862	11.4	9.4	8.7	12.5
1863	11.4	10.7	11.0	11.6
1864	11.5	11.8	12.6	12.5
1865	11.6	13.1	14.5	14.1
1866	11.8	13.4	14.8	14.7
1867	11.8	11.6	11.9	14.8
1868	11.8	13.6	15.4	14.9
1869	11.8	12.9	13.8	14.0
1860–9	115.7	118.9 [3%]	124.7 [8%]	136.2 [18%]
1870	12.0	13.5	14.4	14.0
1871	12.1	13.0	13.4	14.3
1872	12.1	12.9	12.7	14.7
1873	12.1	13.2	14.2	16.5
1874	12.1	15.0	17.1	15.7
1875	12.1	15.2	17.1	14.5
1876	12.2	15.6	17.6	15.3
1877	12.2	13.2	12.9	14.5
1878	12.2	12.9	13.5	12.9
1879	12.2	11.4	10.3	13.4
1870–9	121.3	135.9 [12%]	143.2 [18%]	145.8 [20%]
1880	12.1	12.8	13.4	12.8
1881	12.1	12.6	13.1	12.8
1882	12.0	12.7	12.6	13.9
1883	11.9	13.0	13.6	13.6
1884	11.9	12.0	12.1	12.7
1885	11.8	11.2	10.8	10.4
1886	11.8	9.9	8.6	9.8
1880–6	83.6	84.2 [1%]	84.2 [1%]	86.0 [3%]

APPENDIX 14

Counties Ranked According to Valuation of Land per Acre, Percentage of Land under Tillage, and Valuation of Holdings

The counties are ranked according to tenement valuation per acre, the percentage of land under tillage in 1876, and the tenement valuation of their average holding in 1866; the counties with the highest valuation per acre, the highest percentage of land under tillage, and the highest-valued average holding are ranked first. The provinces are ranked from first to fourth, in the same way.

Valuation is for land exclusive of buildings; tillage includes meadow and clover as well as cereals, green crops, and flax.

Counties	Valuation	Tillage	Holdings
	PROVINCE OF LEINSTER		
Carlow	8 =	8	4
Dublin	1	5	3
Kildare	8 =	14	2
Kilkenny	12	13	11
King's	24	20	16
Longford	15	15	19
Louth	5	3	12
Meath	2 =	19	1
Queen's	16 =	10	15
Westmeath	8 =	22	8
Wexford	13 =	6	14
Wicklow	25 =	23	9
	PROVINCE OF MUNSTER		
Clare	27	29	18
Cork	20 =	21	7
Kerry	31 =	32	21 =
Limerick	7	16	5
Tipperary	13 =	17	10
Waterford	16 =	27	6
	PROVINCE OF ULSTER		
Antrim	11	9	13
Armagh	2 =	1	24
Cavan	16 =	12	26

Counties	Valuation	Tillage	Holdings
Donegal	31 =	26	31
Down	4	2	17
Fermanagh	19	18	20
Londonderry	20 =	7	21 =
Monaghan	6	4	27
Tyrone	23	11	25
PROVINCE OF CONNACHT			
Galway	29	30	29
Leitrim	28	25	30
Mayo	30	31	32
Roscommon	20 =	24	23
Sligo	25 =	28	28
SUMMARY BY PROVINCES			
Leinster	1	2	1
Munster	3	3	2
Ulster	2	1	3
Connacht	4	4	4

Sources: Agricultural Statistics, 1866, p. ix [3958-II], HC 1867-8, lxx. 263; ibid. *1876*, p. 52 [C1749], HC 1877, lxxxv. 580; ibid. *1911*, p. 35 [Cd. 6377], HC 1912-13, cvi. 801.

APPENDIX 15

Counties Ranked According to Quality of their Rural Housing in 1851 and 1881

The counties are ranked according to the percentages of their houses that were second and fourth class in 1851 and 1881, to the number of rooms per house, and to the increase in second-class houses between 1851 and 1881; the counties with the highest percentage of second-class houses, the lowest percentage of fourth-class houses, the most rooms per house, and the biggest increase in the number of second-class houses are ranked first. The provinces are ranked from first to fourth, in the same way.

Civic areas, that is towns with 2,000 and more inhabitants, are excluded; the number of rooms was calculated by assuming that fourth-class houses had one room, third-class houses had three rooms, second-class had 7.5 rooms, and first-class fifteen rooms; the increase in second-class houses between 1851 and 1881 was measured by comparing their percentages in 1851 and 1881.

On the limitations of housing statistics as a measure of wealth see Alan Gailey, 'Changes in Irish rural housing, 1600–1900', in Patrick O'Flanagan, Paul Ferguson, Kevin Whelan (eds.), *Rural Ireland, 1600–1900: Modernization and Change* (Cork, 1987), 86–103.

Counties	Second-class houses		Fourth-class houses		Rooms per houses		Increase of second-class houses
	1851	1881	1851	1881	1851	1881	
PROVINCE OF LEINSTER							
Carlow	6 =	4 =	17	13 =	6 =	5 =	23
Dublin	3	4 =	6	7 =	1	1	28
Kildare	21 =	24 =	22 =	28 =	16 =	17 =	18
Kilkenny	4 =	3	8 =	13 =	4 =	3 =	24
King's	14 =	15 =	14 =	13 =	11 =	11 =	17
Longford	14 =	11 =	14 =	21 =	16 =	17 =	15
Louth	25 =	24 =	19 =	21 =	22 =	23 =	9
Meath	27	28 =	29 =	30	25 =	25	10 =
Queen's	20	21 =	19 =	13 =	20 =	11 =	12
Westmeath	16 =	15 =	18	21 =	14 =	11 =	14
Wexford	8 =	9 =	8 =	13 =	6 =	5 =	26 =
Wicklow	2	1 =	8 =	7 =	2 =	2	26 =

APPENDIX 15

Counties	Second-class houses		Fourth-class houses		Rooms per houses		Increase of second-class houses
	1851	1881	1851	1881	1851	1881	
PROVINCE OF MUNSTER							
Clare	21 =	11 =	22 =	13 =	22 =	20 =	4
Cork	19	18 =	28	25 =	20 =	14 =	13
Kerry	31	31	32	32	31 =	31	2
Limerick	25 =	23	31	31	27 =	26	6
Tipperary	18	9 =	25 =	25 =	18 =	9 =	10 =
Waterford	10 =	7	8 =	7 =	6 =	7	21
PROVINCE OF ULSTER							
Antrim	4 =	8	1 =	1	4 =	8	29
Armagh	13	11 =	7	7 =	14.=	14 =	19 =
Cavan	16 =	18 =	14 =	13 =	18 =	20 =	16
Donegal	24	30	8 =	7 =	22 =	28 =	19 =
Down	1	1 =	1 =	2 =	2 =	3 =	31 =
Fermanagh	8 =	6	8 =	5 =	11 =	9 =	22
Londonderry	6 =	15 =	3	2 =	9	14 =	31 =
Monaghan	12	11 =	5	5 =	11 =	17 =	25
Tyrone	10 =	21 =	4	2 =	10	20 =	30
PROVINCE OF CONNACHT							
Galway	29 =	28 =	27	28 =	29 =	28 =	3
Leitrim	23	18 =	19 =	7 =	25 =	23 =	5
Mayo	32	32	29 =	25 =	31 =	32	7 =
Roscommon	29 =	26	22 =	13 =	27 =	27	1
Sligo	28	27	25 =	21	29 =	28 =	7 =
SUMMARY BY PROVINCES							
Leinster	2	1 =	2	2 =	1 =	1	4
Munster	3	3	4	4	3	3	2
Ulster	1	1 =	1	1	1 =	2	3
Connacht	4	4	3	2 =	4	4	1

Sources: *Census Ire., 1851, General Report*, p. 625 [2134], HC 1856, xxxi. 769; *Census Ire., 1881, General Report* [C 3365], HC 1882, lxxvi. 385; ibid., vol. i, *Province of Leinster* [C 3042], HC 1881, xvii. 1; vol. ii, *Province of Munster* [C 3148], HC 1882, lxxvii. 1; vol. iii, *Province of Ulster* [C 3204], HC 1882, lxxviii. 1; vol. iv, *Province of Connacht* [C 3268], HC 1882, lxxix. 1.

APPENDIX 16

Counties Ranked According to the Quality of their Land and Houses

The counties with the best land and houses were ranked first; the first column is based on the three measures of land (valuation per acre, percentage of land under tillage, and the valuation of the average holding) used above; each was given equal weight; the second column is based on second-class houses, fourth-class houses, and rooms per house in 1851 and 1881; each was given equal weight; the third column is an average of the scores in the six preceding measures. The provinces are ranked from first to fourth in the same way. The difference between Leinster and Ulster in the final column was so small that a slightly different method of calculation would have placed both provinces first equal.

Counties	Land	Houses	Land and houses
	PROVINCE OF LEINSTER		
Carlow	2 =	10	3 =
Dublin	1	2 =	1
Kildare	6	24	15
Kilkenny	11	5	5
King's	24	14	20
Longford	18 =	15	19
Louth	2 =	25	14
Meath	4	28 =	21 =
Queen's	15	18 =	17 =
Westmeath	13	16	13
Wexford	9 =	8 =	6
Wicklow	21 =	2 =	8 =
	PROVINCE OF MUNSTER		
Clare	26	20	25
Cork	16 =	23	23 =
Kerry	29	32	31
Limerick	8	28 =	23 =
Tipperary	14	18 =	16
Waterford	18 =	6	10

APPENDIX 16

Counties	Land	Houses	Land and houses
PROVINCE OF ULSTER			
Antrim	9 =	4	3 =
Armagh	7	12	7
Cavan	20	17	21 =
Donegal	30 =	22	28
Down	5	1	2
Fermanagh	21 =	7	12
Londonderry	16 =	8 =	11
Monaghan	12	11	8 =
Tyrone	23	13	17 =
PROVINCE OF CONNACHT			
Galway	30 =	30	30
Leitrim	28	21	27
Mayo	32	31	32
Roscommon	25	26	26
Sligo	27	27	29
SUMMARY BY PROVINCES			
Leinster	1	2	1
Munster	3	3	3
Ulster	2	1	2
Connacht	4	4	4

Source: this table is based on Appendices 14 and 15 above.

APPENDIX 17

Compensation under Sections 3, 4, and 7 of the Land Act, 1870

The information tabulated in this Appendix is taken from De Moleyns, *Landowner's Guide* (1872), 228, 260–1.

Compensation for disturbance under sections 3 and 7. (Claims for disturbance were made under section 3; claims for good will were made under section 7 ('where any tenant of a holding does not claim or has not obtained compensation under sections one, two, or three of this act...').)

Nature of tenancy	For disturbance	For goodwill
(A) Tenancies existing on 1 Aug. 1870		
Yearly tenancies existing on 1 Aug. 1870, if valued above £100 per annum	None	Allowed
Valued at or under £100 per annum, if the tenant is disturbed by his immediate landlord	Allowed	Allowed
If disturbed by the head landlord	None	Will depend on the special circumstances of the particular case
Leases for terms greater than yearly ones granted before 1 Aug. 1870	None	Allowed
(B) Tenancies created after 1 Aug. 1870		
Yearly tenancies created after 1 Aug. 1870, in holdings valued at or over £50 per annum	Allowed if there is no contract in writing not to claim	Allowed
If valued under £50 per annum	Allowed (contract to forego claim illegal until 1 Jan. 1891)	Allowed

Nature of tenancy	For disturbance	For goodwill
(B) Tenancies created after 1 Aug. 1870		
Leases for terms greater than yearly ones after 1 Aug. 1870:		
(a) under 31 years	Allowed	Allowed
(b) for 31 years and upwards	None	Allowed

Compensation for Improvements under section 4

Nature of tenancy	Claim for improvements	Observations
(A) Tenancies existing on 1 Aug. 1870		
Yearly tenancies existing on 1 Aug. 1870 if no written agreement	Allowed	For all future improvements; but as to improvements made before 1 Aug. 1870, for permanent buildings and reclamation of waste land only; and such other improvements as were made within 20 years before making the claim
If held under a written agreement not expressly excluding the claim for improvements	Allowed	As above
If such claim is expressly excluded	None	No allowance
Where the holding is valued at £50 or upwards and the tenant has contracted in writing not to claim	None	No allowance

Nature of tenancy	Claim for improvements	Observations
(A) Tenancies existing on 1 Aug. 1870		
Leases granted before 1 Aug. 1870, for less than 31 years [if claims not expressly excluded by lease]	Allowed	As yearly with no written agreement (see above)
Leases granted before 1 Aug. 1870, for 31 years and upwards, or for a life or lives, etc., where the lease shall have existed for 31 years before making the claim [where claim is not expressly excluded by the lease]	Allowed	Limited to permanent buildings, reclamation of waste land, and unexhausted tillages and manures, unless otherwise provided by the lease
(B) Tenancies created after 1 Aug. 1870		
Yearly tenancies created after 1 Aug. 1870, valued at £50 or upwards or where the aggregate amount of all the tenants' holdings in Ireland is of that value	Allowed	Unless the tenant has contracted in writing with his landlord not to claim
Valued under £50 per annum	Allowed	Contract not to claim for improvements required for the suitable occupation of the holding prohibited
Leases granted after 1 Aug. 1870 [valued at £50 or upwards]	Allowed	Unless the tenant has contracted in writing not to claim
Leases, for under 31 years, granted after 1 Aug. 1870 [valued under £50]	Allowed	Contract not to claim prohibited
Leases granted after 1 Aug. 1870, for 31 years and upwards	Allowed	Limited to permanent buildings, reclamation of

Nature of tenancy	Claim for improvements	Observations
(B) Tenancies created after 1 Aug. 1870		
		waste lands, and unexhausted tillages and manures [subject to the power of contracting not to claim for any improvement where the valuation exceeds £50]

APPENDIX 18

Expenditure on Nine Estates, 1850–1880

Expenditure on taxes, etc. is given as a percentage of rent receipts. It is an exaggeration to say that every set of estate accounts should be treated as *sui generis*; but naturally methods of book-keeping varied considerably and the headings of expenditure varied as well; Lord Erne, for example, counted curates' salaries as part of his expenditure on tithe rentcharge. The definition of improvements and interest also varied from estate to estate.

More difficult, perhaps, is the propriety of counting certain items as proper charges against the receipts on a particular estate; Lord Erne included the upkeep of Crom in his Fermanagh accounts, although strictly speaking it should have been set against the income from all his estates since he did not maintain a house elsewhere. Some improvements were made on the demesne farms and ideally should be counted not just against rent receipts but against farm income.

The absence of an item does not mean that it did not exist; there is no charge for a house on Sir George Hodson's Cavan estate, nor was there a charge for interest; that does not mean that Sir George was an unencumbered absentee — it simply means that he lived on his Wicklow estate. The following, therefore, is too much a series of discrete vignettes to be reduced to uniformity, tempting though it is to summarize them; its strength is that these were the items of expenditure that landlords and agents usually set against their rent receipts.

A dash (—) indicates that comparable information is not available.

	1850s	1860s	1870s	1851–1880
		ASHTOWN		
Taxes	13	10	8	10
Management	6	5	5	5
Improvements	18	14	8	13
		CLONBROCK		
Taxes	19	13	—	16
Management	4	5	—	5
Improvements	10	11	—	11
Interest	1	2	—	2
House	15	17	—	16
		CROFTON		
Taxes	16	14	13	14
Improvements	21	10	12	14
Interest	29	40	48	39
House	19	20	13	17

APPENDIX 18

	1850s	1860s	1870s	1851–1880
		ERNE		
Taxes	10	11	8	10
Management	7	7	8	7
Improvements	10	9	5	8
House	21	19	22	21
		HALL		
Taxes	15	12	11	13
Management	4	5	5	5
Improvements	9	12	7	9
Interest	5	10	14	10
		HODSON		
Taxes	—	7	7	7
Management	—	6	5	6
Improvements	—	7	7	7
		INCHIQUIN		
Taxes	17	14	15	15
Management	4	4	4	4
Improvements	7	5	5	6
Interest	29	22	28	26
		MURRAY STEWART		
Taxes	14	12	—	13
Management	15	13	—	14
Improvements	40	14	—	27
Interest	5	8	—	7
		RANFURLY		
Taxes	12	11	11	11
Management	6	5	5	5
Improvements	4	7	8	6
House	—	11	16	14

Sources: Ashtown rentals (NLI, MSS 1765–9); Clonbrock, Co. Galway (NLI, MSS 19617–45); Crofton, Co. Roscommon (NLI, MSS 4074–94, 5632–3) Erne, Co. Fermanagh (PRONI, D1939/9/1–3); Hall, Co. Down (PRONI, D2090/3/7–28); Hodson, Co. Cavan (NLI, 16404–6, 16419, 16438–70); Inchiquin, Co. Clare (NLI, MSS 14522–53); Murray Stewart, Co. Donegal (NLI, MSS 5472–84, 5893–903); Ranfurly, Co. Tyrone (PRONI, D1932/2/2–12, 3/2–12, 4/3–10).

APPENDIX 19

Agrarian Outrages and Other Outrages Returned by the Constabulary, 1844–1893

In the table below, threatening letters include notices and other forms of intimidation.

The figures in square brackets give: (1) homicides, firings, etc. as percentages of agrarian outrages; (2) agrarian outrages and other outrages as percentages of total outrages.

Year	Homicides	Firings	Fires	Threatening letters	Others	Total agrarian outrages	Other outrages
1844						1,001	5,326
1845	18	46	113	970	773	1,920	6,168
1846	16	33	73	541	640	1,303	11,077
1847	16	35	108	203	258	620	20,348
1848	7	16	201	267	304	795	13,285
1849	15	20	238	271	413	957	13,951
1845–9	72	150	733	2,252	2,388	5,595	64,829
	[1]	[3]	[13]	[40]	[43]	[8]	[92]
1850	18	18	311	517	498	1,362	9,277
1851	12	13	185	395	408	1,013	8,131
1852	6	15	222	364	300	907	6,917
1853	1	9	97	170	192	469	4,983
1854	5	4	72	114	139	334	4,318
1855	6	5	56	66	122	255	3,946
1856	6	6	51	99	125	287	3,838
1857	4	5	27	78	80	194	3,838
1858	6	1	43	98	87	235	3,257
1859	5	1	35	91	89	221	3,397
1850–9	69	77	1,099	1,992	2,040	5,277	51,902
	[1]	[1]	[21]	[38]	[39]	[9]	[91]
1860	4	6	22	87	113	232	3,299
1861	4	4	25	105	91	229	3,652
1862	8	3	46	211	95	363	4,038
1863	2	6	61	166	114	349	3,483
1864	2	3	63	145	91	304	2,664

APPENDIX 19

Year	Homicides	Firings	Fires	Threatening letters	Others	Total agrarian outrages	Other outrages
1865	4	2	48	73	51	178	2,426
1866	0	3	29	32	23	87	1,877
1867	2	3	31	53	34	123	1,898
1868	4	1	30	72	53	160	2,388
1869	10	16	18	480	243	767	2,386
1860–9	40 [1]	47 [2]	373 [13]	1,424 [51]	908 [33]	2,792 [9]	28,111 [91]
1870	7	11	38	624	649	1,329	3,022
1871	6	6	20	195	146	373	2,524
1872	5	6	28	144	73	256	3,082
1873	5	4	25	137	83	254	2,021
1874	5	4	26	94	84	213	1,883
1875	11	2	10	67	46	136	1,865
1876	5	7	35	97	68	212	1,836
1877	5	4	20	99	108	236	2,067
1878	8	3	40	128	122	301	2,223
1879	10	8	60	553	232	863	2,637
1870–9	67 [2]	55 [1]	302 [7]	2,138 [51]	1,611 [39]	4,173 [15]	23,160 [85]
1880	8	24	210	1,576	767	2,585	3,084
1881	22	66	356	2,606	1,389	4,439	3,349
1882	27	58	281	2,300	767	3,433	2,835
1883	2	9	119	479	261	870	1,665
1884	0	7	110	423	222	762	1,691
1885	7	12	94	512	319	944	1,739
1886	10	16	103	516	411	1,056	2,195
1887	8	19	125	385	346	883	1,837
1888	7	14	73	316	250	660	1,522
1889	1	11	74	232	216	534	1,361
1880–9	92 [1]	236 [1]	1,545 [10]	9,345 [58]	4,948 [31]	16,166 [43]	21,278 [57]
1890	6	15	59	241	198	519	1,415
1891	2	8	77	245	140	472	1,407
1892	4	7	67	219	108	405	1,475
1893	0	7	59	195	119	380	1,625
1890–3	12 [1]	37 [2]	262 [15]	900 [51]	565 [32]	1,776 [23]	5,922 [77]

Sources: National Archives, ICR, returns of outrages, 1844–93.

APPENDIX 20

Counties Ranked According to Serious Crime, 1851–1880

The counties are ranked according to the number of outrages (excluding agrarian outrages) per 10,000 inhabitants; the counties with the lowest rates are ranked first; the counties with the highest are ranked thirty-second. The provinces are ranked from first to fourth, in the same way.

Dublin does not include the metropolitan police area. Belfast, Cork, Galway, Limerick, and Waterford are included with their counties. The ranking of Antrim in 1871–80 is adjusted to exclude the crimes caused by the Belfast riots in 1872. If the riots are included Antrim falls from second place to a position between Carlow (fourteenth) and Cork (fifteenth).

Counties	1851–1860	1861–1870	1871–1880
	PROVINCE OF LEINSTER		
Carlow	13	13	14
Dublin	14	8 =	4
Kildare	31	29	29
Kilkenny	27	24	27
King's	28	26	22
Longford	32	32	28
Louth	2	5	5
Meath	22	27	24
Queen's	23	25	20
Westmeath	29	31	31
Wexford	21	7	7
Wicklow	26	17	21
	PROVINCE OF MUNSTER		
Clare	16	10	11
Cork	15	15	15
Kerry	5	6	13
Limerick	24	22	30
Tipperary	30	30	23
Waterford	20	19	16
	PROVINCE OF ULSTER		
Antrim	1	2	2
Armagh	7	18	17

Counties	1851–1860	1861–1870	1871–1880
Cavan	10	14	18
Donegal	12	12	3
Down	6	1	1
Fermanagh	9	11	8
Londonderry	3	3	6
Monaghan	8	8 =	12
Tyrone	4	4	10
PROVINCE OF CONNACHT			
Galway	18	20	32
Leitrim	25	28	19
Mayo	19	16	25
Roscommon	11	21	9
Sligo	17	23	26
SUMMARY BY PROVINCES			
Leinster	4	4	3
Munster	3	2	2
Ulster	1	1	1
Connacht	2	3	4

Source: National Archives, ICR, returns of outrages, 1851–80.

APPENDIX 21
Counties Ranked According to Agrarian Outrages, 1851–1880

The counties are ranked according to the number of agrarian outrages per 1,000 agricultural holdings; the counties with the lowest rates are ranked first; the counties with the highest are ranked thirty-second. The provinces are ranked from first to fourth, in the same way.

Counties	1851–1860	1861–1870	1871–1880
	PROVINCE OF LEINSTER		
Carlow	16	9	15
Dublin	1	1	1
Kildare	6	14	18
Kilkenny	23	18	13
King's	31	26	27
Longford	32	30	25
Louth	30	21	8
Meath	21	29	21
Queen's	22	17	9
Westmeath	28	32	28
Wexford	15	10	10
Wicklow	10	5	11
	PROVINCE OF MUNSTER		
Clare	17	16	22
Cork	7	11	24
Kerry	2	15	30
Limerick	24	20	32
Tipperary	29	25	20
Waterford	19	13	17
	PROVINCE OF ULSTER		
Antrim	5	3	3
Armagh	26	19	16
Cavan	20	23	19
Donegal	25	22	12
Down	14	2	4
Fermanagh	11	7	2
Londonderry	3	8	7

Counties	1851–1860	1861–1870	1871–1880
Monaghan	18	4	5
Tyrone	4	6	6
PROVINCE OF CONNACHT			
Galway	9	12	31
Leitrim	27	27	26
Mayo	8	31	29
Roscommon	12	24	14
Sligo	13	28	23
SUMMARY BY PROVINCES			
Leinster	4	3	2
Munster	3	2	3
Ulster	2	1	1
Connacht	1	4	4

Source: National Archives, ICR, returns of outrages, 1851–80.

APPENDIX 22

Counties Ranked According to Agrarian Outrages Committed during Four Crises, 1848–1882

The counties are ranked according to the number of agrarian outrages per 1,000 agricultural holdings; the counties with the lowest rates are ranked first; the counties with the highest are ranked thirty-second. The provinces are ranked from first to fourth, in the same way.

Counties	1848–1852	1862–1864	1869–1870	1879–1882
		PROVINCE OF LEINSTER		
Carlow	14	9	13	14
Dublin	1	1	5 =	6
Kildare	3	14	18 =	18
Kilkenny	23	26	11	17
King's	30	30	27	27
Longford	31	32	28	24
Louth	29	15 =	24	10
Meath	12	25	30	13
Queen's	20	13	14	16
Westmeath	28	15 =	32	23
Wexford	17 =	15 =	7	11
Wicklow	9	2	12	12
		PROVINCE OF MUNSTER		
Clare	24	19	16 =	26
Cork	11	20	9	29
Kerry	8	12	18 =	32
Limerick	26	27	16 =	31
Tipperary	32	29	23	28
Waterford	17 =	24	10	20
		PROVINCE OF ULSTER		
Antrim	5	3	4	1
Armagh	25	23	15	4
Cavan	21	22	25	15
Donegal	16	21	21	9
Down	15	8	1	2

Counties	1848–1852	1862–1864	1869–1870	1879–1882
Fermanagh	10	7	8	5
Londonderry	2	10	5 =	3
Monaghan	22	5 =	3	8
Tyrone	6	4	2	7
PROVINCE OF CONNACHT				
Galway	7	11	20	30
Leitrim	27	31	26	25
Mayo	4	5 =	31	22
Roscommon	19	28	22	19
Sligo	13	18	29	21
SUMMARY BY PROVINCES				
Leinster	3	4	3	2
Munster	4	3	2	4
Ulster	2	1	1	1
Connacht	1	2	4	3

Source: National Archives, ICR, returns of outrages, 1851–82.

APPENDIX 23
Spearman Ranking Coefficients of County Ranks

The coefficients below are based on the county ranks in Appendices 3–4 (evictions), 15–16 (houses and land), and 20–2 (ordinary outrages and agrarian outrages). The Spearman ranking coefficient measures the degree to which ranks coincide with each other; complete positive coincidence produces a coefficient of +1.0; complete negative coincidence produces a coefficient of −1.0. The working of the coefficient can be demonstrated by a hypothetical ranking of the four provinces, where characteristic A is compared with characteristics B, C, D, and E.

	A	B	C	D	E
Leinster	1	1	4	1	1
Munster	2	2	3	3	3
Ulster	3	3	2	2	4
Connacht	4	4	1	4	2

The relationship between A and B is perfectly positive (+1.0); the relationship between A and C is perfectly negative (−1.0); the relationship between A and D is reassuringly positive (+0.8). The real world, unhappily, tends to be ambiguous: the relationship between A and E is +0.4. In the appendices above tables were consistently arranged so that the counties with the lowest rates of eviction, the best houses, the best land, and the fewest outrages were ranked first and the counties with the highest rates of eviction etc. were ranked thirty-second. The coefficients below reflect that arrangement.

(1) AGRARIAN OUTRAGES

Agrarian outrages:	Other outrages:	Coefficients:
1851–60	1851–60	+0.45
1861–70	1861–70	+0.71
1871–80	1871–80	+0.69
	Agrarian outrages:	
1851–60	1861–70	+0.63
1861–70	1871–80	+0.69
1851–60	1871–80	+0.28
1848–52	1862–4	+0.71
1862–4	1869–70	+0.55

APPENDIX 23

(1) AGRARIAN OUTRAGES

Agrarian outrages:	Agrarian outrages:	Coefficients:
1869–70	1879–82	+0.56
1848–52	1879–82	+0.34

(2) EVICTIONS

Evictions:	Fourth-class houses:	
1851–60	1851	+0.69
1871–80	1881	+0.57
1851–60	housing index	+0.48
1851–80	fall in the number of houses 1851–81	+0.32

	Agrarian outrages:	
1851–60	1851–60	+0.29
1861–70	1861–70	+0.65
1871–80	1871–80	+0.70
1849–53	1848–52	+0.44
1861–4	1862–4	+0.50
1869–70	1869–70	+0.29
1879–82	1879–82	+0.63

(3) OTHER OUTRAGES

Other outrages:	Other outrages:	
1851–60	1861–70	+0.87
1861–70	1871–80	+0.83
1851–60	1871–80	+0.77
1861–70	housing index	+0.48

(4) LAND AND HOUSES

Land index	housing index	+0.41

(5) THE LAND WAR

Agrarian crime 1879–82	increase in second-class houses 1851–81	−0.56
	evictions 1879–82	+0.63
	evictions as a percentage of the fall in the number of houses 1851–81	+0.75

SELECT BIBLIOGRAPHY

1. Manuscript Material   page
   (a) National Archives   290
   (b) Public Record Office of Northern Ireland   290
   (c) National Library of Ireland   291
   (d) The Library of Trinity College, Dublin   293
   (e) The Registry of Deeds, Dublin   293
   (f) The Valuation Office, Dublin   293

2. House of Commons Sessional Papers
   (a) Royal Commissions, Select Committees, and Special Returns   294
   (b) Land Bills, 1845–1880   297
   (c) Evictions   301
   (d) Judicial Statistics   304
   (e) Agrarian Outrages   305
   (f) Returns under Crime and Outrage Acts, etc.   306
   (g) Agricultural Statistics, 1847–1886   308

3. Official Publications   309
4. Newspapers   309
5. Contemporary Works   310
6. Works of Reference   315
7. Modern Works   315

SELECT BIBLIOGRAPHY

I. MANUSCRIPT MATERIAL

Collections of rentals and accounts are indicated by putting the landlord's name in capitals; acreages etc. of the larger estates are taken from Bateman, *Great Landowners*, U. H. Hussey de Burgh, *The Landowners of Ireland: An Alphabetical List of the Owners of Estates of 500 acres or £500 valuation and upwards in Ireland* (Dublin, 1881), and from *Thom's Directory, 1881*.

(a) National Archives

Chief Secretary's Office: Irish Crime Records; Registered Papers; Official Papers; outrage papers; convict reference files.

Encumbered estates court (landed estates court from 1858) rentals and conveyances.

ERNE (earl of, Crom Castle, Newtownbutler, Co. Fermanagh). Rentals (Co. Donegal), 1848–54, 1868–87.
   These are among the records of the clerks of crown and peace (Co. Donegal); see also below, p. 291.

HAMILTON (James Hamilton, Co. Cavan and Co. Cork). M 5571/1–34.

JOHNSTON (Co. Armagh). M 3508–20.

LE FANU (Joseph Le Fanu, Co. Cavan). M 5634/1–27.

MIDLETON (Viscount, Cahirmone, Midleton, Co. Cork. 9,580 acres, of which 6,475 were in Cork and 3,105 in Surrey). 978/2/3/4.

MILLER (Co. Cavan). M 5860/1–27.

MOORE (Co. Armagh). M 2977.

Valuation Office: letter-books and correspondence.

(b) Public Record Office of Northern Ireland

ABERCORN (first duke of, Baronscourt, Newtownstewart, Co. Tyrone. 78,662 acres, of which 60,000 were in Tyrone, 16,500 in Donegal, and 2,162 in Edinburgh and Renfrew). D623.

ANNESLEY (Earl Annesley, Castle Wellan, Co. Down. 51,060 acres, of which 24,221 were in Cavan, 24,350 in Down, and 2,489 in the Queen's County). D 1854.

ARCHDALE (Mervyn Edward Archdale, Castle Archdale, Lisnarick, Co. Fermanagh. 33,015 acres, of which 27,410 were in Fermanagh and 5,605 in Tyrone). D740.

ATKINSON (Co. Armagh). D1815/3/2–3.

AUCHINLECK (Thomas Auchinleck, Creevenagh House, Omagh, Co. Tyrone. 2,857 acres in Tyrone). D674/230–43.

BELMORE (earl of, Castle Coole, Enniskillen, Co. Fermanagh. 19,429 acres, of which 14,388 were in Tyrone and 5,041 in Fermanagh). D1716.

BLACKER (Major Stewart Blacker, Carrick Blacker, Co. Armagh. 1,466 acres in Armagh). D959/2/2–3.

DUFFERIN (earl of, Clandeboye, Co. Down. 18,238 acres in Down). D1071H.

Dungannon School Estate (commissioners of endowed schools. 1,275 acres in Tyrone). Letter-books of William Wann, agent, 1846–81. D1606/5/3–6.

DUNRAVEN (earl of, Adare Manor, Co. Limerick. 39,755 acres, of which 14,298 were in Limerick, 1,005 in Kerry, 164 in Clare, 23,751 in Glamorgan, and 537 in Gloucester). D3196.

ERNE (earl of, Crom Castle, Newtownbutler, Co. Fermanagh. 40,365 acres, of which 31,389 were in Fermanagh, 4,826 in Donegal, 2,184 in Mayo, and 1,966 in Sligo). D1939.
See above, p. 290, for the Co. Donegal rentals.
GARVAGH (Lord Garvagh, Garvagh Lodge, Co. Londonderry. 15,406 acres, of which 8,427 were in Londonderry, 5,803 in Cavan, and 1,176 in Down). D1550.
GOSFORD (earl of, Gosford Castle, Markethill, Co. Armagh. 18,594 acres, of which 12,177 were in Armagh and 6,417 in Cavan). D1606.
HALL (William James Hall, Narrow Water, Warrenpoint, Co. Down. 6,804 acres, of which 3,648 were in Down, 2,656 in Armagh, and 500 in Louth). D2090.
Correspondence relating to estate of George Vaughan Hart, Kilderry, Co. Londonderry. D3077.
HEYGATE (Sir Frederick William Heygate, bt., Bellarena, Co. Londonderry. 8,845 acres, of which 5,507 were in Londonderry and 3,338 in Donegal). D673.
Correspondence of Robert Knox, agent, mid-1860s. D668.
MCALPINE (James McAlpine, Co. Tyrone. 4,727 acres in Tyrone). D2298.
MANCHESTER (duke of, Tandragee Castle, Co. Armagh. 27,312 acres, of which 12,298 were in Armagh and 15,014 in Cambridge, Bedford, and Huntingdon). D1248.
RANFURLY (earl of, Dungannon Park, Co. Tyrone. 10,153 acres, of which 9,647 were in Tyrone and 506 in Fermanagh). D1932.
SHIRLEY (Evelyn Philip Shirley, Loughfea Castle, Carrickmacross, Co. Monaghan. 28,760 acres, of which 26,386 were in Monaghan and 2,374 were in Warwick and Worcester). D3531.
Letter-book of Alexander Spotswood, 1860–76. D1062/18A.
STRAFFORD (earl and countess, Wrotham Park, Barnet. 14,994 acres, of which 7,647 were in Londonderry and 7,347 were in Bedford, Hertfordshire, Kent, and Middlesex). D1062/1/2.
WHYTE (John Joseph, Loughbrickland House, Loughbrickland, Co. Down. 1,712 acres in Down), D2918.

(c) National Library of Ireland

ASHTOWN (2nd baron, Woodlawn, Co. Galway. 43,643 acres, of which 8,310 were in Galway, 11,273 in Limerick, 9,435 in Waterford, 2,780 in King's County, 4,526 in Tipperary, 841 in Roscommon, 50 in Dublin, 42 in Westmeath, and 6,386 in Yorkshire). MSS 1765–9, 5823–5.
Report on the state of Ireland in 1863 by Sir Henry John Brownrigg, inspector-general of the Irish constabulary. MS 915.
BUTLER (Co. Carlow). MS 14312.
—— (the Misses Anna, Sophia, and Henrietta, Castle Crine, Co. Clare. 11,854 acres, of which 11,389 were in Clare and 465 in Tipperary). MSS 5410–14, 5422.
CLONBROCK (4th baron, Clonbrock, Ahascragh, Co. Galway. 29,550 acres in Galway). MSS 19617–22, 19623–32, 19633–45.
CROFTON (3rd baron, Mote Park, Co. Roscommon. 11,053 acres in Roscommon). MSS 5632–3, 4074–9, 4081–100.
—— (Co. Monaghan). MS 8150.
See also Crofton, below, p. 293.

DEANE (Co. Kildare). MSS 14281-2.
DOMVILE (Sir Charles Compton Domvile, bt., Santry House, Dublin. 6,262 acres in Dublin). MS 11305.
DOPPING (Ralph Anthony Dopping-Hepenstal, Derrycassan, Granard, Co. Longford. 3,269 acres, of which 1,701 were in Longford and 1,568 in Wicklow). MS 9993.
FARNHAM (8th baron, Farnham, Co. Cavan. 25,920 acres in Cavan). MSS 3117-18.
FILGATE (Captain Townely Filgate, Lowther Lodge, Balbriggan, Co. Louth. 2,250 acres in Louth). MS 5874.
FITZWILLIAM (Earl Fitzwilliam, Coolattin Park, Carnew, Co. Wicklow. 115,573 acres, of which 89,891 acres were in Wicklow, 1,532 in Kildare, 325 in Wexford, and 23,995 in Yorkshire, Northampton, Cambridge, Derby, Huntingdon, and Lincoln). MSS 3987, 4972, 4976-99, 5992-9, 6105-17.
FOWLER (Robert Fowler, Rahinston, Enfield, Co. Meath. 8,026 acres in Meath). MS 11414.
GRANARD (earl of, Castle Forbes, Co. Longford. 21,294 acres, of which 14,978 acres were in Longford, 4,266 in Leitrim, and 2,050 in Wexford). MS 11110.
HANDCOCK (Co. Westmeath). MS 14108.
HODSON (Sir George Hodson, bt., Holybrooke House, Bray, Co. Wicklow. 6,827 acres, of which 4,349 were in Cavan, 1,211 in Wicklow, 729 in Meath, 502 in Westmeath, and 26 in Bucks). MSS 16390-6, 16400-7, 16418-19, 16437-70.
HOPKINS (Co. Westmeath). MSS 4821-2.
INCHIQUIN (Sir Lucius O'Brien, 13th baron, Dromoland, Newmarket-on-Fergus, Co. Clare. 20,321 acres in Clare). MSS 14508-77.
JOHNSTON (Co. Leitrim). MSS 9465-6.
KNOX (Co. Roscommon). MS 3178.
Larcom papers. Newspaper cuttings, copies of official correspondence and reports, and comments of Sir Thomas Larcom, under-secretary, 1853-68.
LEITRIM (William Sydney Clements, third earl, 95,007 acres, of which 54,352 were in Donegal, 22,038 in Leitrim, 18,145 in Galway, and 472 in Kildare). MSS 179-80, 3802-12, 5175-8, 5728-33, 5790-2, 5794-805.
LOUGHREA (group of estates near Loughrea, Co. Galway). MSS 2277-80.
MANSFIELD (George Patrick Lattin Mansfield, Morristown Lattin, Naas, Co. Kildare. 5,639 acres, of which 4,542 were in Kildare and 1,097 in Waterford). MS 9634.
MURRAY STEWART (Horatio Granville Murray Stewart, Cally, Gatehouse, Kirkcudbright. 98,269 acres, of which 50,818 were in Donegal and 47,451 in Kirkcudbright and Wigtown). MSS 5472-84, 5893-903.
O'DONNEL (Sir Richard O'Donnel, Newport House, Newport, Co. Mayo. 7,488 acres in Mayo). MSS 5740-1.
Correspondence of Charles King O'Hara and Charles William O'Hara, Cooper's Hill, Ballymote, Co. Sligo, and Richard Beere, agent. MS 20321.
PAUL (Sir Robert Paul, Ballyglan, Co. Waterford. 2,352 acres, of which 1,401 were in Carlow, 708 in Kerry, and 243 in Waterford). MSS 12987-9.
POWERSCOURT (Viscount Powerscourt, Powerscourt, Enniskerry, Co. Wicklow. 53,258 acres, of which 40,986 were in Wicklow, 11,641 in Wexford, and 631 in Dublin). MSS 2740, 3164, 3172, 16376-9, 19202-9, 19210-33, 19246-86.

PRATT (Mervyn Pratt, Cabra Castle, Kingscourt, Co. Cavan. 27,064 acres, of which 17,955 were in Mayo, 8,095 in Cavan, and 1,014 in Meath). MSS 3122, 5088-91.

REYNELL (Richard W. Reynell, Killynon House, Killucan, Co. Westmeath. 1,119 acres, of which 471 were in Fermanagh, 289 in Westmeath, 207 in Wexford, and 152 in Meath). MS 5990.

ST GEORGE (Charles M. St George, Hatfield Manor, Carrick-on-Shannon, Co. Leitrim. 2,957 acres, of which 1,663 were in Leitrim and 1,294 in Roscommon). MSS 4006-11.

Estate and family memoranda of the Sanderson family, Cloverhill, Co. Cavan. MS 9492.

Smith-Barry papers. MS 8819.

TALBOT-CROSBIE (William Talbot-Crosbie, Ardfert Abbey, Co. Kerry. 10,039 acres in Kerry). MSS 5037-9.

TRENCH (Henry Bloomfield Trench, Cangort, King's County. 12,134 acres, of which 4,707 were in Tipperary, 2,113 in King's County, 1,926 in Limerick, 1,581 in Galway, 704 in Clare, 671 in Queen's County, and 432 in Roscommon). MS 2579.

Survey of the Westropp estate in the counties of Clare and Limerick, 1871-7, Robert L. Brown, agent. MS 5397.

(d) The Library of Trinity College, Dublin

College muniments: board minutes, rentals, and papers on the 1851 leasing powers act, including price series. MUN/V and MUN/P.

COURTOWN (earl of, Courtown House, Gorey, Co. Wexford. 23,314 acres, of which 14,426 were in Wexford, 7,395 in Carlow, and 1,493 in Cheshire).

CROFTON (Co. Monaghan). MS 3582.
  See also Crofton, above, p. 291.

(e) The Registry of Deeds, Dublin

Transcripts of leases, mortgages, and releases.

(f) The Valuation Office, Dublin

Cancelled books of the tenement valuation.

2. HOUSE OF COMMONS SESSIONAL PAPERS

The following is a comprehensive list of House of Commons sessional papers for the years 1848 to 1878; some papers published in the years before 1848 and after 1878 are included, where their inclusion was necessary, either because they were referred to above, or because they included matter reproduced in the appendices.

Reports and returns relating to evictions, agrarian crime, etc. are given separately below, pp. 301-8. For full references to the censuses see W. E. Vaughan and A. J. Fitzpatrick (eds.), *Irish Historical Statistics: Population 1821-1971* (Dublin, 1978), 355-7.

(a) Royal Commissions, Select Committees, and Special Returns

Report from Her Majesty's Commissioners of Inquiry into the State of the Law and Practice in Respect to the Occupation of Land in Ireland [605], HC 1845, xix. 1 (earl of Devon, chairman).
—— Minutes of Evidence, pt. i [606], ibid. 57.
—— Minutes of Evidence, pt. ii [616], HC 1845, xx. 1.
—— Minutes of Evidence, pt. iii [657], HC 1845, xxi. 1.
—— Appendix to Minutes of Evidence, pt. iv [672], HC 1845, xxii. 1.
Index to Minutes of Evidence, pt. v [673], ibid. 225.
Return 'Showing the Amount of Average Prices of Agricultural Produce (Arranged in Provinces) of Forty Towns in Ireland, during the Years 1849, 1850, 1851', HC 1852 (307), xlvii. 1.
Copy 'of the Paper [by Robert Phillimore] on the Roman and Foreign Law Considered with Reference to the Relations of Landlord and Tenant in Ireland, Communicated by the Secretary for Ireland to the Members of the Committee on the Irish Land Bills', HC 1852-3 (726), xciv. 605.
Report of her Majesty's Commissioners Appointed to Inquire into the State, Discipline, Studies, and Revenues of the University of Dublin, and of Trinity College; together with Appendices, Containing Evidence, Suggestions, and Correspondence [1637], HC 1852-3, xlv. 1 (Richard Whately, archbishop of Dublin, chairman).
Report from the Select Committee on Destitution (Gweedore and Cloughaneely); together with the Proceedings of the Committee, Minutes of Evidence, Appendix, and Index, HC 1857-8 (412), xiii. 89 (John Bagwell, chairman).
Report of Her Majesty's Commissioners Appointed to Inquire into the Endowments, Funds, and Actual Condition of All Schools Endowed for the Purpose of Education in Ireland ... [2336-I], HC 1857-8, xxii, pt. i, p. 1 (marquis of Kildare, chairman).
—— Evidence, vol. i [2336-II], ibid., pt. ii, p. 1.
—— Evidence, vol. ii with index [2336-III], ibid., pt. iii, p. 1.
—— Papers Accompanying Report, vol. iii [2336-IV], ibid., pt. iv, p. 1.
Report from the Select Committee on the Tenure and Improvement of Land (Ireland) Act; together with the Proceedings of the Committee, Minutes of Evidence, Appendix, and Index, HC 1865 (402), xi. 341 (John Francis Maguire, chairman).
Report from the Select Committee of the House of Lords on the Tenure (Ireland) Bill [HL]; together with the Proceedings of the Committee, Minutes of Evidence, Appendix, and Index, HC 1867 (518), xiv. 423 (marquis of Clanricarde (who sat as Lord Somerhill), chairman).
Report from the Select Committee on General Valuation etc. (Ireland); together with the Proceedings of the Committee, Minutes of Evidence, and Appendix [and index], HC 1868-9 (362), ix. 1 (Hon. Fitzstephen French, chairman).
Two Reports for the Irish Government on the History of the Landlord and Tenant Question in Ireland, with Suggestions for Legislation. First Report Made in 1859; Second, in 1866. By W. Neilson Hancock [4204], HC 1868-9, xxvi. 1.
Reports from Poor Law Inspectors on the Wages of Agricultural Labourers in Ireland [C 35], HC 1870, xiv. 1.

Reports from Poor Law Inspectors in Ireland as to the Existing Relations between Landlord and Tenant in Respect of Improvements on Farms, etc. [C 31], HC 1870, xiv. 37.

Returns Showing the Number of Agricultural Holdings in Ireland, and the Tenure by which they are Held by the Occupiers [C 32], HC 1870, lvi. 737.

Return 'of All Land Holdings Valued at and under Five Pound Yearly... in the Following Poor Law Unions in Ireland: Glenties, Dunfanaghy, Inishowen, Clifden, Oughterard, Belmullet, Newport, Scarriff, Bantry, Castletown, Cahirciveen, Kenmare, Ballycastle', HC 1870 (167), lvi. 769.

Returns 'of the Total Value of Lands Sold under the Encumbered Estates Court (Ireland), to the Latest Date Obtainable [21 Feb.1870]'; *'of the Total Number of Evictions in the Last Three Years for Each County in Ireland'; 'and, of the Average Value of Cattle, Sheep and Pigs, Wheat, Oats, Barley, Bere, or Rye, Beans and Peas, Potatoes, Turnips, Mangold, Flax, Hay, and Butter in Ireland, in the Years 1850, 1860, and* [1866]', HC 1870 (101), lvii. 301.

—— encumbered estates to 10 July 1871 and evictions to 31 Dec. 1870, HC 1871 (383), lviii. 471.

Reports from Her Majesty's Representatives Respecting the Tenure of Land in the Several Countries of Europe, 1869, pt. i [C 66], HC 1870, lxvii. 1.

—— pt. ii, ibid. [C 75], 549.

—— pt. iii [C 271], HC 1871, lxvii. 749.

—— pt. iv, ibid. [C 426], 809.

—— pt. v [C 572], HC 1872, lxii. 695.

Report from the Select Committee of the House of Lords on the Landlord and Tenant (Ireland) Act, 1870; together with the Proceedings of the Committee, Minutes of Evidence, Appendix, and Index, HC 1872 (403), xi. 1. (Lord Chelmsford, chairman).

Return for the Year 1870, of the Number of Landed Proprietors in Each County, Classed according to Residence, Showing the Extent and Value of the Property Held by Each Class... HC 1872 (167), xlvii. 775.

Copy 'of the Letter of Instruction Issued by the Irish Government to the Poor Law Inspectors Relative to the Return of Landed Proprietors (Ireland) Lately Issued', HC 1872 (255), xlvii. 785.

Nominal Return 'of the Municipal Corporations and Boards of Guardians in Ireland that have Sent Petitions to this House in Favour of the Land Tenure (Ireland) Bill', HC 1876 (320), lx. 709.

Summary 'of the Returns of Owners of Land in Ireland, Showing with Respect to Each County, the Number of Owners Below an Acre, and in Classes up to 100,000 Acres and Upwards, with the Aggregate Acreage and Valuation of Each Class', HC 1876 (422), lxxx. 35.

Return of Owners of Land of an Acre and Upwards, in the Several Counties, Counties of Cities, and Counties of Towns in Ireland [C 1492], HC 1876, lxxx. 61.

Copy 'of "a Return of the Names of Proprietors and the Area and Valuation of All Properties in the Several Counties in Ireland, Held in Fee or Perpetuity, or on Long Leases at Chief Rents", Prepared for the Use of Her Majesty's Government...' HC 1876 (412), lxxx. 395.

Report from the Select Committee on [the] *Irish Land Act, 1870; together with the Proceedings of the Committee, Minutes of Evidence, Appendix, and Index*, HC 1877 (328), xii. 1 (George Shaw Lefevre, chairman).

Return 'of the Amount Awarded to Tenants at Land Sessions in Ireland, Exclusive of Costs, under "the Landlord and Tenant (Ireland) Act, 1870", since the Passing of that Measure [1 Aug. 1870] *up to 31 Dec. 1875, with Totals and Gross Totals in Tabular Form...*' HC 1877 (19), lxix. 593.

Report from the Select Committee on [the] *Irish Land Act, 1870; together with the Proceedings of the Committee, Minutes of Evidence, Appendix, and Index*, HC 1878 (249), xv. 1 (George Shaw Lefevre, chairman).

Supplement to the Return of Owners of Land in the Several Counties, Counties of Cities, and Counties of Towns in Ireland. . . . Comprising a Statement of Changes in the Entries in the Return, which on Inquiry Made since the Publication of the Return have been Found to be Necessary [C 2022], HC 1878, lxxix. 501.

Preliminary Report from her Majesty's Commissioners on Agriculture [C 2778], HC 1881, xv. 1 (duke of Richmond and Gordon, chairman).

—— *Minutes of Evidence*, pt. i (12 Feb. to 10 Dec. 1880), ibid. [C 2778-I], 25.

—— *Digest and Appendix to Minutes of Evidence*, pt. i, *with Reports of Assistant Commissioners* [C 2778-II], HC 1881, xvi. 1.

—— *Minutes of Evidence*, pt. ii (23 Feb. to 4 Aug. 1881) [C 3096], HC 1881, xvii. 1.

—— *Minutes of Evidence*, pt. iii (4 Aug. 1881 to 9 Mar. 1882) [C 3309-I], HC 1882, xiv. 45.

—— *Digest and Appendix to Minutes of Evidence*, pts. ii and iii, ibid. [C 3309-II], 493.

—— *Preliminary Report of the Assistant Commissioners for Ireland* [C 2951], HC 1881, xvi. 841.

—— *Assistant Commissioners' Reports* [C 2678], HC 1880, xvii. 1. *Further Reports* [C 3375-I to VI], HC 1882, xv. 1.

—— *Final Report from Her Majesty's Commissioners on Agriculture* [C 3309], HC 1882, xiv. 1.

Report of Her Majesty's Commission of Inquiry into the Working of the Landlord and Tenant (Ireland) Act, 1870, and the Acts Amending the Same [C 2779], HC 1881, xviii. 1 (earl of Bessborough, chairman).

—— *Minutes of Evidence*, pt. i [C 2779-I], HC 1881, xviii. 73.

—— *Minutes of Evidence and Appendices*, pt. ii [C 2779-II], HC 1881, xix. 1.

—— *Index to Minutes of Evidence and Appendices* [C 2779-III], HC 1881, xix. 825.

First Report from the Select Committee of [the] *House of Lords on the Land Law (Ireland) Act; together with Proceedings of the Committee, Minutes of Evidence, Appendix, and Index*, HC 1882 (249), xi. 1 (Earl Cairns, chairman).

—— *Second Report*, ibid. (379), 547.

—— *Third Report*, HC 1883 (204), xiii. 443.

—— *Fourth Report, and Index*, ibid. (279), 653.

Report of the Royal Commission on the Land Law (Ireland) Act, 1881, and the Purchase of Land (Ireland) Act, 1885 [C 4969], HC 1887, xxvi. 1 (Earl Cowper, chairman).

—— Minutes of Evidence and Appendices [C 4969-I], HC 1887, xxvi. 25.
—— Index to Evidence and Appendices [C 4969-II], HC 1887, xxvi. 1109.

(b) Land Bills, 1845–1880

Second Parliament of Queen Victoria, 1841–7

A Bill to Provide Compensation for Tenants in Ireland who have Made, or shall Hereafter Make Improvements on the Premises in the Occupation of Such Tenants, HC 1845 (bill 578), vi. 177.

A Bill for Providing Compensation, in Certain Cases, for Tenants in Ireland who shall Build on or Drain Farms, and to Secure to the Parties Respectively Entitled Thereto the Due Payment of Such Compensation, HC 1846 (bill 383), ii. 367.

A bill to Secure the Right of Occupying Tenants in Ireland, and Thereby to Promote the Improvement of the Soil and the Employment of the Labouring Classes, HC 1847 (bill 127), iv. 85.

Third Parliament, 1847–52

A Bill to Amend the Law of Landlord and Tenant in Ireland, HC 1847–8 (bill 106), iv. 25.
—— as amended by the select committee... ibid. (bill 459), 53.
A Bill to Secure the Rights of Outgoing Tenants in Ireland, HC 1847–8 (bill 155), iv. 551.
A Bill Intituled 'an Act to Amend the Law with Regard to Distress for Arrears of Rent in Ireland', HC 1850 (bill 485), ii. 339.
A Bill to Provide Compensation to Tenants for Improvements Effected by them in Certain Cases, and to Amend the Law of Landlord and Tenant, in Ireland, HC 1850 (bill 64), iii. 493.
A Bill Intituled 'an Act to Amend and Improve the Relations of Landlord and Tenant in Ireland', HC 1850 (bill 551), iii. 531.
—— as amended by the committee... ibid. (bill 668), 539.
A Bill to Provide for the Better Securing and Regulating the Custom of 'Tenant Right' as Practised in the Province of Ulster, and to Secure Compensation to Improving Tenants in Ireland who may not Make Claim under the Said Custom, and to Limit the Power of Eviction in Certain Cases, HC 1850 (bill 431), viii. 323.
A Bill to Provide for the Better Securing and Regulating the Custom of 'Tenant Right' as Practised in the Province of Ulster and to Secure Compensation to Improving Tenants who may not Make Claim under the Said Custom, and to Limit the Power of Eviction in Certain Cases, HC 1852 (bill 47), iv. 371.

Fourth Parliament, 1852–7

A Bill to Consolidate and Amend the Laws Relating to Landlord and Tenant in Ireland, HC 1852–3 (bill 18), iv. 51.
—— As Amended by the Select Committee... ibid. (bill 630), 109.
—— As Amended by the Select Committee and in Committee... ibid. (bill 796), 173.
A Bill to Provide Compensation for Improvements Made by Tenants in Ireland, HC 1852–3 (bill 19), vii. 265.

—— *As Amended by the Select Committee* ... ibid. (bill 574), 287.
—— *As Amended by the Select Committee, and in Committee* ... ibid. (bill 733), 305.
—— *As Amended by the Select Committee, in Committee, and on Recommitment* ... ibid. (bill 807), 321.
A Bill to Provide for the Better Securing of and Regulating the Custom of Tenant Right as Practised in the Province of Ulster, and to Secure Compensation to Improving Tenants who may not Make Claim under the Said Custom, and to Limit the Power of Eviction in Certain Cases, HC 1852–3 (bill 25), vii. 337.
A Bill Intituled 'an Act to Consolidate and Amend the Laws Relating to Landlord and Tenant in Ireland', HC 1854 [bill 130], iii. 381.
A Bill to Provide Compensation for Improvements Made by Tenants in Ireland, HC 1854 [bill 20], vi. 335.
A Bill to Provide Compensation for Improving Tenants and to Consolidate and Amend the Laws Relating to Leasing Powers in Ireland, HC 1854–5 [bill 39], vi. 187.
A Bill to Provide for the Better Securing of and Regulating the Custom of Tenant Right as Practised in the Province of Ulster, and to Secure Compensation to Improving Tenants who may not Make Claim under the Said Custom, and to Limit the Power of Eviction in Certain Cases, HC 1856 [bill 43], vi. 405.
A Bill to Afford Compensation to Tenant Farmers in Ireland for Improvements Made on the Land in their Possession, HC 1857 sess. 1 [bill 35 sess. 1], i, between pp. 416–17 [not printed].

Fifth Parliament, 1857–9

A Bill to Provide Compensation to Tenant Farmers in Ireland for Improvements Made by Them upon Lands in their Occupation, and to Limit the Power of Eviction in Certain Cases, HC 1857 sess. 2 [bill 34], iv. 617.
A Bill to Improve and Amend the Law of Landlord and Tenant with Relation to Emblements and Away-going Crops in Ireland, HC 1857–8 [bill 184], ii. 123.
A Bill to Amend the Law of Landlord and Tenant and to Facilitate the Improvement of Land in Ireland, HC 1857–8 [bill 183], iii. 29.
A Bill to Provide Compensation to Tenant Farmers in Ireland for Improvements Made by Them upon Lands in their Occupation; and to Limit the Power of Eviction in Certain Cases, HC 1857–8 [bill 22], iv. 549.

Sixth Parliament, 1859–65

A Bill to Improve and Amend the Law of Landlord and Tenant in Relation to Emblements and Away-going Crops in Ireland, HC 1860 [bill 88], iii. 151.
A Bill to Consolidate and Amend the Law of Landlord and Tenant in Ireland 1860, HC 1860 [bill 92], iv. 25.
A Bill to Consolidate and Amend the Laws Affecting the Relation of Landlord and Tenant in Ireland (No. 2), ibid. [bill 144], 79.
A Bill to Amend the Law Relating to the Tenure and Improvement of Land in Ireland, HC 1860 [bill 89], vi. 467.
—— *As Amended in Committee* ... ibid. [bill 172], 485.
—— *As Amended in Committee, and on Recommitment* ... ibid. [bill 225], 501.
—— *Amendments Made by the Lords* ... ibid. [bill 322], 517.

A Bill to Provide for the Costs of Certain Proceedings to be Taken under the Landlord and Tenant Law Amendment (Ireland) Act (1860), HC 1861 [bill 217], iii. 53.

A Bill to Amend the Law Relating to the Seizure of Growing Crops in Ireland, HC 1863 [bill 211], ii. 245.

Seventh Parliament, 1866-8

A Bill to Regulate and Improve the Tenure of Land in Ireland between Landlord and Tenant, HC 1866 [bill 190], iii. 301.

A Bill Further to Amend the Law Relating to the Tenure and Improvement of Land in Ireland, HC 1866 [bill 130], v. 353.

A Bill to Enable Contracts to be Made between Landlord and Tenant for the Improvement of Land in Ireland, HC 1867 [bill 32], iii. 329.

A Bill to Regulate and Improve the Tenure of Land in Ireland between Landlord and Tenant, HC 1867 [bill 19], iii. 377.

A Bill to Promote the Improvement of Land by Occupying Tenants in Ireland, HC 1867 [bill 29], vi. 387.

Reprint of the Tenants' Improvements Compensation (Ireland) Bill of Session 1852, HC 1867 [O.86], lix. 355.

A Bill to Suspend for a Limited Period or Periods the Application of the Law of Ejectment in Ireland to Agricultural Tenants Holding from Year to Year, except for Nonpayment of Rent, or upon the Subdivision of Farms, HC 1867-8 [bill 100], ii. 259.

A Bill Further to Amend the Law Relating to the Tenure and Improvement of Land in Ireland, HC 1867-8 [bill 32], iii. 5.

A Bill to Amend the Law Relating to Tenure and Improvement of Land, and to Facilitate and Promote the Sale and Purchase of Land and Tenants' Interests, and the Reclamation of Waste Lands in Ireland, HC 1867-8 [bill 244], v. 245.

Eighth Parliament, 1868-74

A Bill to Amend the Law Relating to the Occupation and Ownership of Land in Ireland, HC 1870 [bill 29], ii. 263.

—— *As Amended in Committee*... ibid. [bill 137], 301.

—— *As Amended in Committee, and on Consideration of Bill as Amended*... ibid. [bill 145], 337.

—— *Lords Amendments to the Irish Land Bill*, ibid. [bill 204], 371.

—— *Amendments Made by the Lords to the Amendments Made by the Commons to the Lords Amendments to the Irish Land Bill, with Reasons of the Lords for Disagreeing to Certain of the Said Amendments*, ibid. [bill 221], 383.

A Bill Intituled 'an Act to Amend the Landlord and Tenant (Ireland) Act, 1870', HC 1871 [bill 215], iii. 9.

A Bill to Amend 'the Landlord and Tenant (Ireland) Act, 1870', so far as Relates to Advances by the Commissioners of Public Works in Ireland to Tenants for the Purchase by them of Holdings Sold in the Landed Estates Court, HC 1872 [bill 98], ii. 597 [not printed].

A Bill to Explain and Amend the Landlord and Tenant (Ireland) Act, 1870, so far as Relates to the Purchase by Tenants of their Holdings, HC 1872 [bill 124], ii. 599.

A Bill to Legalize the Ulster Custom of Tenant Right in Holdings not Agricultural or Pastoral in their Character, HC 1872 [bill 144], vi. 439.

A Bill to Provide Facilities for the Purchase of Lands by Tenants in Ireland, and to Amend and Alter Part ii and Part iii of the Landlord and Tenant (Ireland) Act, 1870, HC 1873 [bill 167], ii. 287.

A Bill to Remove Doubts that have Arisen as to the Provisions of the Landlord and Tenant (Ireland) Act, 1870, as to Notices to Quit, HC 1873 [bill 271], ii. 299.

A Bill to Make Provision for More Effectually Securing the Ulster Tenant Right, and to Amend the Landlord and Tenant (Ireland) Act, 1870, HC 1873 [bill 225], vi. 277.

Ninth Parliament, 1874–80

A Bill to Extend the Provisions of the Landlord and Tenant (Ireland) Act, 1870, to England and Scotland, HC 1874 [bill 47], ii. 537 [not printed].

A Bill to Amend the Landlord and Tenant (Ireland) Act, 1870, HC 1874 [bill 20], iii. 77.

A Bill to Amend the Landlord and Tenant (Ireland) Act, 1870, with a View to Facilitate the Acquisition of Property in Land in Fee and Fee-Farm by Tenants in Ireland, HC 1874 [bill 61], iii. 83.

A Bill to Enable Tenants of Land in Ireland to Acquire Parliamentary Tenant Right in their Holdings, HC 1874 [bill 82], v. 333.

A Bill to Make Provision for More Effectually Securing the Ulster Tenant Right, and to Amend the Landlord and Tenant (Ireland) Act, 1870, HC 1874 [bill 92], v. 501.

A Bill to Facilitate the Creation of a Class of Small Landed Proprietors in Ireland, HC 1875 [bill 148], iii. 187.

A Bill to Amend the Landlord and Tenant (Ireland) Act, 1870, HC 1875 [bill 35], iii. 205.

A Bill to Amend the Landlord and Tenant (Ireland) Act, 1870, HC 1876 [bill 40], iii. 411.

A Bill to Amend the Laws Relating to the Tenure of Land in Ireland, HC 1876 [bill 10], iii. 415.

A Bill to Assimilate the Law in Ireland to the Law in England as to Notices to Quit, HC 1876 [bill 114], v. 275.

—— As Amended in Committee... ibid. [bill 160], 279.

—— As Amended in Committee and on Recommitment... ibid. [bill 226], 283.

—— Lords Amendments... ibid. [bill 283], 287.

A Bill to Facilitate the Proof of the Ulster Tenant Right Custom at the Expiration of Leases in Certain Cases, HC 1876 [bill 84], vii. 235.

A Bill to Protect Agricultural Tenants in Ireland from Capricious Eviction, and to Enable them in Certain Cases to Acquire Security of Tenure, HC 1877 [bill 58], i. 7.

A Bill to Amend the Landlord and Tenant (Ireland) Act, 1870, HC 1877 [bill 51], iii. 27.

A Bill to Amend the Laws Relating to the Tenure of Land in Ireland, HC 1877 [bill 21], iii. 37.

A Bill to Legalize Tenant Right at the End of a Lease in Ireland, HC 1877 [bill 56], vii. 5.

A Bill to Amend the Laws Relating to Tenure of Land in Ireland, HC 1878 [bill 50], iv. 1.

A Bill to Amend the Laws Relating to the Tenure of Land in Ireland, HC 1878 [bill 50], iv. 5.

A Bill for Diminishing the Evils of Absenteeism in Ireland by Giving Facilities for the Purchase of their Holdings to Tenants who may be in Occupation of the Estates of Absentee Proprietors, HC 1878 [bill 115], i. 5 [not printed].

A Bill to Provide for the Equitable Settlement of Rent in Certain Cases of Difference between Landlord and Tenants in Ireland, and to Make Better Provision as to Notices to Quit; and for Other Purposes, HC 1878 [bill 218], iv. 35.

A Bill to Amend the Landlord and Tenant Act (Ireland), 1870, HC 1878 [bill 43], iv. 43.

A Bill to Make Further Provision in Respect of Tenant Right in Ireland at the Expiration of Leases, HC 1878 [bill 31], vii. 353.

A Bill to Secure More Effectively the Tenant Right Custom in the Province of Ulster, HC 1878 [bill 54], vii. 357.

A Bill to Amend the Law Relating to the Landlord and Tenant in Ireland, HC 1878 [bill 109], vii. 367.

A Bill to Provide for the Equitable Settlement of Rent in Certain Cases of Difference between Landlords and Tenants in Ireland, and to Make Better Provision as to Notices to Quit; and for Other Purposes Relating Thereto, HC 1878–9 [bill 26], iii. 489.

A Bill to Amend the Law of Landlord and Tenant in Ireland, HC 1878–9 [bill 51], iii. 499.

A Bill to Amend the Landlord and Tenant (Ireland) Act, 1870, HC 1878–9 [bill 41], iii. 525.

A Bill to Secure More Effectually the Tenant Right Custom in the Province of Ulster, HC 1878–9 [bill 37], vii. 569.

A Bill to Make Further Provision in Respect of Tenant Right in Ulster at the Expiration of Leases, HC 1878–9 [bill 209], vii. 573.

(c) Evictions

Returns 'from the Courts of Queen's Bench, Common Pleas, and Exchequer in Ireland, of the Number of Ejectments Brought in those Courts Respectively, for the Last Three Years, Beginning with Hilary Term 1846, and Ending with Hilary Term 1849; ... and, from the Assistant Barristers' Court of Each County of Ireland, of the Number of Civil Bill Ejectments ...' HC 1849 (315), xlix. 235.

Return 'of All Notices Served [from 14 Aug. 1848 to 19 Feb. 1849] upon Relieving Officers of Poor Law Districts in Ireland, by Landowners and Others, under the Act of Last Session, 11 & 12 Vict., c. 47, Intituled, "an Act for the Protection and Relief of the Destitute Poor Evicted from their Dwellings"', HC 1849 (517), xlix. 279.

Reports and Returns Relating to Evictions in the Kilrush Union [1089], HC 1849, xlix. 315.

Report from the Select Committee on Kilrush Union; together with the Proceedings of the Committee, Minutes of Evidence, Appendix, and Index, HC 1850 (613), xi. 529 (Poulett Scrope, chairman).

A Return 'Giving, in Tabular Form, the Number of Original Civil Bill Ejectment

Processes Entered, and the Number of Copies Served in Each of the Years 1844, 1845, 1846, 1847, 1848, 1849, and 1850...' HC 1851 (322), l. 335.

—— for the counties of Antrim, Galway, Londonderry, Sligo, and Wicklow, ibid. (322–I), 353.

Returns *'of the Number of Actions of Ejectment Brought in the Court of Queen's Bench* [including Actions in the Courts of Common Pleas and Exchequer, and in the Civil Bill Courts] *during the Years 1847, 1848, and 1849...*' HC 1851 (172), l. 629.

Returns, *'from the Assistant Barristers' Court of the Counties of Armagh, Monaghan, and Louth, Giving, in Tabular Form, the Number of Civil Bill Ejectment Processes Entered; the Number of Decrees Pronounced; the Number of Decrees Executed; the Number of Dismisses; the Number of Cases Nilled; the Number of Copies Served... from the Year 1842 to the Year 1852, Inclusive...*' HC 1852 (581), xlvii. 63.

Returns, *'from the Clerks of the Peace of the Several Counties and Counties of Cities in Ireland, of the Number of Civil Bill Ejectments Entered for Hearing in the Courts of the Assistant Barristers, or Chairmen, for Five Years previous to 1 Jan. 1851...* [and] *for Five Years previous to 1 Jan. 1861... Distinguishing the Number of Same Decreed, Dismissed, and Nilled in Each Respective Year*', HC 1861 (552), li. 677.

Copy *'of All Requisitions, Reports, Notices, and Correspondence from or to the Sheriff or Sub-Sheriff of the County of Donegal, and from or to Any Resident Magistrate, Officer of Constabulary, or Relieving Officer, and from or to the Chief or Under Secretary for Ireland, with Reference to a Recent Ejectment of the Lands of Derryveagh, in that County*', HC 1861 (249), lii. 559.

Copies *'of Any Correspondence that has Taken Place between J. G. Adair, Esq., and the Irish Government, on the Subject of Extra Police in the County of Donegal, and of Certain Evictions that have Taken Place in that County; and, Return of the Outrages Specially Reported by the Constabulary as Committed within the Barony of Kilmacrenan, in the County of Donegal, during the Last Ten Years*', HC 1861 (274), lii. 579.

Return, *'in Tabular Form, as to Each County and County of a Town or City in Ireland, of the Number of All Civil Bill Processes and Ejectments Entered for Hearing during the Year 1863*'... HC 1864 (410), xlviii. 559.

Return *'of All Civil Bill Ejectments Entered at the Suit of the Law Life Society before the Chairman of Quarter Sessions of the County of Mayo and the County of Galway, from Hilary Quarter Sessions 1852, up to the Present Time [21 Apr. 1864] Distinguishing the Ejectments of Each Year*', HC 1864 (275), l. 663.

Return *'of Ejectment Processes in the Barony of Farney Entered at Quarter Sessions in the Divisions of Carrickmacross and Castleblayney, County of Monaghan, in Each Year, from 1846 to 1856, distinguishing the Names of the Plaintiffs etc...*' HC 1866 (178), lviii. 95.

Returns *'in Tabular Form, of the Number of Original Civil Bill Ejectment Processes Entered, Heard, and Decided in Each of the Years 1866, 1867, 1868, 1869, and 1870, in and for the Several Counties of Ireland; Distinguishing those Brought for Non-Payment of Rent and on Notices to Quit, and the Number in Each Riding of the County of Cork...*' HC 1875 (260), lxii. 3. [Also gives ejectments and cases under the land act of 1870 for 1871–3.]

Summary '*of the Return Ordered to be Printed on 14 June 1875, Giving Separately the Totals of Columns 2, 3, and 4, for Each County for the Three Years 1868, 1869, and 1870, and for the Years 1871, 1872, and 1873*', HC 1875 (260-I), lxii. 99. [A summary of the preceding paper.]

Return '*of the Number of Stamps for Notices to Quit Issued by Each Stamp Distributor in Ireland from the Time of the Adoption of the Distinctive Die* [16 Oct. 1875] *to 1 June last* [1876]', HC 1876 (409), lx. 711.

Return in '*Tabular Form . . . of the Number of Civil Bill Ejectments, Other than Civil Bill Ejectments for Non-Payment of Rent, Entered, Tried, and Determined, in Each County in Ireland, for Each of the Three Years Ending 31 Dec. 1876*', HC 1878 (25), lxiii. 451.

Return '*of the Total Number of Ejectments Executed in Ireland for Non-Payment of Rent in the Years 1878 and 1879, Compiled from the Volume of Judicial Statistics for 1878, and the Forthcoming Volume for 1879*', HC 1880 (246), lx. 349.

Copy '*of Return Prepared from Reports Made to the Inspector-General of the Royal Irish Constabulary of Cases of Eviction which have Come under the Knowledge of the Constabulary, Showing the Number of Families Evicted in Each County in Ireland in Each of the Four Quarters of the Years 1877, 1878, 1879, First Quarter of the Year 1880, and up to 20 June 1880*', HC 1880 (254), lx. 361.

'*Returns Showing (1) the Number of Families Evicted in Each County in Ireland for Non-Payment of Rent, and the Number of These Families Readmitted as Caretakers for the Years 1877, 1878, 1879, and the Half-Year Ended 30 June 1880; and (2) the Number of Families Evicted for Non-Payment of Rent and Other Causes for the Quarter Ended 30 June 1880*', HC 1880 (317), lx. 367.

Return, '*in Tabular Form . . . of the Number of Civil Bill Ejectments, Distinguishing Ejectments on the Title from those for Non-Payment of Rent, Tried and Determined in Each County in Ireland, for Each of the Three Years Ending 31 Dec. 1879, Exclusive of Ejectments for Premises Situate in Counties of Cities, Boroughs, and Towns under the Act 9 Geo. IV, c. 82 etc*'; *Return,* '*in Tabular Form . . . of the Number of Actions of Ejectment in Superior Courts . . . for Each of the Three Years Ending 31 Dec. 1879 . . .*'; returns '*of the Number of Families Evicted in Each County, Otherwise than for Non-Payment of Rent, in Each of the Three Years Ending 31 Dec. 1879*'; [returns] '*for Each County, of the Number of Land Claims in the Court Certified, under Section 9 of the Land Act, that the Non-Payment of Rent Causing the Eviction had Arisen from the Rent Being an Exorbitant Rent*' . . . HC 1880 (132), lx. 379.

—— for 1877-80, HC 1881 (90) lxxvii. 685.

Return, '*by Provinces and Counties (Compiled from Returns Made to the Inspector-General, Royal Irish Constabulary) of Cases of Evictions which have Come to the Knowledge of the Constabulary in Each of the Years 1849 to 1880, inclusive*', HC 1881 (185), lxxvii. 725.

Return '*of the Number of Notices to Quit Served in the Respective Years from* [16 Oct. 1875] *to 1880, Inclusive, as Shown by the Stamps Issued of the Denomination Required for Such Notices According to the Provisions of the Land Act of 1870*', HC 1881 (53), lxxvii. 755.

Return '*(Compiled from Returns Made to the Inspector-General of the Royal Irish*

Constabulary) *of Cases of Eviction which have Come to the Knowledge of the Constabulary in Each Quarter of the Year Ending 31 Dec. 1880, Showing the Number of Families Evicted in Each County in Ireland during Each Quarter, Number Readmitted as Tenants, and the Number Readmitted as Caretakers'*, HC 1881 (2) lxxvii. 713.
—— to 31 Dec. 1881, HC 1882 (9), lv. 229.
—— to 31 Dec. 1882 [C 3465], HC 1883, lvi. 99.
—— Jan. to Mar. 1883, ibid. [C 3579], 107.
—— Apr. to June 1883, ibid. [C 3770], 111.
—— July to Sept. 1883 [C 3892], HC 1884, lxiv 407.
—— Oct. to Dec. 1883, ibid. [C 3892], 411.
—— Jan. to Mar. 1884, ibid. [C 3994], 416.
—— Apr. to June 1884, ibid. [C 4089], 419.
—— July to Sept. 1884 [C 4209], HC 1884–5, lxv. 29.
—— Oct. to Dec. 1884, ibid. [C 4300], 33.
—— Jan. to Mar. 1885, ibid. [C 4394], 37.
—— Apr. to June 1885, ibid. [C 4485], 41.
—— July to Sept. 1885 [C 4618], HC 1886, liv. 29.
—— Oct. to Dec. 1885, ibid. [C 4619], 33.
—— Jan. to Mar. 1886, ibid. [C 4920], 37.
—— Apr. to June 1886, ibid. [C 4875], 41.
—— July to Sept. 1886 [C 4946], HC 1887, lxviii. 51.
—— Oct. to Dec. 1886, ibid. [C 4947], 55.
—— Jan. to Mar. 1887, ibid. [C 5039], 59.
—— Apr. to June 1887, ibid. [C 5095], 63.
—— July to Sept. 1887 [C 5289], HC 1888, lxxxiii. 433.
—— Oct. to Dec. 1887, ibid. [C 5290], 437.
Return *'of the Number of Writs for Evictions, and for the Recovery of Rent, Issued out of Each Division of the High Court of Justice in Ireland, during Each Three Months, from 1 Jan. 1878 to the Present [31 Dec. 1885]'*, HC 1886 (105), liii. 401.

(d) Judicial Statistics

Judicial Statistics 1863. Ireland: pt. i, *Police, Criminal Proceedings, Prisons*; pt. ii, *Common Law, Equity, Civil and Canon Law* [3418], HC 1864, lvii. 653.
—— 1864 [3563], HC 1865, lii. 657.
—— 1865 [3705], HC 1866, lxviii. 697.
—— 1866 [3930], HC 1867, lxvi. 735; *Supplement to pt. ii, Statistics of Proceedings against Cottier Tenants; Civil Bill Ejectments, and Other Civil Bills Served, etc.* [4071-I], HC 1867–8 lxvii. 947.
—— 1867 [4071], HC 1867–8, lvii. 737.
—— 1868 [4203], HC 1868–9, lviii. 737.
—— 1869 [C 227], HC 1870, lxiii. 753.
—— 1870 [C 443], HC 1871, lxiv. 231.
—— 1871 [C 674], HC 1872, lxv. 235.
—— 1872 [C 851], HC 1873, lxx. 247.
—— 1873 [C 1034], HC 1874, lxxi. 251.

—— 1874 [C 1295], HC 1875, lxxxi. 259.
—— 1875 [C 1536], HC 1876, lxxix. 273.
—— 1876 [C 1822], HC 1877, lxxxvi. 261.
—— 1877 [C 2152], HC 1878, lxxix. 265.
—— 1878 [C 2429], HC 1878–9, lxvi. 569.
—— 1879 [C 2698], HC 1880, lxxvii. 251.
—— 1880 [C 3028], HC 1881, xcv. 243.
—— 1881 [C 3355], HC 1882, lxxv. 243.
—— 1882 [C 3803], HC 1883, lxxvii. 243.
—— 1883 [C 4181], HC 1884, lxxxvi. 243.
—— 1884 [C 4554], HC 1884–5, lxxxvi. 243.
—— 1885 [C 4796], HC 1886, lxxii. 233.
—— 1886 [C 5177], HC 1887, xc. 241.

(e) Agrarian Outrages

A Return 'of the Number of Murders and Waylayings in the Baronies of Upper and Lower Fews, in the County of Armagh, during the Last Six Years; Distinguishing by Name the Persons Killed and Waylaid, and the Place Where the Offence Occurred; also, Giving the Numbers Arrested for Each Offence, and the Result of Any Trial of the Same'; and, 'Copies of the Depositions Taken by the Coroner of Armagh County, at the Inquest Held on the Body of the Late Mr Maulever', HC 1850 (566), li. 517.

Report from the Select Committee on Outrages (Ireland); together with the Proceedings of the Committee, Minutes of Evidence, Appendix and Index, HC 1852 (438), xiv. 1 (Joseph Napier, chairman).

A Return 'of the Number of Murders, Waylayings, Assaults, Threatening Notices, Incendiary Fires, or Other Crimes of an Agrarian Character, Reported by the Constabulary within the Counties of Louth, Armagh, and Monaghan, since 1 Jan. 1849; Distinguishing by Name the Persons Murdered and Waylaid; also, Stating the Numbers Arrested for Each Offence; whether Informations have been Sworn in the Case, and the Result of Any Trial of the Same', HC 1852 (448), xlvii. 465.

Report from the Select Committee of the House of Lords, Appointed to Consider the Consequences of Extending the Functions of the Constabulary in Ireland to the Suppression or Prevention of Illicit Distillation; and to Report Thereon to the House; together with the Minutes of Evidence, and an Appendix and Index, HC 1854 (53), x. 1 (Lord Monteagle, chairman).

Copies 'of Correspondence that has Taken Place between the Irish Government and the Magistrates of the County of Donegal, Relative to the Liberation on Ticket of Leave of Miles Sweeney, a Man Convicted in 1851', HC 1854 (417), liv. 605.

A Return 'of the Outrages Specially Reported by the Constabulary as Committed within the Barony of Kilmacrenan, County Donegal [1851–61], Specifying the Nature of Each Offence etc....' HC 1861 (404), lii. 585.

A Return 'of the Number of Sheep Supposed to have been Killed by Dogs in Each Constabulary District in Ireland, from 1 Jan. 1861 to 1 Jan. 1862', HC 1862 (323), xlvi. 477.

Copy 'of a Resolution on the Subject of the Irish Constabulary, Adopted by the Grand Jury of County of Tipperary, Assembled at Clonmel at the Last Special Commission for that County', HC 1862 (443), xlvi. 481.

Return 'of All Schoolmasters Arrested in Ireland for Ribbonism, Sedition, or Connection with the Fenian Conspiracy, from 1 Jan. 1860 to the Latest Date Ascertainable [9 Apr. 1866]...' HC 1866 (455), lviii. 475.

Copy 'of the Circular Issued to the Irish Magistrates by the Government in which Attention was Directed to the Whiteboy Acts', HC 1867 (201), lix. 377.

Return 'of the Number of Agrarian Murders and Outrages in Ireland Reported to the Inspector-General of Constabulary during the Six Months Ending 1 Dec. 1866; Specifying the Number of Cases in which the Authors of the Crimes have been Made Amenable to Justice', HC 1868–9 (266), li. 411. [Includes a similar return for the period 1 Jan. 1867 to 10 May 1869.]

Copy 'of the Resolutions and Suggestions Made at a Meeting of the Magistrates [24 Mar. 1869] Called by the Vice Lieutenant of Westmeath County, after the Murder of Mr Anketell, Station Master at Mullingar, and Presented to his Excellency the Lord-Lieutenant of Ireland...' HC 1868–9 (215), li. 413.

Return of Outrages Reported to the Constabulary Office in Ireland, during the Year 1869, with Summaries for Preceding Years; and Return of Outrages Reported by the Constabulary in Ireland in the Months of January and February, 1870 [C 60], HC 1870, lvii. 353.

—— for 1870 and for Jan. to Mar. 1871 [C 332], HC 1871, lviii. 477.

Report from the Select Committee on Westmeath, etc. (Unlawful Combinations); together with the Proceedings of the Committee, Minutes of Evidence, and Appendix [and index], HC 1871 (147), xiii. 547 (marquis of Hartington, chairman).

Return 'Showing All Crimes against Human Life, Firing into Dwelling Houses, Administering Unlawful Oaths, Demands for Money, Threatening Letters, or Other Intimidation, Incendiary Fires, Robbery of Arms, etc., which have been Reported by the Royal Irish Constabulary, between 1 Mar. 1878 and 31 Dec. 1879... Distinguishing as far as Possible Agrarian Crimes, and Showing (1) Number and Names of Persons Convicted, (2) Number and Names of Persons Made Amenable, but not Convicted, (3) Number of Cases in which No Person was made Amenable', HC 1880 (6), lx. 1.

Returns 'of Outrages Reported to the Royal Irish Constabulary Office from 1 Jan. 1844 to 31 Dec. 1880', [C 2756], HC 1881, lxxvii. 887. [Gives monthly returns of homicides, threatening letters, etc.]

—— from Jan. 1880 to Jan. 1882, HC 1882 (7), lv. 615.

—— Jan. 1882 to Jan. 1883, HC 1883 (6), lvii. 1047.

Memorandum 'as to the Principle upon which Outrages are Recorded as Agrarian, and Included as Such in the Returns Laid before Parliament', HC 1887 (140), lxviii. 25.

(f) Returns under Crime and Outrage Acts, etc.

Copy 'of Any Report from the Lord-Lieutenant of Ireland to the Secretary of State for the Home Department, with Reference to the Late Proclaiming of a District in the County of Down, under Act 11 & 12 Vict. c. 21', HC 1851 (250), l. 435.

Returns 'of the Baronies in Each of the Several Counties in Ireland in which

Proclamations are Now in Force under the Crime and Outrage Act . . . and, of the Number of Licences to Keep Arms that have been Withdrawn . . . since 1 Jan. 1850', HC 1852–3 (805), xciv. 261.

A Return *'of the Several Counties or Districts, or Baronies of Counties, in Ireland, Proclaimed under the Provisions of the Crime and Outrage Act, from the Period of the Passing of that Act in 1847 to its Discontinuance in the Session of 1856; Specifying the Particular Crime or Outrage for which Each Particular County, District, or Barony, was so Proclaimed, the Date of Each Such Proclamation, and Likewise of the Withdrawal of Such Proclamation';* . . . *'and Similar Return Respecting the Peace Preservation Act, Passed in 1856, and to Expire in 1860'*, HC 1860 (195), lvii. 849.

Return *'Specifying the Date or Dates upon which the Barony of Farney, County Monaghan, was Proclaimed under "the Act for Preventing Crime and Outrage in Ireland"; the Date or Dates upon which Such Proclamation or Proclamations were Revoked; the Date on which the General Election for Said County was Held in the Year 1865; also the Date or Dates upon which the Barony in Question or the Whole of the County of Monaghan was Again Proclaimed under the Peace Preservation Act of Ireland'*, HC 1866 (208), lviii. 421.

Return *'of All Counties or Parts of Counties in Ireland Proclaimed under the Peace Preservation (Ireland) Act, and the Number of Licenses Issued in Each District . . .'* HC 1866 (359), lviii. 435

Returns *'of the Number of All Persons in Custody in Ireland under the Habeas Corpus Suspension Act who were Released from Imprisonment between 1 Feb. 1866 and 1 Mar. 1867* . . . *, and, of the Number Arrested in Ireland under the Habeas Corpus Suspension Act from 1 Feb. 1866 to 1 Mar. 1867* . . .*'* HC 1867 (304), lvii. 729.

Return of *'Outrages Reported to the Office of the Chief Secretary in Dublin to have Taken Place in the King's County, and the Counties of Westmeath, Meath, and Tipperary, since the Passing of the Peace Preservation Act (1870)'* [from Apr. 1870 to Feb. 1871], HC 1871, lviii (76). 473.

Returns *'Specifying the Districts in Ireland to which the Provisions of the Peace Preservation (Ireland) Act (1870), have been Applied as "Proclaimed Districts", Distinguishing Such Districts as have been Specially Proclaimed under Part II of the Same Act'; 'and, of All Arrests which have been Made under the Authority of the Same Act, of All Orders which have been Made under the Provisions of the Same, whether Made by the Lord-Lieutenant of Ireland, or by Justices of the Peace, and of All Grand Jury Presentments Made in Cases of Murder, Maiming, or Other Personal Injury under the Provisions of the Same Act'* [to 2 Mar. 1871], HC 1871 (239), lviii. 517.

—— to 9 May 1873, HC 1873 (207), liv. 391; ibid. (207-I), 399.

Copy of Orders and Regulations Made by the Lord-Lieutenant; and, List of Persons Detained under the Warrant of the Lord-Lieutenant under Part I of the *'Protection of Life & Property in Certain Parts of Ireland Act, 1871'*, HC 1871 (342), lviii. 525.

List of Persons Detained in Prison under the Warrant of the Lord-Lieutenant under the Authority of Part I of *'the Protection of Life & Property in Certain Parts of Ireland Act, 1871'*, on 1 Aug. 1871, HC 1871 (432), lviii. 529.

—— on 1 Aug. 1872, HC 1872 (381), l. 275.

—— on 1 Mar. 1873, HC 1873 (92), liv. 407.
—— on 1 July 1873, HC 1873 (298), liv. 405.
—— on 1 Apr. 1874, HC 1874 (91), liv. 527.
Returns 'of the Number of Searches Made during the Past Two Years in the County of Westmeath, under Section 15 of the Peace Preservation Act, and the Result of Such Searches'; and 'of the Number of Persons Arrested for Being out of their Houses at Prohibited Hours, and what was Done with them', HC 1873 (321), liv. 403.
Returns 'Specifying as to Each County and County of City or Town in Ireland, the Portions which are at Present [20 Apr. 1874] under the Operation of Proclamations under the Peace Preservation Acts, or Any of them, Distinguishing in Each Case the Districts which are Specially Proclaimed under the Second Part of the Peace Preservation Act, 1870...' HC 1874 (231), liv. 529.
Return 'of All Applications Made to the Grand Jury of Each County in Ireland for Compensation, under the Ninth Section of the Peace Preservation Act, Specifying the Names of Applicants, the Cause for which Compensation was Claimed, and the Amount Applied for...' HC 1875 (449), lxii. 159.
Return 'of All Warrants Issued by the Lord-Lieutenant or Other Chief Governor of Ireland, since 1 Jan. 1865, Requiring Any Collector of Grand Jury Cess to Levy and Collect Any Sum for Additional Police in Any Proclaimed District...' HC 1875 (450), lxii. 169.
Return 'of All Arrests Made under "the Protection of Life and Property Act, 1871", since the Passing of the Act, Distinguishing Nature of Offence; Duration of Imprisonment; County and Parish', HC 1875 (180), lxii. 183.
Return, 'for Each County in Ireland, of the Portions of Such County which are Now Exempt from the Operation of Any Proclamations under Any of the Acts Known as the Peace Preservation Act, or under "the Protection of Life & Property in Certain Parts of Ireland Act, 1871"...' [on 27 Feb. 1877]. HC 1877 (167), lxix. 605.
—— on 7 Aug. 1878, HC 1878–9 (70), lix. 369.

(g) *Agricultural Statistics, 1847–1886*

Returns of Agricultural Produce in Ireland, in the Year 1847 [923], HC 1847–8, lvii. 1; pt. ii, stock [1000], ibid. 109.
—— 1848 [1116], HC 1849, xlix. 1.
—— 1849 [1245], HC 1850, li. 39.
—— 1850 [1404], HC 1851, l. 1.
The Census of Ireland for the Year 1851, pt. ii, Returns of Agricultural Produce in 1851 [1589], HC 1852–3, xciii. 1.
Returns of Agricultural Produce in Ireland, in the Year 1852 [1714], HC 1854, lvii. 1.
—— 1853 [1865], HC 1854–5, xlvii. 1.
—— 1854 [2017], HC 1856, liii. 1.
—— 1855 [2174], HC 1857, sess. 1, xv. 81.
—— 1856 [2289], HC 1857–8, lvi. 1.
The Agricultural Statistics of Ireland for the Year 1857 [2461], HC 1859, sess. 1, xxvi. 57.

The Agricultural Statistics of Ireland for the Year 1858 [2599], HC 1860, lxvi. 55.
—— 1859 [2763], HC 1861, lxii. 73.
—— 1860 [2997], HC 1862, lx. 137.
—— 1861 [3156], HC 1863, lxix. 547.
—— 1862 [3286], HC 1864, lix. 327.
—— 1863 [3456], HC 1865, lv. 125.
—— 1864 [3766], HC 1867, lxxi. 201.
—— 1865 [3929], HC 1867, lxxi. 491.
—— 1866 [3958-II], HC 1867-8, lxx. 255.
—— 1867 [4113-II], HC 1868-9, lxii. 645.
—— 1868 [C 3], HC 1870, lxviii. 439.
—— 1869 [C 239], HC 1871, lxix. 347.
—— 1870 [C 463], HC 1872, lxiii. 299.
—— 1871 [C 762], HC 1873, lxix. 375.
—— 1872 [C 880], HC 1874, lxix. 199.
—— 1873 [C 1125], HC 1875, lxxix. 131.
—— 1874 [C 1380], HC 1876, lxxviii. 131.
—— 1875 [C 1568], HC 1876, lxxviii. 413.
—— 1876 [C 1749], HC 1877, lxxxv. 529.
—— 1877 [C 1938], HC 1878, lxxvii. 511.
—— 1878 [C 2347], HC 1878-9, lxxv. 587.
—— 1879 [C 2534], HC 1880, lxxvi. 815.
—— 1880 [C 2932], HC 1881, xciii. 685.
—— 1881 [C 3332], HC 1882, lxxiv. 93.
—— 1882 [C 3677], HC 1883, lxxvi. 825.
—— 1883 [C 4069], HC 1884, lxxxv. 313.
—— 1884 [C 4489], HC 1884-5, lxxxv. 1.
—— 1885 [C 4802], HC 1886, lxxi. 1.

3. OFFICIAL PUBLICATIONS

A Collection of the Public General Statutes, Passed... in the Reign of Her Majesty Queen Victoria... London, 1848-1887.
General Valuation of Rateable Property in Ireland... Dublin, 1849-64. [There are collections in the National Library of Ireland, the library of Trinity College, Dublin, the National Archives, and the Public Record Office of Northern Ireland. Each collection is bound in a different way.]
Hansard's Parliamentary Debates: Forming a Continuation of the 'Parliamentary History of England, from the Earliest Times to the Year 1803'. 3rd series, 356 vols. London, 1831-91.

4. NEWSPAPERS

The Ballinrobe Chronicle and Mayo Advertiser
Ballymena Observer
The [Irish] Farmers' Gazette and Journal of Practical Husbandry
Freeman's Journal
The Galway Vindicator and Connaught Advertiser

Impartial Reporter
The Irish Law Times and Solicitors' Journal: A Weekly Newspaper, and Gazette of Legal Proceedings
The Irishman
The Londonderry Standard
The Mayo Constitution
The Nation
The Northern Whig
The Penny Dispatch
Saunders's News-Letter and Daily Advertiser
The Tipperary Advocate
The Tipperary Free Press
The Warder

5. CONTEMPORARY WORKS

ALLINGHAM, WILLIAM, *Laurence Bloomfield in Ireland: A Modern Poem* (London and Cambridge, 1864).

ANKETELL, WILLIAM ROBERT, *Landlord and Tenant: Ireland. Letters by a Land Agent on: I Agricultural Leases, II Tenants' Improvements, III Tenant Right, IV Fixity of Tenure, V Tenants' Claims, VI Covenants, VII Capricious Evictions, VIII Valuation Rents, Corn Rents, IX Peasant Proprietorship, X Settled Estates—Montgomery's Act, XI Scotch Land Tenure, XII the Irish Land—Mr Campbell's Proposals, XIII Landlord and Tenant—an Agent's Proposal. Appendix: A Model Case of Ulster Tenant Right* (Belfast, 1869).

BAILEY, W. F., 'The Ulster Tenant Right Custom; its Origins, Characteristics and Position under the Land Acts', *Jn. Stat. Soc. Ire.* 10 (1893-4), 12-22.

BALDWIN, THOMAS, *An Introduction to Practical Farming*, 7th edn. (Dublin, 1880).

—— *Handy Book of Small Farm Management* (Dublin, [1871]).

BALL, JOHN, *What Is to be Done for Ireland?*, 2nd edn. (London, 1849).

BARRINGTON, RICHARD M., 'The Prices of Some Agricultural Produce and Cost of Farm Labour for the Past Fifty Years', *Jn. Stat. Soc. Ire.* 9 (1886-7), 137-53.

—— 'Notes of the Prices of Irish Agricultural Produce Illustrated by Diagrams', *Jn. Stat. Soc. Ire.* 9 (1892-3), 679-702.

BARRY, JAMES F., *A Chapter of Irish History; or, Land Tenure in Ireland* (Dublin and London, n.d.).

BAXTER, ROBERT, *The Irish Tenant Right Question Examined by a Comparison of the Law and Practice of England with Law and Practice of Ireland* (London, 1869).

BAYLDON, JOHN, *Bayldon's Art of Valuing Rents and Tillages, and the Tenant's Right on Entering and Quitting Farms...*, corrected and revised by John Donaldson, 6th edn. (London, 1844).

BEDFORD, eleventh duke of. See Russell, H. A.

BENCE JONES, WILLIAM, *The Life's Work in Ireland of a Landlord who Tried to Do his Duty* (London, 1880).

BLACKWOOD, FREDERICK TEMPLE HAMILTON-TEMPLE-, first marquis of Dufferin and Ava, *Contributions to an Inquiry into the Present State of Ireland* (London, 1866).

—— *Irish Emigration and the Tenure of Land in Ireland* (London, 1867).
[Bombay civilian,] *The Land Question in Ireland, Viewed by a Bombay Civilian* (London and Dublin, 1870).
BROWN, ROBERT E., *The Book of the Landed Estate* (London and Edinburgh, 1869).
BROWNRIGG, SIR HENRY JOHN, *Examination of Some Recent Allegations Concerning the Constabulary Force in Ireland, in a Report to his Excellency the Lord-Lieutenant* (Dublin, 1864).
BUTLER, THOMAS, *The Agricultural Output of Ireland, 1908. Report and Tables prepared in Connection with Census of Production Act, 1906* (London, 1912).
BUTT, ISAAC, *Land Tenure in Ireland: A Plea for the Celtic Race* (Dublin, 1866).
—— *The Irish People and the Irish Land* (Dublin, 1867).
—— *A Practical Treatise on the New Law of Compensation to Tenants in Ireland, and the Other Provisions of the Landlord and Tenant Act, 1870; with an Appendix of Statutes and Rules* (Dublin, 1871).
CAIRD, SIR JAMES, *High Farming under Liberal Covenants, the Best Substitute for Protection*, 3rd edn. (Edinburgh and London, 1849).
—— *The Irish Land Question*, 2nd edn. (London, 1869).
CAMPBELL, GEORGE, *The Irish Land* (London and Dublin, 1869).
—— *The Progress of the Land Bill* (London, 1870).
CARLETON, J. W., *The Jurisdiction and Procedure of the County Courts in Ireland* (Dublin, 1878).
CHERRY, RICHARD R., and WAKELY, JOHN, *The Irish Land Law and Land Purchase Acts, 1881, 1885 and 1887* (Dublin, 1888).
CLIFFE LESLIE, T. E., *Land Systems and Industrial Economy of Ireland, England, and Continental Countries* (London, 1870).
CLIVE, GEORGE, *Some Evidence on the Irish Land Question* (Hereford, 1870).
CONNOLLY, JAMES, 'Notes of Some Points in Irish Agricultural Statistics', *Jn. Stat. Soc. Ire.* 7 (1878), 254–6.
COULTER, HENRY, *The West of Ireland: Its Existing Condition and Prospects* (Dublin, [1862]).
DAVITT, MICHAEL, *The Fall of Feudalism in Ireland: Or the Story of the Land League Revolution* (London and New York, 1904).
DEAN, GEORGE ALFRED, *A Treatise on the Land Tenure of Ireland, and Influences which Retard Irish Progress* (London, 1869).
DE LASTEYRIE, JULES, *A Few Observations upon Ireland. Translated from the* Revue des deux mondes, *15 Dec. 1860 by C.E.H. and F.H.N., and Dedicated, with Permission, to his Grace the Duke of Leinster* (Dublin, 1861).
DE LAVERGNE, LÉONCE, *The Rural Economy of England, Scotland and Ireland* (London and Edinburgh, 1855).
DE MOLEYNS, THOMAS, *The Landlord's and Agent's Practical Guide*, 1st edn. (Dublin, 1860); 2nd edn. (Dublin, 1860); 4th edn. (Dublin, 1862); 6th edn. (Dublin, 1872); 7th edn. (Dublin, 1877). ['landlord' was replaced by 'landowner' in the title after the 1st edn.]
—— *The Landed Property Improvement and Landlord and Tenant Consolidation Act, 23 & 24 Vict. cc 153 and 154* (Dublin, 1860). [This work is described as the 3rd edn. of *The Landowner's Practical Guide*.]
DENTON, J. BAILEY, *The Farm Homesteads of England* (London, 1864).

DONNELL, ROBERT, *Practical Guide to the Law of Tenant Compensation and Farm Purchase under the Irish Land Act* (London, 1871).
—— *Chapters on the Leaseholders' Claim to Tenant Right and Other Tenant Right Questions, with Land Act Reports* (Dublin, 1873).
—— *Reports of One Hundred and Ninety Cases in the Irish Land Courts; with Preliminary Tenant Right Chapters* (Dublin, 1876).
DUFFERIN, first marquis of. See Blackwood.
FERGUSON, WILLIAM DWYER, AND VANCE, ANDREW, *The Tenure and Improvement of Land in Ireland, Considered with Reference to the Relation of Landlord and Tenant and Tenant Right* (Dublin, 1851).
FISHER, JOSEPH, *The Position and Prospects of Ireland* (Waterford, 1855).
—— *How Ireland may be Saved; or the Injurious Effects of the Present System of Agriculture on the Prosperity of Ireland and the Social Position of the Irish People* (London, 1862).
FITZGERALD, JAMES F. V., *A Practical Guide to the Valuation of Rent in Ireland; with an Appendix Containing some Extracts from the Instructions Issued to Valuators in 1853, by the Late Sir R [ichard] Griffith, bt.* (Dublin, 1881).
—— *Some Practical Suggestions Concerning the Land Law (Ireland) Bill. [For private circulation only]*, (Dublin, 1881).
FITZGIBBON, GERALD, *The Land Difficulty of Ireland* (London and Dublin, 1869).
FURLONG, JOSEPH SMITH, *A Treatise of the Law of Landlord and Tenant as Administered in Ireland* (Dublin, 1845).
—— *The Law of Landlord and Tenant as Administered in Ireland*, 2nd edn. by Edmund R. Digues La Touche (2 vols.; Dublin, 1869).
GAMBLE, L. W., *Compensation for Improvements Made by Tenants in Ireland. When and How Far it should be Secured by Law* (London, 1867).
GODKIN, JAMES, *The Land War in Ireland* (London, 1869).
GRAY, SIR JOHN, *The Irish Land Question: Speech of Sir John Gray, Delivered in the Free Trade Hall, Manchester, on 18 October 1869* (London and Dublin, 1869).
GRIFFITH, RICHARD, *Outline of the System according to Which the General Valuation of Ireland under 6 & 7 Wm IV, cap. 84 is Carried into Effect* (Dublin, 1844).
—— *Instructions to Valuators and Surveyors Appointed under 15th and 16th Vict., cap. 63, for the Uniform Valuation of Lands and Tenements in Ireland* (Dublin, 1853).
GRIMSHAW, THOMAS WRIGLEY, *Facts and Figures about Ireland, Comprising a Summary and Analysis of the Principal Statistics of Ireland for the fifty years, 1841–90* (London and Dublin, 1893).
—— 'A Statistical Survey of Ireland from 1840 to 1888', *Jn. Stat. Soc. Ire.* 9 (1888), 321–61.
HAMILTON, JOHN, *Sixty Years' Experience as an Irish Landlord: Memoirs of John Hamilton, DL, of St Ernan's, Donegal* (London, [1894]).
HANCOCK, WILLIAM NEILSON, *The Tenant Right of Ulster, Considered Economically...* (Dublin, 1845).
—— *Impediments to the Prosperity of Ireland* (London, 1850).
—— *Report on the Supposed Progressive Decline of Irish Prosperity* (Dublin, 1863).
—— *Report on the Landlord and Tenant Question in Ireland, from 1860 till 1866; with an Appendix, Containing a Report on the Question from 1835* (Dublin, 1866).

—— *Report on the State of Ireland in 1874* (Dublin, 1874).
HENDERSON, W. D., *The Irish Land Bill* (Belfast, 1870).
HERON, DENIS CAULFIELD, 'Historical Statistics of Ireland', *Jn. Stat. Soc. Ire.* 3 (1862), 235-7.
—— *Historical Statistics of Ireland*, 2nd edn. (London, 1863).
HEWITT, JAMES, third Viscount Lifford, *Thoughts on the Present State of Ireland* (London, 1849).
HILLARY, SIR AUGUSTUS W., *A Letter to the Rt. Hon. Lord John Russell, First Lord of the Treasury, Suggesting a Plan for the Adjustment of the Relation between Landlord and Tenant in Ireland* (London and Dublin, 1849).
HUSSEY, S. M., *The Reminiscences of an Irish Land Agent* (London, 1904).
HUTTON, HENRY DIX, 'The Land Question Viewed as a Sociological Problem', *Jn. Stat. Soc. Ire.* 3 (1862), 293-313.
—— *The Prussian Land Tenure Reform and a Farmer-Proprietary for Ireland* (Dublin, 1867).
—— *History, Principle, and Fact, in Relation to the Irish Question* (London and Dublin, 1870).
—— *Handy Book of Farm Tenure and Purchase under the Landlord and Tenant (Ireland) Act, 1870* (Dublin, 1870).
[Irish Constabulary,] *The Constabulary Manual; or Guide to the Discharge of Police Duties* (Dublin, 1866).
—— *Standing Rules and Regulations for the Government and Guidance of the Royal Irish Constabulary*, 3rd edn. (Dublin, 1872).
[Irish Land Agent,] *A Demurrer to Mr Butt's Plea by an Irish Land Agent* (Dublin, 1867).
[Irish Landlord,] *Fixity of Tenure, a Dialogue. By an Irish Landlord* (London, 1870).
The Irish Land Question and the Twelve London Companies in the County of Londonderry (Belfast, 1869).
[Irish Peer,] *The Irish Difficulty by an Irish Peer* (Dublin, 1867).
JOHNSTON, WILLIAM [of Ballykilbeg,] *Ribbonism, and its Remedy: A Letter Addressed to the Rt. Hon. the Earl of Derby, First Lord of the Treasury* (Dublin, 1858).
LANSDOWNE, sixth marquis of. See Petty-Fitzmaurice.
LANKTREE, JOHN, *The Elements of Land Valuation, with Copious Instructions as to the Qualifications and Duties of Valuators* (Dublin and Edinburgh, 1853).
LAVELLE, FR. PATRICK, *The Irish Landlord since the Revolution* (Dublin, 1870).
—— *The War in Partry; or, Proselytism and Eviction on the Part of Bishop Plunket of Tuam* (Dublin, 1861).
—— *Partry and Glenveagh: A Letter to the Rt. Hon. E. W. Cardwell, MP, Chief Secretary for Ireland* (Dublin, 1861).
LEADHAM, I. S., *Coercive Measures in Ireland, 1830-1880* (London, [1880]).
LE QUESNE, CHARLES, *Ireland and the Channel Isles; or, a Remedy for Ireland* (London, 1848).
'LEX', *Doings in Partry: A Chapter of Irish History in a Letter to the Rt. Hon. the Earl of Derby, KG* (London, 1860).
LIFFORD, third Viscount. See Hewitt.
[LOCKE, JOHN,] *Ireland: Observations on the People, the Land and the Law, in 1851; with Especial Reference to the Policy, Practice and Results of the*

Incumbered Estates Court. Appendices, Tables, 3rd edn. (Dublin and London, 1852).

LONGFIELD, MOUNTIFORT, 'Address by the President, Hon. Judge Longfield, at the Opening of the Eighteenth Session', *Jn. Stat. Soc. Ire.* 4 (1865), 129-54.

—— *Systems of Land Tenure in Various Countries: Series of Essays Published under the Sanction of the Cobden Club* (London, 1870).

MACAULAY, JAMES, *Ireland in 1872: A Tour of Observation. With remarks on Irish Public Questions* (London, 1873).

MACDONALD, DUNCAN GEORGE FORBES, *Estate Management (New Edition of 'Hints on Farming' in a Separate Volume),* 10th edn. (London, 1868).

MACDONALD, W., 'On the Relative Profits to the Farmer from Horse, Cattle, and Sheep Breeding', *Journal of the Royal Agricultural Society of England,* 12 (1876), 1-11.

MCDONNELL, RANDAL W., 'Statistics of Irish prosperity', *Jn. Stat. Soc. Ire.* 3 (1862), 268-78.

[MACDONNELL, ROBERT,] *Irish Nationality in 1870, by a Protestant Celt,* 2nd edn. (London and Dublin, 1870).

MACLAGAN, PETER, *Land Tenure and Land Culture in Ireland* (London and Edinburgh, 1869).

MALONE, SYLVESTER, *Tenant Wrong in a Nutshell; or, a History of Kilkee in Relation to Landlordism during the Last Seven Years* (Dublin, 1867).

MILLER, THOMAS, *The Agricultural and Social State of Ireland* (Dublin, 1858).

MOSSE, R. B., *Ireland, its State, its Evils, and its Remedies: A Letter Addressed to the Rt. Hon. the Earl of Roden, KP* (London, 1849).

MULHALL, MICHAEL G., *History of Prices since the year 1850* (London, 1885).

—— *Dictionary of Statistics* (London, 1884); 2nd edn. (London, 1892).

O'BRIEN, R. BARRY, *The Parliamentary History of the Irish Land Question, from 1829 to 1869; and the Origin and Results of the Ulster Custom* (London, 1880).

O'CONNOR MORRIS, WILLIAM, *Letters on the Land Question of Ireland* (London, 1870).

—— *The Irish Land Act, 33 & 34 Vict., cap. 46, with a Full Commentary and Notes* (Dublin, 1870).

PETTY-FITZMAURICE, H. W. E., sixth marquis of Lansdowne, *Glanerought and the Petty-Fitzmaurices* (London, 1937).

PIM, JONATHAN, *The Land Question in Ireland: Suggestions for its Solution by the Application of Mercantile Principles to Dealings with Land* (Dublin, 1867).

PORTER, J. G. V., *The State of Ireland in 1866: Its Chief Evils, and their Best Possible Remedies* (Dublin and London, 1866).

PRINGLE, R. O., 'A Review of Irish Agriculture', *Journal of the Royal Agricultural Society of England,* 8 (1872), 1-76.

PURDON, W. S., *Purdon's Practical Farmer, the Principles and Practice of Agriculture, including Tillage Farming and Management of Stock* (Dublin, 1863).

REARDON, THOMAS D., AND ROCHE, CECIL R., *The Irish Land Code and Labourers' Acts* (Dublin, 1886).

RICHEY, ALEXANDER G., *The Irish Land Laws* (London, 1880).

ROSS, DAVID, 'The Tenant Right of Ulster, What it is, and How Far it should be Legalized and Extended to the Other Provinces of Ireland', *Jn. Stat. Soc. Ire.* 3: 24 (July 1863), 390-404.

RUSSELL, H. A., eleventh duke of Bedford, *A Great Agricultural State, Being the Story of the Origin and Administration of Woburn and Thorney* (London, 1897).
RUSSELL, ROBERT, *Ulster Tenant Right for Ireland; or, Notes upon Notes Taken During a Visit to Ireland in 1868*, 2nd edn. (London and Edinburgh, 1870).
SAMUELSON, BERNHARD, *Studies of the Land and Tenantry of Ireland* (London, 1870).
SENIOR, NASSAU WILLIAM, *Journals, Conversations, and Essays Relating to Ireland* (2 vols.; (London, 1868).
SIGERSON, GEORGE, *History of the Land Tenures and Land Classes of Ireland, with an Account of the Various Secret Agrarian Confederacies* (London and Dublin, 1871).
SPROULE, JOHN, *Facts and Observations on the Irish Land Question* (Dublin, 1870).
—— *A Chapter of Irish Landlordism* (Dublin, 1873).
STEPHENS, HENRY, *The Book of the Farm*, 2nd edn. (2 vols.; Edinburgh and London, 1851).
THOMPSON, H. S., *Ireland in 1839 and 1869* (London and Dublin, 1870).
TRENCH, GEORGE F., *Are the Landlords Worth Preserving? or, Forty Years Management of an Irish Estate* (London and Dublin, 1881).
TRENCH, WILLIAM STEUART, *Realities of Irish Life* (London, 1868).

6. WORKS OF REFERENCE

BATEMAN, JOHN, *The Great Landowners of Great Britain and Ireland*, 4th edn. (London, 1883); repr. with an introduction by David Spring (Leicester, 1971).
BENCE-JONES, MARK, *Burke's Guide to Country Houses*, i. *Ireland* (London, 1978).
BURGH, U. H. HUSSEY DE, *The Landowners of Ireland: An Alphabetical List of the Owners of Estates of 500 Acres or £500 Valuation and upwards, in Ireland* (Dublin, 1881).
BURKE, SIR BERNARD, *A Genealogical and Heraldic History of the Landed Gentry of Great Britain and Ireland*, 6th edn. with supplement (2 vols.; London, 1882).
COCKAYNE, G. E., *Complete Peerage of England, Scotland, Ireland, etc., Extant, Extinct, or Dormant* (8 vols.; Exeter, 1887–98); rev. edn. by Vicary Gibbs and others (13 vols.; London, 1910–49).
STEPHEN, LESLIE, and LEE, SIR SIDNEY, *Dictionary of National Biography from the Earliest Times to 1900* (63 vols.; London, 1885–1900); Supplement (3 vols.; 1901); repr. (22 vols., 1908–9).
Thom's Almanac and Official Directory of the United Kingdom and Ireland (Dublin, 1845–).

7. MODERN WORKS

BARRINGTON, THOMAS, 'A Review of Irish Agricultural Prices', *Jn. Stat. Soc. Ire.* pt. 101 [1925–7], 249–80.
BELL, J[ONATHAN], 'The Improvement of Irish Farming Techniques since 1750: Theory and Practice', in Patrick O'Flanagan, Paul Ferguson, Kevin Whelan (eds.), *Rural Ireland, 1600–1900: Modernization and Change* (Cork, 1987), 24–41.
BELL, JONATHAN, and WATSON, MERVYN, *Irish Farming: Implements and Techniques, 1750–1900* (Edinburgh, 1986).
BEW, PAUL, *Land and the National Question in Ireland, 1858–82* (Dublin, 1978).
—— 'The Land League Ideal: Achievement and Contradictions', in P. J. Drudy

(ed.), *Irish Studies*, 2. *Ireland: Land, Politics and People* (Cambridge, 1982), 77–92.
—— and WRIGHT, FRANK, 'The Agrarian Opposition in Ulster Politics, 1848–87', in Clark and Donnelly (eds.), *Irish peasants: Violence and Political Unrest, 1780–1914* (Manchester, 1983), 192–229.
BLACK, R. D. COLLISON, *Economic Thought and the Irish Question, 1817–1870* (Cambridge, 1960).
—— *A Catalogue of Pamphlets on Economic Subjects, Published between 1750 and 1900 and Now Housed in Irish Libraries* (Belfast, 1969).
BOYLE, JOHN W., 'A Marginal Figure: The Irish Rural Laborer', in Clarke and Donnelly (eds.), *Irish Peasants: Violence and Political Unrest 1780–1914* (Manchester, 1983), 311–38.
BRADY, J. C., 'English Law and Irish Land in the Nineteenth Century', *Northern Ireland Legal Quarterly*, 23:1 (Spring 1972), 24–47.
—— 'Legal Developments, 1801–79', in W. E. Vaughan (ed.), *A New History of Ireland*, v. *Ireland under the Union, I. 1801–70* (Oxford, 1989), 451–81.
BRADY, SEAMAS, 'The Secret Diaries of Lord Leitrim', *Irish Press*, 2–7 Oct. 1967.
BUCKLEY, K., 'The Fixing of Rents by Agreement in Co. Galway, 1881–5', *IHS* 7: 27 (Mar. 1951), 149–79.
BURN, W. L., 'Free Trade in Land: An Aspect of the Irish question', *Trans. Royal Hist. Soc.* 4th ser. 31 (1949), 61–74.
CLARK, SAMUEL, 'The Social Composition of the Land League', *IHS*, 17: 68 (Sept. 1971), 447–69.
—— 'The Political Mobilization of Irish Farmers', *Canadian Review of Sociology and Anthropology*, 22: 4, pt. 2 (Nov. 1975), 483–99.
—— *Social Origins of the Irish Land War* (Princeton, NJ, 1979).
—— 'The Importance of Agrarian Classes: Agrarian Class Structure and Collective Action in Nineteenth-Century Ireland', in P. J. Drudy (ed.), *Irish Studies*, 2. *Ireland: Land, Politics and People* (Cambridge, 1982), 11–36.
—— 'Landlord Domination in Nineteenth-Century Ireland', *UNESCO Yearbook on Peace and Conflict Studies, 1986* (Paris, 1988), 5–29.
—— and DONNELLY, JAMES S., jun. (eds.), *Irish Peasants: Violence and Political Unrest, 1780–1914* (Manchester, 1983).
CONNELL, K. H., 'The Land Legislation and Irish Social Life', *Econ. Hist. Rev.* 2nd ser. 11: 1 (Aug. 1958), 1–7.
COLLINS, M. E., *The Land Question, 1879–1882* (Dublin, 1974).
COUSENS, S. H., 'Emigration and Demographic Change in Ireland, 1851–1861', *Econ. Hist. Rev.* 2nd ser. 14: 2 (Dec. 1961), 275–88.
CRAWFORD, E. MARGARET, 'Indian Meal and Pellagra in Nineteenth-Century Ireland', in J. M. Goldstrom and L. A. Clarkson (eds.), *Irish Population, Economy, and Society: Essays in Honour of the Late K. H. Connell* (Oxford, 1981), 113–33.
CROTTY, RAYMOND D., *Irish Agricultural Production: Its Volume and Structure* (Cork, 1966).
CURTIS, L. P., jun., 'Incumbered Wealth: Landed Indebtedness in Post-Famine Ireland', *AHR* 85: 2 (Apr. 1980), 332–67.
—— 'Stopping the Hunt, 1881–2: An Aspect of the Irish Land War', in C. H. E. Philpin (ed.), *Nationalism and Popular Protest in Ireland* (Cambridge, 1987), 349–402.

DEWEY, CLIVE, 'Celtic Agrarian Legislation and Celtic Revival: Historicist Implications of Gladstone's Irish and Scottish Land Acts, 1870–86', *Past & Present*, no. 64 (Aug. 1974), 30–70.
DONNELLY, JAMES S., jun., *Landlord and Tenant in Nineteenth-Century Ireland* (Dublin, 1973).
—— 'The Journals of Sir John Benn-Walsh Relating to the Management of his Irish Estates, 1823–64', *Cork Hist. Soc. Jn.* 79: 230 (1974), 86–123; 80: 231 (1975), 15–42.
—— *The Land and the People of Nineteenth-Century Cork: The Rural Economy and the Land Question* (London, 1975).
—— 'The Irish Agricultural Depression of 1859–64', *Ir. Econ. & Soc. Hist.* 3 (1976), 33–54.
—— 'Production, Prices, and Exports, 1846–51' and 'Landlords and Tenants', in W. E. Vaughan (ed.), *A New History of Ireland*, v. *Ireland under the Union, I. 1801–70* (Oxford, 1989), 286–93, 332–49.
DUFFY, PATRICK, 'Irish Landholding Structure and Population in the Mid-Nineteenth Century', *Maynooth Review*, 3: 2 (Dec. 1977), 3–27.
DUNLEAVY, J. C. and G. W., 'The Hidden Ireland of Irish Landlords: Manuscript Evidence of Oral Traditions', *Anglo-Irish Studies*, 4 (1979), 47–58.
FEENEY, PATRICK, 'Ballysaggart Estate: Eviction, Famine, and Conspiracy', *Decies*, no. 27 (Autumn, 1984), 4–12.
FEINGOLD, W. L., 'The Tenants' Movement to Capture the Irish Poor Law Boards, 1877–1886', *Albion*, 7: 3 (Dec. 1975), 216–31.
—— *The First Hurrah: The Rise of Tenant Leadership in the Irish Localities, 1870–1886* (St Louis, Mo., 1976).
—— 'Land League Power: The Tralee Poor-Law Election of 1881', in Samuel Clark and James S. Donnelly (eds.), *Irish Peasants: Violence and Political Unrest, 1780–1914* (Manchester, 1983), 285–310.
—— *The Revolt of the Tenantry: The Transformation of Local Government in Ireland, 1872–1886* (Boston, 1984).
FITZPATRICK, DAVID, 'The Disappearance of the Irish Agricultural Labourer, 1841–1912', *Ir. Econ. & Soc. Hist.* 7 (1980), 66–92.
—— 'Class, Family and Rural Unrest in Nineteenth-Century Ireland', in P. J. Drudy (ed.), *Irish Studies*, 2. *Ireland: Land, Politics and People* (Cambridge, 1982), 37–75.
FLETCHER, T. W., 'The Great Depression of English Agriculture, 1873–1896', *Econ. Hist. Rev.* 2nd ser. 13: 3 (May 1961), 417–32.
GAILEY, ALAN, 'Changes in Irish Rural Housing, 1600–1900', in Patrick O'Flanagan, Paul Ferguson, Kevin Whelan (eds.), *Rural Ireland, 1600–1900: Modernization and Change* (Cork, 1987), 86–103.
GARVIN, TOM, 'Defenders, Ribbonmen and Others: Underground Political Networks in Pre-Famine Ireland', in C. H. E. Philpin (ed.), *Nationalism and Popular Protest in Ireland* (Cambridge, 1987), 219–63.
GOLDSTROM, J. M., 'Irish Agriculture and the Great Famine', in J. M. Goldstrom and L. A. Clarkson (eds.), *Irish Population, Economy, and Society: Essays in Honour of the Late K. H. Connell* (Oxford, 1981), 155–71.
GUTTMAN, J. M., 'The Economics of Tenant Rights in Nineteenth-Century Irish Agriculture', *Economic Inquiry*, 18 (July 1980), 408–24.

HAZELKORN, ELLEN, 'Reconsidering Marx and Engels on Ireland', *Saothair*, 9 (1983), 79–88.
HOOKER, ELIZABETH R., *Readjustments of Agricultural Tenure in Ireland* (Chapel Hill, NC, 1938).
HOPPEN, K. THEODORE, 'Tories, Catholics, and the General Election of 1859', *Hist. Jn.* 13 (1970), 48–67.
—— 'Landlords, Society, and Electoral Politics in Mid-Nineteenth-Century Ireland', *Past & Present*, no. 75 (May 1977), 62–93.
—— 'National Politics and Local Realities in Mid-Nineteenth-Century Ireland', in Art Cosgrove and Donal McCartney (eds.), *Studies in Irish History Presented to R. Dudley Edwards* (Dublin, 1979), 190–227.
—— *Elections, Politics, and Society in Ireland, 1832–1885* (Oxford, 1984).
—— 'The Franchise and Electoral Politics in England and Ireland, 1832–1885', *History*, 70 (1985), 202–17.
—— *Ireland since 1800: Conflict and Conformity* (London and New York, 1989).
—— 'Landownership and Power in Nineteenth-Century Ireland: The Decline of an Élite', in Ralph Gibson and Martin Blinkhorn (eds.), *Landownership and Power in modern Europe* (London, 1991), 164–80.
HORN, PAMELA L. R., 'The National Agricultural Labourers' Union in Ireland, 1873–9', *IHS* 17: 67 (Mar. 1971), 340–52.
HUGHES, T. JONES, 'Landholding and Settlement in the Counties of Meath and Cavan in the Nineteenth Century', in Patrick O'Flanagan, Paul Ferguson, Kevin Whelan (eds.), *Rural Ireland, 1600–1900: Modernization and Change* (Cork, 1987), 104–41.
HUTTMAN, JOHN P., 'The Impact of Land Reform on Agricultural Production in Ireland', *Agricultural History*, 46: 3 (July 1972), 353–68.
JORDAN, DONALD, 'Merchants, "Strong Farmers" and Fenians: The Post-Famine Political Élite and the Irish Land War', in C. H. E. Philpin (ed.), *Nationalism and Popular Protest in Ireland* (Cambridge, 1987), 320–48.
KENNEDY, LÍAM, 'Regional Specialization, Railway Development, and Irish Agriculture in the Nineteenth Century', in J. M. Goldstrom and L. A. Clarkson (eds.), *Irish Population, Economy, and Society* (Oxford, 1981), 173–93.
—— 'Farmers, Traders, and Agricultural Politics in Pre-Independence Ireland', in Clark and Donnelly (eds.), *Irish Peasants: Violence and Political Unrest, 1780–1914* (Manchester, 1983), 339–73.
—— 'The Rural Economy, 1820–1914', in Líam Kennedy and Philip Ollerenshaw (eds.), *An Economic History of Ulster, 1820–1940* (Manchester, 1985), 1–61.
KIERNAN, V. G., 'The Emergence of a Nation', in C. H. E. Philpin (ed.), *Nationalism and Popular Protest in Ireland* (Cambridge, 1987), 16–49.
KIRKPATRICK, R. W., 'Origins and Development of the Land War in Mid-Ulster', in F. S. L. Lyons and R. A. J. Hawkins (eds.), *Ireland under the Union: Varieties of Tension: Essays in Honour of T. W. Moody* (Oxford, 1980), 201–35.
KOLBERT, C. F., and O'BRIEN, T., *Land Reform in Ireland: A Legal History of the Irish Land Problem and its Settlement* (Cambridge, 1975).
LANE, P. G., 'The Encumbered Estates Court, Ireland, 1848–1849', *Economic and Social Review*, 3 (1972), 413–53.
—— 'The General Impact of the Encumbered Estates Act of 1849 on Counties

Galway and Mayo', *Galway Archaeological and Historical Society Jn.* 33 (1972-3), 44-74.

—— 'The Management of Estates by Financial Corporations in Ireland after the Famine', *Studia Hib.* 14 (1974), 67-89.

—— 'The Impact of the Encumbered Estates Court upon the Landlords of Galway and Mayo', *Galway Archaeological and Historical Society Jn.* 38 (1981-2), 45-58.

LEE, JOHN, 'Richard Griffith's Land Valuation as a Basis for Farm Taxation', in G. L. Herries Davies and R. Charles Mollan (eds.), *Richard Griffith, 1784-1878: Papers Presented at the Centenary Symposium Organised by the Royal Dublin Society, 21 and 22 Sept. 1978* (Dublin, 1980), 77-101.

LEE, JOSEPH, 'The Land War', in Liam de Paor (ed.), *Milestones in Irish History* (Dublin and Cork, 1986), 106-16.

LOWE, W. J., 'Landlord and Tenant on the Estate of Trinity College, Dublin, 1851-1903', *Hermathena*, 120 (1976), 5-24.

MACCABE, DESMOND, 'Magistrates, Peasants, and the Petty Sessions Courts: Mayo 1823-50', *Cathair na Mart*, 5: 1 (1985), 45-53.

MACCARTHY, ROBERT BRIAN, *The Trinity College Estates, 1800-1923: Corporate Management in an Age of Reform* (Dundalk, 1992).

MCCOURT, EILEEN, 'The Management of the Farnham Estates during the Nineteenth Century', *Breifne*, 4: 16 (1975), 531-60.

MAC GIOLLA CHOILE, Breandán, 'Fenians, Rice and Ribbonmen in County Monaghan', *Clogher Record*, 6: 2 (1967), 221-52.

MCMAHON, KEVIN, and MCKEOWN, THOMAS, 'Agrarian Disturbances around Crossmaglen, 1835-55', *Seanchas Ardmhacha*, 9: 2 (1979), 302-32; 10:1 (1981), 149-75; 10:2 (1982), 380-416.

MCMINN, J. R. B., 'The Social and Political Structure of North Antrim in 1869', *Glynns*, 10 (1982), 11-22.

MARNANE, DENIS G., *Land and Violence: A History of West Tipperary from 1660* (Tipperary, 1985).

MATSUO, TARO, 'Researches in Irish Land Laws Undertaken by Japanese Bureaucrats Facing the Tenancy Question in the 1920s', *Hosei University Economic Review*, 46 (1978), 2-3.

MORAN, GERARD P., 'Absentee Landlordism in Mayo in the 1870s', *Cathair na Mart*, 2: 1 (1982), 30-52.

—— 'An Assessment of the Land League Meeting at Westport, 8 June 1879', *Cathair na Mart*, 3: 1 (1983), 54-9.

—— 'Mayo and the General Election of 1874', *Cathair na Mart*, 4: 1 (1984), 69-73.

—— 'Famine and the Land War: Relief and Distress in Mayo, 1879-81', *Cathair na Mart*, 5: 1 (1985), 54-66; 6: 1 (1986), 111-27.

—— *The Mayo Evictions of 1860: Patrick Lavelle and the 'War' in Partry* (Cathair na Mart, 1986).

MURPHY, DESMOND, 'The Land War in Donegal, 1879-1891', *Donegal Annual*, 32 (1980), 476-86.

MURRAY, A. C., 'Nationality and Local Politics in Late Nineteenth-Century Ireland: The Case of County Westmeath', *IHS* 25: 98 (Nov. 1986), 144-58.

—— 'Agrarian Violence and Nationalism in Nineteenth-Century Ireland: The Myth of Ribbonism', *Ir. Econ. & Soc. Hist.* 13 (1986), 56–73.

O'CONNOR, R., and GUIOMARD, C., 'Agricultural Output in the Irish Free State Area before and after Independence', *Ir. Econ. & Soc. Hist.* 12 (1985), 89–97.

Ó GRÁDA, CORMAC, 'Agricultural Head Rents, Pre-Famine and Post-Famine', *Economic and Social Review*, 5: 3 (Apr. 1974), 385–92.

—— 'The Investment Behaviour of Irish Landlords, 1850–75: Some Preliminary Findings', *Agric. Hist. Rev.* 23: 2 (1975), 139–55.

—— 'Irish Agricultural Output before and after the Famine', *Journal of European Economic History*, 13: 1 (Spring 1984), 149–65.

—— *Ireland before and after the Famine: Explorations in Economic History, 1800–1925* (Manchester, 1988).

O'NEILL, T. P., 'The Irish Land Question, 1830–50', *Studies*, 44 (Autumn 1955), 325–36.

ORRIDGE, ANDREW W., 'Who Supported the Land War? An Aggregate-Data Analysis of Irish Agrarian Discontent, 1879–82', *Economic and Social Review*, 12: 3 (Apr. 1981), 203–33.

O'SHEA, JAMES, *Priest, Politics and Society in Post-Famine Ireland: A Study of County Tipperary, 1850–1891* (Dublin and Atlantic Highlands, NJ, 1983).

PALMER, NORMAN DUNBAR, *The Irish Land League Crisis* (New Haven, Conn., 1940).

PALMER, STANLEY H., *Police and Protest in England and Ireland, 1780–1850* (Cambridge, 1988).

PHELAN, M. M., 'Fr Thomas O'Shea and the Callan Tenant Protection Society', *Old Kilkenny Review*, NS 2: 2 (1980), 49–58.

POMFRET, JOHN E., *The Struggle for Land in Ireland, 1800–1923* (Princeton, NJ, 1930).

PROUDFOOT, LINDSAY, 'The Management of a Great Estate: Patronage, Income and Expenditure on the Duke of Devonshire's Irish Property, c. 1816–1891', *Ir. Econ. & Soc. Hist.* 13 (1986), 32–55.

ROBINSON, OLIVE, 'The London Companies as Progressive Landlords in Nineteenth-Century Ireland', *Econ. Hist. Rev.* 2nd ser., 15: 1 (Aug. 1962), 103–18.

—— 'The London Companies and Tenant Right in Nineteenth-Century Ireland', *Agric. Hist. Rev.* 18 (1970), 54–63.

ROBINSON, PHILIP, 'From Thatched to Slate: Innovation in Roof Covering Materials for Traditional Houses in Ulster', *Ulster Folklife*, 31 (1985), 21–35.

SOCOLOFSKY, HOMER E., *Landlord William Scully* (Lawrence, Kan., 1979).

SOLOW, B. L., *The Land Question and the Irish Economy, 1870–1903* (Cambridge, Mass., 1971).

—— 'A New Look at the Irish Land Question'. *Economic & Social Review*, 12: 4 (July 1981), 301–14.

STEELE, E. D., *Irish Land and British Politics: Tenant Right and Nationality, 1865–1870* (Cambridge, 1974).

TAYLOR, LAWRENCE J., 'The Priest and the Agent: Social Drama and Class Consciousness in the West of Ireland', *Comparative Studies in Society and History*, 27: 4 (Oct. 1985), 696–712.

THOMPSON, FRANCIS, 'The Landed Classes, the Orange Order and the Anti-Land

League Campaign in Ulster, 1880–81', *Éire-Ireland*, 22: 1 (Spring 1987), 102–21.
TOWNSHEND, CHARLES, *Political Violence in Ireland: Government and Resistance since 1848* (Oxford, 1983).
TURNER, MICHAEL, 'Towards an Agricultural Prices Index for Ireland, 1850–1914', *Economic and Social Review*, 18: 2 (Jan. 1987), 123–36.
—— 'Output and Productivity in Irish Agriculture from the Famine to the Great War', *Ir. Econ. & Soc. Hist.* 17 (1990), 62–78.
VAUGHAN, W. E., 'Landlord and Tenant Relations in Ireland between the Famine and the Land War, 1850–1870', in L. M. Cullen and T. C. Smout (eds.), *Comparative Aspects of Scottish and Irish Economic and Social History 1600–1900* (Edinburgh, 1977), 216–26.
—— 'Agricultural Output, Rents and Wages in Ireland, 1850–80', in L. M. Cullen and F. Furet (eds.), *Ireland and France, 17th–20th Centuries: Towards a Comparative Study of Rural History* (Paris, 1980), 85–97.
—— 'An Assessment of the Economic Performance of Irish Landlords, 1851–81', in F. S. L. Lyons and R. A. J. Hawkins (eds.), *Ireland under the Union: Varieties of Tension. Essays in Honour of T. W. Moody* (Oxford, 1980), 173–99.
—— 'Richard Griffith and the Tenement Valuation', in G. L. Herries Davies and R. Charles Mollan (eds.), *Richard Griffith, 1784–1878: Papers Presented at the Centenary Symposium Organized by the Royal Dublin Society, 21 and 22 Sept. 1978* (Dublin, 1980), 103–22.
—— 'Farmer, Grazier and Gentleman: Edward Delany of Woodtown, 1851–99', *Ir. Econ. & Soc. Hist.* 9 (1982), 53–72.
—— *Sin, Sheep and Scotsmen: John George Adair and the Derryveagh Evictions, 1861* (Belfast, 1983).
—— *Landlords and Tenants in Ireland, 1848–1904* (Studies in Irish Economic and Social History, 2; Dundalk, 1984).
—— 'Ireland c. 1870', in Vaughan (ed.), *A New History of Ireland*, v. *Ireland under the Union, 1. 1801–70* (Oxford, 1989), 726–800.
—— 'Potatoes and Agricultural Output', *Ir. Econ. & Soc. Hist.* 17 (1990), 79–92.
WALKER, BRIAN M., 'The Land Question in Elections in Ulster, 1868–86', in Clark and Donnelly (eds.), *Irish Peasants: Violence and Political Unrest 1780–1914* (Manchester, 1983), 230–68.
—— *Ulster Politics: The Formative Years, 1868–86* (Belfast, 1989).
WINSTANLEY, MICHAEL J., *Ireland and the Land Question, 1800–1922* (London and New York, 1984).

INDEX

Abbotsford, Selkirkshire 106
Abercorn, duke of 71–2, 228
Abercorn estate 71–2, 75, 133
Acheson, Mrs Anne 170
Achill, Co. Mayo 150, 152, 155
act of union 1800, 219–20
Adair, John George 26, 30, 36, 38, 106, 107–8
Adair estate, Co. Donegal 139, 142
Adare, Co. Limerick 1, 121
agents 5, 38, 168, 180
  contact with tenants 111–12
  powers of 33, 41
  and rent collection 65–6, 113, 114–15
  risks of 138
  role of 108–12
  and tenant right 87–93
  training of 110–11
agrarian crime 15, 18, 19, 63
  causes of 156–61
  coercion acts 140–1, 161, 184; *see also* habeas corpus; Peace Preservation Act 1870; Westmeath act
  concealment of criminals 184–9
  constabulary returns 279–80
  counties ranked by 283–6
  decline in 163–4
  definitions of 141–50
  firings 145–6, 189
  importance of 161–76
  during land war 209, 211, 212
  see also homicides and assassinations; Spearman ranking coefficients threatening letters
agriculture:
  calculations of output 53–4, 247–50
  depressions 19, 23, 114, 157, 159–60, 209–13, 227
  distribution of agricultural incomes 8–9
  improvements encouraged 121–2
  lack of organization 203–4
  machinery 128
  output and rents 62, 115–17
  output increases 50–2
  post-famine output 16–18
  potato failures 117, 249
  use of surplus 225

agriculturists 122
Alexander, Mrs Cecil Frances 228
Allingham, William 17, 191
American civil war 2, 14, 82, 215
amnesty meetings 179
Ancient Order of Hibernians 199
Anderson, Messrs 136
Anketell, Thomas 171, 194
Annesley, Lord 109, 110, 112
Annesley estate 109
Annual Register 15
Antrim, County 1, 4, 12, 111–12, 134
  agrarian crime 156, 157
  ranked according to: agrarian outrages 283, 285; evictions 233, 235; rural housing 270, 272; serious crime 281; valuation, tillage and holdings 267, 272
  tenant right 76, 98
approvers 169, 186, 197, 200
Archdale estate, Co. Fermanagh 48, 76, 119–20
Archdall, William 170
Archerstown, Co. Westmeath 153
Armagh, Co. Armagh 13
Armagh, County 39, 50, 136
  agrarian crime 138, 188, 192
  estate management 109, 112
  ranked according to: agrarian outrages 283, 285; evictions 233, 235; rural housing 270, 272; serious crime 281; valuation tillage, and holdings 267, 272
  rents 56, 63, 117
  Ribbonism 190, 196
  TCD leasing powers act 258
  tenant right 76
  valuations 58
Armstrong, Messrs 89
Arran, Lord 45
arrears 15, 19, 28, 64, 157
  on 12 estates 241–3
  evictions 29–30, 32
  fluctuations in 115–17
  and payment of rents 113–17
  post-famine 17–18
arrears act 1882, 23, 209, 225

INDEX

Arva, Co. Cavan 3
Ashbourne act 1885, 209
Ashtown, Lord 122
Ashtown estate, Co. Galway 17, 48, 79, 115, 264
   annual rents, arrears and receipts 239–40, 242–3, 245–6
   estate expenditure 277
assassinations:
   analysis of 142–6
   difficulty of conviction 185–7, 189
   and Ribbonism 196–8, 201–2
   threatening letters 150–1
Athavallie, Co. Mayo 182
Athlone, Co. Westmeath 20
Aughamullen, Co. Tyrone 40–3
Austin v. *Scott* 95, 96–7

Bagehot, Walter 105, 107
bailiffs 40, 45, 153–4, 168, 175
   attacks on 5, 177–8, 187, 189, 197
   and evictions 22, 34, 38
   role of 15, 112–13
   threats to 181–2, 207
Baker, Captain George Cole 103, 142, 162, 189, 202, 207
Baker, Revd William 162, 207
Baldwin, Thomas 83–4, 127
Balla, Co. Mayo 182
Ballina, Co. Mayo 77, 202
Ballinagore, Co. Westmeath 152
Ballinamallard, Co. Fermanagh 2
Ballindrait, Co. Donegal 119
Ballinrobe, Co. Mayo 77, 182
Ballycohey, Co. Tipperary 139
   'battle' of 34, 108, 142, 151, 185, 218
Ballyconnell, Co. Cavan 162, 181, 188
Ballykilbeg, Co. Down 192
Ballylehane, Queen's County 38
Ballyman, Co. Wicklow 56
Ballymena, Co. Antrim 95
Baltiboys, Co. Wicklow 1–2, 66, 129
Banbridge, Co. Down 11
Bandon, earl of 5
banking 116, 117, 128, 213
bankruptcy court 99
Baronscourt, Co. Tyrone 228
Barrett, Peter 145
Barrington, Richard M. 252
Barrington farm, Fassaroe 247, 248
Barry, Captain William 171, 173
Bateman, John 13, 123
Bateson, Sir Thomas 56
Bateson, Thomas 162, 182, 185, 188, 190
Bateson estate 58, 60
Bath estate, Co. Monaghan 109, 201
Bayldon, J. S. 59, 252

Bayly, J. U. 188
Beckham, Thomas 151, 189
Bedford, duke of 123, 125
Beere, Richard 112
Beers, Wiliam 173–4
Belfast 191, 199, 200
Belfast Banking Co. 90
Belfast Hibernian Benevolent Society 199
Belle Isle, Co. Fermanagh 2
Bellegrove, Queen's County 107–8
Belmore, Lord 4, 49, 56, 134
Belmore estate, Co. Tyrone 60
Belturbet Agricultural Society 16
Bence-Jones, Mark 2
Bence Jones, William 44
benefit societies 199
Benn-Walsh, Sir John 16–17, 58, 62 n., 105, 111, 112, 264
Benn-Walsh estate 47
Beragh, Co. Tyrone 49, 56
Beresford, Lord John George, archbishop of Armagh 257
Bergin, James J. 199
Berridge estate 37–8
Berry, Francis 188
Bessborough commission 44, 72
Bingham, Arthur Shaen 12
Bingham estate, Co. Mayo 204
Birr Castle, King's County 228
Blackditch, Co. Wicklow 57
Blacker, St John Thomas 256
Blacker, William 222
Blacker estate 17, 48, 116
   annual rents, arrears, and receipts 239–40, 242–3, 245–6
Blake, James 36
Blake, Captain Maurice 170
Blake, Valentine 170
Blakiston–Houston estate 45
Blayney, Lord 162
Blessington, Co. Meath 4
Blosse, Sir Robert Lynch 182
Blunden, John 161
board of works 121, 124, 126, 127
boards of guardians 36
Bond, J. W. MacGeough 97
Boycott, Captain 109, 110, 178
boycotting 178–9
Boyle, Pat 197
Brabazon, Lady Theodosia 132
Braddel, Walter 151
Bradshaw, Hugh 144, 152, 162, 186
Brassington, Charles 49
Brassington & Gale 57, 58, 60, 124
Breen (assassin) 197
Brennan, Michael 194
Brett, James 143

Brett, John 143
Brew, Sub-Inspector 175
Bridge, Patten Smith 142, 146, 189
Brien, Redmond 186
Broderick, Mr 147
Brookeborough, Co. Fermanagh 2
Brown, Robert E. 105
Brown, Robert L. 61, 102
Browne, Captain 182
Browne, Fr. James 170
Brownehall, Co. Mayo 182
Brownrigg, Sir Henry John 142, 154, 193, 194
Buchanan, Charles 142
Buckley, John 179
Buncrana, Co. Donegal 30
Burke, Sir Bernard 221
Burke, J. C. R. 20
Butler, Lady 21 n.
Butler, Thomas 247
Butler estate, Co. Clare 61, 108
Butt, Isaac 37, 228
Byrne, Head Constable 191
Byrne, Judith 79
Byrne, William 171

Cahir, Co. Tipperary 223-4
Cahir Castle 223
Caird, James 85
Caledon, Co. Tyrone 1, 121
Caledon, Lord 121
Callaghan (tenant) 58 n.
Callow Hill, Co. Fermanagh 121
Campbell, Alice 186
Campbell, George 44, 69, 76-7, 80-1
Cannadine, David 125
Canthill, Mrs N. 120
Cardwell, Edward 192
caretakers 22-3, 37, 38
Carew, Lord 5
Carew, S. F. 184
Carey, James 184
Carlisle, Lord 104, 175
Carlow, County 77
 ranked according to: agrarian
  outrages 283, 285; evictions 233, 235;
  rural housing 269, 271; serious
  crime 281; valuation, tillage and
  holdings 267, 271
Carr, John 150
Carraher v. *Bond* 97
Carton, Co. Kildare 1
Carty, William 188
Castle Archdale, Co. Fermanagh 2
Castle Coole, Co. Fermanagh 1, 4
Castle Crine, Co. Clare 61, 108
Castlebar, Co. Mayo 77

Castledaly, Co. Westmeath 207
Castlemaine, Lord 148, 205
Castlereagh, Co. Down 182
Castlestuart, earl of 45
Castletown, Co. Louth 186
Castletown House, Co. Kildare 1
Castlewellan, Co. Down 191
Cavan, Co. Cavan 3
Cavan, County 12, 17, 39, 40, 82, 107, 206-7, 277
 agrarian crime 143, 147, 148, 162, 181
 estate expenditure 118, 119, 135
 estate management 108-9, 109, 112
 estate sales 136-7
 evictions 30, 31, 38
 ranked according to: agrarian
  outrages 283, 285; evictions 233, 235;
  rural housing 270, 272; serious
  crime 282; valuation, tillage and
  holdings 267, 272
 rent collection 113
 rents 18, 55-6, 57, 58, 64, 65
 tenant right 76, 88, 91, 92
Cavanagh, Michael 173
Cave estate 47
Chaloner, Robert 57
Chambré, Merideth 188
charities 119-20
Charles II, King 11
Chelmsford committee 89, 98, 99
Chichester estate 12
Chief Secretary's Office 147, 229
church act 160
Church of Ireland 14, 119-20, 203, 215, 217
 disestablished 13, 133
 and landlords 11, 220
civil bill courts 94, 98
civil bills 24-5, 31, 32, 66, 210, 213, 232
 number of processes and executions 232
 see also ejectments
Civil war 226, 227
Clare, County 108, 117-18, 126
 agrarian crime 187
 evictions 25, 26, 36, 37
 ranked according to: agrarian
  outrages 283, 285; evictions 233,
  235; rural housing 270, 271; serious
  crime 281; valuation, tillage and
  holdings 267, 271
 rents 73-4
 valuations 61
Claremorris, Co. Mayo 77, 178
Clarendon, Lord 257
Clark, Samuel 209, 210
Clarke, Charles 142
Classiebawn, Co. Sligo 1

clearances 25-7
Clements, Hon. Charles 256, 257
Clinan House, Co. Westmeath 151
Clonbrock, Lord 2
Clonbrock estate, Co. Galway 17, 50, 130
　annual rents, arrears and receipts 239-40, 242-3, 245-6
　estate expenditure, 277
Clonbur, Co. Galway 165
Cloneyhaigue, Co. Westmeath 194
Close, Charles Maxwell 256
Clough, Co. Down 191
Coalisland, Co. Tyrone 30
coercion acts 140-1, 141, 161, 184
　see also habeas corpus; Peace Preservation Act 1870; Westmeath act
Coffey, J. C. 98
Colebrooke, Co. Fermanagh 2
Colgan, Owen 151-2
Collum, John 40
Coltsman, Daniel 28
combinations 65, 179-80, 183
　difficulties of combining 202-6
Comerford, Professor R. V. 214
Connacht 81
　Fenianism 214
　ranked according to: agrarian outrages 284, 286; evictions 234, 236; rural housing 270, 272; serious crime 282; valuation, tillage and holdings 268, 272
　Ribbonism 193
　tenant right 80
Connell, K. H. vii–viii, 46
constabulary 14-15, 31, 162, 163, 167, 211
　agrarian crime returns 138, 141-2, 147-50, 158, 279-80
　and concealment of criminals 184-9
　control of 139, 165, 166, 219
　detection rate 187
　eviction returns 21, 25, 27, 29, 229-30
　and evictions 20, 35, 36, 168, 179-80, 204
　on Leitrim estates 103, 105
　and magistrates 173-4
　obstacle to combinations 204-5
　powers of 164
　and Ribbonism 189-91, 193-6
　summary jurisdiction act 168
Constabulary Office 141, 142
Conyngham, Marquis 37, 99
Coolattin, Co. Wicklow 1
Coolavin, princes of 221
Cootehill, Co. Cavan 191
Corboy, Terence 188

Cordner, Edward 90
Cork, County 3, 208
　agrarian crime 147, 178, 180
　ranked according to: agrarian outrages 283, 285; evictions 233, 235; rural housing 270, 271; serious crime 281; valuation, tillage and holdings 267, 271
　rents 17, 47, 264
　tenant right 77, 95
　valuations 58
Cormack, Thomas 152
Cormack brothers 188
corn laws 11, 13
Corrigan (assassin) 197
Costello estate, Co. Westmeath 207
Counsel, Lawrence 152
Counsel, Miss 152
Coutts & Co. 134, 135, 136
Cowper, Lord 123
Cowper commission 21, 53, 54, 123, 248
Coyle, Bryan 144
Crawford, William Sharman 68
Crime and Outrage (Ireland) Act 1847, 141
Crimean war 14, 15, 16, 17, 263
Crofton, Revd James 143, 172-3, 189
Crofton estate, Co. Roscommon 48, 116, 130, 134
　annual rents, arrears and receipts 239-40, 242-3, 245-6
　estate expenditure 277
　improvements 125
Crom, Co. Fermanagh 132, 277
Cronin, J. L. 205
Crosbie estate, Co. Kerry 50, 79
Crotty, Charles 170, 189
Cully, Thomas 147
Cuming, Dr Thomas 133, 135, 136
Curling, Charles 128
Curling, Edward 61, 110, 128
Curraghmore, Co. Waterford 106
Currey, Francis 110
Curtis, Professor L. P. 131
Curtis (Ribbonman) 197

Daly, James 183
Daly, John 188
Daly, Tim 207
D'Arcy, G. J. N. 173
Davidson, Mrs 92
Davigan, Pat 175-6
Davis, Humphrey 163, 187-8
Davitt, Michael 183, 214, 215
Day, William Marshall 35
de Lavergne, Léonce 53
de Moleyns, Thomas 105, 113
de Montmorency, Revd Waller 121

Deane estate, Co. Kildare 114
Defenderism 199
Delany, Edward 6, 11
Delin, Alice 167
demesnes 1, 8, 121, 228
Denton, J. Bailey 105, 125, 127
Derg faction 180
Derry 111, 133
Derrylin, Co. Fermanagh 121
Derryveagh, Co. Donegal 185
  evictions 5, 26, 27, 30, 34, 36, 38, 70, 106, 218
Despard, Captain 110
Devlin, Anne 56
Devlin, Charles 56
Devon, Lord 110
Devon commission 44, 69, 70, 110, 133
Devonshire, duke of 3, 110, 123
Devoy, John 214
Digby, Lord 167
Digby estate, King's County 109
disease 164
Disraeli, Benjamin 13, 106, 221–2
distraint 31, 206
disturbance, compensation for 94, 95–6, 273–4
dog regulation act 164, 165, 168
Doherty, Fr. 105
Doherty, Mrs 75
Doherty (murderer) 144
Domvile, Sir Charles Compton 59
Donegal, County 1, 3, 67, 103, 104, 106, 118, 221
  agrarian crime 139, 144, 146
  estate expenditure 119
  evictions 26, 27, 30, 34, 36, 38
  game preservation 99
  improvements 121, 122, 126
  ranked according to: agrarian outrages 283, 285; evictions 233, 235; rural housing 270, 272; serious crime 282; valuation, tillage and holdings 268, 272
  rent collection 115
  rents 17, 18, 45, 48, 50, 56, 61, 86
  Ribbonism 191, 193
  TCD leasing powers act 258
  tenant right 71–2, 74, 76, 88, 97
  turbary rights 99–100
  valuations 58
Donnell, Robert 69, 73
Donnelly, Professor J. S. ix, 47–8, 208, 209, 211
Donoghue, Florence 28
Donoghue, James 28
Donoghue, Sub-Inspector 190
Dowling, Francis 172, 173, 194–5

Down, County 1, 89, 95
  agrarian crime 138, 157
  improvements 121
  ranked according to: agrarian outrages 283, 285; evictions 233, 235; rural housing 270, 272; serious crime 282; valuation, tillage and holdings 268, 272
  rents 48, 62 n.
  resistance to landlordism 182–3
  tenant right 76, 97–8
  valuations 58
Downshire, marquis of 1, 4, 45, 67, 182, 189
drainage 121, 127, 128–9
Dromoland Castle, Co. Clare 228
Druids, Ancient Order of 192
Drum Manor, Co. Tyrone 228
Drumkeeran, Co. Fermanagh 169
Drumlish, Co. Longford 169
Drumminis, Co. Armagh 90
Dublin 12, 220
Dublin, County:
  agrarian crime 156, 157
  ranked according to: agrarian outrages 283, 285; evictions 233, 235; rural housing 269, 271; serious crime 281; valuation, tillage and holdings 267, 271
  tenant right 77
  valuations 59
Dublin Castle 14, 160, 166, 174, 175
Dublin Gazette 258
Dublin University, *see* Trinity College
Dufferin, marquis of 4, 6, 117, 129, 205
  expenditure of 118–19, 120, 132–3
  on tenant right 68, 69, 72, 73
Duffy, 'Captain' 143, 172–3, 180, 201
Duffy faction 180
Dun, Finlay 44
Dundas, Robert 136, 137
Dundrum, Co. Down 4
Dungannon, Co. Tyrone 3, 13, 104–5, 181
Dungannon Royal School estate, Co. Tyrone 39–40, 41, 63, 89
  rents 56, 64–5, 73, 116
  valuations 57, 58, 59
Dungiven Castle, Co. Londonderry 228
Dunleer, Co. Westmeath 189
Dunne, Patrick 173
Dunne, Thomas 181
Dunraven, Lord 4, 61, 107, 121, 124
Dunraven estate, Co. Limerick 49, 58, 124
Durham letter 215
Dwyer, Patrick 186–7
Dwyer, Thomas 162
Dysart, Co. Westmeath 185

Eastwood, James 180, 186, 188, 196, 197, 205
ecclesiastical titles act 215
Edge, Dr Samuel 161–2, 167
Edward of Saxe-Weimar, Prince 137
ejectments 29, 31–2, 37–8, 162, 204, 206, 213
  numbers of 100, 210, 232, 237
  procedures 21–5
  see also evictions; notices to quit
elections 4, 13, 18, 101, 215, 218, 228
  and evictions 33
  franchise 203
  landlord candidates 133
  landlords' influence 13
  meetings 179
Ellard, Louisa Martha 166
Elliott, John 92
Ely, marquis of 76
emigration 92, 164, 171, 211, 217
encumbered estates acts 133, 218
encumbered estates court 9, 18, 20, 27
endowed schools 13
  commissioners of 39–40, 42, 63, 89, 109
  royal commission on 64
England 33, 39, 52, 121, 187, 219
  crime rate 138, 140
  estate expenditure 125, 128, 130
  improvements 123
  labourers' unions 183
  labourers' wages 7
  landlordism's decline 228
  rents 46, 115, 226
Ennis, Co. Clare 95
Enniscrone, Co. Sligo 150
Enniskillen, Co. Fermanagh 3, 13, 121, 191
Enniskillen, Lord 120
entails 124
Erne, earl of 1, 119, 122, 126, 132, 277
  farm machinery 128
  income 118
Erne estate, Co. Donegal 17, 18, 48, 50
  annual rents, arrears and receipts 239–40, 242–3, 245–6
  rent collection 115
  rents 116
Erne estate, Co. Fermanagh 48, 128
  estate expenditure, 278
  improvements 121, 122
Erne estate, Co. Mayo 109
Erne estate, Co. Sligo 109
estate management 2, 18, 103–37, 218, 222–3
  and agrarian crime 161–2
  arrears and payment of rents 113–17
  and evictions 29–34
  expenditure 2, 117–23, 277–8
  interest payments 118, 277–8
  lack of investment 218
  landlords' indebtedness 124, 125, 130–7, 277–8
  low expenditure on improvements 124–30
  reasons for few improvements 124–30
  role of agents 108–12
  and tenant right 87–93
  valuation and rent increases 57–61
  writings on 105–6
estate papers 10, 39–40, 47, 48, 70–1, 79, 90–2, 107
Evans, William 169
Evening Mail 165
evictions 5, 15, 16, 18, 19, 84, 101, 107–8, 129, 206, 207, 215, 218
  after land act (1881) 226
  agents' powers of 93
  and agrarian crime 157, 158–9, 162
  clearances 25–7
  collusive evictions 28
  and constabulary 20, 35, 36, 168, 179–80, 204
  counties ranked by 233–6
  effects of 25, 28–9
  and estate management 29–34
  financial losses 38–9
  numbers of 20–9, 23, 100, 209, 230–1
  obstacles to 34–9, 177–9
  post-eviction occupiers attacked 143, 149, 178–9
  publicity 36–8
  and rent increases 63–4
  squatters 92
  and tenant right 68, 70, 80
  threats of 29–32
  see also ejectments; notices to quit; Spearman ranking coefficients

factions 166, 180–1
Fallon, Martin 200
farmers' clubs 179
Farney, Co. Monaghan 37, 162, 192
Farnham, Lord 88
Farnham estate, Co. Cavan 88, 107
Fassaroe, Co. Wicklow 247, 248
Feingold, William L. 210
Fenianism 174, 191, 206, 211, 214, 215, 217
Fenton, Mr 189
Ferguson, W. D. and Vance, A. 67
Fermanagh, County 1, 2, 106, 109, 128, 277
  agrarian crime 157, 170
  estate expenditure 118, 119–20, 132
  evictions 25
  housing 83 n.

Fermanagh (cont.)
  improvements 121
  ranked according to: agrarian outrages 283, 286; evictions 233, 235; rural housing 270, 272; serious crime 282; valuation, tillage and holdings 268, 272
  rents 48
  Ribbonism 195, 198
  tenant right 76, 81
  valuations 58
Fermoy, Co. Cork 179
Fetherston Haugh, J. H. 142, 151, 161, 173, 180, 184, 189
Fetherston Haugh, Richard 155, 162
Filgate, Fitzherbert 67
Finnegan, James 196, 197
firearms 144, 145–7
firings at the person 145–6, 189
First World War 226, 227
Fitzgerald, Francis 144, 151, 180, 188–9
Fitzgerald, J. F. V. 252
Fitzgerald, Thomas 59
Fitzwilliam, Earl 1, 29–30, 57, 105
  expenditure 120
Fitzwilliam estate 57, 79
  improvements 122
  valuation 60
flax cultivation 81–2
Fosberry, George 181
Fox, Wilson 250
Freeman's Journal 21
freemasonry 192
Friel v. *The earl of Leitrim* 95, 97
friendly societies 192
Fyfe, Mr (bailiff) 88

gale day 30
Galway, County 2, 199
  agrarian crime 145, 157, 189
  evictions 20–1, 27, 35, 36, 37–8
  indebtedness 211
  ranked according to: agrarian outrages 284, 286; evictions 234, 236; rural housing 270, 272; serious crime 282; valuation, tillage and holdings 268, 272
  rents 17, 48
Galway Vindicator 161
Gamble (tenant) 103
gambling 135
game, preservation of 99
Gardiner, Miss 189
Gardner, Edward 98
Gardner, Robert 98–9
Gartlaney, Catherine 41
Gartlaney, Eliza 40–1
Gartlaney, Laurence 40, 41
Gartlaney, Michael 30, 40–3, 65
Gartlaney, Owen 40, 41
Garvagh, Lord 70, 115, 125
Garvagh estate, Co. Londonderry 17, 48, 114, 116, 125–6
  annual rents, arrears and receipts 239–40, 242–3, 245–6
Garvin, Professor Tom 191
Gavan Duffy, Charles 206, 215, 222–3
Geashill, King's County 167, 192
Germany 219
Gerrard, J. N. 20
Gibstown, Co. Meath 20
Gillardstown House, Co. Westmeath 169
Gladstone, W. E. vii, 6, 13, 44 n., 80, 101, 173, 183, 214, 215, 229
Glasnevin model farm 84, 85
Glengall, Lady 223–4
Glengall, Lord 223
Glin, knights of 221
Golding, Edward 154
Gorey, Co. Wexford 3
Gorman, Darby 34, 189
Gorman, Patrick 186–7
Gosford, Lady 136
Gosford, Lord 3, 14, 39–40, 92, 107, 109, 138, 168
  indebtedness 130, 133, 134–7
  jointures 132, 136
  rents 45, 56, 63, 64
  and tenant right 90
  valuations 58
Gosford Castle, Co. Armagh 134
Gosford estate 91–2, 105
  valuation 60
Gosford estate, Co. Armagh 87, 109, 112, 136
  improvements 122
  rent collection 117
  rents 63
  tenant right 90
Gosford estate, Co. Cavan 57, 58, 109
  rents 64, 65
  sold 136–7
Graham, Sir James 132–3
Graham estate 134
grand juries 166
Grange, Co. Cork 58 n.
Grant, Revd J. Brabazon 152
Gray, Sir John 21, 53, 80, 82–5
great famine 19, 23, 28–9, 51, 55, 114, 211
  arrears 115, 242
  clearances and evictions 24–6
  crime 138, 163 n., 279
  rent receipts 245
  rents 239

Green, Revd T. W. 152
Greene, John Ball 51
Greig, William 124
Greville, Fulke 173
Griffith, Sir Richard 58
  Instructions 59–60, 250, 251, 254
  and TCD leasing powers act 50–1, 256, 258–9
  tenement valuation 45, 51, 54, 60, 251–5, 264
Grimshaw, T. W. 53
Grocers' Co. 123, 128
Guinness, Mahon, Hardy, & Co. 108–9
Gweedore, Co. Donegal 45, 221

habeas corpus, suspension of 140, 189, 195
  see also Westmeath act
Hall, Roger 115
Hall estate, Co. Down 48, 92, 115
  accounts 118
  estate expenditure, 278
  annual rents, arrears and receipts 239–40, 242–3, 245–6
  rent collection 113–14
Hamilton, Lord Claud John 133
Hamilton, G. A. 257
Hamilton, John 105
Hamilton, Richard 103–4, 112
Hamilton, W. J. 77
Hamilton estate 48, 115, 116
  annual rents, arrears and receipts 239–40, 242–3, 245–6
Hancock, John 67, 70, 110
Hancock, W. N. 53, 55, 91, 99
  on eviction statistics 229
  and TCD leasing powers act 260
  on tenant right 67–8
Handcock, Miss 148
hanging gale 113
hangings 36, 151, 186, 188–9, 202
  petitions 181
  reprieve offered 200–1
Hanlon, Mary 186
Harcourt, Sub-Inspector 169
Harris, Charles 189–91
Head, Sir Francis 12, 168, 192
Headford Castle, Co. Galway 35
Henderson, W. D. 67
Henrietta Street, Dublin 217
Henry, Revd Robert 138
Henry estate, Co. Tipperary 151
Hertford, marquis of 111
Hibernia Funeral Society 199
Hill, Benjamin 168
Hill, Lord George 30, 45, 221
Hillsborough, Co. Down 3, 4, 121
Hinds, Charlotte 12, 162, 181, 188

Hodgens, Patrick 197, 200–1
Hodson, Sir George 82, 92, 107, 108–9, 112, 118, 277
  expenditure 119
  improvements 122
  memorial to 206–7
Hodson estate 31
Hodson estate, Co. Cavan 30, 92, 108–9, 277
  annual rents, arrears and receipts 239–40, 242–3, 245–6
  estate expenditure, 278
  bailiff 112
  memorial 206–7
  rent collection 113, 115, 117
Hodson estate, Co. Wicklow 277
  estate expenditure 118
Holden, John 181
Holland, Daniel 111
Holybrooke Park, Co. Wicklow 118
Holywood, Co. Down 182
home rule 13, 215, 218, 228
homicides and assassinations 5, 12, 49, 129, 139, 159, 162
  perpetrators hanged 188–9
Hooker, Eligabeth R. vi
Hope, George 152
Horan, Patrick 175–6
Hornidge, G. J. 153, 161, 172
horses 84, 85, 128
housing 122, 211, 217
  country houses 1–2
  designs by Denton and Stephens 127
  labourers 225
  ranking of counties 269–72
  rural 83
  small farms 126–7
Houston, E. C. 80
Howley, Patrick 174
Hunt, Charles 201
Hunter, James 150, 174, 181
Hunter, William 110–11
hunting 99, 120, 132, 182
Huntly, marquis of 135
Hussey, Samuel 109, 110
Hussey family 184–5
Hyland, John 142
Hynds, James 171, 173

Illustrated London News 1, 5, 21
improvements:
  compensation for 95, 274–6
  estate expenditure 119–23, 134, 277–8
  by landlords 18
  landlords' low expenditure on 124–30
  reluctance of tenants 84–6
  and rent increases 45–6

improvements (cont.)
  sale of 68
  and tenant right 74, 83
  Thomas Baldwin on 83–5
Inchiquin, Lord 107, 126, 226
  expenditure 117–18, 119, 278
  indebtedness 130–1, 220
Inchiquin estate, Co. Clare 17, 79, 106–7, 130
  arrears and receipts 242–3, 245–6
  estate expenditure 278
  improvements 125, 126
  jointures 132
  rent collection 115, 116
Indian mutiny 14, 15
insurance schemes 128, 131, 133, 138
Irish Farmers' Gazette 16, 39, 54
Irish Land Committee 123 n., 250 n.
Irish language 110
Irish Law Times & Solicitors' Journal, The 95
Irish Loyal & Patriotic Union 80
Irish parliamentary party 15, 18, 209
Irish Republican Brotherhood, 214
Irwin, Thomas Staples 104–5

Jackson, J. D. 201
Jenkins, James 'Flower Pot' 190
Jeremy, Isaac 138
Johnston, James 99–100
Johnston, Robert 89, 95
Johnston, William, of Ballykilbeg 192
Johnston estate, Co. Armagh 56
Jonesborough, Co. Armagh 138
Jordan, Revd W. T. 15
journalists 220
Joy, Mr (agent) 105
juries:
  coroner's 38, 185, 203
  grand 9
  petty 141, 187, 203

Keady, Thomas 10
Kearney, Brian 187
Kearney, Fr. 205
Keelaghan (tenant) 172
Kells, Co. Meath 3
Kelly, Mrs 144
Kemmis, William 186
Kenmare, Co. Cork 3
Kennedy, Captain 25
Kenny, James (assassin) 185
Kenny, James (tenant, Tuite estate) 173
Kenny (witness) 169
Kent and Sussex Labourers' Union 183
Kenyon, Fr. John 15
Kerry, County 107
  agrarian crime 143, 156, 157
  estate management 109
  evictions 28, 36
  indebtedness 211
  land league 210
  ranked according to: agrarian outrages 283, 285; evictions 233, 235; rural housing 270, 271; serious crime 281; valuation, tillage and holdings 267, 271
  rents 50
  TCD leasing powers act 258
  tenant right 79
  valuations 58
Kesh, Co. Fermanagh 14, 170
Kidd, Revd Henry 90
Kiernan, V. G. 52–3
Kilcoosh, Co. Galway 20, 22, 24, 26, 39, 183
Kildare, County 1, 4
  agrarian crime 148
  housing 83 n.
  ranked according to: agrarian outrages 283, 285; evictions 233, 235; rural housing 269, 271; serious crime 281; valuation, tillage and holdings 267, 271
  rent collection 114
  tenant right 77
Kildare Street Club 12
Kildoney, Co. Cork 178
Kilkee, Co. Clare 37
Kilkenny, County 35, 38
  agrarian crime 143, 165
  improvements 121
  ranked according to: agrarian outrages 283, 285; evictions 233, 235; rural housing 269, 271; serious crime 281; valuation, tillage and holdings 267, 271
  tenant right 77
Killarney, Co. Kerry 28
Killucan, Co. Westmeath 184
Killymackan, Co. Fermanagh 121
Kilmacanogue, Co. Wicklow 57
Kilmaine, Lord 182
Kilrush, Co. Clare 24, 25, 36
King's County 1, 4, 109
  agrarian crime 140, 157, 171
  evictions 27
  ranked according to: agrarian outrages 283, 285; evictions 233, 235; rural housing 269, 271; serious crime 281; valuation, tillage and holdings 267, 271
  Ribbonism 192
Kingscote, Captain 174, 181
Kingsisland, Co. Tyrone 40–3
Kingston estate, Co. Limerick 186–7

Kirk, James 180, 186, 188, 196
Kirwan, Patrick 142, 144
Knockbride, Co. Cavan 148
Knockninny, Co. Fermanagh 121
Knox estate, Co. Roscommon 17, 114, 115, 116, 122
  annual rents, arrears and receipts 239–40, 242–3, 245–6
  jointures 132
Kyle, William Cotter 40

labourers 27, 49, 204, 225
  cost of labour 1850–86, 248–50
  decline in numbers 209–10
  lack of organisation 183
  neglect of 10
  numbers 7
  share of agricultural output 8
labourers' unions 183
Lambert, Captain T. E. 145, 185–6, 189
Lamph, Michael 91
Lamph, William 91
land act 1870, 6, 24, 34, 46, 68, 160, 215
  compensation under 273–6
  effects of 41, 42, 100–2, 206, 213–14, 218
  leading cases 95–9
  Lord Leitrim blamed for 38, 104
  and tenant right 78, 93–102
  weaknesses of 217
  see also disturbance; improvements; leases; town-parks
land act 1881, 23, 28, 46, 209
  effects of 226–7
  and tenant right 80
land bill 1877, 51
land bonds 228
land cases reserved, court for 94–5, 96, 97
land commission 131
land league 1, 23, 54, 191, 209, 210, 211, 212
land purchase 209, 227–8
land registration 9
land war 19, 23, 51, 55, 114, 138, 140, 160, 163
  causes of 208–16
  crime during 156, 157
  effects of 225–7
  and labourers 10
landed estates court 136
Landed Property (Ireland) Improvement Act 1860, 86, 120, 124
landlords 4–8, 9–11, 98, 104–5, 149–50
  and 1870 land act 100
  absenteeism 2, 3
  and agents 111–12

alien 11–13
attacks on 142–3, 145–7, 159, 188–9
and combinations 205–6
decline of gentry 227–8
deference towards 33, 106, 207, 226
effects of agrarian crime 161–2
extravagance of 132–3
family charges and jointures 131–2
incomes of 8–9, 115–17, 117–20
indebtedness of 31, 124, 125, 130–7
interest payments 130–1, 136, 277–8
as magistrates 165–8
no mass movement against 202–8
non-violent resistance to 206–7
numbers of 3–4, 6
powers of eviction 24, 31–4
prosecuted for assault 35–6
relations with constabulary 14–15, 173–5
survival of 217–18
and tenant right 93
weak position of 213, 215–16, 218–24
see also estate management; magistrates
Lanesborough, Lord 106
Lanktree, John 253
Lansdowne, marquis of 107, 112
Lansdowne estate, Co. Kerry 109
Laois, County, see Queen's County
Larcom, Sir Thomas 3, 174–5, 193, 201, 219
Lavelle, Fr. Patrick 2, 5–6, 14, 37, 44, 156
Lavelle, Peter 181–2
Law Life Society 37
Lawless, Michael 180
leases:
  under 1870 land act 100
  usefulness of 107–8
Leeds 220
Lefroy, Thomas 256
Leinster:
  ranked according to: agrarian outrages 284, 286; evictions 234, 236; rural housing 270, 272; serious crime 282; valuation, tillage and holdings 268, 272
  Ribbonism 193
  tenant right 80
Leinster, duke of 1, 3, 14, 100
Leitrim, County 3
  agrarian crime 144, 149
  evictions 27
  and Lord Leitrim 104
  ranked according to: agrarian outrages 284, 286; evictions 234, 236; rural housing 270, 272; serious

Leitrim (*cont.*)
   crime 282; valuation, tillage and holdings 268, 272
   rents 48, 86
   Ribbonism 193
Leitrim, earl of 5, 30, 32, 36, 38, 129, 146, 256
   estate management 103–5, 112
   murder of 139, 142, 146, 151, 185, 189
   rackrenting 86
   rents 50
   and tenant right 97
Leitrim estate, Co. Donegal 48, 50
   management of 103–5
   tenant right prohibited 76, 97
   valuations 58
Letterkenny, Co. Donegal 191
Liberal Party 13, 101, 160, 179, 219, 228, 257
Lifford, Co. Donegal 119
Limerick 142
Limerick, County 4, 49
   agrarian crime 186–7
   housing 83 n.
   improvements 121, 124
   ranked according to: agrarian outrages 283, 285; evictions 233, 235; rural housing 270, 271; serious crime 281; valuation, tillage and holdings 267, 271
   rents 73–4
   resistance to landlordism 181
   valuations 58, 61
Lisbellaw, Co. Fermanagh 2
Lisnaskea, Co. Fermanagh 121
literacy 154, 164, 211
Lloyd, Mr 188
loan societies 128
London 12, 81, 220
London companies 3, 13, 109, 126
Londonderry, County 3, 13, 87, 125
   agrarian crime 157, 165
   estate management 109
   evictions 27
   ranked according to: agrarian outrages 283, 286; evictions 233, 235; rural housing 270, 272; serious crime 282; valuation, tillage and holdings 268, 272
   rents 17, 44–5, 47, 48, 56
   tenant right 72, 76, 97, 98
   valuations 60
Long, Michael 186–7
Longfield, Mountifort 67, 68, 73, 257
Longford, County:
   agrarian crime 152, 157, 169
   ranked according to: agrarian outrages 283, 285; evictions 233, 235; rural housing 269, 271; serious crime 281; valuation, tillage and holdings 267, 271
   resistance to landlordism 177–8
   Ribbonism 193, 200
lord-lieutenant:
   powers of 141, 171, 200–1, 221
Louth, County:
   agrarian crime 138, 186, 188, 192
   housing 83 n.
   ranked according to: agrarian outrages 283, 285; evictions 233, 235; rural housing 269, 271; serious crime 281; valuation, tillage and housing 267, 271
   Ribbonism 196, 198
Lowe, Professor W. J. 53
Lucan, Lord 148
Lucas, Frederick 215
lunacy 211
Lurgan, Lord 12, 67
lynch law 165, 219
Lyons, Tom 186

McArdle, Patrick 197
McAteer family 92
McCarthy, Fr. William 179
McCooey, Patrick 180, 186, 188, 196, 197, 202
McCormick, S. F. 5
McDermott estate, Co. Mayo 187
MacDonald, Duncan George Forbes 105
McDonald, George 183
McDonnell, William 88
McDonough, Michael 139
McEntaggart, Barney 197
McGrath, Peter 89
McGuinness, Neddy 197
MacHale, Archbishop 37
McKim, John 142
MacKnight, James 215
MacLagan, Peter 80, 81
Maclise, Daniel 106
MacMahon, Marie Edmé Patrice Maurice de 4
McMahon, Pat 226
McMahon, Patrick 197
McMahon, Thomas 226
MacMenemin, Denis 191
MacNaboos faction 180
McParlin, James 90
McSharry, Andrew 144
McTernan, Captain 147
McVeagh, Michael 169
Magherafelt, Co. Londonderry 95

magistrates 6, 14, 35, 139, 219–20, 224
  bargaining 170–3
  and constabulary 173–4
  landlords as 3, 4, 163, 165–8, 222
  lay magistracy abolished 227
  stipendiary magistrates 139, 166, 167, 174
  summary jurisdiction act 164–5
  see also petty sessions
Maguire, John Francis 215
Mahaffy, John Pentland 12
Maher family 180
Mahers faction 180
Malowney, William 171–2, 173, 180, 194–5
Manchester, duke of 135, 137, 228
Manly, Samuel 120
Manners, Lord John 12
market tolls 205
Markethill, Co. Armagh 3, 88
Markree House, Co. Sligo 228
Martin estate, Co. Galway 20
Mayo, County 1, 12, 118, 126, 199, 217
  agrarian crime 148, 152, 155, 157, 159, 162, 170, 184, 189, 202
  estate management 109
  evictions 24, 26
  ranked according to: agrarian outrages 284, 286; evictions 234, 236; rural housing 270, 272; serious crime 282; valuation, tillage and holdings 268, 272
  rent collecting 204
  resistance to landlordism 178, 181–2
  tenant right 77
Mayo, earl of 4, 12, 146
Meagher, Fr. Thomas 21
Mealia, James 171
Mealy, Walter 143
Meath, County 1, 146
  agrarian crime 140, 167, 171, 184, 189
  housing 83 n.
  ranked according to: agrarian outrages 283, 285; evictions 233, 235; rural housing 269, 271; serious crime 281; valuation, tillage and holdings 267, 271
  rents 53 n.
  tenant right 77
Meehan, Margaret 197
memorials 11, 174, 181, 206–7
middlemen 65, 73
  and TCD leasing powers act 256–60
Midland Great Western Railway 194
Midleton estate, Co. Cork 17, 48, 116, 117

rents, arrears and receipts 239–40, 242–3, 245–6
Milford, Co. Donegal 103
militia 20, 167
Mitchell, Arthur 184, 187–8
Mitchell, Patrick 142
M'Noun v. Beauclerk 95, 97
Moate, Co. Westmeath 154, 207
model farm, Glasnevin 84, 85
Mohill, Co. Leitrim 146
Monaghan, County 111
  agrarian crime 138, 153, 154, 162, 182, 185, 188, 192
  estate management 109
  ranked according to: agrarian outrages 284, 286; evictions 233, 235; rural housing 270, 272; serious crime 282; valuation, tillage and holdings 268, 272
  rents 63
  Ribbonism 190
  select committee on 196
  tenant right 76
Monahan, James Henry 257
Moody, T. W. 214
Mooney, Pat 197
Moore, Charles 34
Moore, George Henry 214
Moore, Revd John 109, 110–11
Moore, William 91
Moorefort, Co. Tipperary 34
Morris, Mr Justice 153–4
Morris, William O'Connor 44, 68, 76
Morrow, Samuel 34, 142, 189
mortgages 90, 98, 131, 133, 134, 136, 208
Mote Park, Co. Roscommon 118
Mountcashell, Lord 105, 133–4
Mountcashell estate, Co. Antrim 133–4
Mulhall, Michael 21
Mullaghmore, Co. Sligo 77
Mullingar, Co. Westmeath 171, 180, 184–5, 194, 200
Munster:
  ranked according to: agrarian outrages 284, 286; evictions 234, 236; rural housing 270, 272; serious crime 282; valuation, tillage and holdings 268, 272
  tenant right 80
Murphy, Bartly 38
Murphy, James 207
Murray, Dr A. C. 198, 201
Murray, Patrick 171
Murray Stewart, H. G. 121
Murray Stewart estate, Co. Donegal 3, 17, 18, 56, 99

Murray Stewart estate (*cont.*)
  improvements 121, 122, 126, 127
  estate expenditure 278
  income from 130
Murray Stewart estate, Scotland 115
Myers, Mary 223

Napier, Joseph 257
Narrow Water House, Co. Down 115, 118
Nation, The 174
Neill, Mrs 162
new departure 213, 214–15
New Ross, Co. Wexford 5
Newcastle Mutual Assurance Club 128
Newport, Co. Tipperary 95
newspapers 220
Newton, Courtenay 69–70, 100
Newtownbutler, Co. Fermanagh 106
Nicholson, J. A. 171, 189
Nicholson, Samuel 57, 58, 60
Norwich 220
notice to quit 29–30, 31–4, 65, 162
  under 1870 land act 100
  numbers 24 n.
  and tenant right 89, 92
  use of by Lord Leitrim 32, 103–4
Nottingham 220
Nugent, Joseph 194
Nugent, Lt.-Colonel 173
Nulty, Bishop 167, 177, 198, 199, 204, 205

Oakes, Thomas 194
O'Brien, Lady 132
O'Brien, Murrough 45
O'Brien, William 144
O'Connell, Daniel 219
O'Donnell, Sir George 174, 181
O'Donoghue, the 214, 215
Offaly, County, *see* King's County
O'Hagan, Lord 141
O'Hara, William 168
O'Hara family 112
O'Hara (sub-sheriff) 20
Oldcastle, Co. Meath 53 n.
O'Malley, Fr. Edward 139
O'Malley, Sir Samuel 26
O'More, Rory 199
O'Neill, Lord 12
Oola, Co. Limerick 166
Orange order 166, 199
Order of St Patrick 221
ordnance survey 164
Orkney, earl of 36
Ormond, marquis of 77, 188
Ormsby, William 150
Orridge, Andrew W. 212
Otway, Captain Robert Jocelyn 15

Overend, Gurney, & Co. 117
Owen, William 189

Pakenham estate, Co. Antrim 98
Palmerston, Lord 1, 77
papal states, collapse of 215, 217
Parnell, Charles Stewart 13, 191, 209, 214, 215
Parsonstown, King's County 3, 183
Partry, Co. Mayo 14, 26
  evictions 36–7
party processions act 1850, 166
peace preservation act 1870, 141, 153, 161, 168–9, 187
Peel, Sir Robert 13, 25
Perren, Richard 123
Perry, Messrs. 152, 172, 173, 194
petty sessions 3, 4, 30, 104, 164–5, 170, 182, 194–5
  during land war 226
Phillips, Dr 147
Pike, William 155
Pirie, Lord 222
Pirie (bailiff) 40
Pius IX, Pope 14, 215
Plunket, Lord, bishop of Tuam 26–7, 37
Pollok, Alan 27
Pollok estate 36
Pomfret, J. E. v–vi, vii, viii, 46, 47, 52, 215–16
poor law 217, 219
poor law commissioners 4, 105, 112
poor law guardians 11, 104, 203, 210
poor law inspectors, reports of:
  on auctions 87–8
  on Leitrim estate 103–4, 105, 112
  on rents 45–6
  on tenant right 68, 76–8
poor law rates 9, 215
Portacarron lease 102 n., 208
Portarlington, Lord 28
Portglenone, Co. Antrim 96
Portsmouth, Lord 77
poteen-makers 184
Powerscourt, Lord 56–7, 107
Powerscourt estate, Co. Wicklow 10, 56–7, 58, 79, 122
  expenditure 120
  improvements 124
  valuation 60
Powerscourt House, Co. Wicklow 1, 2
Pratt estate, Co. Cavan 17, 18, 38, 55–6
Prendergast, J. P. 5
Presbyterian church 133, 203, 220
Presbyterians 11, 14
priests 11, 14
  and combinations 204–5

Pringle, R. O. 120–1, 122
Provincial Bank 130–1
Prunty, Mr 88
pseudonyms 152–3
   see also threatening letters
public health act 1878, 164
public houses 11, 30, 141, 164, 167, 179, 181, 201

Queen's County 109
   agrarian crime 161–2, 167, 189
   evictions 38
   ranked according to: agrarian outrages 283, 285; evictions 233, 235; rural housing 269, 271; serious crime 281; valuation, tillage and holdings 267, 271
   tenant right 77
Quilter, Honoria 143
Quilter, John 143
Quilter, Thomas 143
Quin, Barney 196, 197
Quinlan, Mrs 111

rackrenting 5, 48–9, 52–3, 66, 68, 86, 209
Ranfurly, Lord 69, 100, 118, 119, 123
   estate expenditure 278
rate collectors 175–6
Rathcormack, Co. Cork 152
Rathnew, Co. Wicklow 57
Reade, William Morris 172–3, 202
reaping-machines 11
Redditch 220
Redesdale, Lord 257
rents 13, 15, 33–4, 44–66, 134, 164, 215, 217, 227
   abatements 9, 134, 162
   and agrarian crime 158, 160
   and cost of labour 250
   effects of 1870 land act 101–2
   fixing of increases 47–9, 55–63, 263–6
   flexibility of 61–3, 222–3
   high rents as stimulus 86–7
   insurance of 214
   letting by proposal 56–7
   movement of 238–40
   obstacles to increases 63–6
   post-famine recovery 17–18
   potential rent increases 61–2, 265–6
   question of 44–8
   receipts 244–6
   resistance to 177
   significance of increases 49–55
   size of increases 46–8, 239–40, 249, 265–6
   stabilized 226
   and TCD leasing powers act 256–60, 261–2, 265–6
   and tenant right 68–9, 71, 73–4, 97–8
   tests of 50–1
   see also arrears; rackrenting; valuations
Reynell family 121
Ribbonmen 140, 166, 169, 171, 180, 183
   Charles Harris's revelations 189–91
   and clergy 204–5
   connection with Hibernians 199
   constabulary report on 195–6
   contemporary accounts 191–2
   George Tallbot's description 199–200
   modus operandi 196–8
   number of cases 193, 195
   occupations of suspects 194
   W. S. Trench on 200–1
Richmond and Gordon, duke of 44
Richmond (valuator) 58–9, 60
Robinson, Olive viii, 47–8
Rockism 198
Rockview, Co. Westmeath 155, 162
Roman Catholic church 14, 133, 203
   Catholic landlords 11
   and combinations 204–5
   and landlords 220
Roscommon, County 17, 118, 122, 132
   ranked according to: agrarian outrages 284, 286; evictions 234, 236; rural housing 270, 272; serious crime 282; valuation, tillage and holdings 268, 272
Roscrea, Co. Tipperary 27–8
Ross, David 68
Rosse, earl of 183, 228
Rossmore, Lord 166
Roundstone, Co. Galway 139
royal commissions 40, 53
Rush, James Bloomfield 138
Russell, Alic 103
Russell, Marcus G. 155–6
Russell, Robert 67, 77
Rutledge (valuator) 60
Ryan, Martin 188

St Ernan's, Co. Donegal 105
St George, Richard 35
St George estate 120
St Patrick's College, Maynooth 14, 133
St Patrick's Fraternal Society 199
Salters' estate, Co. Londonderry 44–5, 56, 89
Samuelson, Bernhard 46
Sanderson estate, Co. Cavan 91
schools 13, 14, 119
Scotland 33, 39, 81, 106, 121
   rent collection 115

Scotland (*cont.*)
  rents 226
  valuations 59
Scott, Major Thomas 97
Scott, Sir Walter 106
Scully, Vincent 179
Scully, William 11, 150, 189, 202, 204
  'battle' of Ballycohey 34, 108, 139, 142, 151, 185, 218
  sued for assault 35, 38–9
secret societies 191, 192, 194, 195, 197–9
  see also Ribbonism
Seed, Stephen 196
Seery, James 153
Semple, Revd Edward 169–70
Senior, Nassau William 72, 73
Shanahan, Fr. 28
Shanahan, James 144
Sheehy, Alderman 142
sheriff's sales 99
Shiels, John 144
Shirley estate, Co. Monaghan 63, 111
shopkeepers 3, 5, 128, 209–10, 211, 213, 220–1
Simmons, Alfred 183
Slator, Bevan 151, 153, 163
Sligo, County 1, 109, 118
  agrarian crime 150
  ranked according to: agrarian outrages 284, 286; evictions 234, 236; rural housing 270, 272; serious crime 282; valuation, tillage and holdings 268, 272
  Ribbonism 191
  tenant right 77
Sligo, marquis of 117, 205; 228
small farms 11, 124, 204, 217, 224–5
  competition for 75
  high productivity 86–7
  horses 85
  problems of 125–6
Smith, Colonel Henry 2, 129
Smith, Elizabeth 2, 66
Smith, Philip 88
Smith Barry papers 75
Smyth, Revd Mitchell 165
Smyth, Sydney 165
Solow, B. L. ix, 46–8, 52–3
Spearman ranking coefficients 287–8
special constables 203
Spencer, Earl 125
Spotswood, Alexander 60, 70, 87, 89, 109
squatters 92
Standard Life Assurance Co. 133, 135
Stannus, Walter 111–12
Stephens, Henry 61, 62, 105, 127
Stephens, James 215
Stewart, Robert 104

Stewart of Ards estate, Co. Donegal 88
Strabane, Co. Tyrone 95
Stritch, A. J. R. 174, 202, 220
Stronge, Sir James 50, 256
Styles estate, Co. Donegal 99
sub-sheriffs 15, 20, 29, 162, 168, 175
  and evictions 21–2, 36, 38, 41–2
sub-tenants 8, 30, 34, 225
  disputes with 11, 143, 158
Sullivan, A. M. 3, 34, 36
Sullivan, Darby 28
summary jurisdiction act 164–5, 168
Sutton, John 57
Sweeney, Hugh 74
Swineford, Co. Mayo 77, 152, 153

Talbot, George 199–200
Tandragee Castle, Co. Armagh 228
Tarleton, Captain Rowland 150, 152, 207
taxation 13, 224, 277–8
TCD leasing powers act 1851, 50, 53, 62, 63, 127, 256–60
  difficulties with 54–5
  rents based on 261–2, 263, 264, 265
Teahan, Bridget 35, 38
Teahan, Patrick 35
Teemore, Co. Fermanagh 121
Temple, Hon. Reginald Temple Harris 148
Templederry, Co. Tipperary 15
Templetown, Lord 154
tenancies 225
  annual 7, 33–4
  and evictions 21–2
  lease-breaking 27
  let by proposal 56–7, 87
  need for security 9–10
  subdivision 89
  tenant right sales 87–9
  three Fs 32, 159, 225
  see also sub-tenants; tenant right
tenant league 18, 177, 178–9, 214–15
tenant protection societies 178
tenant right 31, 67–102
  definitions of 67–76
  and estate management 87–93
  extent of 76–80
  and land act 1870, 93–102
  leasehold tenant right 96–7
  and prosperity 80–7
  sales of 71–3
  value fixed 227
tenant right legislation 28
tenants 6–7
  and 1870 land act 100
  contact with agents 111–12
  difficulties of combining 177–83, 202–6, 217

tenants (*cont.*)
  disputes among 31, 143, 158
  disputes with landlords 149–50
  disputes with sub-tenants 11, 143, 158
  and estate improvements 128–30
  indebtedness 211, 213, 215
  landlord-tenant relationship 9–11
  legal protection of 34–5
  non-violent resistance 206–7
  obstacles to rent increases 63–6
  religion of 14
  subdivision 89
  threatening letters 154–5
  see also improvements; rents
tenement valuation 9, 60–1, 164
  calculations of value of production 251–5
  counties ranked by valuation per acre 267–8
  rents 45, 49, 51–2, 54
  in Ulster 71
Thiebault, Gustavus 144, 151
Thomas, W. 120
Thompson, H. S. 46, 68, 69–70
Thompson, James 120
Thompson, R. J. 123, 226
Thom's Directory 2
Thornton, 'Culloville' 197, 200
threatening letters 142, 146, 148, 162, 170, 180, 188, 194–5, 207
  see also pseudonyms
Tighe, Robert 170
Tinahely, Co. Wicklow 189
Tipperary, County 15, 223–4
  agrarian crime 142, 144, 151–2, 156–7, 184, 186, 188
  evictions 25, 34
  leases 108
  ranked according to: agrarian outrages 283, 285; evictions 233, 235; rural housing 270, 271; serious crime 281; valuation, tillage and holdings 267, 271
  resistance to landlordism 178
  tenant right 76, 77, 99
  town-park 96
tithe war 138
Tobin, 'Foxey' Tom 190
Tory faction 180
Tory party 13, 18, 174, 218
Tottenham estate 10
town commissioners 11
town-parks 95–6, 100
Townshend, Charles Uniacke 72, 73, 99
trade unions 179, 192, 202, 204, 206, 217
Tralee, Co. Kerry 36, 210
Tramore, Co. Waterford 95

Trench, George Frederick 50, 51
Trench, Thomas Weldon 167
Trench, William Steuart 63, 109, 110, 111
  accounts system 107
  and agrarian crime 162, 166
  attacks on 188, 197–8
  breaks leases 27
  evictions 37
  improvements 129
  Realities of Irish Life 44, 192, 200–1
  and Ribbonmen 192, 197, 201
Trench family 109, 112
Trinity College, Dublin 9, 11–12, 13, 50, 67, 104
  see also TCD leasing powers act
Trollope, Anthony 106, 147
Tucker, Mrs Anne 147
Tuite, Joseph 173
turbary rights 99–100
Tyrone, County 4
  agrarian crime 148
  Gartlaney eviction 39–43
  housing, 83 n.
  improvements 121
  ranked according to: agrarian outrages 284, 286; evictions 233, 235; rural housing 270, 272; serious crime 282; valuation, tillage and holdings 268, 272
  rents 49, 56, 57, 63, 64–5
  tenant right 71–2, 73
  town-parks 96
  valuations 58, 60
Tyrone Protestant Orphan Society 119
Tyrrelspass, Co. Westmeath 194

Ulster 47, 75, 213
  evictions 70
  Fenianism 214
  land act 1870 and tenant right, 96–101
  ranked according to: agrarian outrages 284, 286; evictions 234, 236; rural housing 270, 272; serious crime 282; valuation, tillage and holdings 268, 272
  rents in 68–9, 71
  Ribbonism 193
  tenant right 76, 77–83, 93
Ulster Bank 135
Ulster Custom, *see* tenant right
United States of America 185, 186, 200, 214

vaccination 164
Valuation Office 51, 58, 59–60, 258
valuations 156
valuators 57–60

Vaughan Charity, Kesh 170
Versailles 228

wages 248, 250, 260
Wales 140, 187
Wales, prince of 135
Wallace, John 31, 92
Walsh, Fr. David 178
Walsh (tenant) 199
Wann, James 14
Wann, William 30, 63, 105, 107, 124, 205
  on bailiffs 112–13
  debt management 109, 130, 133, 134–7
  Gartlaney eviction 39–43
  and improvements 129
  rent collection 116–17
  rent increases 56, 64–5
  tenant right sales 88–9, 90–1
  tenant right succession 91–2
  uninsured 138, 139
  and valuations 58–9
War of independence 226, 227
Warburton, Captain 190
Warburton, Richard 189
Waterford, County 3, 4, 77, 83 n., 106
  ranked according to: agrarian outrages 283, 285; evictions 233, 235; rural housing 270, 271; serious crime 281; valuation, tillage and holdings 267, 271
Waterford, marquis of 106
Waters, Thomas 143, 171, 172
Waterstown, Co. Westmeath 148
West, Elizabeth 20
Westmeath, County 3, 32, 144
  agrarian crime 142, 148, 151–2, 155, 159, 161–2, 168–9, 171, 173, 180, 183–5, 189, 192–5
  ranked according to: agrarian outrages 283, 285; evictions 233, 235; rural housing 269, 271; serious crime 281; valuation, tillage and holdings 267, 271
  rents 49

resistance to landlordism 178, 182
Ribbonism 140, 189, 193, 194–5, 199–200, 201–2, 205
  select committee on 196, 198
Westmeath act 1871, 140, 161, 170–1, 172, 173, 194
Westminster, marquis of 123
Westport, Co. Mayo 152
Westport House, Co. Mayo 228
Wexford, County 5, 29, 77
  ranked according to: agrarian outrages 283, 285; evictions 233, 235; rural housing 269, 271; serious crime 281; valuation, tillage and holdings 267, 271
Whig faction 180
Whig party 219
White (tenant) 89
Whiteboyism 190, 191, 193, 198, 199
Whyte, John 11
Wicklow, County 1, 2, 66, 277
  agrarian crime 189
  estate expenditure 118
  evictions 29
  housing 83 n.
  improvements 124, 129
  ranked according to: agrarian outrages 283, 285; evictions 233, 235; rural housing 269, 271; serious crime 281; valuation, tillage and holdings 267, 271
  rents 56
Williamson, John 98
Williamson v. The earl of Antrim 96
wills 90–2
Wilson, Robert 104
Winter, Samuel 173
Wodehouse, Lord 35
Woodbrook, Co. Roscommon 1
Woodhouse, Mr 74
Woodstock, Co. Wicklow 2, 10
Woodtown, Co. Meath 6, 11

yachting 119, 132–3, 135
Young Men's Christian Association 119